Oracle Press™

OCA Oracle Solaris 11 System Administration Exam Guide

(Exam 1Z0-821)

D1561051

Oracle Press™

OCA Oracle Solaris 11 System Administration Exam Guide

(Exam 1Z0-821)

Michael Ernest

New York Chicago San Francisco Lisbon London Madrid
Mexico City Milan New Delhi San Juan Seoul Singapore Sydney Toronto

Cataloging-in-Publication Data is on file with the Library of Congress

OCA Oracle Solaris 11 System Administration Exam Guide (Exam 1Z0-821)

1234567890 DOC DOC 109876543

ISBN: Book p/n 978-0-07-177571-7 and CD p/n 978-0-07-177572-4 of set 978-0-07-177574-8

MHID: Book p/n 0-07-177571-4 and CD p/n 0-07-177572-2 of set 0-07-177574-9

Sponsoring Editor Meghan Riley Manfre	**Copy Editor** Bart Reed	**Illustration** Lyssa Wald, Howie Severson
Editorial Supervisor Jody McKenzie	**Proofreader** Susie Elkind	**Art Director, Cover** Jeff Weeks
Project Editor Rachel Gunn	**Indexer** Ted Laux	**Cover Designer** Pattie Lee
Acquisitions Coordinator Stephanie Evans	**Production Supervisor** James Kussow	
Technical Editor Tim Wort	**Composition** Apollo Publishing Services	

To my wife, Jocelyn, who waited through no small number of late nights
as I struggled to write something just a little "gooder."

Michael Ernest was once left alone for three weeks with a shelf of abandoned O'Reilly books and a SPARC IPX computer, complete with a dedicated 435MB drive and 48MB of RAM. He discovered a passion for Sun Microsystems technology to add to his passion for adult learning and has enjoyed teaching and writing computing courses since 1995. He formed Inkling Research, a group of contract service professionals, in 1999.

Michael has written exam items and consulted on both the Oracle Certified Professional (1Z0-822) and the Oracle Certified Master Java EE 6 Architect (1Z0-807) exams. A certified Solaris and Java instructor for 18 years, he has written courses for Sun Microsystems and Oracle on diverse topics, including Solaris 10 Performance Management, What's New in Solaris 11, and Java EE Design Patterns.

Michael lives in the San Francisco Bay Area. A continuous learner by nature, he practices Kung Jung Mu Sul and studies widely, including philosophy, operating systems internals, and emerging practices in software development and systems management.

About the Technical Editor

Tim Wort is a consultant and trainer. As a consultant for Sun Microsystems, he wrote and contributed to various Solaris Security and Solaris Administration courses. In addition, Tim contributed to and developed test exams for Solaris 8 through Oracle Solaris 11 Certified Administration exams and the Solaris 10 Certified Security Administration exam. His background includes senior network and security administrator for a multinational company and Linux administration. Tim has been working with Solaris and Linux since 1989, and he is an honors graduate of the Denver Institute of Technology.

About LearnKey

LearnKey provides self-paced learning content and multimedia delivery solutions to enhance personal skills and business productivity. LearnKey claims the largest library of rich streaming-media training content that engages learners in dynamic media-rich instruction, complete with video clips, audio, full-motion graphics, and animated illustrations. LearnKey can be found on the Web at www.LearnKey.com.

CONTENTS AT A GLANCE

CONTENTS

PREFACE

This book includes the key topics you need to know for a well-rounded and comprehensive introduction to administering the Solaris 11 operating system. It begins with the information you need to install it and guides you step by step through all its core technologies and concerns: booting the machine; managing files, processes, and users; securing the system against unauthorized users; monitoring and managing system activity; managing storage and network resources; and, finally, understanding the composition of and uses for a Solaris Zone. Read this book to the end, and you will have a broad grasp of the elements that make up a system administrator's everyday work.

The primary objective of this study guide, however, is to prepare you for the Oracle Certified Associate, Oracle Solaris 11 System Administrator exam (1Z0-821). It will familiarize you with the body of knowledge the exam will test. It also includes technology discussions that the exam topics rely on but aren't tested. These topics are included so the book will remain a useful reference once you've passed the exam.

These discussions, specifically the chapters on projects, resource management, system logging, managing core files, and network virtualization, will also give you a small jump on topics that are covered by the Oracle Certified Professional, Oracle Solaris 11 System Administrator exam (1Z0-822). In some cases, potentially overlapping discussion in this book is brief because the OCA exam does not require so much detail, or because some information falls specifically within the OCP exam objectives.

In This Book

This book is organized as an in-depth review for the Oracle Certified Associate, Oracle Solaris 11 System Administration exam (1Z0-821). It is suitable for anyone who has user-based experience in a UNIX-based operating system (Linux, HP-UX, AIX, BSD) or Solaris itself. A Windows server–based administrator may also find this book useful as a crossover guide in preparation for adopting the Solaris 11 platform.

Each chapter covers a specific aspect of Solaris 11 technology. In some cases, a Solaris 11 technology covers a broad enough area that it merits two chapters. ZFS, for example, is a technology that addresses both file system and storage management. Solaris 11 network configuration has undergone a substantial change, providing separate tools for IP interface and data link administration. Accordingly, each of these topics is covered with two chapters of treatment.

To put it bluntly, I disagree with the architects of the exam objectives for the OCA and OCP topics. I believe you'll appreciate how the Solaris Zones operate far better if you first learn about Solaris projects and resource controls. Accordingly, I've included these chapters in the guide, even though they do not appear on the OCA exam. If you take a literal view of the exam and have no interest beyond what you need to know to pass it, you can skip these chapters. I think you'll be a much better administrator if you read them, but it's up to you.

All 17 chapters are designed so the concepts that drive each technology are presented first. Tools and practices you can apply come second. The chapters are kept brief to emphasize learning points and to reduce the focus on memorizing tables or documenting obscure usage or problems. The exams for Solaris 11 have filtered out so-called "memory stunt" questions to discourage this kind of learning. The certification team is more interested in testing your knowledge and ability to apply Solaris technology within the confines of a knowledge-based test.

On the CD

For more information on the CD-ROM, please see the Appendix at the back of the book.

Exam Readiness Checklist

At the end of the Introduction, you will find an Exam Readiness Checklist. This table will help you cross-reference the official exam objectives with the objectives as they are presented and covered in this book. The checklist may also help you gauge your current grasp of each objective before you begin to study. Check your progress from time to time and make sure you spend more time on difficult or unfamiliar sections. The references map to the objectives as the vendor presents them.

In Every Chapter

We've created a set of chapter components that call your attention to important items, reinforce important points, and provide helpful exam-taking hints. Take a look at what you'll find in every chapter:

■ Every chapter begins with **Certification Objectives**—what you need to know in order to pass the section on the exam dealing with the chapter topic. The Objective headings identify the objectives within the chapter, so you'll always know an objective when you see it!

■ **Exam Watch** notes call attention to information about, and potential pitfalls in, the exam. These hints are based on information available to the test writers (including the author). You won't get hints on specific exam questions, but you will get guidance on key areas of study.

■ **On the Job** notes describe the issues that come up most often in real-world settings. They provide a valuable perspective on certification- and product-related topics. They point out common mistakes and address questions that have arisen from on-the-job discussions and experience.

■ **Inside the Exam** sidebars highlight some of the most common and confusing problems that students encounter when taking a live exam. Designed to anticipate what the exam will emphasize, these sidebars help ensure you know what you need to know to pass the exam. You can get a leg up on how to respond to those difficult-to-understand questions by focusing extra attention on these sidebars.

■ The **Certification Summary** is a succinct review of the chapter and a restatement of salient points regarding the exam.

 ■ The **Two-Minute Drill** at the end of every chapter is a checklist of the main points of the chapter. It can be used for last-minute review.

 ■ The **Self Test** offers questions similar to those found on the certification exams. The answers to these questions, as well as explanations of the answers, can be found at the end of each chapter. By taking the Self Test after completing each chapter, you'll reinforce what you've learned from that chapter while becoming familiar with the structure of the exam questions.

Some Pointers

Once you've finished reading this book, set aside some time to do a thorough review. You might want to return to the book several times and make use of all the methods it offers for reviewing the material:

1. *Reread all the Two-Minute Drills*, or have someone quiz you. You also can use the drills as a way to do a quick cram before the exam. You might want to make some flash cards out of 3×5 index cards that have the Two-Minute Drill material on them.

2. *Reread all the Exam Watch notes and Inside the Exam* elements. These notes come from someone who helped write the exam. Use them to set your focus on the right knowledge base.

3. *Retake the Self Tests.* Taking the tests right after you've read the chapter is a good idea, because the questions help reinforce what you've just learned. However, it's an even better idea to go back later and do all the questions in the book in one sitting. Pretend that you're taking the live exam. When you go through the questions the first time, you should mark your answers on a separate piece of paper. That way, you can run through the questions as many times as you need to until you feel comfortable with the material.

ACKNOWLEDGMENTS

Isn't this a strange place, the acknowledgements section? Why would you read it before you read the book itself? It's like thanking everyone for making a boat that has yet to hit water. This part is *scary* for me, after all. I don't know yet if anyone's found it everything they hoped it would be.

That said, there was a lot of effort required just to get this guide to market. I hope you'll take the time to note these people for that work. Meghan Manfre, the sponsoring editor at McGraw-Hill, invited me to this project and guided me oh-so-diplomatically as I fell off the deadline wagon time and again. Stephanie Evans, promoted to associate acquisitions editor near the end of this project (w00t!), managed the chapter-by-chapter development. Her positive, forward-going spirit kept me away from hand-wringing over missed deadlines and focused on the achievable. Thank you both.

I met Tim Wort, this book's technical editor, when I got my start in technical training years ago. As both a fellow instructor and a thoroughgoing reviewer, I enjoy his notes because I get as much instruction as I do correction. I don't want to write books that prove how much I know, but to teach others what I can. It's a pleasure and a privilege to have an editor who operates on the same premise and who cares more about useful material than wondering out loud if I know what I'm talking about. Thanks, Tim.

Rachel Gunn managed the book's production to the final stage and Bart Read copyedited the material, helping to make every sentence count and make the whole thing easy to look at. Thanks to you both for taking the time to help make a better product.

It is my hand, ultimately, that uncorrected the errors they caught, ignored their good advice, or allowed some passage to stand that they felt needed another pass. Should you find quirks of writing and factual errors in this book, they are my mistakes and mine alone.

INTRODUCTION

Welcome to the first and best choice you can make in a prep guide for the OCA Solaris 11 exam! This material has been written and tested by two instructors with over 30 years of experience in administering, training, and writing course materials and test questions for the Solaris platform, starting with Solaris 2.5. In that time, Solaris technology has undergone such profound changes and advances that Solaris 11 makes older releases look like toys. The complexity is far greater. The tools provided to administer the system and observe its operations are much more sophisticated. The hardware they support has increased in power and range of ability by orders of magnitude. No one is asking where it will end, but in what manner it will grow next.

Certification testing has also changed. I remember sitting through a Solaris 7 Admin II exam, trying to remember which complex and obscure nistbladm command invocation would accomplish a described task. Today, that sort of question is called a *memory stunt*, a test of a candidate's recall, and it is removed from the question pool when the reviewers spot it. What's the new idea? That the Solaris OCA exam, as well as the OCP exam, should emphasize instead your understanding of the technology and which tools help you apply those concepts.

Exam Structure

The exam administration includes 75 questions. You are given up to two hours to complete the exam. The stated minimum pass percentage, at publication time, is 64 percent, or 48 correct answers. Oracle, however, reserves the right to change the difficulty of the exam items and adjust the passing rate accordingly. Before registering, you should consult Oracle's website and confirm the current standard.

The high-level exam objectives include:

- Installing Oracle Solaris 11 using the interactive installer
- Updating and managing software packages
- Setting up and administering user accounts
- Administering services
- Controlling access to systems and files
- Managing system processes and scheduling system tasks
- Setting up and administering data storage

- Administering a physical network
- Administering Oracle Solaris Zones

The number of questions posed for each objective, known as the *weighting*, is not disclosed. To prepare, you should consider all objectives equally important. The amount of information available on each topic could imply its relative importance, but generally the weightings reflect the certification team's focus on new technology over existing practices. That is, it's reasonable to expect there may be more questions on managing a zone than there will be on, for example, adding users to the system. That said, all you can really count on is the fact that weighting is not even across all topics.

Exam Relevance

The Oracle certification group wants to make sure this credential, when earned, signals to a prospective employer that you know how to apply Solaris 11 to a given task. The OCA exam should challenge your comprehensive grasp of the technologies that make up Solaris 11—on an introductory level for the Associate exam, and on a detailed, advanced level for the Professional exam. Of course, you can finish your assigned tasks faster if you know exactly what to type, but it's more important from a testing perspective to demonstrate knowledge than recollection.

Think of the OCA exam as your way to demonstrate a competent but basic level of understanding of the Solaris 11 operating environment. With the credential, you can demonstrate you understand Solaris 11 well enough to assist experienced administrators in configuring and monitoring Solaris-based systems. You can claim you'll be able extend those skills, too, because you have a fundamental but comprehensive understanding of its key technologies.

You'll notice in this book that most chapters are divided into a discussion of concepts and relationships among technologies first and applications second. This arrangement is no accident. If you understand how and why you might configure additional storage for a system, and you know the relevant commands, the difference between knowing exactly what to type and where to find that information gets smaller. The exam questions, similarly, will focus on your familiarity with the practices and tools that pertain to a specific task. Some questions may test your ability to distinguish from among several command invocations which one is right, but most questions will test whether you know the right practice or tool for a certain task.

Planning the Next Step

Passing the Associate exam is a required step to preparing for the Oracle Certified Professional certification. I for one don't think it's a status to be taken lightly.

As an item contributor to this exam myself, I can tell you it will be difficult for many people to pass. At the Professional level, we do not test for competence, but mastery. It's fully expected that only diligent, practicing Solaris administrators with significant experience will have the knowledge and understanding needed to pass the exam. I fully expect the number who will possess this credential to be small and correspondingly more noticeable for having it. It will be a real investment in time and money, but there's no question in my mind the people who achieve this certification will have a valuable addition to their resumes.

Consult Oracle's website for Solaris 11 certification. It's no longer as easy as signing up for the exams and passing them, which is too bad for those who'd like to test themselves and have something to show for their efforts. This program is now serious business, however, and is not inappropriate for an industrial exam and not a small asset to employers who require certified professionals for their staff.

Using This Guide for Preparation

You may notice this book is a bit shorter than most volumes of its type. I have not detailed the options for each and every command that might appear on the exam. The ones you should know very, very well before taking the exam are of course included, but there are also more than a few hints, by way of using related commands, throughout the text. Don't assume any of these examples are incidental because they are not fully documented. Pay attention instead to every reference to documentation that's made. As an Associate candidate, you should refer to source material any time you're unsure of your understanding or think you should have more information.

For the sake of brevity and to discourage memory drills, this book emphasizes concepts over command options and standard practices over subtle gotchas. This Associate exam itself provides straightforward questions and avoids, if not completely eliminates, trick questions. It does, however, favor candidates who have a broad command of the objectives and have taken the time to review online documentation, man pages, and the material included in any required course. As you read this guide, focus on the domain under discussion. Follow the command examples and test yourself with the review questions. Use the practice exams to get a feel for the difficulty level you can expect. Cramming probably won't help you; experience through regular practice and research, on the other hand, will help reinforce the core knowledge you need, not just for the exam but for using the technology as well.

Exam IZ0-821

Exam Readiness Checklist				Beginner	Intermediate	Advanced
Official Objective	**Study Guide Coverage**	**Ch #**	**Pg #**			
Installing Oracle Solaris 11 Using an Interactive Installer						
Plan for an Oracle Solaris 11 Operating System Installation	Planning Installation	1	2			
Install the Oracle Solaris 11 Operating System by Using an Interactive Installer	Installing Solaris 11	2	31			
Verify the Operating System Installation	Installing Solaris 11	2	54			
Troubleshoot Installation Issues	Installing Solaris 11	2	54			
Access Open Boot PROM	Understanding the Boot Model	3	65			
Updating and Managing Software Packages						
Explain the Image Packaging System (IPS)	Adding and Updating Software	12	348			
Update the Oracle Solaris 11 Operating System by Using IPS	Adding and Updating Software	12	357			
Manage Software Packages by Using Package Manager and the Command-line Interface	Adding and Updating Software	12	361			
Administer Boot Environments Using Package Manager and the Command-line Interface	Adding and Updating Software	12	357			
Troubleshoot Software Update Issues	Adding and Updating Software	12	356			
Administering Services						
Explain the Role of the Service Management Facility (SMF)	Administering the Services Management Facility (SMF)	8	228			
Administer SMF Services	Administering the Services Management Facility (SMF)	8	244			
Boot and Shut Down a System	Understanding the Boot Model	3	74			
Troubleshoot service and boot issues	Understanding the Boot Model	3	84			

Exam Readiness Checklist

Official Objective	Study Guide Coverage	Ch #	Pg #	Beginner	Intermediate	Advanced
Controlling Access to Systems and Files						
Control Access to Systems	Securing Systems and Files	5	126			
Control Access to Files	Securing Systems and Files	5	138			
Use Authentication	Securing Systems and Files	5	148			
Troubleshoot Access and Authentication Issues	Securing Systems and Files	5	149			
Setting Up and Administering User Accounts						
Explain Key User Management Concepts	Managing Users and Groups	6	177			
Set Up User Accounts	Managing Users and Groups	6	167			
Manage User Accounts	Managing Users and Groups	6	177			
Manage User Initialization Files	Managing Users and Groups	6	183			
Use Shell Metacharacters	Managing Users and Groups	6	188			
Configure User Disk Quotas	Understanding File Systems	4	110			
Troubleshoot User Account and Quota Issues	Managing Users and Groups	6	177			
Administering a Physical Network						
Explain Basic Networking Concepts	Managing Network IP Interfaces	16	471			
Configure a Network Interface	Managing Network IP Interfaces	16	493			
Administer a Network Interface	Managing Network IP Interfaces	16	493			
Verify Network Operation	Managing Network Data Links	15	456			
Determine Datalink Availability	Managing Network Data Links	15	450			
Troubleshoot Network Issues	Managing Network IP Interfaces	16	493			

Exam Readiness Checklist

Official Objective	Study Guide Coverage	Ch #	Pg #	Beginner	Intermediate	Advanced
Managing System Processes and Scheduling System Tasks						
Manage System Processes	Managing Processes	7	200			
Schedule System Administration Tasks	Managing Processes	7	214			
Troubleshoot Process Issues	Managing Processes	7	211			
Monitor System Logs	Using the System Log for Troubleshooting	13	394			
Explain the Use of Core Files, Core Dump Files, and Crash Dump Files	Administering Process and Kernel Crash Data	14	408			
Setting Up and Administering Data Storage						
Describe ZFS	Understanding File Systems	4	101			
Administer ZFS Storage Pools	Configuring Additional Storage	11	328			
Administer ZFS File Systems	Understanding File Systems	4	98			
Administer ZFS Snapshots and Clones	Understanding File Systems	4	114			
Troubleshoot File Systems and Storage Issues	Configuring Additional Storage	11	338			
Administering Oracle Solaris Zones						
Explain Oracle Solaris Zones	Administering Zones	17	504			
Determine the Current Zones Configuration and Resource Utilization on the System	Administering Zones	17	514			
Administer an Oracle Solaris Zone	Administering Zones	17	516			
Troubleshoot Zone and Resource Utilization Issues	Administering Zones	17	507			

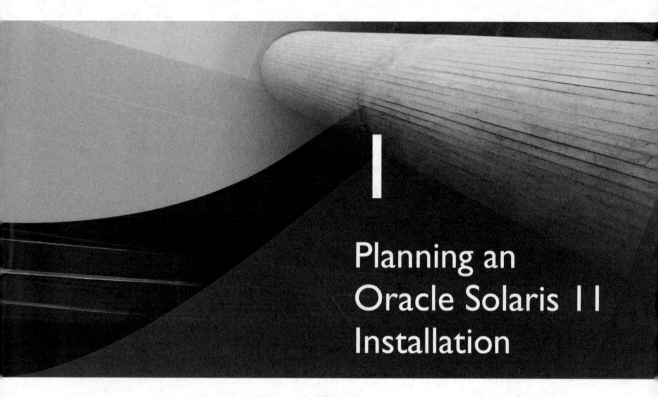

1
Planning an Oracle Solaris 11 Installation

T he Oracle Solaris operating system has been a powerful workhorse in workstation and server-based computing for over two decades now. Since the release of Solaris 10 in 2005, the OS has undergone profound changes, in ways that both distinguish it from the overall UNIX market and maintain pace with it. For one, while Solaris is well known and widely used in the high-end server market, running on SPARC hardware, it has also become much easier to install on laptops and other PC hardware. The explosion in virtualization technology has made it easy for computing professionals to run multiple Solaris versions on a single machine, either a session at a time or concurrently. Most recently, Solaris itself has proliferated, spawning an OpenSolaris codebase that is the parent to new operating environments such as Illumos and SmartOS. In short, installing and running this world-class operating system couldn't get much easier and less expensive, or more appealing as a skill set. Anyone with recent computer hardware can install Solaris and learn to use it through everyday hands-on practice. You can walk into the Oracle Certified Associate Solaris System Administrator exam armed with as much experience, as well as knowledge, as you choose to obtain.

This study guide is written with that goal in mind: to prepare you for the OCA Solaris 11 System Administrator exam. But there is also a larger purpose: to help you become a knowledgeable, competent Solaris administrator who can operate, configure, and maintain Solaris-based systems, and who can discuss how those systems support their users and applications. This chapter assumes you know little about Solaris, but by the end of this guide you should be able to identify and interact with every primary Solaris technology an Oracle Certified Associate is expected to know. More importantly, you'll be able to administer a Solaris system with confidence.

CERTIFICATION OBJECTIVE 1.01

Why Plan Your Solaris 11 Installation?

Many UNIX-based operating systems are promoted on the premise that they "just work." And it's a great concept—both for casual and professional users. After all, a modern OS can make many reasonable assumptions about the hardware you've got: the smallest disk the hardware is likely to have, the likely minimum complement of RAM, the built-in networking components (including wireless transceivers), and so on. In that vein, you can *probably* install Solaris 11 on a current laptop without much preparation and expect it to work out of the box.

As a systems administrator, however, one who is supporting a multitude of users and their applications, you're expected to know the following:

- How much disk space Solaris 11 requires
- How much RAM Solaris 11 requires
- Which physical devices Solaris 11 supports
- What conditions or limits are known to affect how the OS runs

We can list that information easily enough; in fact, these questions are all answered in the next section. You're also expected to know how to configure the system during the installation process, which we cover in the next chapter. It's not tricky stuff: Every operating system needs to keep time, of course. The installation process therefore asks you to confirm or correct that time. The system also needs a name, it needs to know your language of choice, and so on. All of these elements influence the system's behavior and presentation after booting. Knowing what values you entered and why, and what behavior to expect as a result, will go a long way to making your first login a straightforward event, utterly lacking in mystery.

Once you've gone through this process a few times, you won't think much about the minimum requirements. Systems administration, however, is almost never about feeling personally comfortable with your system's operations. It's about maintaining systems you can delegate confidently to others when the time comes. Obtaining that goal means following accepted practices and conventions and, when you add or configure something outside the standard practice, documenting those differences for others. You don't just want *your* login to look and feel familiar. You want every authorized user to have that same experience.

INSIDE THE EXAM

Installation Categories

Generally, installation is the first step in a variety of tasks an administrator performs. For the purposes of the exam, Oracle organizes these tasks into the following categories and sequences them into a workflow:

- Installing the Operating System
- Updating Software
- Managing Users
- Configuring Security
- Managing Processes

- Administering Services
- Administering Storage
- Administering Networking
- Administering Zones
- Monitoring the System

Some tasks, such as installing the operating system, are natural prerequisites to other tasks. This guide is organized with that order in mind. Simpler topic areas come before complex ones, and topics that depend on other topics come later.

In Solaris 11, more has been done to make acquiring, installing, and using Solaris easier than in any previous release. Some tools, such as the Hardware Compatibility List (HCL), have been around for a long time. The ability to install a Solaris image to a USB stick and boot from it, just to see how things fly, is new. Also, more recent virtualization software products, such as VirtualBox, make it possible to install Solaris on top of a host operating system. Oracle enhances that approach by providing appliances—preconfigured Solaris 11 images—that you can download and import directly into a VirtualBox virtual machine.

None of these options, with the exception of the HCL, are things you need to know for the exam. They will, however, save you a lot of time getting started with Solaris. They also make it easier to demonstrate how Solaris can support many users running many applications in a variety of configurations.

With Users in Mind

Most people who rely on computer systems don't think about the operating system very much. They think, and rightfully so, about the things that directly affect their jobs: the applications they count on. The operating system could be a big bar of aluminum with a blinking green light for all they know (or care). They may speak in terms such as *high availability* (when to expect work to get done), *high throughput* (how much work is getting done), and *low response time* (how fast work is getting done). But most users only know they want those things. They don't know (or need to know) how to achieve them. The users you support as a system administrator don't want to know why system availability is only at "three nines," or why throughput is lower than expected, or why response time is slow. They just want the system to work when they call on it. They want it to process a lot of data, and they want it done as quickly as possible.

To demonstrate value, a systems administrator must relate the role of the operating system to the quality of service users expect in a way that matters to them. Figure 1-1 depicts a high-level view of these relationships; it may help you remember that an administrator's primary work often concerns managing services and resources most users can't even see.

FIGURE 1-1

Role of the operating system

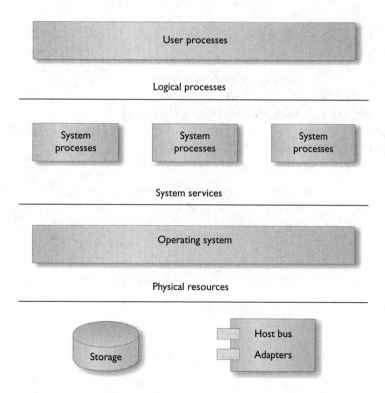

CERTIFICATION OBJECTIVE 1.02

Identifying Pre-installation Tasks

Circling back to the installation prerequisites mentioned earlier, you should list four tasks when asked to name the key parts of the pre-installation process. There's a fifth, however, that will serve you well to remember and is the last item included on this list:

1. Identify system requirements.
2. Identify installation requirements.
3. Identify networking options.
4. Check device drivers.
5. Review documentation and release notes.

a t c h *An Associate-level exam isn't designed to test a subtle understanding of the topic. In many cases, the questions you're given just make sure you've done your homework.*

Let's review these one at a time. They're not rocket science, but in preparing for the exam, sometimes the trick is knowing how simple the answers to some questions should be.

Identify System Requirements

Every mainstream operating system requires storage and RAM to function. Some experienced administrators with an enthusiasm for experimenting will have their own ideas of the "real" minimum values to run Solaris. The numbers you should recite for the exam are the numbers that Oracle documents. If it helps to say, "according to Oracle…" when memorizing them, by all means do so. Table 1-1 lists Oracle's storage recommendations for Solaris 11.

	Storage Type	Minimum Capacity
TABLE 1-1	Persistent (disk or file based)	13GB
Solaris 11 Storage Recommendations	RAM	1GB

You don't have to be so careful to say "persistent" storage. I just want to be sure you know that the storage space Oracle calls for doesn't change for a virtual machine. If you experiment with installations, you'll find you don't need even half this size to set up a working instance of Solaris 11. In reality, 13GB is an estimate that allows lots of room for other needs, including a kitchen-sink installation of Solaris utilities, application and user software (databases, development kits, favorite middleware products), data and user files, software updates, and so on.

The recommended amount of RAM you need, on the other hand, is a very conservative estimate. You can run Solaris 11 on 1GB of RAM if you aren't making truly heavy demands on the system, but you'll feel a loss in response time pretty quickly once you load it down. I run Solaris 11 from time to time on VirtualBox and allocate 1.5GB for demos that include an application server or database. I'd give it more if I had the RAM to spare. Think of 1GB as the bare minimum.

on the
ob

In reality, these numbers aren't much cause for worry. Modern hardware platforms that Solaris 11 supports usually have ample disk space and RAM available.

Identify Installation Requirements

Each major release of Solaris, alas, retires support for some older hardware platforms. Usually these changes affect SPARC platforms more than X86 because of the expense involved in replacing systems. This event is preceded, sometimes years ahead of time, by end-of-life (EOL) announcements that give customers a heads-up to plan for future maintenance and purchases.

With the acquisition of SPARC and Solaris technologies by Oracle, recent announcements of this sort also signal a strategic shift in support for these products. Solaris 11 is the first major release under Oracle's watch. Accordingly, platform and service support have changed to align with Oracle's policies for customer support. Table 1-2 delivers the news.

The X86 platform requirements for 64-bit hardware came out with Solaris 10, which is great news for anyone who wants to try Solaris 11 on existing hardware. The license and support services that Oracle offers, however, have changed quite a bit. You can find out more about Oracle service contracts, which include support for technical services and software patches, by browsing www.oracle.com/technetwork/server-storage/solaris11/solaris-service-409058.html.

Solaris grew up on SPARC processors, of course, but many versions of SPARC have come and gone over the years. The minimum platform requirements for Solaris 11 shift focus to the most recent hardware models; older SPARC systems are still supported with Solaris 10. It appears as if the focus will be on SPARC for high-end application demand. The future for Solaris on bare-metal X86 doesn't seem to be a big concern, so it may be that the interest is focused on virtualization on commodity hardware. If these developments concern your own enterprise, it's important to keep an ear to the ground concerning them.

To boot on X86 systems now, Solaris has relied on a proprietary version of a popular open source tool called the Grand Unified Bootloader (GRUB) since 2006. If you're already familiar with GRUB, what you know about it applies to booting Solaris. There are proprietary extensions, however, that adapt to Solaris-specific boot components. These technologies have been added to the GNU version of GRUB. The GNU version itself has no support for these same extensions. If you just want to load Solaris on a disk alongside other operating systems—in a configuration known as *multibooting*—you'll need to use the Solaris-specific version of GRUB to make it all work.

TABLE 1-2   Computing Hardware Supported by Solaris 11

Hardware Platform	Minimum Model	Other Requirements
X86	64-bit support only	Component support based on driver availability
SPARC	M-Series (Enterprise) and T-Series (Servers)	Open Boot PROM (OBP) 4.17 or better

On SPARC, a facility called the OpenBoot PROM (OBP) provides a suite of diagnostic tools and facilities, including a bootloader, to boot the operating system. OBP version 4.17, the minimum required version, has been available since 2005. The supported SPARC platforms certainly have this requirement covered.

Identify Networking Options

Solaris was designed from the start to support network connectivity. Even the early SPARC systems included a network transceiver in support of Sun Microsystems' philosophy that the network is the computer. However, it is not required, as documentation sometimes seems to imply, that you have a network adapter to install Solaris. If you do, and are connected to a network that provides services Solaris can use, the installation process can proceed much faster and more conveniently.

If you have an acceptable complement of hardware, as detailed earlier, you can next decide if you'd like to configure your system's network resources manually or automatically. The automatic process, as you'll see in the next chapter, is almost completely hands off. Consequently, there's not much to learn by observing it. If you want to configure the process manually to understand what's involved, you'll need the following:

- An IP address for your station
- The IP address of a local gateway or router (to connect to other networks)
- A naming service, such as DNS

on the job

You may need to get these values from the network administrator in your environment.

Depending on your choice for the naming service, there may be additional information the install wizard asks for to connect to that service (such network location and authorization). I detail the cases you need to know for the OCA exam in the next chapter.

Choosing Manual or Automatic Configuration

If you prefer, you can configure your network setup after installation; choose the approach that is more convenient for you. It's expected that you'd want to use manual configuration for a server setup in a controlled network environment. Fixing an IP address to a server makes it easier for client systems to locate and remember, so it's a good choice for any system that many users will rely on.

For a workstation, automatic configuration is a much easier way to go. Whether you are based in a home or office network, it's very likely that Dynamic Host Configuration Protocol (DHCP) and Domain Name Service (DNS) are already in place. If so, automatic configuration can discover these services and configure them for your system to use, no questions asked. You can also undo or disable this configuration easily if it doesn't work out. I discuss configuring for network access in Chapter 16, "Managing Network Resources."

Check Device Drivers

Unlike the Linux kernel, which grew up on commodity hardware, the Solaris kernel grew up in a culture of commercial applications and high-end demand. For many Linux users, as a result, the very idea that you need to check for support for certain hardware devices breaks the principle that "things just work." It helps to remember that X86 is a second home for Solaris, and although a number of devoted engineers (and open-minded executives) went to great lengths to put Solaris in the hands of more X86 users, it has been a work in progress for some time to realize the same model achieved by branded Linux products such as Ubuntu and Red Hat.

SPARC is Solaris's first home. Naturally, it's not a concern to check for device driver software on SPARC-compliant devices. If your company has purchased M-Series or T-Series systems in particular, the hardware that ships with them include driver software as part of the bargain. It doesn't mean that any component that fits in a card slot on a SPARC system is supported, however. Sometimes people will try, though, just to see.

For X86 systems, it's a different story. Oracle provides support for many common devices out of the box. It also still documents the availability of some additional drivers for X86 to support that user community. Many of these drivers are provided directly by the hardware vendors themselves. Still other drivers are supplied by third parties to promote the use of a specific device with Solaris.

Also, many hardware components, despite their wide deployment on X86 platforms, have not captured the interest of developers who write device driver code. In many of these cases, a driver is available for the component, but it only works with a 32-bit kernel. As a result, there's wider device support for Linux (running a 32-bit kernel) than Solaris (which no longer supports it).

In short, if you have Solaris 11 on a supported SPARC system, you're set for device drivers. Otherwise, you should check your target system carefully against the

Oracle Solaris 11/11 Hardware Compatibility List web page before committing to a bare-metal installation (go to www.oracle.com/webfolder/technetwork/hcl/index.html). This page provides a list of systems and components that are either certified or known to work with Oracle Solaris 11/11.

on the **job**   *The LiveCD installer (discussed later in this chapter) includes the Device Driver Utility. If you boot your target machine with a LiveCD, you can use the Device Driver Utility to see if the machine's components are all supported by the version of Solaris 11 your LiveCD is based on.*

Review Documentation and Release Notes

Three documents in particular should pique every Solaris 11 administrator's interest right away:

- Oracle Solaris 11 What's New
- Oracle Solaris 11 Release Notes
- End of Features (EOF) for the Oracle Solaris 11 Release

The first two are PDF documents you can download. They are part of an Information Library for the Solaris 11/11 release you can browse, at http://docs.oracle.com/cd/E23824_01/, under the heading "Getting Started with Oracle Solaris 11." The End of Features (EOF) document is new to this set. At this writing, it is available as a web page only: www.oracle.com/technetwork/systems/end-of-notices/eonsolaris11-392732.html.

Together the What's New and the Release Notes documents describe the features added to Solaris since the last release, the known issues with installing, running, and updating the OS, and any features that were removed. The EOF document lists many utilities and services that have been associated with Solaris for years, along with changes to the kernel code that alter the way various other well-known services rely on it. If you have used Solaris in the past and are brushing up your knowledge for the exam, read the EOF document thoroughly. You may find that any number of tools and services you expect to find in Solaris no longer exist.

on the **job**   *Although it's not given as a task specific to the exam, you should always review documentation and release notes for any new software you install. Every release of Solaris comes with a complete set of documentation.*

CERTIFICATION OBJECTIVE 1.03

Identifying Installation Options and Differences

With all the preliminary checks and information covered, you have two decisions to make: which installer to use and how to configure your disk if you're installing to bare metal. For each decision you have a few options.

Installer Images

Oracle provides three installation images for the Solaris 11/11 release, as shown in Table 1-3.

If you want to run Solaris for your own use on a laptop or other PC hardware, you'll want a graphical windowing system. The Live Media image suits that purpose. If you want to run a Solaris server, to which users connect remotely, you probably don't need or want a desktop. The Text Install image provides terminal support only and consequently is a smaller image that consumes less memory and CPU.

on the Job

It's simple to add graphics support to a Text Install–based system. It's even simpler to disable graphics support in a Live Media–based install, so you don't have to think of these choices as a fork in the road.

| TABLE 1-3 | Solaris 11/11 Downloadable Installation Images |

Install Image	Platforms Supported	Image Size
Live Media	X86 only	821MB
Text Install	SPARC/X86	526/430MB
Automated Installer	SPARC/X86	353/272MB

I've also listed the Automated Installer (AI) image in Table 1-3 so you're aware of it. When you're ready to automate Solaris installs in your environment, or customize and execute remote installations, you'll need the AI image to do it. Using AI is considered an advanced skill and is covered as part of the OCP Solaris System Administrator exam. Although you're free to install the AI image, we do not discuss it further in this text.

Some additional images should be considered as well. Once you get comfortable using Solaris or want to practice using it in different configurations, consider the options listed in Table 1-4.

Storage

You have a few ways to install Solaris software to a disk: You can install to the whole disk, to part of it (a partition), or, if you are using a virtualization technology, to a file. The reasons for dedicating a whole disk to a Solaris 11 install won't become clear until Chapter 4. Until then, I'll just say that using a whole disk is the best way to go.

You can also install to one partition on a disk, although the reasons for taking this approach have diminished. Separating application and user data from system files is one reason familiar to many Windows users. With Solaris, however, this defensive scheme for protecting data in case the OS gets trashed isn't necessary. Multibooting is another motivation, although virtualization tools make it easy to store a working

| TABLE 1-4 | Alternative Solaris 11 Images Available for Download |

Image Type	Purpose
Repository	Can be used to create a local software package server
USB Install	Can be installed to a flash drive and used to boot other systems
Virtual Machine	Preconfigured with key software additions

operating system as a file in a host operating system that runs the hardware. If you prefer the multibooting model anyway, remember that Solaris requires its own version of GRUB to participate. Also, it does not support multibooting unless it is installed in the first partition of the boot disk.

If you're just starting with Solaris on X86 and you're going to install to bare metal, use the Live Media image. You'll want a desktop scheme with menus of familiar tools at hand to help you explore. Although few chapters in this guide rely on graphical interfaces, you will want to have a web browser, a word processing tool, and other familiar utilities at hand while you learn. If you change your mind or don't need a desktop to help you, you can always disable the windowing system.

Conversely, here are also some good reasons to use the Text Installer image:

- To limit disk space, memory, and CPU consumption
- To emulate the SPARC user environment (that is, terminal windows access only)
- To add and maintain server-oriented processes (databases, web containers)
- To access the system remotely most or all of the time

In such cases, by all means use the Text Installer. If you change your mind, you can add the graphics software packages (for X86) and enable the desktop service later.

If you want to prepare yourself for all possible contingencies, including more elaborate experiments with your current Solaris instance, use the Automated Installer image. The Automated Installer image itself falls outside the scope of this book, but when the OCP exam guide becomes available, or if you investigate AI services on your own, you'll be ready to go. If you prefer, you can read ahead in Chapter 12 to learn about the Image Packaging System (IPS). You can use that information to add the solaris-auto-install package to your installation.

If you really want to have a good time and have disk space to spare, you can create a separate virtual machine for each install type in VirtualBox and compare them. If you also have RAM and CPU to spare, you can even run them side by side. (Oracle sets up the labs for its Solaris administration courseware using this approach.) You won't see a great deal of difference between the Text and Live Media install processes, however. One runs in a terminal window; the other is graphical. One assumes you're going to assign an IP address statically; the other assumes you want it done for you. That's about it.

In the next chapter, we walk through the installation process using the Live Media image, but I also note differences with the Text Installer as they occur in the configuration process. Also, we walk through the installation process using the Live Media image, and I note differences with the Text Installer as they occur in the configuration process.

Identifying Differences Between the Live Media and Text Installers

As mentioned, the primary difference between these installer options is support for a graphical windowing system. Of the two installers, only the Text Installer is suitable for SPARC. Both images are suitable for installing Solaris to one system at a time. The other differences reviewed in the chapter are summarized in Table 1-5.

TABLE 1-5   Differences Between Live Media and Text Installer

Resource	Live Media Installer	Text Installer
Software packages	Base install + graphics support	Base install
Network configuration	Automatic	Manual or automatic
Memory consumption	Higher (for graphic support)	Lower (no desktop)

CERTIFICATION OBJECTIVE 1.04

Conducting a Test of Installation Requirements

Let's say you'd like to test multiple X86 systems and their devices for compatibility with Solaris 11. You could burn the image to media and then carry it to whichever system you'd like to test. If you're especially concerned about leaving the system's boot disk untouched, this is an easy, noninvasive approach.

Because only M-Series and T-Series hardware are supported, it's never a question whether Solaris will run on	*SPARC. Both systems, as shipped, exceed the minimum requirements for running Solaris 11 by a wide margin.*

If you don't care what's currently on the system, you can just install to bare metal, pick the appropriate configuration settings as you go, and see what there is to see. If carrying around a DVD seems tedious or prone to loss, you can also boot a system using a Solaris 11–bootable flash drive. This approach won't alter your system disk either, so you can test quickly for support of your system's components. When you're done, you can boot back to the system's current OS and get on with life.

To transfer the USB Install image to a flash drive using Oracle's instructions, you need a program called usbcopy. This program runs on various flavors of Solaris and Linux, so it's not much help if you're not already using one of these operating systems.

On Windows, you can use the OpenSolaris Live USB Creator program, which can be downloaded from http://genunix.org or one of its mirror sites. All you have to do is identify your target flash drive and select the .usb file from Oracle's Solaris download page. Although I don't walk through that process in this study guide, I have followed the instructions given and have booted a laptop to Solaris 11/11 from my 2GB flash drive without a hitch. Note that you may have to change the system's boot firmware to recognize your flash drive at boot time. Once that's done, the boot program takes care of itself.

on the **job**

If you use the OpenSolaris Live USB Creator program, you will need a root password to run the Device Driver Utility that comes with the installer. The user account in the installer program is jack; the password is also jack. The password for the root account is solaris.

If you have just one machine to work with, however, and you can't afford to be away from your e-mail or other web apps, use VirtualBox instead. Create a virtual machine for Solaris 11 and configure it to use either install image (Text or Live Media). Oracle recommends this approach and uses it to conduct its own Solaris training courses. As long as you have enough memory and CPU to support one or more virtual instances, this is the most convenient way to go.

INSIDE THE EXAM

A Guide to Using VirtualBox

I recommend the article "Taking Your First Steps with Oracle Solaris," (www.oracle.com/technetwork/articles/servers-storage-admin/o11-112-s11-first-steps-524819.html) as a rough guide to using VirtualBox. In particular, note the discussion in this article regarding the Device Driver Utility. Study the output from this program on your own system carefully. If there are unsupported devices on your target system—for example, your wireless transceiver—installing Solaris 11 to a virtual machine instead can spare you a great deal of inconvenience.

CERTIFICATION OBJECTIVE 1.05

Reviewing the Installation Process

The installation process is itself a logical sequence of smaller programs. Although they aren't called out during the process itself, identifying these stages now will help you better understand how to automate Solaris 11 installation when the time comes.

The installer is itself a working copy of Solaris 11. When booted, the session goes through the following steps:

1. Builds a logical tree of the boot system's devices
2. Asks the user to select a keyboard layout
3. Asks the user to specify a language of choice for the session
4. Loads drivers for all recognized devices
5. Assigns itself a hostname (solaris)
6. Invokes the installation process (Text Installer only)
7. Automatically logs in (as user jack) to a desktop session (Live Media only)

on the job

The Live Media session gives you plenty of room to explore Solaris services and features. You can do many things during this session that you can do in a normally installed session. The difference is that it runs only in memory. Any operation that relies on reading from or writing to disk requires additional configuration.

The screenshot in Figure 1-2 shows the desktop that appears once the installer loads.

As shown in the figure, the desktop icons along the left include Install Oracle Solaris, GParted Partition Editor, and Device Driver Utility. The Install Oracle Solaris utility begins the installation process and uses a wizard to govern configuration.

FIGURE 1-2   LiveCD Installer desktop

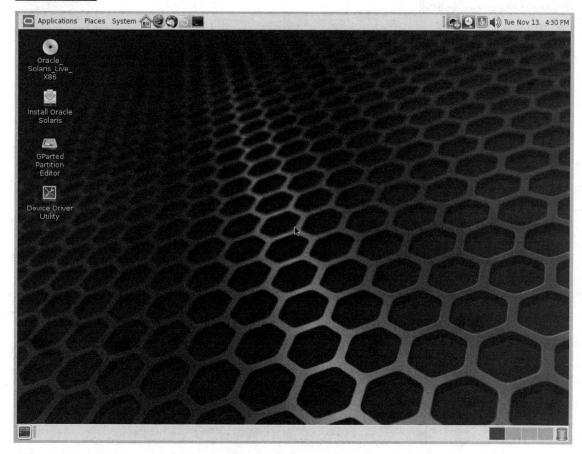

We'll cover this sequence in full in the next chapter. The partition editor lets you carve up your boot disk before starting the installation process. This is a helpful tool if you want to use only a portion of your target disk to host Solaris 11. The Device Driver Utility reports on the system's components and which software drivers support them.

Generating a Device Driver Utility Report

1. Using a LiveCD Desktop, double-click the Device Driver Utility icon.

2. At the prompt, enter the user or role you want to use.

3. The utility will now scan the device tree, which is a privileged operation.

4. You'll be asked for the administrative password. Enter **solaris**.

5. Once you're authenticated, the utility will report on each device it recognizes on the system. Figure 1-3 shows a report from a Dell Precision M6300.

FIGURE 1-3

Example of a
Device Driver
Utility Report

6. Watch the output of the report. As the report progresses, the screens it goes through aren't persisted.

7. Check for a pink-highlighted line, indicating lack of support for one of your components. If you miss this line, you'll have to run the utility again.

CERTIFICATION SUMMARY

Planning is the first step an administrator takes to document the information and decisions used to start the process of an operating system installation. Knowing the minimum requirements, major configuration options, platform support, and testing tools prepares the administrator to make clear choices and rule out options that aren't supported. With experience, the administrator can contribute effectively to a larger effort of provisioning new systems. In addition, an administrator is also better prepared to configure systems for casual use.

✓ TWO-MINUTE DRILL

Why Plan Your Solaris 11 Installation

❑ Oracle documents the requirements for disk space, memory, and hardware platform to install Solaris 11. You're expected to know these requirements for the exam.

❑ A Solaris 11 administrator is expected to maintain systems in support of user processes and therefore needs to relate the system's features and services to the tasks users need to perform.

Identifying Pre-installation Tasks

❑ Solaris 11 will run on both SPARC and X86 platforms. Only the M-Series and T-Series systems are supported for SPARC. Support for X86 is handled on a device-by-device basis.

❑ Solaris 11 supports manual and automatic network configuration. The manual form allows the installation administrator to assign a fixed IP address to the system. The automatic form allows the system to discover addressing and naming services on the network.

❑ Oracle provides a Device Driver Utility with the installation programs that can identify each system component and the driver that supports it. This utility will also identify any components for which no driver support is known to exist.

❑ The three primary installer options are called Text Installer, Live Media for X86, and the Automated Installer. The first two are included on the OCA exam; the third falls within the scope of the OCP exam.

❑ The Text Installer image is smaller and consumes fewer run-time resources because it does not include desktop windowing software. It supports both SPARC and X86 platforms.

❑ The Live Media for X86 installer includes desktop software. It is only available for X86 platforms.

Reviewing Installation Options and Differences

❑ The Text Installer image is complete and sufficient to prepare for the exam, except for learning the Live Media install sequence and initial desktop arrangement. Unless your hardware resources are truly constrained, prefer the Live Media image.

❑ You can add windowing support to a Text Install or disable windowing in a Live Media install. Neither image commits you to one user interface.

❑ The Live Media installer provides a graphical desktop system and supports X86 platforms only. The Text Installer provides terminal support and will install to both X86 and SPARC platforms.

❑ Both Live Media and Text Installer are suitable for installing to one system at a time. To install to multiple systems concurrently, the Automated Installer image is available for both platforms.

Conducting a Test of Installation Requirements

❑ Testing the install process on bare metal (X86) consumes the fewest hardware resources. You can transfer any Solaris install image to a USB flash drive and boot the target with it.

❑ Using VirtualBox, you can install any Solaris image to a virtual machine and run it on top of the host operating system. This approach consumes more memory and CPU, but allows the host operating system direct control of the hardware.

❑ You can customize GRUB and use the GParted utility to create and run a multiboot system. Multibooting is helpful when you prefer running one operating system at a time to hosting virtual machines on top of one.

Reviewing the Installation Process

❑ The install image is a working Solaris session that runs in memory. It includes a default non-root user account (jack). The root password is solaris.

❑ Several tools are available in the Live Media installer to assist with configuration. These tools include a partition editor, a device driver utility, and a wizard to walk you through the installation process.

SELF TEST

Use the following questions to test your recall and understanding of the chapter's material.

Why Plan Your Solaris 11 Installation

1. Complete the following statement: The operating system _____.
   A. Controls and manages physical resources
   B. Is mostly a collection of device drivers
   C. Provides at least one network connection
   D. Is something only the systems administrator can see

2. Which document or tool will tell you if your X86 system is completely supported by Oracle Solaris 11/11? (Choose all that apply.)
   A. The Device Driver Utility
   B. The OpenBoot PROM
   C. The Hardware Compatibility List
   D. GRUB

Identifying Pre-installation Tasks

3. What is the minimum RAM requirement for running Solaris 11?
   A. 821MB
   B. 13GB
   C. 1GB
   D. About half of Oracle's recommended amount

4. Which two services are needed to support automatic network configuration in Solaris?
   A. The hardware clock and DHCP
   B. OBP 4.17 or better and DNS
   C. DNS and DHCP
   D. The hardware clock and OBP 4.17 or better

Identifying Installation Options and Differences

5. Which install image will run on SPARC?
   A. Text Installer
   B. Live Media
   C. VirtualBox
   D. Automated Installer

6. Which supplemental download image provides all the available Solaris packages in a single bundle?
   A. AI
   B. USB Image
   C. Repository
   D. Virtual Machine Appliance

7. Which of the following resources will support a Solaris 11 installation?
   A. A VirtualBox virtual machine
   B. A bare-metal X86 system with 64-bit support
   C. A Windows system with 20GB of available disk space
   D. Any SPARC hardware

Conducting a Test of Installation Requirements

8. Which installer supports a desktop windowing system and runs on SPARC?
   A. Live Media for SPARC
   B. Automated Installer
   C. Text Installer
   D. None of the above

Reviewing the Installation Process

9. What information is required from the user before starting a Live Media session?
   A. Location of the boot disk
   B. Keyboard layout
   C. Screen resolution settings
   D. Logging in as jack with the password solaris

10. What is the account and password for the installer program?

    A. root/cangetin

    B. jack/jill

    C. scott/tiger

    D. jack/jack

SELF TEST ANSWERS

Why Plan Your Solaris 11 Installation

1. ☑ **A.** The operating system's job is to gather the physical resources of the system and coordinate them for the benefit of users and their applications.
   ☒ **B, C,** and **D** are incorrect. **B** is incorrect because the operating system manages physical resources through device drivers, but there's a great deal more to it. **C** is incorrect because the OS supports network connectivity but does not depend on it. **D** is incorrect because almost any user can point to evidence of the OS at work, if they know what to look for.

2. ☑ **A** and **C.** The Device Driver Utility supports Live Media installer users who want to check their hardware before starting the installation process. The Hardware Compatibility List has been the authoritative document for supported hardware devices since the late 1990s.
   ☒ **B** and **D** are incorrect. **B** is incorrect because the OpenBoot PROM is part of the SPARC platform; it has nothing to do with testing for device support. **D** is incorrect because GRUB manages booting for X86 systems and has nothing to do with testing for device support.

Identifying Pre-installation Tasks

3. ☑ **C.** Oracle recommends 1GB of RAM as a minimum to run Solaris 11.
   ☒ **A, B,** and **D** are incorrect. **A** is the size of the Live Media image. **B** is the recommended disk space for the installation. **D** amounts to 512MB of RAM, which is too little memory to run Solaris 11 and be happy about it.

4. ☑ **C.** The automatic network configuration option relies on DNS and DHCP services.
   ☒ **A, B,** and **D** are incorrect; the options given, other than DNS and DHCP, play no role in automatic network configuration.

Identifying Installation Options and Differences

5. ☑ **A** and **D.** The Text Installer is specifically intended for the SPARC platform; the Automated Installer image supports both platforms.
   ☒ **B** and **C** are incorrect because Live Media and VirtualBox are only available on the X86 platform.

6. ☑ **C.** The Repository image is provided to let administrators serve software packages from their own network.
☒ **A, B,** and **D** are incorrect. The Automated Installer supports administrators who want to configure custom, automated installations. A USB image is only suitable for launching an installation process; it is not a complete repository of Solaris 11 software. A virtual machine appliance is a premade installation customized for a specific purpose, such as database management.

7. ☑ **A and B.** VirtualBox supports several operating systems as guest machines, not just Solaris. A bare-metal X86 system may have individual components that aren't supported by a Solaris 11 driver, such as certain wireless transceivers, but the essential components for installing are covered for many standard systems.
☒ **C and D** are incorrect. **C** is incorrect because it does not specify the underlying hardware. **D** is incorrect because Solaris 11 supports only M-series and T-series class SPARC hardware.

Conducting a Test of Installation Requirements

8. ☑ **D.** There is no out-of-the-box support for running a desktop on SPARC.
☒ **A, B,** and **C** are incorrect because no support exists for a desktop session on a SPARC machine.

Reviewing the Installation Process

9. ☑ **B.** Before the desktop session can start, the user must select a keyboard layout and a language.
☒ **A, C,** and **D** are incorrect. **A** is incorrect because the installer session does not require a disk. **C** is incorrect because the installer only allows screen settings through the GRUB menu, as you'll see in the next chapter. **D** is incorrect because you are not required to log into any installer-based session.

10. ☑ **D.** The Live Media desktop session does not allow direct login as root, so a user account has to be available to access the desktop. The predefined login name and password are both jack.
☒ **A, B,** and **C** are incorrect because they are not configured in the Live Media or Text Installer images. The username jack is used during the installation process, as you will learn later. The username scott is for one of the predefined accounts of an Oracle database instance.

2

Installing Oracle Solaris 11

W e're now ready to install Oracle Solaris 11 and observe the configuration flow. We know from the previous chapter that the Text Installer image, intended for servers with no graphic console attached, is a subset of the Live Media for X86 installer. All the software we get with the Live Media image is a thin superset of the Text Installer image. There are, however, some differences in the installation process worth noting. We'll review them once we've worked through the complete Live Media install process.

If you've installed Solaris before, you might be surprised how brief the Live Media configuration is. You'll define the default language and keyboard layout, the disk(s) to use, the time zone, and a non-root user. There's not much else to do but watch, wait, and review the logged results. A great deal of manual configuration that used to be necessary, including configuration of network services, has been automated so that "things just work" when you're getting started with Live Media. The Text Installer offers only a bit more control over configuration. After that, if you want to customize the process in detail, you'll need to use the Automated Installer. This approach involves a substantial learning curve, but it's worth it if you have a specific setup you need to apply to several systems. Until that time comes, though, you don't have a lot you need to do to get Solaris 11 up and running.

Don't worry about writing to disk before you're ready. All configuration work resides in the memory of your session. When it's complete, you'll be asked to initiate the actual process. You can even use the system while you're configuring the install to browse the Internet or use other Solaris tools. The Live Media gives you a full session, minus the applications that require disk-based resources.

If you're still worried about overwriting important content on disk, however, using VirtualBox is as safe as it gets. VirtualBox allows you to use a single file as the repository for your operating environment, so all you need is enough space on the disk. We'll use it in this chapter in part to show that it does not affect the nature of the installation one bit, but also because it's a bit more convenient for capturing the screen than with a bare-metal install. If you prefer to install directly to your target system's boot disk, you should have no trouble following along.

Using the LiveCD GUI Installer

If you haven't already downloaded the Oracle Solaris 11/11 Live Media for X86 image, do so now. The URL is www.oracle.com/technetwork/server-storage/solaris11/downloads, or you can enter **Solaris 11 download** in your search engine of choice. Accept Oracle's license agreement to enable the download; you'll have to create an account on Oracle's site if you don't already have one. You can use the file sol-11-1111-live-x86.iso by attaching it to a virtual machine you define in VirtualBox. Or you can burn it to a CD, DVD, or thumb drive (total size is 821MB). Remember, you'll need specific software to install the image to a thumb drive so that you can boot from it.

Once you boot from the ISO, you'll see the Grand Unified Bootloader (GRUB) menu options, shown in Figure 2-1, after a short pause.

FIGURE 2-1	Live Media Installer GRUB menu

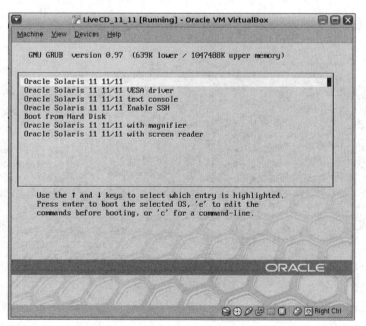

Use the arrow keys to move the selection bar. This action will disable the timer. If you do nothing, the install process starts itself in 30 seconds. If you need accessibility support, choose the appropriate option for you. We'll follow the default option here: Oracle Solaris 11 11/11. Highlight the option and press the ENTER key.

You'll next see a text-based screen that identifies the boot image and prints the line "SunOS Release 5.11 Version 11.0 64-bit." The system follows this with a message that it is probing for devices. This phase identifies system hardware and assigns a driver to each component that is recognized. Assuming the essential system components each match an available driver, you'll then see the messages "Preparing image for use" and "Done mounting image." So far, so good.

Next, the boot program identifies your keyboard attachment type (such as USB) and asks you to specify the layout and the language you want to use. The defaults are US-English and English, respectively, but you can choose from several alternatives.

Once you've made your selections, the boot program assigns itself the hostname solaris. You'll see a console login after another short pause. Ignore this prompt and wait: The Live Media graphic environment will start up in a few more seconds and replace the text console with a display like the one in Figure 2-2.

FIGURE 2-2   Live Media Installer GRUB menu

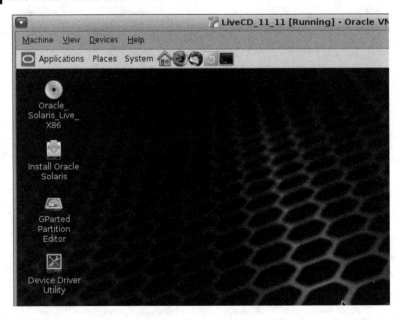

If you followed the instructions in Chapter 1 to test your target system for driver support, you've now arrived full circle. You can use the Device Driver Utility now if you haven't already. When you're done with it, use the Install Oracle Solaris application to initiate configuration.

CERTIFICATION OBJECTIVE 2.02

Reviewing the LiveCD Desktop

The LiveCD desktop consists of the server grill backdrop and four shortcut icons:

- Oracle_Solaris_Live_X86
- Install Oracle Solaris
- GParted Partition Editor
- Device Driver Utility

You'll also see menus for Applications, Places, and System, along with icon picks for your home directory, the Firefox browser, the Thunderbird mail client, the Package Manager, and the Terminal-spawning application.

If you have not already investigated the icon-based picks that are right-justified in the menu bar, including the date/time applet, feel free to review them now. Any application that does not need to store changes to an on-disk file will work as you'd expect. The installation process begins once you select the Install Oracle Solaris application, either by double-clicking or right-clicking and choosing Open from the pop-up menu.

The Installation Wizard separates the process into six panels:

- Welcome
- Disk
- Time Zone
- Users
- Installation
- Finish

The Disk panel discovers the target media for you, but it's also useful in the event you want to incorporate multiple disks or partitions into the installation. The Time Zone panel lets you establish the clock and offset from GMT. It's not important that you pick the zone to match your location, but the system must have one as a reference point. The Users panel lets you identify a non-root user for your first login. The Installation panel reviews the information provided in the previous panels.

CERTIFICATION OBJECTIVE 2.03

Conducting an Installation

The Welcome screen appears in Figure 2-3. The links you see here point to Internet-based URLs. If you click on one, such as Release Notes, make sure you're connected to a network; otherwise, you'll spend some time waiting for the access attempt to time out. The process may stall as the browser attempts to resolve the link. Click the Next button when you wish to continue.

FIGURE 2-3   Live Media Install Welcome panel

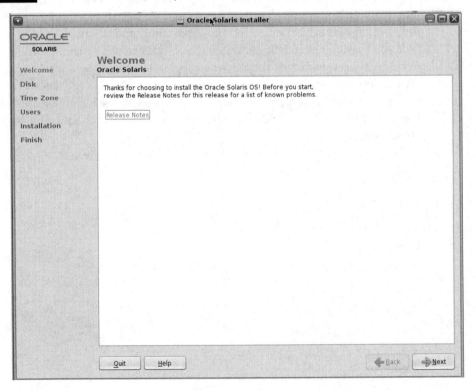

The Disk panel, shown in Figure 2-4, defines the storage currently attached to the computer. If you are using VirtualBox, the disk geometry is determined by the size of the file and the virtual attachment type you specified for it (such as SATA or IDE). By default, the boot drive is assumed to be your primary storage target.

The Recommended Size and Minimum Size settings given for installation are 7.0GB and 5.0GB, respectively. These are recommendations, not hard limits. If you provide less space, the installation will proceed as planned, but you risk exhausting the disk space before the installation completes. If a discovered disk is too small, you'll see a caution icon on top of the disk icon. If you select such a disk, you'll get a message telling you it's too small for an installation. You will want some additional disk capacity for software and data you're going to add later anyway. Choose the option Use the Whole Disk unless you are planning to support a multiboot configuration. Click the Next button.

Figure 2-5 shows the Time Zone, Date and Time panel. You have two ways to select the time zone. You can select a dot on the map that represents a key city in your time zone. Or, you can select the region, location, and time zone via the drop-

FIGURE 2-4   Live Media Install Disk panel

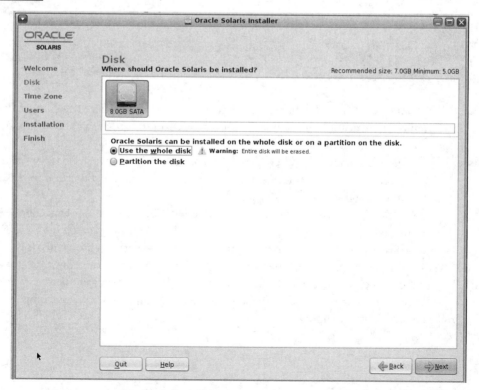

FIGURE 2-5   Live Media Time Zone, Date and Time panel

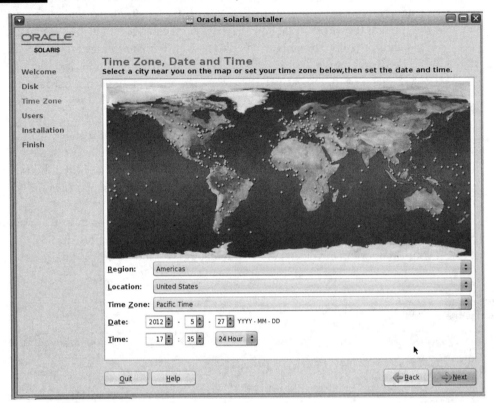

down boxes below the map. If the date and time do not reflect the current time, adjust them accordingly. Choose 12-hour or 24-hour format, as you wish. Click Next when you are done.

Figure 2-6 shows the Users panel. You are required to give an identity for a non-root user who will have access to root privileges after the installation. In this panel, you also give the system a hostname.

In Oracle Solaris 11, the root user can be implemented as a role account. A role is just like a user account, except you cannot log in with it. If root is a role, everyone on the system with root privileges has to log in first with their own account, then switch to root privileges when they need to use them. Security administrators have a much easier time tracking individuals on the system as long as they identify themselves on entry. Making root a role makes it impossible on a system with several administrators to appear effectively anonymous.

FIGURE 2-6   Live Media Users panel

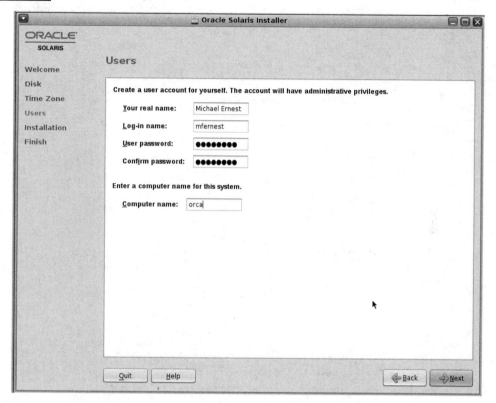

You'll also notice the password you provide must include one or more numeric characters. This requirement doesn't add much protection, as far as password strength is concerned, but it's sufficient to disallow common words that are easy to guess.

The name you assign to this system doesn't matter as much as if you were installing a server or other machine that you'd configure with a static IP address. In that case, an administrator may provide a name that is associated to the static IP recorded in a network lookup table. Assuming the name is for your own identification, something short but memorable is fine. Click the Next button when you are done with this panel.

Figure 2-7 shows the Installation panel, which reviews the information entered in the previous panels. Review the choices you've made and make sure they're what you want. Once you click the Install button, the only way to avoid writing the disk

FIGURE 2-7 Live Media Installation panel

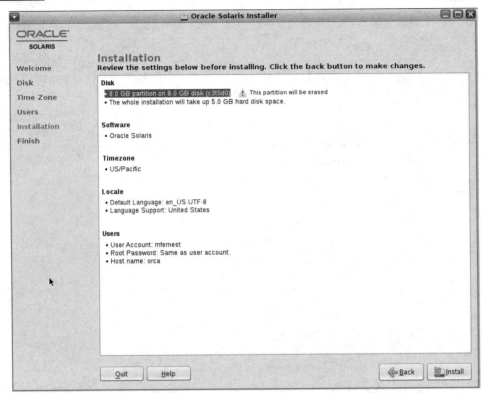

is by aborting the install program before it does anything. Use the Back button to return to any panels you'd like to correct. If the information is right, you're ready to install. That's it!

The Live Media install process is short for two reasons. First, Solaris 11 does not have bundled software packages (called *metaclusters* in prior Solaris versions) to select and modify. It's a one-size-fits-all software package with the Live Media or Text installers. Using a tool called the Automated Installer, you can assemble custom images for a one-time installation, but that is an advanced topic.

Second, the Live Media install process assumes you're installing Solaris for individual use. Using a process called Network Auto-Magic (NWAM), the install session discovers resources available on the local network, such as a Dynamic Host Configuration Protocol (DHCP) server, to configure the network interface. In fact, NWAM will work like this on each boot of the system to try and adapt the system to its local network environment.

Once you click the Install button, the Installing panel appears, as shown in Figure 2-8. The process may take 15 minutes or so, depending on your disk's throughput and other system resources. The progress meter that appears at the bottom of the Installer window gives you a rough idea of the total time the install will take. (Bear in mind that a number of accounting tasks are included in the last percent, so the 99-percent mark takes a bit longer to complete than expected.)

FIGURE 2-8   Live Media Installing panel

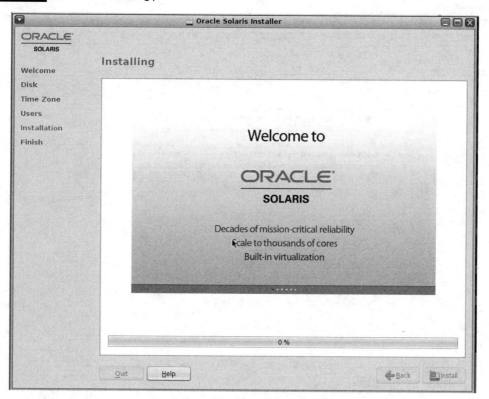

Reviewing the Installation Log

Once the installation process completes, the Finished panel appears, as shown in Figure 2-9.

This panel includes a link to the installation log, which is an in-memory transcript written to the install disk just before rebooting. If you click this link, a scrolling window of logged activity appears, similar to what's shown in Figure 2-10.

FIGURE 2-9   Live Media Finished panel

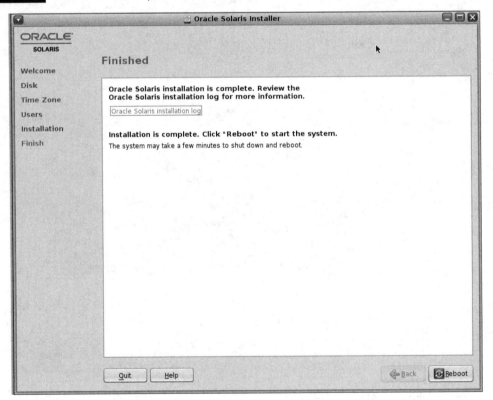

FIGURE 2-10   Post-installation log

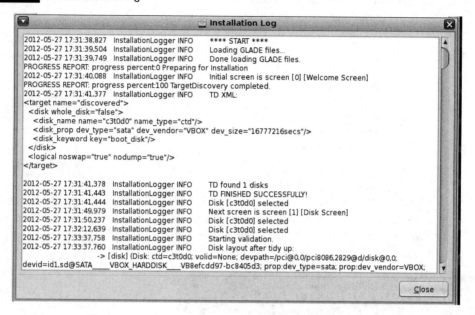

Notice a timestamp is included with some lines. You can use these times to determine the full duration of the install process and time required by individual steps. These steps include:

- Progressing through the wizard panels
- Identifying the target disk and layout calculations
- Creating space swap and dump (crash file) areas
- "Transferring files to /a" messages
- Checkpoint messages on file transfers

It's well worth your time to understand the process as logged. It's perhaps not so interesting when you're trying to digest a ton of other information all at once, but when you have to fix problems at this level, knowledge is the only expedience that will matter to you. If you know what a correct installation process looks like, you will not have to rely on error messages entirely to explain why the process took a left turn. Take some time with this file until you can make sense of the individual steps.

When the PROGRESS REPORT statements get to 99 percent, some scripted configuration activities take place to finalize the installation. These activities are intuitively named:

- generate-sc-profile (sc = system configuration)
- initialize-smf (smf = Services Management Facility)
- boot-configuration
- apply-sysconfig
- boot-archive
- create-snapshot

When you're finished reviewing the log, click the Reboot button. Before the system restarts, it will copy this content to the /var/sadm/system/logs/install_log file. You can review it again once after the system reboots and you log in.

CERTIFICATION OBJECTIVE 2.05

Logging In for the First Time

After the reboot, the GRUB menu will appear again. This time select Boot from Hard Disk. This action transfers control from GRUB on the install media to the GRUB setup that is now on your installed disk. This menu will look like Figure 2-11.

Again, the boot process starts automatically after 30 seconds if there is no keyboard input to interrupt it. Just attempting to move the cursor will disable the timer even though there are no other options to select. The sequence of events is more or less the same as booting from the install media: The system probes for physical devices, assigns drivers to manage them, and so on. Unlike the install process, it will read the default keyboard layout and language from the boot disk

FIGURE 2-11   GRUB menu on the installed disk

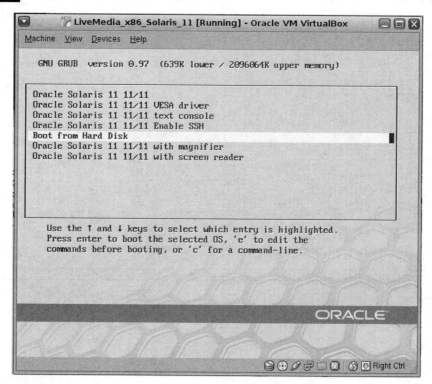

itself and prepare accordingly. While this initialization is going on, you'll see a grey screen with a faint honeycomb pattern in the background, similar to Figure 2-12.

Pressing the ENTER key will dismiss this graphic screen, revealing a console interface. If you do this soon after booting starts, you may see a number of SMF service descriptions tallying their way to 193. SMF services document and track the life cycles and dependencies of system services as well as some Userland applications. The descriptions mentioned are configurations read in from various XML files. They're used to populate a services database that establishes a dependency graph

FIGURE 2-12   Boot disk loading screen

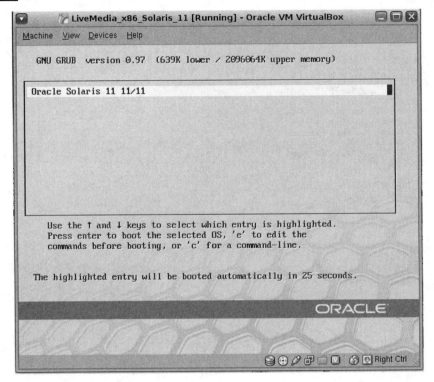

among them. This graph provides a start order for the services, based on their known dependencies. The graph also isolates these dependency chains from unrelated services, which means different chains can start up concurrently and help speed up the boot process. Your Solaris install builds this graph during the first bootup. Although the graph is checked on each subsequent boot for amendments, these boots typically take less time.

You will again see a login prompt on this console. Ignore it and wait for the graphic display to appear and provide a login console. Figure 2-13 shows this login interface.

FIGURE 2-13

Graphic login
screen

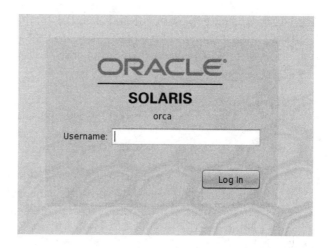

If you're following along on your own system, you'll see the accessibility options
represented by the disability icon in the lower-right corner. (It is cropped from
Figure 2-13 to save page space.) When clicked, it displays a list of preferences
suitable for users who need nonstandard displays and keyboards suited to their
needs. Figure 2-14 is the dialog box that displays these choices.

FIGURE 2-14

Universal Access
Preferences
dialog box

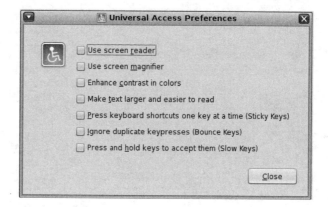

Once you enter a username and click Log In, the screen will change to present the additional controls shown in Figure 2-15.

Three options appear at the bottom of the screen. From left to right, these options let you select:

- Language
- Keyboard layout
- Session type (GNOME or xterm)

You can use these controls to modify your desktop session for localization and preferred appearance. Figure 2-16 shows the languages that are available at this stage of the process. After choosing one, you can complete your login with the password you established at the install configuration.

Login screen after a username is entered

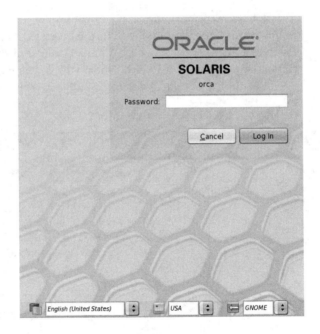

FIGURE 2-16

Language choices available at initial login

This screenshot shows the Live Media image is still mounted in the virtual machine that's hosting Solaris 11. The shortcut icons along the left side of the screen include:

- Oracle_Solaris_Live_X86
- Start Here
- Add More Software

Across the menu bar you see the same menu choices and icons as in the Live Media session. Again, feel free to explore these. We'll cover them in this study guide as they become relevant to the topics being presented. When you're finished exploring, log out using the System | Log Out *username* selection from the menu bar.

CERTIFICATION OBJECTIVE 2.06

Reviewing Text Installer Differences

A full walkthrough of the Text Installer is more than we need just to review the differences. The most obvious change is cosmetic: a terminal-based screen control in place of a full graphical mode. We should also note some configuration changes in the setup because they demonstrate some of the changes in preference you might want when managing a server instead of an individual setup.

At the first boot, the Text Installer begins a short countdown to its own installer. This lag provides a moment to alter the boot options, if you wish. Once started, the installer needs you to supply the keyboard layout and language, just like the Live Media installer did. The initial menu that follows that configuration is shown in Figure 2-17.

Option 1 will start the install configuration wizard. The welcome screen in the Text Installer, shown in Figure 2-18, tells you the location of the installation log in this session: /system/volatile/install_log. (The Live Media installer uses the same location, it just doesn't reveal it.)

FIGURE 2-17	
Text Installer initial menu	

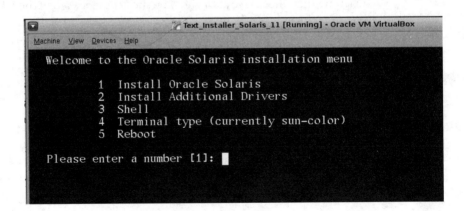

FIGURE 2-18

Text Installer
welcome screen

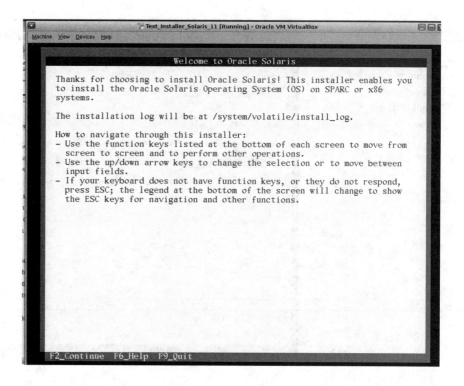

Assuming the keyboard layout permits, the Text Installer uses F keys for screen navigation: F2 to go forward, F3 to go back, F9 to quit. Other F keys are mapped as they become relevant in the current screen. If you don't have F keys, the program will map an alternative key combination, such as ALT+2. You'll use arrow keys to highlight a choice on the current screen. Pressing F2 (or the mapped alternative) accepts the choice.

Following the disk configuration in the sequence, the Text Installer prompts you for the computer name and network configuration, as shown in Figure 2-19.

Text Installer
computer name
and network
configuration
screen

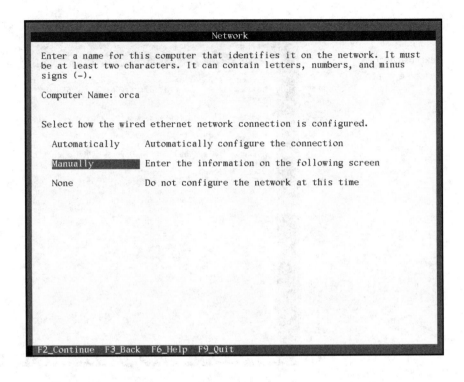

If you're installing a server, the name you give here may be one assigned by
a network administrator. Select the Manually choice to set up other network
identifiers and resources. F2 will take you to the Manually Configure: net0 screen.

The network interface identifier net0 is new. In prior versions of Solaris, network
interfaces were assigned a name to match the device driver, along with an instance
number. It's part of Solaris admin lore to recall interface names gone by: le0, hme0,
eri0, bge0, and so on. Starting with Solaris 11, however, you can name network
interfaces as you wish. Solaris 11 uses "net" by default. This makes for a uniform
display of resources, which is a good thing. Unfortunately, it also obscures, at least
for veteran users, the properties that are particular to certain drivers.

Once you provide a legal IP address, subnet, and router, the next screen will ask if
you want to configure the Domain Name Service (DNS), as shown in Figure 2-20.

If you want to add DNS services right away, the installer gives you space for three
IP addresses, as shown in Figure 2-21.

FIGURE 2-20

Text Installer
network
configuration
screen

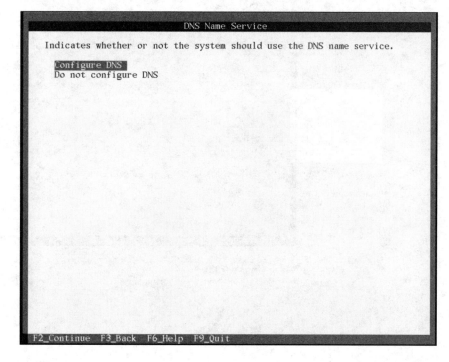

```
                            Manually Configure: net0

   Enter the configuration for this network connection. All entries must
   contain four sets of numbers, 0 to 255, separated by periods.

      NIC:          net0                   Settings will be applied to this
                                           interface
      IP Address:                          Must be unique for this network

      Netmask:      255.255.255.0          Your subnet use may require a
                                           different mask
      Router:                              The IP address of the router on this
                                           subnet

  F2_Continue   F3_Back   F6_Help   F9_Quit
```

FIGURE 2-21

Text Installer
DNS server
configuration
screen

```
                              DNS Name Service

   Indicates whether or not the system should use the DNS name service.

      Configure DNS
      Do not configure DNS

  F2_Continue   F3_Back   F6_Help   F9_Quit
```

The following screen, DNS Search List, lets you add default domain names. These can be used to resolve unqualified hostnames. If, for example, you'd like to make it a little easier to connect to a machine named khan in the fedofplanets. com domain, you can add this domain to the configuration. If a user on this system identifies the remote system only as "khan," the default domain will be added to the search for that machine's IP address. You can leave this list empty with no ill consequences; it just provides search convenience.

The Alternate Name Service screen, shown in Figure 2-22, lets you define supplemental lookup services to DNS (or in place of it, if you choose not to configure DNS).

The Time Zone: Regions and Date and Time screens follow. These are straightforward and virtually the same as the corresponding Live Media screens. However, the Users screen, shown in Figure 2-23, has some important differences.

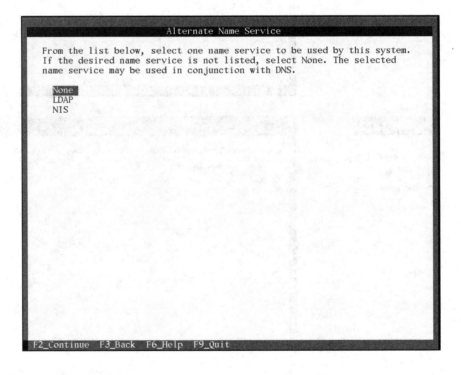

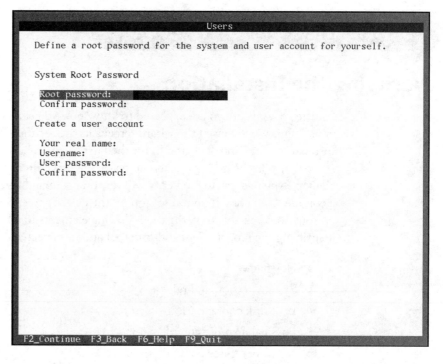

FIGURE 2-23

Text Installer
Users screen

Unlike the Live Media panel, here you're allowed to specify different passwords for the root role and the non-root user. The purpose for this arrangement isn't obvious, but if you supply a root password and leave the user account blank, the root role will be configured silently as a user account you can log into directly. If you prefer to keep root as a role, the passwords for both accounts may be the same, but this is not required. Both passwords must contain at least one numeric character or they'll be rejected.

The Installation Summary screen is the last in the flow. Visual differences aside, the rest of the process is about the same as with the Live Media installer. Once the installation completes, quit the installer process to view the installation log, or reboot and review the file after logging in.

If you're interested in seeing all the differences between Live Media and Text Installer, you can download the Text Installer and walk through each screen carefully. Installation time is considerably shorter because the program doesn't have to build a graphics environment and there is less software to install.

CERTIFICATION OBJECTIVE 2.07

Verifying the Installation

For the OCA exam, you're expected to know how you can verify the installation upon login. We reviewed the wizard screens in the sections "Reviewing the Installation Log" and "Logging In for the First Time." Those screens detailed the accessibility, keyboard layout, and language options currently set. The remaining elements you're expected to verify will rely on command-line tools. You'll only need a console screen or a terminal session on the desktop to execute these commands.

You should be able to verify the following elements in a Solaris 11 system by identifying the proper command-line tool and its expected output:

■ Hostname
■ System version and release
■ Boot disk configuration
■ Physical memory complement
■ Network service configuration
■ Network interface configuration

To do this from the desktop, you need a terminal window. There are several ways you can open one, including:

■ Right-clicking the backdrop. Choose Open Terminal from the menu that appears.
■ Clicking the icon that looks like a terminal screen on the menu bar.
■ Choosing Applications | Accessories | Terminal from the menu bar.

The hostname command should return the name you assigned your system during configuration:

```
$ hostname
orca
```

The uname -a command will report six fields of version and release information, including:

- Operating system (SunOS)
- Hostname
- Technical OS release number (5.11)
- Marketing release number (11.0)
- Hardware platform (i86pc i386 for X86 systems)
- Processor type (i86pc)

```
mfernest@orca:~$ uname -a
SunOS orca 5.11 11.0 i86pc i386 i86pc
```

You may notice there are seven fields of output instead of six. The fifth and sixth fields both report the hardware platform for X86 systems.

The /etc/release file contains version information that, unlike the uname command, does not come from the kernel itself. It's just a text file you can display using the cat utility:

```
mfernest@orca:~$ cat /etc/release
                 Oracle Solaris 11 11/11 X86
Copyright © 1983, 2011, Oracle and/or its affiliates.  All rights reserved.
            Assembled 18 October 2011
```

To get the total amount of memory available on your system, use the prtconf command and the grep utility:

```
mfernest@orca:~$ prtconf | grep Memory
Memory size: 4095 Megabytes
```

You have yet to learn about SMF services in detail, but using the svcs utility is the easiest way to verify the network services you have running. For now, just follow the syntax provided. We'll cover this command-line tool and SMF services in general in a later chapter:

```
mfernest@orca:~$ svcs network/physical
STATE          STIME    FMRI
disabled       6:14:09  svc:/network/physical:nwam
online         6:14:34  svc:/network/physical:upgrade
online         6:14:42  svc:/network/physical:default
```

This output shows the physical:nwam service is disabled. The physical:upgrade and physical:default services are online. The physical:default service manages a static IP configuration. The physical:nwam service, which once provided automatic configuration when connected to a network, is used to create network definitions for systems that connect to multiple networks.

Another big change in Solaris 11 has to do with the tools that report various layers of network resources. Solaris 11 has the ipadm command, which just manages IP interfaces. Along with several other tools like it, ipadm uses subcommands that all have a verb-object form, such as show-addr:

```
# ipadm show-addr
ADDROBJ          TYPE      STATE        ADDR
lo0/v4           static    ok           127.0.0.1/8
net0/_b          dhcp      ok           10.0.2.15/24
lo0/v6           static    ok           ::1/128
net0/_a          addrconf  ok           fe80::221:70ff:fec6:e4f8/10
#
```

The IP interfaces that have been defined for the system are listed as address objects in which the addresses themselves are one property. This output shows the IP addresses and subnets for net0. net0/_b is an IPv4 address object, and net0/_a is an IPv6 address object. Don't worry about the other fields included for now. We'll address them in detail when we focus on network services.

CERTIFICATION SUMMARY

The installation process, in particular for the Live Media installer, requires very little information to do its work. You just need to understand the installation sequence. Understanding the Text Installer differences helps you appreciate the intent of each installer type: Live Media for personal/workstation use, and Text Installer for server installation, including manual network configuration and possibly reverting root back to a user account. You also need a passing knowledge of the tools that help you verify the setup after the fact.

TWO-MINUTE DRILL

Using the LiveCD GUI Installer

❏ The Live Media for X86 and Text Installer images are both available for download from Oracle's website. You must have an Oracle support account (free) and agree to the license requirements.

❏ A Solaris 11 administrator should know the required elements to get to the Live Media desktop and the name and purpose of each utility that appears on the desktop.

Reviewing the LiveCD Desktop

❏ The application that starts the install process is called Install Oracle Solaris.

❏ You have access to the full services of a Solaris session as long as the tools do not require disk-based resources to operate properly.

Conducting an Installation

❏ For the certification exam, expect to recite the name of each panel that makes up the install wizard and what items you're expected to configure on it.

❏ The Live Media installer requires you to supply a non-root user account because root will be implemented as a role.

Reviewing the Installation Log

❏ The log report timestamps key operations in the installation process, marks the navigation of panels in the wizard process, and lays out the geometry of the boot disk, as well as tracks the progress by percentage of the install.

❏ Final tasks to prepare the new system for boot include writing a system configuration profile, initializing SMF, creating a boot archive, and taking a snapshot of the installation process.

Logging In for the First Time

❏ Two new applications appear on first login: Start Here and Add More Software.

❏ You can change the window session from GNOME to xterm. You can also change the keyboard layout and language, but only after you've entered a username.

Reviewing Text Installer Differences

❏ The Text Installer lets you choose manual or automatic network configuration.

❏ The Text Installer gives you the option of configuring the root account either as a role or a user who can log in directly to the system.

Verifying the Installation

❏ You need the hostname, uname, and prtconf commands to confirm the system's identity and to release information and memory resources.

❏ The network services physical:default and physical:nwam provide for static and dynamic IP configuration, respectively. Both can be disabled.

SELF TEST

Use the following questions to test your recall and understanding of the chapter material. Although these questions emphasize preparation for the OCA Solaris exam, one or two of them may test your recall of any material in this chapter.

Using the LiveCD GUI Installer

1. Which two values must you supply before the Live Media for X86 installer can initiate a desktop session?
   A. Keyboard attachment
   B. Time zone
   C. Language
   D. Keyboard layout

Reviewing the LiveCD Desktop

2. Which three actions are supported in a Live Media Desktop session?
   A. Using a web browser
   B. Examining device drivers
   C. Saving configuration changes to a file
   D. Opening a terminal console

Conducting an Installation

3. Which three options are configuration panels that are included in the Live Media installation wizard?
   A. Users
   B. Disk
   C. Network
   D. Installation

4. What is the difference between a role and a user account?

  A. A user account must have an exclusive password.

  B. A role account cannot log into the system.

  C. Only root can be a role.

  D. All non-root accounts must be users.

Reviewing the Installation Log

5. Which of the following activities execute to finalize a Solaris 11 installation?

  A. apply-sysconfig

  B. archive-snapshot

  C. boot-services

  D. initialize-smf

Logging In for the First Time

6. Which two settings can you change before entering a password through the Solaris login screen?

  A. Time zone

  B. Keyboard layout

  C. Accessibility options

  D. Password

Reviewing Text Installer Differences

7. Which directory holds the installation log before rebooting?

  A. /var/sadm/install/logs

  B. /system/volatile

  C. /var/adm/log

  D. /sbin/volatile

8. Which installation option(s) is/are available with the Text Installer but not the Live Media installer?

  A. Disk/partition configuration

  B. Naming network interfaces

  C. Adding software packages

  D. Configuring Domain Name Services

Verifying the Installation

9. Which command-line utility can you use to determine the physical memory available on your system?

A. memconf

B. uname -a

C. prtconf

D. svcs

10. How many addresses will Solaris 11 assign to a network interface by default?

A. One

B. Two

C. Three

D. Four

SELF TEST ANSWERS

Using the LiveCD GUI Installer

1. ☑ C and D. The system requires you to give defaults for the keyboard layout and language before it initiates the session.
   ☒ A and B are incorrect. The system determines the keyboard attachment automatically. The time zone isn't required until it's time to install the operating system.

Reviewing the LiveCD Desktop

2. ☑ A, B, and D. A LiveCD desktop session is like any other Solaris 11 session except it has no disk-based file system.
   ☒ C is incorrect because all files in the desktop session are backed by a read-only image.

Conducting an Installation

3. ☑ A, B, and D. You are required to specify all three elements before you can install Solaris 11 using the Live Media installer.
   ☒ C is incorrect. Network configuration is automatic with the Live Media installer. There is no option to configure it manually.

4. ☑ B. Role and user accounts behave in exactly the same way in every respect except one: You can only assume a role account after logging in with a user account first.
   ☒ A, C, and D are incorrect. A is incorrect because passwords don't have to be exclusive. In fact, in the Live Installer, the root role and first user account must have the same password. C is incorrect because a role is not exclusive to the root account; a role is simply the means by which Solaris 11 prevents a user from logging in as root. D is incorrect because any user account can be converted to a role, and vice versa.

Reviewing the Installation Log

5. ☑ A and D. These services are listed in the installation log once the progress reaches 99 percent. It's important to identify these services by name. If they are absent from the log, something has gone very wrong with the process and should be investigated.
   ☒ B and C are incorrect. These options are mangled versions of their original names. They are intended to remind you that knowing the exact names of these services is important.

Logging In for the First Time

6. ☑   **B and C.** These options appear on the login screen after you enter a username.
    ☒   **A and D** are incorrect. The time zone and user password can only be set during the installation phase or after logging in.

Reviewing Text Installer Differences

7. ☑   **B.** Both the Live Media and Text Installer use the /system/volatile directory to store the log during the installation. This directory is mounted on an in-memory file system because file writes can't be made to the install image.
    ☒   **A, C, and D** are incorrect. **A** and **C** are valid Solaris 11 directories but reside on disk-based file systems that are mounted as read-only during installation. **D** is a mash of well-known directory names and does not exist by default on Solaris 11.

8. ☑   **D.** You can configure DNS as well as other aspects that go with assigning a static IP to the system's network interface.
    ☒   **A, B, and C** are incorrect. Disk configuration is available through either installer. Neither installer lets you modify the installed software bundle or name your network interfaces, although you can do both tasks once the system is installed.

Verifying the Installation

9. ☑   **C.** The prtconf utility prints a great deal of information used during the system startup. Physical memory is just one component.
    ☒   **A, B, and D** are incorrect. The name memconf is made up and does not correspond to an available utility. The uname utility prints out information on the operating system release and hardware platform. The svcs utility is useful for learning the state of existing services but does not report static system information such as available RAM.

10. ☑   **B.** By default, Solaris 11 will assign each network interface IPv4- and IPv6-compliant addresses. In the Live Media installer, the configuration is automatic. In the Text Installer, the generated IPv6 address is shown. This address is based on data supplied with the network interface itself.
    ☒   **A, C, and D** are incorrect for the reasons just given.

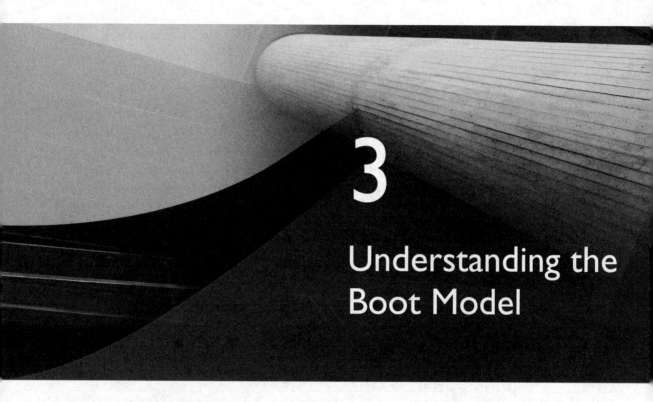

3
Understanding the Boot Model

Back in the old days, running Solaris on a PC was a novelty. The platform you'd run Solaris on was a SPARC-based system. However, with a little help, Solaris could run on an Intel processor supported by some, but not all, peripheral components. You used a piece of software called the Device Configuration Assistant (DCA) to load specific drivers to help bootstrap the system—and voilà! It wasn't something most people could do on their own without some arcane knowledge and maybe some expert help, but plenty of people did it. That's the way it was, and we liked it! We loved it!

Today, the Solaris world has turned on its head. I don't have numbers to show whether more people run Solaris on X86 than on SPARC today, but far more people know X86 hardware. Solaris 11 installs just as easily on it as any other operating system—minus a few peripheral devices here and there. I find myself in a strange position writing this chapter. After years of teaching Solaris on SPARC systems, I now teach it on X86 machines or VirtualBox. The SPARC boot model has become the rare platform (at least for me) and the X86 boot model the common case. We'll treat the two platforms accordingly in this chapter.

CERTIFICATION OBJECTIVE 3.01

Booting on SPARC Systems

Modern SPARC systems rely on a specification called OpenBoot, also known as the IEEE-1275 Standard for Boot Firmware. It defines a machine-independent Basic Input Output System (BIOS) that promotes the machine from its Power-On Self-Test (POST) diagnostics to a boot-ready state. Once the system chassis is powered, the POST inspects the system's onboard components. If the key components (CPU, RAM, and other system controllers) are found in working order, the firmware establishes an initial machine state suitable for testing components individually, configuring the firmware environment, or booting a kernel program. From that state, the system can initiate a boot process automatically, if so configured, or present a console prompt. If you have direct console access to a SPARC system, the prompt will appear like this:

```
ok
```

The environment behind this access point is a configurable and programmable session run by the OpenBoot PROM (OBP). Many small utilities are supported. For example, there is a banner utility that executes once the POST is complete. It reports the platform type, the amount of physical memory available, the OBP firmware version, the chassis serial number, and a few other details. You can also call it from the ok prompt. Other tools available here support diagnosing component states and listing or modifying your firmware's boot configuration. It's a rich environment for managing system components. Your PC hardware supports a similar facility. It's just available in a different way, usually by holding down an F key while the PC initializes.

on the
job

If you want to learn about these facilities in depth, consult the OpenBoot 4.x Command Reference Manual, which is available at http://docs.oracle.com/cd/ E19253-01/816-1177-10/816-1177-10.pdf.

The OBP boot utility sets up a SPARC system to accept and execute the core Solaris operating program called kernel. Although you can't execute it as a command, it's listed in a man page that describes how it works and what arguments it accepts—more on that later. Machine-level booting is a complex procedure in detail, but the process reduces to four distinct phases:

- OpenBoot PROM phase
- Booter phase
- Ramdisk phase
- Kernel phase

The Solaris 10 Update 1 release, first distributed in 2005, introduced a boot execution model that brings the SPARC and X86 implementations closer together. The DCA software I mentioned in the introduction, among other artifacts, is a thing of the past. If you didn't notice anything particular during the install process in the last chapter, that's the point of the current model. Now the last three phases are the same for both hardware platforms, so we'll cover the phase that is unique to SPARC here, using the boot utility, and discuss the remaining phases in the section "Booting on X86 Systems."

If you call the boot program, the OpenPROM boot phase starts by looking for a file system reader. If you're booting from a disk, you first need that disk's layout. The boot disk stores a partition map, called a VTOC, at sector 0. After reading it, the utility will find and load a file reader from sectors 1–15, an area called the *boot block*. It can then find and read a file called the *boot archive*, a collection of configuration files and driver code that prepares the system to load and execute the kernel program.

It sounds clean from a high level, but the process depends on a raft of settings stored in the OBP environment. You can change them if they are misconfigured, but that's about all you can do without deeper knowledge of the firmware. If the hardware isn't right for some reason, you can turn off the power, reseat your memory chips, cable connectors, and interface cards, turn on the power, and cross your fingers. If the system firmware isn't right, you can modify the settings and try again. Consult your hardware documentation for those procedures.

Assuming no lower-level problems exist, the boot utility will pass the OBP environment values to the kernel program. (The man page for the kernel program lists all the arguments it can receive. There's no mystery to it.) By calling boot -a, for example, you can invoke an interactive session to override values that are passed as defaults to the kernel. You don't need to learn this interaction for the exam, but here's a digest of what it looks like:

```
ok boot -a
Boot device: <path_to_default_device> File and args: -a
Name of system file [/etc/system]:<OS identification messages>
Retire store [/etc/devices/retire_store] [/dev/null to bypass]
root filesystem type [zfs]:
Enter physical name of root device [path_to_default_device]
```

At each one of these prompts you could provide an alternate value. You will rarely, if ever, do that, except for the name of the system file. If you've modified the /etc/system file such that the boot process panics while trying to read it, you could enter /dev/null (or a backup file, if you made one) to bypass it.

You can also override the default running state or logging level of a Solaris 11 system using boot -m. The first -m option has the following form:

```
boot -m milestone=<milestone>
```

The legal values for the milestone are:

- none
- all
- single-user

- multi-user
- multi-user-server

I'll have more to say about SMF milestones in Chapter 10. The setting none is useful if you have to raise the system to a point where you can repair the services facility itself, or fix other files needed to boot properly.

You might want to change the logging level to isolate the cause of adverse behavior in the previous session, or just change the level of detail for the next one. The second option for boot -m looks like this:

```
boot -m [ quiet | verbose | debug ]
```

You can pick one option, hit ENTER, and enjoy the quiet, verbosity, or debuggery that follows.

To reboot quickly on a SPARC system, you can apply the Fast Reboot feature that comes with Solaris 11. Owing to differences in the first phase, this feature operates by default on X86 platforms. For SPARC, you can invoke it in a terminal session with reboot -f.

CERTIFICATION OBJECTIVE 3.02

Booting on X86 Systems

On X86 systems, the Solaris 11 boot model relies on the BIOS that ships with the target hardware. Instead of using a VTOC and boot block, X86 systems use the BIOS to call the Master Boot Record (MBR), a 512-byte construct that includes support for a partition table and bootstrap code. The MBR provides support for multibooting, a practice of putting multiple operating systems on a single disk. That capability on SPARC is moot.

The X86 counterpart to the OBP's boot utility is the Grand Unified Bootloader (GRUB), which we used in the last chapter. Like the OBP, several utilities are available within GRUB itself. If you press C before the system has a chance to boot, you'll be dropped into a command-line environment with this prompt:

```
grub>
```

It's not stated on the screen, but Solaris 11 uses a modified version of GNU GRUB 0.97 you can't replace with the software you can download from www.gnu.org/software/grub/. The two are close enough for most uses, but if you're already fluent with standard GRUB, you might be surprised by some utilities that are unique to Solaris and some that are, for various technical reasons, disabled.

GRUB supports tab completion for commands, which can come in handy. If you press TAB at the prompt, all available commands will be output, as shown in Figure 3-1. Press ESC to return to the main menu.

GRUB supports boot sessions with different criteria, which are then shown as menu choices you can select to start a session (refer to Figure 2-2 and Figure 2-11 in Chapter 2). Instead of pressing ENTER to select one, you can press E to see the details of the highlighted choice. Figure 3-2 shows the settings for the Oracle Solaris 11 11/11 choice that's given for a new installation.

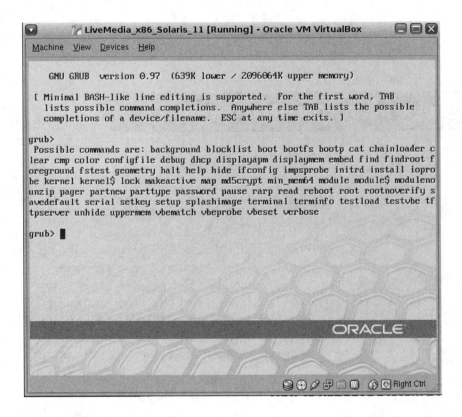

FIGURE 3-1

Available commands in the GRUB utility

Boot details for
the Solaris 11
11/11 GRUB
entry

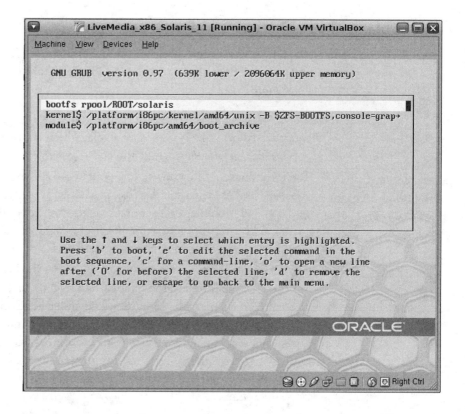

```
                    LiveMedia_x86_Solaris_11 [Running] - Oracle VM VirtualBox
  Machine  View  Devices  Help

     GNU GRUB  version 0.97  (639K lower / 2096064K upper memory)

   ┌─────────────────────────────────────────────────────────────────────┐
   │ bootfs rpool/ROOT/solaris                                             │
   │ kernel$ /platform/i86pc/kernel/amd64/unix -B $ZFS-BOOTFS,console=grap→│
   │ module$ /platform/i86pc/amd64/boot_archive                            │
   │                                                                       │
   │                                                                       │
   │                                                                       │
   │                                                                       │
   │                                                                       │
   │                                                                       │
   └─────────────────────────────────────────────────────────────────────┘
       Use the ↑ and ↓ keys to select which entry is highlighted.
       Press 'b' to boot, 'e' to edit the selected command in the
       boot sequence, 'c' for a command-line, 'o' to open a new line
       after ('O' for before) the selected line, 'd' to remove the
       selected line, or escape to go back to the main menu.


                                                          ORACLE
```

The variable bootfs locates the file system reader. The kernel$ variable locates
the kernel program and can include additional parameters to pass to it, such as the
console type. This variable is set to graphical by default for Live Media installations.
The full line is cut off in the screenshot and on most displays, but if you press E
again with the line highlighted, it will appear in an edit mode that lets you run the
cursor over the complete line. The module$ variable locates the boot archive file, as
mentioned in the "Booting on SPARC Systems" section.

Use the ESC key to get to the main menu. You can use the ENTER key to start the
session whenever you'd like.

The Solaris Boot Design and Process

Once you start the boot process, either from an OBP or a GRUB menu, the remaining phases are the same on each platform. Let's take each phase in turn and provide more detail.

- **Booter phase**   It's at this point the boot archive file gets read. It comes in sequence before a file system is available, which is why the system needs a special file reader, identified by the bootfs variable, to begin with.

- **Ramdisk phase**   The ramdisk component is a file in ISO format that is mounted and used as a stand-alone, read-only file system. It contains drivers and configuration files that set up the earliest stages of initializing the kernel program. Placing critical startup files in the ramdisk makes it possible to establish a platform-agnostic booting model as early as possible.

- **Kernel phase**   After the bootstrapping is done, the kernel program starts. It starts out by mounting to the ramdisk and reading in driver modules. One of those drivers supports the root file system and can attach it to the root device specified in the system setup. After some amount of further initialization, the kernel unmounts from the ramdisk, continues working on the root file system, and drops the ramdisk itself from memory. Once initialized, the kernel program can call other programs that build the system to a user-accessible state.

Managing the Boot Archive

The boot archive is a collection of files derived from the full root (/) file system of a Solaris 11 instance. Using it supports a boot model that's consistent between the SPARC and X86 platforms, to the degree possible, and improves booting efficiency. When you install Solaris 11, the system creates the archive by copying key files from the root file system. During any given session, a configuration change might affect one of these files, so it's important to keep the boot archive copy in sync with the root file system copy before shutting down. The system will perform this task automatically as part of a graceful shutdown process. From time to time, however, you might want to inspect the archive or update it immediately after making changes, just to be safe.

Solaris 11 provides the bootadm utility to manage all four tasks. It only supports two of these tasks on a SPARC platform: update-archive and list-archive. On X86 platforms, the bootadm utility also supports the set-menu and list-menu subcommands for managing the GRUB menu list.

You can see the list of archived files any time using the list-menu subcommand. This operation is privileged, however. You can invoke the command from your default user account with sudo and your password (or the root password if it's different from yours), as shown here:

```
$ sudo bootadm list-archive
Password: <enter password>
boot/acpi/tables
boot/solaris/bootenv.rc
...
platform/i86pc/ucode/GenuineIntel
platform/i86pc/ucode/AuthenticAMD
```

You'll see a variety of files from the boot, etc, and platform directories. Some files will vary per platform, but they are all concerned with information that comes into play early in the boot process.

The update-archive subcommand checks these files in the root file system against their archive counterparts. If any of the former have changed, the result will look like this:

```
$ sudo bootadm update-archive
updating //platform/i86pc/boot_archive
updating //platform/i86pc/amd64/boot_archive
```

The sudo utility doesn't require a password if you use it again within a few minutes of the previous command. Also, we see there are platform-specific versions of the file. Also, if you run this process yourself, you'll notice it doesn't finish quickly if it needs to repack the files. If you want to see more information, use the -v switch for verbose output.

The list-menu subcommand reports the location and contents of text file menu.lst. You don't need superuser privilege to invoke it:

```
$ bootadm list-menu
the location for the active GRUB menu is: /rpool/boot/grub/menu.lst
default 0
timeout 30
0 Oracle Solaris 11 11/11
```

The default setting indicates which indexed menu item will be chosen when the menu is first presented. The timeout setting allows 30 seconds before triggering a boot. You can set this lower to reduce the delay (or to 0 if you want to disable it). Each menu choice, preceded by its index number, follows after that.

With the set-menu subcommand, which does require superuser privilege, you can change the settings using a key-value pair, as shown:

```
$ sudo bootadm set-menu timeout=15
```

Have a look at the menu.lst file through an editor if you want more detail as well as some notes on alternate settings. It's a good idea to make a backup of this file if you decide to experiment.

Listing Logged-in Users

Prior to shutting down your system, it's a good idea to list the open sessions, see who else is currently connected, and provide some kind of warning. If you have remote users accessing an HTTP server or some other stateless service, you won't see them, and there aren't many ways to warn them from a console session. If, however, you have users connected via services such as telnet or a secure shell, you can use the system to identify their sessions and send a warning through that channel.

Solaris 11 has the who command, as do many UNIX variants. It supports numerous options for reporting. Consult the man page to review the choices. The default report includes the user's identity, the name of their terminal connection, the date and time they logged in, and where they're connecting from, as shown:

```
$ who
mfernest    vt/2        Jun 30 08:03    (:0)
mfernest    pts/3       Jul  3 15:38    (192.168.15.100)
mfernest    pts/2       Jul  2 15:58    (:0.0)
```

In this example, I have three active sessions. One is connected from another system, as indicated by the IP address. That connection might appreciate some fair warning, particularly if the user has a file open with unsaved edits.

Shutting Down the System

You have many options for changing the system's running state, including shutting it down. There are as many ways to refer to these options, too. I just call them "init states," after the init command, but there are also namesake commands, such as reboot, shutdown, and halt, that do the same work, with a few differences.

Using the init command, you change the state of your session as you see fit. Table 3-1 lists the arguments for init that have such an effect. You can learn the other options by consulting the man page.

On SPARC, an init 0 command should return you to the ok prompt. Firmware mode in this case refers to the OBP. For X86 systems, you'll end up at the GRUB menu unless you enter the system configuration menu for your machine. Most platforms use an F key combination during the BIOS check to allow access. On a VirtualBox installation, you may appear to stall, but if you hit the ENTER key once or twice, it should return to the GRUB menu.

It's not a common practice to switch back and forth among the user states (s or S, 2 and 3) except to test new applications and services. Usually it's sufficient to use init 6 to reboot the system and cycle through these states in proper order. To get into more detail, I refer to these user states as milestones in Chapter 10.

It's not common to boot or switch to administrator mode (1), but the system will stop here if it can't continue booting. This problem may occur if, for example, the kernel can't read the boot archive or mount the root file system. It's different from the single-user level, which is a healthy state but restricts access to the local console. Administrator mode exists so you can effect necessary repairs.

Think carefully before using init 5 on a remote system. If you can't quickly or easily restore power to it, this option is not for you. I can't say how often people use init 6, or its namesake command reboot, on a system that supports many users, but certainly for dedicated user systems it's fine.

TABLE 3-1	init Command Argument	Mode or Action
init Command Arguments That Change the System State	0	Firmware
	1	System administrator
	2	Multiuser (allows remote connections)
	3	Multiuser with services
	4	Unspecified
	5	Shutdown and power off
	6	Reboot
	S or s	Single user

For servers, or on any system multiple users rely on, the shutdown command is a good tool. With it you can post a notice to any user who has a state connect and can receive a terminal message. The shutdown command lets you define a grace period before shutdown occurs and includes a message facility that warns users when that time will expire. A sample invocation looks like this:

```
$ sudo shutdown -g 600 -i 6 "Save your files!"
```

In this example, I set a grace period for 600 seconds (10 minutes) and tell the system to change to init state 6 (reboot). The default values for these settings are 60 seconds and single user state, respectively. I also included a message I want added to the utility's default warning, which is issued to everyone using a terminal connection. By default, the system prompts the issuing user to revoke the command at certain intervals; consult the man pages for these values. You can disable this prompt with the -y switch.

The remaining states, or run levels, all have counterparts in the Services Management Facility (SMF) called milestones. We discuss these in detail in Chapter 10.

The commands halt and poweroff are the same program code. They accept the same arguments and are documented on the same man page. It's a programmer trick that makes the program do slightly different things depending on the name used to invoke it.

If you prefer these namesake commands to using the init command's numeric arguments, that's fine. They are not, however, synonymous with the init command states. The init command is tied into the process of starting services on your system, but is also integral to shutting them down gracefully. That is, when you call the init 0 command, you're instructing the system to work its way down to that level of service. Utilities such as halt and reboot are exactly what they sound like: a call to change the state of the system right away. The shutdown command lets you impose a delay and warn logged-in users before it is executed, but by default it just shuts down the system where it stands.

CERTIFICATION OBJECTIVE 3.03

Managing Boot Environments (BEs)

Solaris 11 has a new default root file system called ZFS. The ZFS file system first appeared in Solaris 10 Update 2, which was released in June 2006. In Solaris 10

Update 6, released in October 2008, it became an option for the root file system. Now it is the default (and only) choice.

It may sound like a step back to have fewer options than more, but ZFS is really more than just a file system. I have more to say about that in Chapter 4. As an integral part of the operating system, it supports other bedrock features that would be hard-pressed to work, or work as well, without it. Support for boot environments (BEs) is one of them.

The concept behind boot environments began with a product called Live Upgrade. Live Upgrade supports what are called *alternate boot environments (ABEs)*, copies of the root file system that can be used as alternate boot devices. You could upgrade or patch an ABE with the system running on a different boot environment. Then, when you want, you could switch to it. If all goes well, you have reduced the cost of upgrading or patching your root file system to a reboot instead of taking it offline for the maintenance work.

With BEs, it's the same, except you don't need additional partitions. Instead, you use ZFS's snapshot capability to capture a point-in-time view of the file system. You name it and track it. Using the utility Package Manager or beadm, you can manage the list of BEs you create. Now you can add or update multiple software packages, configure security or other key services, or just mess the system up. By rolling back to a working BE, it all goes away. By choosing a more current snapshot, your changes come back.

Two tools manage BEs: The Package Manager GUI provides fewer options and isn't much fun without two or three BEs already made. The beadm utility gives you full command of your BEs, so I'll discuss that first.

Using the beadm Utility to Administer Boot Environments

The beadm utility supports the following subcommands:

- activate
- create and destroy
- list
- mount and unmount
- rename

INSIDE THE EXAM

The exam may ask you how to verify a BE once it is created. This means listing it. The beadm utility does not support actual verification, such as sanity testing or integrity checks, of a BE.

You can create a BE simply by naming one:

```
$ sudo beadm create ocach3
$ beadm list
BE        Active Mountpoint Space  Policy Created
--        ------ ---------- -----  ------ -------
ocach3    -      -          181.0K static 2012-07-04 01:36
solaris   NR     /          4.32G  static 2012-05-27 17:40
```

There are now two images of BEs. The ocach3 BE is a clone of the active BE. The difference between them amounts to all changes to the root file system since it was created, about 181K, which includes some metadata for tracking the ocach3 BE. The Active column for the solaris BE reports NR, indicating this is the active BE (N) and is also the active BE after reboot.

You can create BEs based on any other BE, active or inactive. If you want to examine an inactive BE, you can even mount it to an available directory on the active BE!

You can rename the ocach3 image if you like:

```
$ sudo beadm rename ocach3 beupdate1
$ sudo beadm activate beupdate1
$ beadm list
BE          Active Mountpoint Space  Policy Created
--          ------ ---------- -----  ------ -------
beupdate1   R      -          4.32G  static 2012-07-04 01:36
solaris     N      /          409.0k static 2012-05-27 17:40
```

Notice the change in space allocation. Now that the beupdate1 BE is scheduled to activate on reboot, it assumes responsibility for the file system. The solaris BE reports 409K as the effective difference between the install image and the current state of the file system. Because metadata is involved, these numbers can be hard to reconcile to actual file changes. It's more important to understand the overall cost of each BE on disk than to account for it exactly.

On X86 systems, these operations also update the GRUB menu. If you performed the preceding operations, you'd see the change on your system as shown:

INSIDE THE EXAM

```
$ bootadm list-menu
the location for the active GRUB menu is: /rpool/boot/grub/menu.lst
default 1
timeout 15
0 Oracle Solaris 11 11/11
1 beupdate1
```

The default setting now points to the new BE that appears in the list. You can examine the menu.lst file to see the setting details. The bootfs setting will reflect the name of the BE; the other settings should match what's given for the original BE.

On reboot, unless you select the solaris BE from the GRUB menu, the BE listing will look like this:

```
$ beadm list
BE         Active Mountpoint Space  Policy Created
--         ------ ---------- -----  ------ -------
beupdate1  NR     /          4.39G  static 2012-07-04 01:36
solaris    -      -          11.69M static 2012-05-27 17:40
```

The solaris BE has grown a bit more to accommodate all the data blocks on disk that preserve its snapshot. As the active BE changes more of the file system data it inherited, the ZFS file system duplicates the original data blocks and updates the duplicate with the changes. The original blocks remain assigned to the original BE.

Without a BE to reference the original blocks, the root file system has no reason to track them. Destroying a BE releases the metadata that references its data blocks. If another BE references those same blocks, only the metadata is lost. Even if a destroyed BE is the sole owner of some data blocks, the system doesn't delete them. It just stops tracking them and considers their space available for future use.

The beadm utility can also create a *snapshot* of a BE. Let's say you want to take a read-only image of the current BE before making some changes. If all goes well, you won't need that image and you can discard it. If something goes wrong, however, you want to start over with the image you had, not boot to an alternate. A snapshot provides that service.

For the sake of illustration, I'll create a snapshot of the solaris BE I have, then list the snapshots currently on my system:

```
$ sudo beadm create solaris@test
$ beadm list -s
BE          Active Mountpoint Space  Policy Created
--          ------ ---------- -----  ------ -------
beupdate1   NR     /          4.39G  static 2012-07-04 01:36
solaris     -      -          11.69M static 2012-05-27 17:40
$ beadm list -s
BE/Snapshot                        Space    Policy  Created
-----------                        -----    ------  -------
beupdate1
    beupdate1@2012-07-04-08:36:13  27.65M   static  2012-07-04 01:36
    beupdate1@install              148.64M  static  2012-05-27 18:12
solaris
    solaris@test                   0        static  2012-07-04 03:13
```

The -s option to the list subcommand lists the snapshots of all BEs. If you name the snapshot you want, you'll get output just for that entity. Notice each BE has at least one snapshot supporting it. There are a few system events that prompt this behavior automatically.

The space consumed by snapshots grows as the clones on top of it change more data blocks. You can delete copies you don't need. You can also create a new BE from a snapshot instead of the current BE—just name it as part of the create subcommand.

Once a BE represents an image you can no longer use, you can destroy it, as shown:

```
$ sudo beadm create temp
$ beadm list
BE          Active Mountpoint Space  Policy Created
--          ------ ---------- -----  ------ -------
beupdate1   NR     /          4.41G  static 2012-07-04 01:36
solaris     -      -          11.69M static 2012-05-27 17:40
temp        -      -          149.0K static 2012-07-04 07:00
$ sudo beadm destroy temp
Are you sure you want to destroy temp?  This action cannot be undone(y/[n]): y
```

```
$ beadm list
BE          Active Mountpoint Space  Policy Created
--          ------ ---------- -----  ------ -------
beupdate1   NR     /          4.41G  static 2012-07-04 01:36
solaris     -      -          11.69M static 2012-05-27 17:40
```

You can also remove snapshots this way; just name one. If any snapshots are associated with a BE, this command removes them automatically, so be sure you don't want any as BEs before you commit. If you're sure, you can override the confirmation prompt by using the -F option. If the BE is mounted, use the -f option to force unmount and delete in one action.

Marking a BE as active or active on boot protects it from any operations that try to change its state, which includes renaming and destroying. Sometimes that's confusing. For example, if you have two BEs, one marked active and the other marked active on reboot, you can't rename or destroy either one.

Other rules are listed in the man pages that refer to delicate or complex uses of BEs. If you're working with an important, complex system, confine yourself to simple cases until you're quite sure of these arrangements. At the very least, you should review all of the "EXAMPLES" section in the beadm man page to appreciate the full scope of this utility.

Using Package Manager to Administer Boot Environments

The system will create new BEs when it is prompted by software upgrades. I review the motivation and the mechanism for that service in Chapter 12. It's for that reason the Package Manager provides some support for BE management.

There are three ways you can invoke the Package Manager:

- Click the icon in the menu bar.
- Choose System | Administration | Package Manager from the menu bar.
- Call the packagemanager program from the command line.

Figure 3-3 shows the menu pick option. The icon for the Package Manager is the light blue box with the circular arrow to the right of the System menu. With either choice, your login environment automatically raises your privilege so you run the program as root.

FIGURE 3-3

Menu option
for selecting the
Package Manager
utility

If you run the packagemanager program from the command line as a non-privileged user, you'll see this error:

```
$ packagemanager
WARNING: packagemanager
Unable to setup log:
 [Errno 13] Permission denied: '/var/tmp/packagemanager_info.log'
  All info messages will be logged to stdout
 [Errno 13] Permission denied: '/var/tmp/packagemanager_error.log'
  All errors and warnings will be logged to stderr
```

Remember to use the sudo command. Many users get impatient with this practice and use the sudo command to call a shell program instead of specific commands. This raises the privilege of all subsequent operations in that shell. You did not learn how to do that from me.

You'll also discover that using sudo when putting a command in the background (by using & at the end of the command) may appear to hang your current session. If it has been a while since your last sudo command, you'll be prompted for the password. If the job is in the background, you won't see it. Bring the job to the foreground, answer the prompt, and then you can push the job to the background again.

Managing BEs is a side task for the Package Manager, so it's not obvious where to find it. You can get to it by choosing File | Manage Boot Environments menu or typing ALT-F B. You can delete and rename any BE that is not marked active or active on boot. The panel enforces this rule by graying out prohibited actions. You can activate any BE you like.

Figure 3-4 shows the two BEs, solaris and beupdate1, on my system. If you have the same, try selecting the solaris BE and click the radio button for Active on Reboot. The OK button at the lower right will become available to commit the choice. You can also rename it if you rebooted after activating the beupdate1 BE.

If you do make a change, the Package Manager produces a confirmation dialog panel. It will dismiss the Manage Boot Environments panel if you choose OK. It seems that while the panel implicitly lists BEs, it does not refresh this list on its own. It is therefore not a useful monitor for ongoing BE activity from other sessions. If you raise the panel again, however, any changes made by you—and possibly other privileged users—will appear.

FIGURE 3-4

The Manage Boot
Environments
panel in Package
Manager

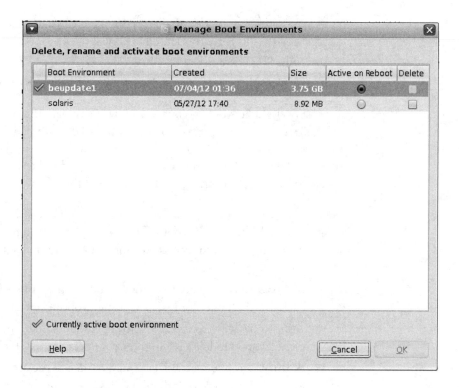

CERTIFICATION OBJECTIVE 3.04

Troubleshooting Boot Problems

The artifacts used in each boot phase, when misconfigured or corrupted, will certainly gum up the works. Solving all of the problems we can identify here falls outside the scope of the OCA exam. That said, solving these issues is the easy part. It's not quick if you don't know how to fix what's broken, but once you're certain where the trouble lies, you do know what you need to know to take the next step.

Isolating your problem is always the first step. That's very hard if you don't know how the system is organized, what sequence of actions you rely on for the system to boot correctly, or where key files happen to be. For the boot model, the list of concerns we can specify include:

- **SPARC/X86:** A successful POST
- **SPARC:** Properly configured OBP variables
- **X86:** Properly configured BIOS/GRUB settings
- **SPARC/X86:** Syncing the boot archive with the root file system

Most of the time, you'll go out of your way to create these problems here. The OCA exam doesn't expect you to know what to do with bad physical components, corrupted driver configurations, and other low-level technical details. The best advice is to know what a proper booting system looks like without needing that system for reference. To that end, I recommend the following precautions as good practice:

- **SPARC:** Know what your OBP environment settings should be. These can vary with your hardware, so consult your platform documentation and your system.
- **SPARC:** Know the boot -a process and the files it uses for defaults. Refer back to the chapter for instructions on working around a bad /etc/system file.
- **X86:** Know what the menu.lst file should look like, specifically the bootfs, kernel$, and module$ settings for your default GRUB choice.
- **Both:** When in doubt, use bootadm to update the archive. You can learn the format and content of individual files over time, but knowing how to update the boot archive goes a long way.

- **Both:** For multiple users, be gracious when shutting down the system. Plan ahead and give fair warning. For your own sake, be doubly cautious with connected users who have privileged access.
- **Both:** Confirm the BE marked active on boot before rebooting.

CERTIFICATION SUMMARY

Booting is conceptually one process, but the hardware details can be quite different. To prepare for this portion of the exam, pay attention to differences in technology between SPARC and X86 systems and the role the technology component plays on each platform. Remember that the OBP only has to support running Solaris on a SPARC machine. The GRUB utility, on the other hand, is a general-purpose bootloader for which Solaris is just one of the supported operating systems.

These differences also change the features a utility such as beadm can support and the complement of files that are incorporated into the boot archive. If you keep these elements straight, you're more than halfway to succeeding with exam questions on this topic.

TWO-MINUTE DRILL

Booting on SPARC Systems

❏ The OpenPROM Boot phase is unique to SPARC systems.

❏ If booting is not automatic from the OBP session, use the boot utility to initiate it.

Booting on X86 Systems

❏ The boot phases common to both platforms are called the booter, ramdisk, and kernel phases.

❏ The boot archive file is a critical component. Its files must match their counterparts in the root file system to guarantee a correct and complete boot.

Managing Boot Environments (BEs)

❏ The Package Manager program can list, rename, activate, and destroy eligible BEs.

❏ The beadm utility can create, mount, and unmount BEs in addition to what the Package Manager can do. It can also create snapshots of BEs suitable for making new BEs.

❏ On X86, new BEs are automatically added to the GRUB file menu.lst.

Troubleshooting Boot Problems

❏ Focus on the setting and files you rely on for proper booting. If you know how their contents should appear, you'll be more effective at isolating trouble. Learning to fix them quickly takes time, but such tasks are specific and achievable.

SELF TEST

The following questions will help measure your understanding of the material presented in this chapter. Some questions have more than one correct answer. When this is the case, the question states how many options are correct.

Booting on SPARC Systems

1. Which one of the following phases is specific to booting on a SPARC system?
   A. The ramdisk phase
   B. The ok phase
   C. The OpenBoot PROM phase
   D. The POST phase

2. Which two options does the boot -m argument support?
   A. Setting the logging level
   B. Passing an argument the kernel program accepts
   C. Enabling interactive mode
   D. Setting the milestone level

Booting on X86 Systems

3. Which of the following is a required component to boot Solaris 11 on an X86 system?
   A. A boot block area
   B. A user-keyed selection from the GRUB menu
   C. A user account with privileged access
   D. A ramdisk

4. Which option is a valid function of the bootadm command?
   A. Delete an alternate boot archive
   B. Activate a boot archive
   C. Edit the GRUB menu file settings
   D. Rename the current boot archive

Managing Boot Environments (BEs)

5. What does it mean if a boot environment is marked active on boot?
   A. It is active and currently mounted.
   B. It cannot be destroyed.
   C. It has no snapshots.
   D. It cannot be mounted.

6. Assuming there are two BEs—one marked active, the other marked active on boot—which function can you execute with Package Manager?
   A. Listing BEs
   B. Renaming BEs
   C. Destroying BEs
   D. Mounting BEs

7. Which statement describes a function you cannot perform with the beadm utility?
   A. Destroy a snapshot of the BE marked active
   B. Deactivate the current BE
   C. Clone an inactive BE
   D. Mount a snapshot

Troubleshooting Boot Problems

8. Which three options are supported by the shutdown command?
   A. You can override the administrator prompts to abort the countdown.
   B. You can suppress the utility's default warning message.
   C. You can set a grace period.
   D. You can transition to any init state.

9. Which statement correctly describes a difference between single-user mode and administrator mode, as defined by init command arguments?
   A. Single-user mode prevents remote users from connecting.
   B. The system may stop at administrator mode if something's wrong.
   C. The system cannot stop at single-user mode unless something's wrong.
   D. Administrator mode lets you repair the system.

10. Which three options are valid logging states you can select using boot -m?

A. quiet

B. verbose

C. default

D. debug

SELF TEST ANSWERS

Booting on SPARC Systems

1. ☑ **C.** The OpenBoot PROM phase occurs after the POST completes and before the bootstrapping process begins.

    ☒ **A** is incorrect because the ramdisk phase is common to both platforms. **B** is incorrect because it does not identify a proper phase. **D** is incorrect because a POST, although a common process to both platforms, is not considered part of the booting model.

2. ☑ **A and D.** The boot -m option allows the user to specify one of three logging levels: quiet, verbose, or debug. With a milestone= parameter added, the user can change the default milestone.

    ☒ **B and C** are incorrect. **B** is incorrect because the kernel accepts different arguments using different switches or syntax from the OBP's boot program. **C** is incorrect because interactive mode is established with boot -a.

Booting on X86 Systems

3. ☑ **D.** The ramdisk phase is synonymous with reading the boot archive file.

    ☒ **A** is incorrect because the boot block area is associated with a SPARC install. **B** is incorrect because GRUB can time out and start automatically with the default selection. **C** is incorrect because booting does not rely on user accounts. The system will still boot; you just won't be able to log into it.

4. ☑ **C.** The set-menu option of the bootadm command won't edit the entire contents of the menu.lst file, but it will let you change default and timeout settings.

    ☒ **A, C, and D** are incorrect. Each one refers to a feature of the beadm command. I just replaced the term *boot environment* with *boot archive*.

5. ☑ **B.** The BE marked active on boot will become active and is mounted on the next reboot.

    ☒ **A** is incorrect because it describes the BE that is currently marked active. **C** is incorrect because snapshots are irrelevant to the BE's active status. **D** is incorrect because any unmounted BE can be mounted.

Managing Boot Environments (BEs)

6. ☑ **A.** Package Manager lists the BEs one time when the Manage Boot Environments command is chosen.
   ☒ **B** and **C** are incorrect because these options can't be used when all available BEs have one of the two active status marks. **D** is incorrect because the Package Manager doesn't perform mounting.

7. ☑ **D.** You cannot treat a snapshot as if it was a BE. You'd have to make a BE from it first.
   ☒ **A** is incorrect because snapshots aren't usable as BEs. B is incorrect because deactivating a BE only affects its status after reboot. **C** is incorrect because you can make (or clone) a BE with any other BE. Cloning the active BE is just the default behavior.

Troubleshooting Boot Problems

8. ☑ **A, C,** and **D.** The switches -y, -g, and -i, respectively, manage the capabilities described by these options.
   ☒ **B** is incorrect. You can supplement the shutdown utility's warning message with your own, but you cannot disable its standard warning.

9. ☑ **B.** You can get to administrator mode using init 1, but it's more likely the system will stop here when it cannot continue the boot process.
   ☒ **A** is incorrect because both modes disallow remote connection. **C** is incorrect because you can get to single-user state with init s or init S. **D** is incorrect because you can repair the system from any run level you can get to.

10. ☑ **A, B,** and **D.** These three choices are the documented acceptable settings with the boot -m command.
    ☒ **C** is incorrect because it is sufficient to provide no option for default logging.

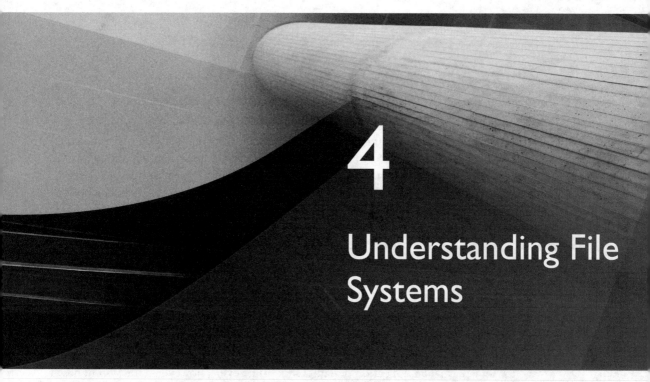

4

Understanding File Systems

File systems do something that looks quite simple at first glance: They convert an amount of storage space into an index of objects we call *files*. Files have names and locations (called *directories* on UNIX systems and *folders* on other systems). Each file contains data that some user or process uses to perform a task. Most users think about a file this way: what it's called, where it is, what content is in it, and how to open it (an editor for plain text, a browser for HTML-formatted content, an e-mail client for messages, and so on). Processes that rely on configuration files or repositories of specially formatted content, such as a database, do the same thing. The file system, it seems, just makes files available. That's a sufficient view for an everyday user. It's even okay for a user to imagine that every file sits on a disk, or a "drive," somewhere in the world.

Solaris administrators, on the other hand, have to know that there are several different file system types that support different forms of media. Locally attached disks, DVDs, remotely available volumes, and even physical memory can be used to make file systems. The high-level *service* is the same: providing names and locations for some particular collection of data. Under the covers, however, a file system has to define how this logical view of storage, the file, maps to some kind of physical storage, such as a disk. A file system also has to provide controls the administrator can use to take it offline, repair it and return it to service, or change properties, such as making it read-only, to suit user requirements.

In this chapter, your primary exam goal is to learn and use a specific file system called ZFS. It is, as it bills itself, "the last word in file systems." But before I discuss that, there is plenty to know and appreciate about the other file systems available to you in Solaris 11. It's a shame, in my view, they're not all fair game for the exam. You want to know them, not only so you can understand all the features your Solaris system has to offer, but so the users you support get the benefits of all that knowledge.

I break them down into three categories: disk based, network based, and virtual. As I detail file systems of special interest or utility along the way, I'll also build up a list of features you'd want most file systems to have and then show you how ZFS handles them. I think you'll find it hard to live without ZFS by the end of this chapter.

CERTIFICATION OBJECTIVE 4.01

Understanding Disk-based File Systems

Most people think their files live on a disk somewhere. Among technical professionals, there are more people comfortable with the idea of remote storage, network drives, and all that. The so-called cloud has brought more consumers around to using storage "somewhere out there." Still, the concept for most boils down to some disk at some location most people think of as the place files go.

The Solaris operating system, and UNIX systems in general, promote this simple, if not entirely accurate, view. The design of the system hides the details of every file system implementation in kernel code so that any user, human or automated, needs only a location and a name to identify any one file. But if you've ever tried to read a DVD from a CD-ROM drive, or wanted to access files written on a Windows machine through another operating system, you know there's a little more to it.

The file system is one piece in a chain of services that translate a raw unit of storage, called a *block*. Most of these blocks become data blocks, or spaces a file can allocate to store its content. A smaller number of blocks will store metadata the file system needs for internal tracking. To make that possible, the system first has to recognize the disk as a device attached to the computer. If it has driver code it can match to the device, mission accomplished. Using the driver, the system reads the disk's firmware and determines a *geometry* for it. The geometry provides an organization for all the blocks, also called *sectors,* that a device has.

One sector is a mere 512 bytes of space, or half of 1 kilobyte, so it takes 2,000 sectors to support a megabyte, 2,000,000 sectors for a gigabyte, and 2,000,000,000 sectors for a terabyte. The geometry (configuration) of the device supplies a unit of measure called a *cylinder* that groups these blocks into even multiples.

Say you have a disk with 5,000,000 blocks. The geometry divides this collection into 1,000 cylinders, each of which contains 5,000 blocks. If the system has to retrieve block 472,134, it can divide this number by the cylinder multiple to get to cylinder 94 and then use the remainder (2,134) as an offset from the cylinder's starting point. That's faster work than counting off a block at a time. Minus a slew of important technical details, that's how every file system has to go about finding a block.

Now, how does a file system *relate* any one block to an individual file? How are all the blocks managed, or indexed, so the file system can track millions of these relationships, including tiny files that don't even require 512 bytes as well as massive files that consume millions of them? It's an interesting question when studying file systems themselves. In this book, you only need to know that file systems relate storage blocks to an organization of directories (folders, if you're a Windows or Mac person), which themselves contain files. In UNIX systems, in fact, a directory is just a special kind of file that stores the name of a file whose metadata and data are on the disk.

Each file system driver supports one kind of format. Some are tied to a medium, such as a CD or DVD; others to a file system type that's used on other systems. A few key file systems are listed here and described:

- **hsfs** High Sierra, also known as ISO 9960 format
- **pcfs** File Allocation Table (FAT) file system
- **udfs** Universal Disk Format, also known as ISO/IEC 13346
- **ufs** UNIX FS, based on Berkeley fast file system
- **zfs** ZFS, Solaris 11 default file system

hsfs supports the ISO 9660 format for CD-ROMs. It also supports format variations known by the market names Rockridge (Version 2) and Joliet extensions. The driver will detect these variations in a CD's physical format and adjusts accordingly.

pcfs supports specifications for FAT 12, FAT 16, and FAT 32 file systems. It has been used in the past to support Windows files and to prepare files for transfer to a Windows machine.

udfs supports reading and writing to DVDs and optical disks. It also supports the ISO 9960 format but cannot overwrite CD-R media.

ufs was Solaris's default file system for a very long time, and it has gone through considerable design changes and modifications over that time. You may find documentation still for special-purpose file systems that refer to ufs as their base model. It is, of course, a highly versatile design that has lived a long and useful life. In Solaris 11, it is relegated to supporting legacy ufs file systems, which still account for a significant amount of stored data worldwide.

CERTIFICATION OBJECTIVE 4.02

Understanding Network-based File Systems

A network-based file system performs two tasks: It has to translate the way a file system is presented on its host to some form a client system can support. It also has to present the file system in such a way that the remote user doesn't need to understand the translation process in order to use the files.

Keeping the look of a file simple—an object with a name and location—is a paramount goal. Network file systems thus help to make files from a remote machine appear as local ones. Users may know the files they need are stored on a remote machine, but under normal operation they don't have to think about it.

The Network File System (NFS) provides a platform-neutral format. Any two systems that implement NFS can share files with each other. Naturally, the server and client in this arrangement have to discuss file access and changes—opening, closing, reading, and updating files—so NFS includes a *protocol,* or command language, that defines a proper channel of communication. NFS is a popular choice, both for sharing read-only data from a source system and for serving files to multiple subscribers at the same time. Network-attached storage (NAS) devices use this protocol as well—implemented in firmware, or a dedicated chip, or whatever the vendor has chosen to do.

Windows operating systems, alas, don't include NFS. On Solaris, you can share files to Windows clients instead using the Common Internet File System (CIFS). The protocol is called smb, which is short for Server Message Blocks, and has been part of the Windows networking scheme, under different names and iterations, for many years now. It's common at many sites to rely on Windows machines for desktops and UNIX-based systems for servers—and for particularly detailed requirements, pulling the two together can be tricky. Using NFS instead, unfortunately, is often a cost-prohibitive workaround.

 on the Job

A popular open-source tool called Samba also supports UNIX-to-Windows file sharing over the network.

Understanding Virtual File Systems

The Solaris operating system has evolved a great deal, both to meet changes in technology and to address innovations in the support model for administrators. In Solaris, the engineers have paid particular attention to letting administrators *observe* their Solaris systems while keeping the intrusion to a minimum. One way they support that observability is through a variety of virtual file systems. Each of these systems exposes some aspect of internal operation as viewable files that the operating system itself maintains. Each one of these file systems is intended for use by administrators, either in human-readable form or through a specific utility.

Virtual file systems fill two basic roles. One, they organize binarized data or some other resource into an observable, accessible form. Two, they employ file system semantics to make the underlying resource navigable as a hierarchy. The resource doesn't even have to include its own files. It could be empty disk space. Or it could be a file that contains other files, such as a ZIP archive. It can even be some part of kernel memory, such as a common data structure, that the engineering team exposes to make some aspect of the system easier to observe.

The benefits of translating arbitrary data into its own file system, from a performance and safety perspective, are hard to overestimate. A virtual file system turns any logical data structure, such as the state of a running process, into a visible and navigable hierarchy of objects. Most of the virtual file systems that Solaris supports provide a read-only view of some hard-to-observe part of the system. They're safe to use in the sense that the underlying data isn't affected by viewing their file-based representations. The performance benefit derives from precluding the need for more intrusive and labor-intensive tools, such as kernel-loaded modules that mine low-level data along with a dedicated utility to report it.

Most virtual file systems, however, aren't designed with end users as their direct consumer and therefore aren't necessarily friendly to casual browsing. Sometimes even using the tools provided requires training to understand their output. Consequently, you won't be tested on these file systems for the OCA exam. As a working administrator, you should know them by name, know what they do, and, most importantly, realize these resources aren't stored to disk, just memory. These file systems are listed in Table 4-1.

File System Type	Object Type or Usage	Location
ctfs	SMF service contracts	/system/contract
fdfs	File descriptors	/dev/fd
fifofs	First-in, first-out data pipe	Not visible
lofs	Loopback virtual file systems	Various
mntfs	Table of mounted file systems	/etc/mnttab
objfs	Kernel-loaded modules/drivers	/system/object
procfs	Running processes	/proc
sharefs	Exported (shared) file systems	/etc/dfs/sharetab
specfs	Special device access	Not visible
swapfs	File-based swap space	/tmp, /var/run, /etc/svc/volatile

TABLE 4-1   Solaris 11 Virtual File Systems

I'll have more to say about some of these file systems in later chapters. The ctfs (contract) file system relates directly to Chapter 10. I'll say more about the procfs file system in Chapter 7.

Some of these file systems support behind-the-scenes services that are "user transparent" or support troubleshooters concerned with the booting process and kernel code. These include the fdfs, fifofs, objfs, and specfs file systems. You're not expected to know what these file systems do just yet, so they are not covered further in this book. The remaining elements in the table, however, all have some particular feature or utility you should be aware of.

The loopback file system (lofs) is an interesting device. It has two related functions: one, it can present an existing file (or files) under an alternate path name. Solaris 11 itself uses it to present the code library file libc.so.1, which is needed by every running process, as a mounted file system. The following command shows you the particulars:

```
$ df -h /lib/libc.so.1
Filesystem  size  used  avail capacity   Mounted on
/usr/lib/libc/libc_hwcap1.so.1
            50G   8.7G  41G   18%        /lib/lib.so.1
```

The actual file, /usr/lib/libc/libc_hwcap1.so.1, has an implementation-specific name and location in the file system hierarchy. The conventional location for all shared library files is the /lib directory. The lofs driver has been used to give the file an alias with the standard name and location that a Solaris application developer expects. There's nothing in the df utility's output to show that the lofs driver manages this dual identity, but it fits the driver's description perfectly.

Two, you can use lofi to manage any file that contains a file system. The lofiadm utility will work on any file that assumes the format of a *block device*, a technical term for space managed by a file system. You can mount the file to an available directory and inspect its contents without extracting them. This technique will work with any recognized format, including ISO 9960 format, FAT, and ufs. The man page for lofiadm even has step-by-step examples for creating file systems from scratch.

The mntfs and sharefs file systems have a simple purpose. Each one provides a table of mounted and NFS-exported file systems, respectively. You can read them as text if you like, but the mount command, used without arguments, will give you a cleaner report of the mounted file systems than dumping the /etc/mnttab file's contents to the screen.

SCENARIO & SOLUTION

The Solaris 11 image you downloaded from Oracle's site is in ISO 9960 format. The format itself is simply a collection of files suited for burning directly to media. To inspect its contents or just use it as a virtual CD, you can use a lofi driver to mount it, like this:	```$ file /sol-11-1111-live-x86.iso```
	```sol-11-1111-live-x86.iso: ISO 9660 filesystem image - El Torito```
	```$ sudo lofiadm -a /sol-11-1111-live-x86.iso```
	```/dev/lofi/1```

You must specify the file to the lofiadm utility by its absolute path. The lofiadm command then returns a device interface you can use to mount the image to the file system.	```$ sudo mount -F hsfs -o ro /dev/lofi/1 /mnt```
	```$ df -h /mnt```
	```Filesystem size used avail capacity Mounted on```
	```/dev/lofi/1 821M 821M ok 100% /mnt```
	```$ ls /mnt```
	```<contents of top-level-directory>```

The swapfs file system has been around the longest and predates the idea of using virtual file systems as widely as Solaris does now. It provides a view of the swap space allocated in a system so users and processes have a "scratch" file system space useful for storing transient data. If you list the contents of the /tmp directory, you'll see a few files, usually with a suffix of mixed-case characters or numbers. Some application installation processes will unpack their files into the /tmp directory before assembling them. Any files remaining in the /tmp directory when the system shuts down are automatically cleaned out.

The file systems mounted on the directories /var/run and /etc/svc/volatile specialize in this same behavior. Rather than drop any and all transient data in the /tmp directory, Solaris uses these locations for temporary files to the boot-up process and services that support long-running processes. These two locations aren't intended for end users at all, but may be used by experienced administrators to confirm whether some system process is properly configured and healthy.

All these file systems amount to a lot of information. There's quite a few of them, for starters, and plenty more to say about some of them, especially the ufs file system. If you end up working at a site with a great deal of legacy data, on a scale that's impractical to transfer to a more recent file system type, you'll need to learn more to support it. In the long term, however, you can expect most sites will retire their ufs-based data for more efficient and feature-rich technologies. ZFS is one of those successors, and there's quite a bit you have to know about it to prepare for the exam.

CERTIFICATION OBJECTIVE 4.04

Understanding ZFS

I must say it feels very, very odd to describe the ufs file system in just a paragraph or two after decades of using it. The ufs files system has enjoyed a long, long run. However, it's time to move on, and ZFS is an outstanding replacement. Before I do, I'll say on behalf of old-school Solaris administrators everywhere, ufs isn't dead just because the exam doesn't mention it. You may well see it at a site with a very large amount of stored legacy data. Then again, you might not see it at all. Time will tell.

One thing you miss by omitting the details of ufs is its history, much of which informs the many innovations ZFS has incorporated into file system management, making it so much easier and so much different. ZFS is the result of deep and careful thinking about managing disk-based data. It provides a solution that wipes out much, if not most, of the work I used to do installing and managing disk storage and file systems. When ZFS first came on the scene, in fact, more than one expert commented it would put a lot of admins out of work.

What Is ZFS?

A number of features combine to make ZFS a world-class file system that makes managing on-disk data easier, safer, and more efficient.

First, ZFS *consolidates storage and file system management*. It uses two key commands to do this: zpool and zfs. This concept alone is novel for file systems. But if you're practicing on a system with a single disk, such as a laptop or a VirtualBox machine, there's not much to do but see output from the zpool command on your one disk. For that reason, it makes sense to discuss these utilities separately. Other than an overview of your root file system from a zpool perspective, this chapter focuses on what you can do with the zfs command. I'll have more to say about the zpool command and all its uses in Chapter 11.

Second, ZFS provides *effectively limitless scalability*. It's not infinite capacity, of course: It just might as well be. ZFS can address a 128-bit range of storage. In pure capacity terms, that amounts to 256 quadrillion zetabytes, a bit more than you're using right now. In fact, it's a bit more than everyone is using right now. Jeff Bonwick, the mastermind behind ZFS, implemented this range as a comment on how much power we'd all need to hold that much data. His phrase "enough to boil the oceans of the world" tells you that well before we run out of ZFS space, we'll have much bigger problems to deal with.

Third, ZFS *never overwrites a file on disk*. In most file systems, modifying a file means overwriting its blocks to change their content. In that event, there is always a risk of corrupting those blocks with incomplete writes. On recovery, you hope your file system has enough metadata to put the file back to a sane state. ZFS's transactional model for writing guarantees the file's sanity. You might still lose data you tried to store, but the file itself will always have a before or after state, not an in-between state. This action protects the state of your file from power loss, crashes, and other events that can disrupt writes to disk.

Those are some big wins for file system administrators, but that's just the start of what ZFS provides. As you'll learn in Chapter 11, ZFS doesn't think about disks when making file systems; instead, it thinks about *pools*. The pool is a common space, supplied by one or more storage devices, from which you can allocate as many file systems as you like. There is no space you have to declare, no mount point you have to claim in advance. Each file system has dozens of configuration properties you won't find in other operating systems, most of which you can change any time you want, *without taking the file system out of service*. As you read in the section "Administering ZFS File Systems" later in the chapter, you don't have to unmount or mount a file system. One reason you might want to, though, is just to prove you can. Otherwise, it's one of many actions that ZFS makes almost obsolete.

Let's start by looking at ZFS file systems and the space they require. Try this command on your own Solaris 11 system:

```
$ zfs list -o name,used
NAME                          USED
rpool                         5.29G
rpool/ROOT                    3.79G
rpool/ROOT/solaris            3.75G
rpool/ROOT/solaris/var         338M
rpool/dump                     416M
rpool/export                  55.2M
rpool/export/home             55.1M
rpool/export/home/mfernest    55.1M
rpool/swap                    1.03G
```

Each row lists the names of the file systems, which are ordered hierarchically under the pool name. (Notice that file systems themselves may be organized under one another.) Each file system can independently account for the space it consumes. The value may range from several kilobytes to several gigabytes on a given system. There isn't a minimum, other than the least amount of metadata necessary to initialize the file system itself, which is roughly 30KB on the Solaris 11 default setup. Now let's look at the pool size using the following command:

```
$ zpool list -o name,size
NAME    SIZE
rpool   7.94G
```

If your setup follows what's shown in Chapter 2, you'll have one entry, named rpool, and the disk space you fed to the installer program, minus a little overhead. If you run this command again without the -o switch and its following arguments, you'll also see the FREE and CAP columns to tell you how much space is left and what percentage of the pool has been consumed so far. File systems just know how much space they use. Pools show how much space they have, both used and free.

Each file system also has its own set of properties. In the next section, you'll learn how to manipulate them. As a feature, most properties are *inherited* by one file system that is located under another. For the sake of a complete hierarchy, a pool is also the "parent" file system of any file systems it contains. The properties are passed along to each file system and can be changed by anyone with the right authorization. You can therefore create a pool, configure all the properties of that file system as you see fit, and then create any number of file systems in that pool. Each one will inherit the property changes the parent had when it was created.

on the **Job**

One way you can use this behavior is to designate one area in a pool for a specific use or purpose, such as user home files or a test area for application development. Customize the parent file system according to the users' needs and then create file systems underneath it as they are requested. Each one will inherit the parent's configuration.

One killer feature of ZFS is its ability to *create on-disk snapshots of any file system in linear time*. You can make what looks like a copy of a ZFS file system by declaring a snapshot. It may consume 40Kb or 4GB; the snapshot will take about the same time. Once made, a snapshot is a *point-in-time copy* of that file system. It does not change over time, even as you add, remove, or modify files. Snapshots make it possible to *roll back* a file system to that point in time and use it as if nothing had changed. This feature has profound implications for data backup and recovery, protecting data against buggy applications, quickly reproducing test environments, and more.

In addition, you can use a snapshot to *clone* a file system. Whereas a snapshot is a read-only version of a file system, a clone is a copy of the snapshot you can modify as you see fit. Because it takes a negligible amount of time to create, in particular when compared to straight copying, rapidly spawning clones turns file system duplication into a minor task. Boot environments (BEs), as discussed in Chapter 3, are just clones of the root file system.

You'll learn how to exploit these features in the next two sections.

CERTIFICATION OBJECTIVE 4.05

Administering ZFS File Systems

At the heart of a ZFS file system's configuration is its property list. Every file system can be customized through property settings. Many of these settings don't interfere with the file system's availability, making the administrator's job less tedious. A ZFS administrator can make most changes on the fly, avoiding the unmount-change-remount sequence that many other file system types require. Many zfs subcommands just read and modify these property settings for you, incorporating additional checks and steps that raise them from a mere convenience to a robust aid.

The "command subcommand" paradigm has become more common in Solaris releases over the years. More and more key tools report a usage error unless you supply a correct subcommand; the zfs command is one of them:

```
$ zfs
missing command
For more info, run: zfs help
$ zfs help
The following commands are supported:
allow        clone       create      destroy     diff        get
groupspace   help        hold        holds       inherit     key
list         mount       promote     receive     release     rename
rollback     send        set         share       snapshot    unallow
unmount      unshare     upgrade     userspace
For more info, run: zfs help <command>
```

There are 28 subcommands in all, which you can review by typing in **zfs help** yourself. In this section, we cover a few that are important for general use, and dig deeper on subcommands an OCA Solaris administrator is expected to know well.

Using the zfs Command

I don't believe you should have to memorize all 28 subcommands; fortunately, neither do the exam's question writers. You should know, in general terms, what you can do using the zfs command, and even then it takes time to absorb and appreciate all those functions. For the OCA exam, you should know by heart the subcommands for performing the following operations:

- Listing the ZFS file systems
- Creating and destroying them
- Renaming them
- Getting and setting their properties
- Mounting and unmounting them

You should also be able to identify the correct outcome of each subcommand when it succeeds, the known conditions under which it could fail (if any), and the property state that the file system retains when those failures occur.

Listing ZFS File Systems

Earlier you saw the list subcommand used with the -o switch to print out the NAME and USED columns only. You can see the default output by leaving off the switch:

```
$ zfs list
NAME                          USED   AVAIL  REFER  MOUNTPOINT
rpool                         5.29G  2.53G  40.5K  /rpool
rpool/ROOT                    3.79G  2.53G    31K  legacy
rpool/ROOT/beupdate1          50.7M  2.53G  3.24G  /
rpool/ROOT/beupdate1/var      4.88M  2.53G   182M  /var
rpool/ROOT/solaris            3.75G  2.53G  3.24G  /
rpool/ROOT/solaris/var         338M  2.53G   182M  /var
rpool/dump                     416M  2.54G   403M  -
rpool/export                  54.5M  2.53G    32K  /export
rpool/export/home             54.5M  2.53G    32K  /export/home
rpool/export/home/mfernest    54.4M  2.53G  54.4M  /export/home/mfernest
rpool/swap                    1.03G  2.56G  1.00G  -
```

INSIDE THE EXAM

The parts of the exam that test command knowledge do their best not to test and reward memorization. The Oracle certification program has a candidate's understanding of the technology as its foremost concern.

Obscure command-line semantics are explicitly weeded out of the question set. That said, you'll need to identify plain uses of the key tools to succeed with the questions that test your understanding of the technology.

The default output includes the mount point of the file system in the far-right column and the space available to the file system in the AVAIL column. Under default settings, the amount available reflects what's left in the underlying pool. If you want to limit this size, you can use a property called quota. An example is given in the section "Listing and Modifying Properties."

The REFER column (short for *referenced*) is not as intuitive. This column shows how much data is *accessible* by the file system, which may be shared with other file systems. This is an odd way to put it, but consider a snapshot briefly. It works by referencing existing blocks in a file system rather than copying them. When you first make a snapshot, it only uses the space it needs for metadata, including its property set and pointers to the data in use by the active file system. A snapshot can use little disk space but refer to much more.

You can reduce list output by declaring a specific file system; use a value from the NAME column to do this. It's common when starting out to use the mount point instead because it is more familiar, but this won't work. If you also want to see all the file systems organized under a given name, use the -r switch. The example that follows shows a single listing for the rpool/export file system followed by a listing with its children:

```
$ zfs list rpool/export
NAME            USED   AVAIL   REFER   MOUNTPOINT
rpool/export   57.3M   2.52G    32K    /export
$ zfs list -r rpool/export
NAME                          USED   AVAIL   REFER   MOUNTPOINT
rpool/export                 57.3M   2.52G    32K    /export
rpool/export/home            57.3M   2.52G    32K    /export/home
rpool/export/home/mfernest   57.3M   2.52G   57.3M   /export/home/mfernest
```

The -o switch lets you reduce the output to just the columns you specify. Columns are named in all lowercase letters and separated by commas with no spaces between.

Creating and Destroying File Systems

To create a new ZFS file system, specify the pool it will belong to and name it—that's all. By default, it inherits the properties of the file system that is its immediate parent. The default mount point for the file system will include the pool name, as shown here. Mounting is automatic.

```
$ sudo zfs create rpool/friendly
$ zfs list rpool/friendly
NAME             USED   AVAIL   REFER   MOUNTPOINT
rpool/friendly    31K   2.50G    31K    /rpool/friendly
```

You can also nest a new file system in one or more directories if you want. The create subcommand supports the -p switch, which behaves like the mkdir -p command, creating the intermediate directories without complaint. The zfs create -p command will create the intermediate file systems instead:

```
$ sudo zfs create -p rpool/this/that/other
$ zfs list -r rpool/this
NAME                      USED   AVAIL   REFER   MOUNTPOINT
rpool/this                95K    2.51G    32K    /rpool/this
rpool/this/that           63K    2.51G    32K    /rpool/this/that
rpool/this/that/other     31K    2.51G    31K    /rpool/this/that/other
```

To remove a file system, provide its full name with the destroy subcommand. It's an automatic habit for some people to use the mount point instead, but this won't work. The pool name is an essential part of the identifier because ZFS never assumes there is only one pool on any machine. If you want to destroy a file system that has children, you'll need to include the -r switch; otherwise, the zfs command will complain:

```
$ sudo zfs destroy rpool/this
cannot destroy 'rpool/this': filesystem has children
use '-r' to destroy the following datasets:
rpool/this/that/other
rpool/this/that
$ sudo zfs destroy -r rpool/this
$ zfs list rpool/this
cannot open 'rpool/this': dataset does not exist
```

A destroy subcommand can fail for other reasons, such as the file system won't unmount (because it is busy) or it has indirect dependents. An indirect dependent is a child filesystem that resides in another hierarchy, including any clones. You can force a file system to unmount using the -f switch. The -R switch will trace all indirect dependents and delete them.

on the
Job

Do take care when destroying a ZFS file system, particularly one with multiple children. Once the file system is destroyed, it's gone. There is no supported method for recovering it.

Renaming File Systems

Relieving the administrator from managing the mount state on the command line comes up time and again with ZFS. It's less typing, of course, but the joy of convenience can also make you forget effects that could upset a user. The rename subcommand provides a good example. It's trivial to use, and unmounting is not necessary:

```
$ zfs list rpool/friendly
NAME               USED   AVAIL   REFER   MOUNTPOINT
rpool/friendly     31K    2.51G   31K     /rpool/friendly
$ sudo zfs rename rpool/friendly rpool/lukewarm
$ zfs list rpool/lukewarm
NAME               USED   AVAIL   REFER   MOUNTPOINT
rpool/lukewarm     31K    2.51G   31K     /rpool/lukewarm
```

The mount point change, which follows by default, will surprise any user or process that's using the old mount point. ZFS deletes mount points it no longer needs, which could put that user or process in an unknown state. Whereas an explicit unmount step might remind you to notify your users, ZFS makes the process quiet. It's something you have to keep in mind before you act.

Rename operations don't move data in the sense of copying it; they update the properties of the file system and silently manage the mount change. A rename operation is only valid within the target file system's pool; you can't rename a file system into another pool.

You can change a file system's parent when renaming it, but there's a necessary test you might find surprising: ZFS has to make sure there's enough space under the hierarchy you want to move to! Because you're moving data that's already in the pool, why would you have make sure there's room just to rename it? As it turns out, one of your file system properties is a quota, which you can use to limit the space available to a file system. If the file system you're renaming is 500MB, and the quota of the target parent is 400MB, the rename won't work. If that's the case, renaming fails and the file system stays put.

You can change the mount point of a file system without renaming it; just set the mountpoint property as shown in the section "Listing and Modifying Properties." You can't rename the file system and maintain the current mount point in one step. Following the rename, change the mountpoint property back to its old value.

The unmount operation implied by a rename may fail if a file system remains busy during the request. If unmounting does not succeed, the renaming operation will also fail and no change will take place.

Listing and Modifying Properties

ZFS has been available since Solaris 10 Update 4, and has seen steady improvements and modifications since that release. One of those changes is an increasing number of properties. The list has expanded from about 30 since the initial release to about 50. With properties, you can modify any file system to suit a particular purpose.

The subcommands for managing properties directly are get and set. Using get, you can retrieve one, some, or all of a file system's properties. To keep things manageable, I'll just use short lists and discuss key properties in this section. For an exhaustive list of properties and their meanings, consult the documentation for the Solaris 11 11/11 Release. If you just want to see the full property list for a file system, use the get all subcommand, as follows:

```
$ zfs get all rpool/lukewarm
NAME             PROPERTY       VALUE                 SOURCE
rpool/lukewarm   type           filesystem            -
rpool/lukewarm   creation       Thu Aug 16 17:25 2012 -
rpool/lukewarm   used           31K                   -
rpool/lukewarm   available      2.50G                 -
rpool/lukewarm   referenced     31K                   -
rpool/lukewarm   compressratio  1.00x                 -
rpool/lukewarm   mounted        yes                   -
rpool/lukewarm   quota          none                  default
rpool/lukewarm   reservation    none                  default
<more>
```

The first nine properties are listed here, described by the file system name, property name, current value, and source. There is also a type for each property value; it's used internally by ZFS to validate change requests. The SOURCE column indicates the origin of the setting. A dash shows the value is set by ZFS and is not subject to inheritance. The properties quota and reservation list their source as default, meaning they've inherited the value from their immediate parent. If the source is set to local, the property was changed on the file system with the set subcommand. Other possible values for the source include inherited (a value received from a non-immediate parent) and temporary.

The properties that appear to have no source reflect the file system's managed state. Properties used, available, and referenced are read and reported by the list subcommand. The creation property tells you when the file system was made.

Notice the type property, which says the object we're looking at is a file system. The more general term for most objects in a ZFS pool is *dataset*. A dataset can also be a snapshot or a *volume*, a specialized storage object used to present a fixed amount of space. A clone may be a writable snapshot or volume, but it is not considered a dataset.

Table 4-2 presents a sample of ZFS properties to learn first, both to use ZFS as an entry-level administrator in the field and to prepare for the exam.

The compression property is a fun one to start with. When it's set to on, the file system applies a compression algorithm to every new write at the block level. This setting doesn't have to synchronize with ongoing file writing; you just turn it on. ZFS has no problem storing files that have been partially compressed, partially written in whole. The file system itself will report the real size of the file. It uses another read-only property, compressratio, to express on-disk savings as an inverse of the file's stored size. That is, if I write a 100MB text file with compression on, and the resulting storage cost is 50MB, the compressratio value should be 2.00x, or the inverse of 1/2 the actual size.

To turn compression on, use the set subcommand:

```
$ sudo zfs set compression=on rpool/lukewarm
```

TABLE 4-2   Short List of ZFS Properties

Property Name	Value Range	Purpose
compression	off, on	Reduces the disk space required
mountpoint	<*path*>, none, legacy	Location or directive for managing mount control
quota	none, <*size*>	Maximum space allocatable
readonly	off, on	Permission to modify contents
reservation	none, <*size*>	Guaranteed space allocatable
sharenfs	off, on	Shared over the network using NFS

Copy in some text files, which typically compress very well. You can check on the compressratio value from time to time and see how you're doing:

```
$ sudo zfs get compressratio rpool/lukewarm
NAME                  PROPERTY        VALUE    SOURCE
rpool/lukewarm        compressratio   2.08x    -
```

The zfs command man page has 16 different examples of its use, including an example using compression. Use these examples to familiarize yourself with its other uses and to learn more about the properties.

Mounting and Unmounting ZFS File Systems

Mounting is one operation that's often implied by other operations such as creating, renaming, and destroying file systems. In the early days of ZFS, it was also an operation that received a lot of user testing, especially among administrators not quite ready to abandon their current processes. As I mentioned before, sometimes removing a step from a well-known process exposes a hidden assumption—such as having to notify users of a mount change—that you now have to think through consciously.

Most of the time, however, ZFS will invoke this process for you, save you time, and increase the availability of the file system to users and processes; that's all to the good. If you want to manage mount states and operations yourself, you can also do that.

The mount subcommand lists currently mounted file systems in a simple format that's easier to read than the list subcommand's output:

```
$ zfs mount
rpool/ROOT/solaris              /
rpool/ROOT/solaris/var          /var
```

```
rpool/export                /export
rpool/export/home           /export/home
rpool/export/home/mfernest  /export/home/mfernest
rpool                       /rpool
rpool/lukewarm              /rpool/lukewarm
```

Used with the -a switch, it invokes mount operations on all ZFS file systems that are currently unmounted but have a valid mountpoint property setting. If the property is set to none, the file system is off limits to mount. Barring an operational error, this invocation returns silently even if no file systems are mounted.

One reason you might set the mountpoint property to none is to make a file system that contains a properties configuration only, and you don't want to use it for storage. A file system configured this way can have mountable child file systems that inherit all the other properties a parent has set.

```
$ sudo zfs set mountpoint=none rpool/lukewarm
$ zfs mount rpool/lukewarm
cannot mount 'rpool/lukewarm': no mountpoint set
$ sudo zfs create rpool/lukewarm/milk
$ sudo zfs set mountpoint=/beverage rpool/lukewarm/milk
$ zfs mount
...
rpool/lukewarm/milk         /beverage
```

To use a temporary mount point that expires once a file system is unmounted, use the mount subcommand with -o and then assign the mountpoint property to the location:

```
$ sudo zfs unmount rpool/lukewarm/milk
$ sudo zfs mount -o mountpoint=/newdrink rpool/lukewarm/milk
cannot mount '/newdrink': mountpoint does not exist
$ sudo zfs mount -o mountpoint=/mnt rpool/lukewarm/milk
$ zfs mount
...
rpool/lukewarm/milk         /mnt
```

Notice that unlike persistent mount points, ZFS will not create a temporary one. If the target directory doesn't exist, the operation will fail. The next time the file system is mounted, ZFS will revert to the existing setting.

on the job

The legacy setting for the mountpoint property lets the administrator configure mounting by hand. The value was originally made available so that long-time users of ufs file systems and the /etc/vfstab file could handle their new ZFS file systems the same way as other file systems.

CERTIFICATION OBJECTIVE 4.06

Using ZFS Snapshots and Clones

You learned to use the beadm utility in Chapter 3, which you now know uses the clone feature of ZFS to drive its work. That's just one example of the many ways Solaris 11 has integrated its innovative technologies to form a more versatile system. The beadm utility itself isn't even a binary executable; it's a script, written in the Python programming language. Somewhere in its makeup, it simply delegates the work of making clones to ZFS itself.

This won't help you understand what the zfs snapshot and clone subcommands do, but that's okay. There isn't a whole lot to see from the zfs command line either. For the exam, you need a clear conceptual grasp of snapshots and clones, and you need to know how to list, make, and destroy them. I covered the conceptual explanation earlier; that just leaves the how-to, which I'll cover now.

Listing Snapshots and Clones

If you have BEs on your system, you must have clones. And if you have clones, you must have snapshots supporting them—it's that simple. And snapshots are easy to recognize; they all have an @ symbol somewhere in their name. So why don't you see them in the output of a zfs list command? One consequence the ZFS designers saw coming was that administrators would probably make a lot more file systems, and that meant reporting on them could get cumbersome pretty quickly. Still, they didn't do a whole lot about that in ZFS's infancy.

Now, however, it's clear that people who use ZFS love snapshots. Because they hold a specific version of the file system in place, you can use them without interfering with the active file system, even while it's under heavy use. You can use a snapshot to make a backup and use the file system at the same time—that's the holy grail of backup administration right there, to save data off to archive storage and use it at the same time. It's built into ZFS; all you have to do is use it—and people do.

And the snapshots add up. For Solaris 11, it was decided snapshots should not be included in the default output of a list. You can specify them one of two ways with the -t option. Use the argument snap or snapshot to list just the snapshots, or use the all argument to lump them in with everything else:

```
$ zfs list -t snap
NAME                                             USED   AVAIL  REFER  MOUNTPOINT
rpool/ROOT/beupdate1@2012-07-04-14:53:37         3.76M    -    3.24G  -
rpool/ROOT/beupdate1/var@2012-07-04-14:53:37     2.76M    -    183M   -
rpool/ROOT/solaris@install                       149M     -    2.99G  -
rpool/ROOT/solaris@2012-07-04-08:36:13           5.99M    -    3.24G  -
rpool/ROOT/solaris@test                          4.21M    -    3.24G  -
rpool/ROOT/solaris/var@install                   150M     -    302M   -
rpool/ROOT/solaris/var@2012-07-04-08:36:13       4.42M    -    183M   -
rpool/ROOT/solaris/var@test                      1.02M    -    182M   -
```

I haven't created any snapshots yet, so all I have to show are the ones made on my system's behalf. The @ symbols you see separate the name of the file system from its mnemonic identifier. The identifier can be a named event, a timestamp, or some other arbitrary string that recalls what the snapshot was made for, or when, or some other guide.

Snapshots don't grow in the sense of accumulating more files, so they do not report an AVAIL column value. The space they report in the USED column is the sum of the data blocks they have protected as the active portion of the file system has made changes to their current view. The more blocks modified by the active file system, the more blocks a snapshot has to retain so it can restore the view of the file system it captured. The REFER column shows how much data can be accessed through the snapshot, and therefore represents all the blocks the snapshot still has in common with the current version of the file system.

A clone has the same effective role as an active file system. Whereas the active file system may view a snapshot as a kind of fallback, for a clone it is more like the base on which it can build differences in the form of deleted, modified, and new files. For an active file system, an unpopulated file system is a kind of beginning it can built on, and a snapshot is a milestone along the way. For a clone, a snapshot is the beginning.

If a file system is a clone, its origin property will contain the name of a snapshot. You can query all your file systems at once for a property value by not specifying a final argument:

```
$ zfs get origin
```

The origin property tracks the relationship between a snapshot and one or more clones so that a request to delete a snapshot can first be checked against the origins of all file systems in the pool. If there is a match, then a clone needs the snapshot in question. It cannot then be deleted without the clone also being deleted.

If you prefer to see snapshots in default output of the zpool list command, you can modify the property of the pool that controls this. The property name is listsnapshot, and it can be turned on or off:

```
$ sudo zpool set listsnapshot=on rpool
```

For a small practice installation like the one I've been using so far, it's one less step and easier to see all the datasets at one time. You can turn this property off if you decide it's filling up your screen with more information than you can process at one time.

Creating and Destroying Snapshots

To create a snapshot, add an identifier to an existing file system, starting with the @ symbol, and put it after the snapshot subcommand:

```
$ sudo zfs snapshot rpool/lukewarm@5am
$ zfs list -t snap rpool/lukewarm@5am
NAME                  USED   AVAIL   REFER   MOUNTPOINT
rpool/lukewarm@5am      0       -    38.6M   -
```

You can also take a recursive snapshot by using the -r switch. This captures all the child file systems of the target dataset and applies the same identifier:

```
$ sudo zfs snapshot -r rpool/export@bay
$ sudo zfs list -t snap
NAME                                    USED   AVAIL   REFER   MOUNTPOINT
...
rpool/export@bay                          0       -     32K    -
rpool/export/home@bay                     0       -     32K    -
rpool/export/home/mfernest@bay         158K       -    92.2M   -
```

In this example, I've taken a snapshot of the rpool/export file system, which contains a home file system, which in turn contains my personal file system. The snapshots share one identifier to remind me they were made at the same time. The used space declared by my file system accounts for metadata needed to track 92MB worth of data. If and when I make a change to this file system, the active version of the file system will read and copy the original block of data that needs modification. It will write those modifications to the copy and then track the updated block. The snapshot will track the original block.

Duplicating existing data and updating the copy is called *copy-on-write.* ***The existing data is never at risk because the original block is never modified. A snapshot tracks the original data. Copy-on-write minimizes the risk of corrupted data due to interrupted block modifications.***

Creating and Destroying Clones

All you need to create a clone is a snapshot and a target for the clone name. For end users, there's no meaningful difference between a file system and a clone. For the administrator, a clone is an entity that adds a dependency to a snapshot, which in turn depends on the active version of the file system it captured. When it comes time to tear things down, you'll want to work your way backwards carefully. Creating is the easy part:

```
$ sudo zfs clone rpool/lukewarm@5am rpool/tepid
```

You can only clone in the same pool, naturally, and by default the mount point will be the string following the pool qualifier in the last argument. You can write to a cloned file system right away. With a snapshot as its base, the space consumed by any clone depends on the number of blocks it changes over time. Aside from the dependency noted in a clone's origin property, it has the same properties as a file system.

The dependency chain doesn't go any further out than a clone, so destroying one is simple:

```
$ sudo zfs destroy rpool/tepid
```

Practical applications for this technology help people create the illusion of far greater storage capacity than they really have. Much of that impression stems from the fact that most of what we store just doesn't change that much. You'll be able to see the benefit, using the tools you've learned so far, once you have all the foundation material you need to learn about Solaris zones.

In this book, zones are the technology point at which all the other technologies I'm covering come together. You'll see how ZFS is used to create new zones immediately by cloning a core set of software into a new virtual environment. Eliminating the costs associated with disk-to-disk copying of large file sets pays off time and again, but you might never like it as much as when you can make a new operating environment inside your Solaris 11 machine in about the time it takes to tell someone else what you're tuning.

CERTIFICATION SUMMARY

In this chapter, you reviewed the kind of service a file system provides and the various types that Solaris supports. You also took a detailed look at its flagship file system technology, ZFS. To prepare for the exam, review the types available through ZFS—file systems, volumes, snapshots, and clones—and learn the various properties that govern their working state. You'll be expected to understand the purpose of key properties, as described in this chapter, and identify the outcomes of the zfs commands I've described.

TWO-MINUTE DRILL

Understanding Disk-based File Systems

❑ The smallest unit of measure for disk space is a sector. Sectors are grouped into cylinders for easier management.

❑ Prior to ZFS, the default file system in Solaris was ufs.

Understanding Network-based File Systems

❑ NFS is a multiple-platform protocol used by system and storage servers to share files with client machines.

❑ The smb protocol allows Solaris to share its file system space with Windows systems.

Understanding Virtual File Systems

❑ Virtual file systems can translate disk space, files, or kernel data structures into a hierarchical system of user- and process-readable objects.

❑ The swapfs file system is backed by disk in the form of swap space and provides processes with file-based storage in the /tmp directory. It also backs file systems located at /var/run and /etc/svc/volatile, which are intended for system use only.

Understanding ZFS

❑ ZFS has two major commands. The zpool command manages storage; the zfs command manages file systems made from that storage.

❑ ZFS provides virtually unlimited scalability, a transaction model for writing files to disk, and the ability to make snapshots and clones from any file system.

Administering ZFS File Systems

❑ ZFS file systems have a set of properties the zfs command uses to report on and modify their state. This scheme makes it possible for some operations, such as creating and renaming file systems, to use operations such as mounting, and in a transparent fashion.

❑ Most file system properties can be read and modified through the get and set subcommands. When a new file system is created, it will inherit the current properties of the file system it is organized under.

Using ZFS Snapshots and Clones

❑ Snapshots capture a working file system at a point in time and preserve all the storage blocks necessary to maintain that image.

❑ Clones derive from snapshots and make it possible to create data almost immediately and start working with it.

SELF TEST

The following questions will help measure your understanding of the material presented in this chapter. Some questions have more than one correct answer. When this is the case, the question states how many options are correct.

Understanding Disk-based File Systems

1. Which file system was the default used for Solaris before ZFS?
   A. udfs
   B. ufs
   C. rootfs
   D. specfs

Understanding Network-based File Systems

2. Which statement correctly identifies a difference between the nfs and smb file systems?
   A. Only smb has a protocol.
   B. NFS only works with UNIX systems.
   C. Either one could work with a properly configured Windows client.
   D. They are mutually exclusive; if you're using one, you can't use the other.

Understanding ZFS

3. Which three ZFS objects are considered datasets?
   A. File system
   B. Clone
   C. Volume
   D. Snapshot

4. Which statement describes ZFS's transaction model?
   A. Updated data is always written to duplicated blocks.
   B. Nothing in the pool is ever overwritten.
   C. It is a property you can set to guarantee disk writes.
   D. Each write to disk is tracked with a two-commit process.

Administering ZFS File Systems

5. Which command line will set the temporary mount point /mcdoodle for a zfs file system rpool/cheese (currently unmounted)?
   A. zfs set mountpoint=/mcdoodle rpool/cheese
   B. zfs set -t mountpoint=/mcdoodle rpool/cheese
   C. zfs mount -o mountpoint=/mcdoodle rpool/cheese
   D. zfs set mount -t mountpoint=/mcdoodle rpool/cheese

6. What does the compressratio property do?
   A. It lets the user set the desired compression rate on a file system.
   B. It reports the percentage of conserved storage space on a pool.
   C. It reports internal statistics on a pool.
   D. It reports the inverse of stored size divided by actual size on a file system.

7. Which zfs operations, if successful, will invoke a mount operation? (Choose two.)
   A. snapshot
   B. rename
   C. set mountpoint=legacy
   D. create

8. Which statement correctly defines the quota or reservation property?
   A. A reservation value has to be larger than a quota value.
   B. A reservation set on a child file system reduces the space available to its parent.
   C. It is possible to set quotas so that some pool space is never allocated.
   D. Setting a quota requires a file system to be mounted.

9. Which ZFS property cannot be modified with the set subcommand?
   A. mounted
   B. mountpoint
   C. readonly
   D. sharenfs

10. Which of the following is a valid mountpoint property setting?
    A. path
    B. legacy
    C. enabled
    D. origin

SELF TEST ANSWERS

Understanding Disk-based File Systems

1. ☑ **B.** UFS, short for Unix File System, was the default root and data file system in Solaris for many years.

   ☒ **A, C,** and **D** are incorrect. **A** is a driver that supports reading DVDs and legacy CD-ROM formats. **C** is not a file system driver at all; it's a directive that's listed in the /etc/system file. **D** is a special-purpose driver that is critical to the early booting process.

Understanding Network-based File Systems

2. ☑ **C.** Windows machines have built-in support for the smb protocol, but they can also be configured with third-party software to accept files from an NFS server.

   ☒ **A, B,** and **D** are incorrect. **A** is incorrect because both systems require a protocol to communicate with clients over a network. **B** is incorrect because it conflicts directly with the right answer. **D** is incorrect because there's no system limit that prohibits using nfs and smb on one system at the same.

Understanding ZFS

3. ☑ **A, C,** and **D.** The only object listed that is not considered a dataset is a clone.

   ☒ **B** is incorrect. Although a clone behaves as a file system, it is not considered a dataset in its own right.

4. ☑ **A.** One facet of the ZFS's write model is that any change committed to a file invokes a copy-on-write action in ZFS. The blocks intended for change copy their contents to new blocks. The updates are then merged with those duplicates and tracked as "new" file blocks replacing the old.

   ☒ **B, C,** and **D** are incorrect. **B** is incorrect because it goes too far. Live data blocks are never overwritten in ZFS. Any space that doesn't contain active blocks can be written to after they've been discard from a previous file change. **C** is incorrect because the ZFS transaction model is not a user-managed feature. **D** is incorrect because the key action is copy-on-write, not two-phase commit.

Administering ZFS File Systems

5. ☑ **C.** The only way to establish a temporary mount point is through the mount subcommand with the -o option. This syntax isn't made clear in many references except the zfs man page.
☒ **A, B,** and **D** are incorrect. **A** and **B** are incorrect because you cannot set a temporary option using the set subcommand. **D** is incorrect because several zfs subcommands support a -t switch, but only to specify the dataset type.

6. ☑ **D.** The compressratio property reflects the current savings of actual file size divided by the stored file size and is expressed as a multiple, or the inverse stored file size divided by the actual file size.
☒ **A, B,** and **C** are incorrect. **A** is incorrect because compressratio is a read-only property. **B** and **C** are incorrect because compressratio is not a pool property.

7. ☑ **B** and **D.** The rename and create subcommands, by default, establish a new mount point for the target file system, which then must be moved to a new mount point or set to it for the first time.
☒ **A** and **C** are incorrect. **A** is incorrect because snapshots don't require mounting. **C** is incorrect because setting a file system's mount point to legacy makes mounting a manual operation.

8. ☑ **B.** Any time a file system sets a reservation, the amount reserved is deducted from the entire pool size, thus affecting the available space to every other file system, including the parent.
☒ **A, C,** and **D** are incorrect. **A** is logically impossible; zfs will not allow a file system to reserve more pool space than it is allowed to use. **C** is incorrect because setting low quotas would keep the file systems from using the pools themselves, but it would prevent the creation of volumes or new objects using the space. **D** is incorrect because setting quotas does not affect the availability of a file system.

9. ☑ **A.** The mounted property is derived from the results from a mounting or unmounting operation.
☒ **B, C,** and **D** are incorrect. These are all properties that can be managed by the administrator using the set subcommand.

10. ☑ **B.** The legacy setting allows an administrator to performing mounting and unmounting manually.
☒ **A, C,** and **D** are incorrect. **A** is incorrect because an actual file path may suffice for a value, but the term *path* itself means nothing. **C** and **D** are incorrect because neither value applies to the mountpoint setting.

5

Securing Systems and Files

Building a strong security profile in a networked environment is a tall order. For one, the challenge has a built-in chicken-and-egg problem. Before you even turn on your computer for the first time, you have to trust the firmware and software on it. The moment you connect to a network, you have to trust that it's a safe thing to do. The moment you execute an application, you have to trust that it is not itself malicious and is not designed to introduce malicious agents into your system's environment. You can spend a lot of time just listing the vulnerabilities of any system you use and learning how to secure yourself against them.

But security administration is not, for most of us, the practice of proofing systems against every conceivable attack. It is instead an economic question: How do you best apply finite resources (you and your organization's time and money) to a seemingly infinite problem (all the ways a user can gain unauthorized access to your systems)? Addressing the problem calls for planning as well as tactics. One strategy is to arrange your systems so the effort required to penetrate them persuades hackers to find more vulnerable targets. Some people like to say, "You don't have to outrun the fastest lion, just the slowest gazelle." Others like to throw up barricades of a sort, or put their resources into detecting and identifying unwelcome users. There are as many ways to combat attacks as there are to perpetrate them.

This chapter guides you through the mechanisms by which most UNIX operating environments control access to the system and its data, and the framework Solaris implements to secure a host system. This framework is, by design, composed of many options that allow administrators to choose the model they require, bearing in mind that the more complex the security scheme, the more knowledge and effort necessary to maintain it.

CERTIFICATION OBJECTIVE 5.01

Controlling System Access

Every administrator should be familiar with the three pillars of a security plan. The first pillar concerns letting only users (or remote systems) you trust access your system, and letting those users do only what you allow them to do. This domain is called *authentication and authorization*. The second pillar, *encryption*, protects the communication between two authenticated parties. The third pillar you rely on ensures that data passed between two parties hasn't been corrupted in some way. This is called *message integrity*, but is also known informally as *signing*, and involves providing a secure digital key that can verify some bundle of data as unchanged. When you connect to a secure HTTP site, your browser affects these services in the form of server authentication, session encryption, and checksums passed between the browser and server to ensure the data hasn't been altered. These facilities provide assurance for a safe commercial transaction (typically, across unsecured networks). Often, it is only after the session is protected that login data, using passwords, is accepted by the site.

As you'll see, the services aren't much different in a proper Solaris setup. Just the roles change; that is, users are known to the administrator. And although the Solaris implementation has particular files and locations it uses to implement these services, you will find that every operating system you work with uses about the same schemes with differing implementations.

Understanding the Authentication and Authorization Model

The default authentication process for a Solaris user has two phases, generally known as *weak* and *strong authentication*. So-called weak authentication refers to a form of self-identifying information that, by itself, isn't verified. Your username is an example of weak authentication; no system can know or prove that the username you provide is in fact one you've been assigned. Your password is an example of strong authentication. There are various degrees of strength and varying methods for ensuring only you could provide it. A string of characters that is difficult to guess is one example. A password that is randomly generated, with the help of a handheld device, is stronger. A fingerprint or retina scan is even stronger. All three are means of proving identity. The stronger the method, usually, the more complex or expensive it will be to implement.

The username/password combination is the default mechanism in Solaris because it can satisfy many site requirements without adding complexity. The mechanism is simple: Any time you start a new user session, the login process executes and asks you for a name and password. The name you enter has to match an entry in the /etc/ password file (described in Chapter 6). The password you enter gets checked against the user's encrypted password, which is kept in the /etc/shadow file. If the password you enter matches the corresponding /etc/shadow value, the login program sets up a working environment for the session and passes control of it to you. As described in Chapter 6, the user entry in the /etc/passwd file determines the first program that is run when a user logs in.

To avoid giving any information, the login process does not indicate whether a given username or password is incorrect. If either one is wrong, the system indicates after both values are entered that authentication has failed. This approach prevents the system from hinting whether one or both elements entered are wrong.

The login process allows the user four more chances before it will log the event and reset the login process. If you are attempting to log in from a remote machine, your session is dropped and you'll have to reconnect. If you are logging in from a desktop console, you'll see a dialog box with the message "Authentication Failed" that has to be cleared before you can try again.

Additional checks against the password also may occur. The system can, for example, determine after a successful login whether the user account should be locked, perhaps because it is a temporary account or has not been used for several weeks. The process may seem counterintuitive, but Solaris does not actively check a user account for these conditions; it always waits until someone tries to access it. The means to *expire* an account are built in to the structure of an /etc/shadow record. Default values for the minimum number of characters in a password, as well the minimum and maximum time a password remains valid, can be configured in the /etc/default/passwd file. See Chapter 6 for more details.

Understanding Password Strength

The /etc/default/passwd file also supports a variety of so-called *complexity tunables* that let you configure the required characters of a password: How many alphabet characters (as well as how many lowercase and uppercase ones), numeric characters, special characters, and so on, may all be defined to prevent users from using dictionary words and other easy-to-guess strings as passwords. These settings all contribute to a password's *strength* by imposing more requirements on the strings a user can submit. These specific properties are also discussed in Chapter 6.

Each user's password is stored in encrypted form in the /etc/shadow file; even an administrator cannot read it or reverse-engineer it. If intruders get hold of an encrypted password, however, they can figure it out by matching that string to one that is produced by encrypting a machine-generated character combination. All it takes is a looping program to generate strings until the match is found.

To make matters worse, the built-in encryption scheme uses the first eight characters only for any supplied password. It doesn't matter if you use more characters or increase the required minimum length (using the proper setting in the /etc/default/passwd file). If there are only combinations of six to eight characters to figure out, an intruder can calculate the cost of a brute-force attempt to crack it—which is modest, in current compute-power terms—and decide if it's worth the time.

Fortunately, Solaris 11 changes the default encryption algorithm from the built-in one, called __unix__, to a more rigorous one called SHA256. SHA stands for Secure Hashing Algorithm. The value 256 refers to the number of bits used in the algorithm's *digest length,* which establishes a relative degree of safety. The more bits used in the digest length, the greater the protection. Solaris also provides a way to change the encryption model, either back to the traditional form or to something else. This configuration rests in two files in the /etc/security directory: the policy.conf file, which maintains the current settings, and the crypt.conf file, which keeps a list of the available schemes.

The policy.conf file includes nine configuration settings, or *keys,* that establish default security attributes for all users. Table 5-1 lists them for your review.

TABLE 5-1 Configurable Settings in the /etc/security/policy.conf File

Policy Key	Default Value	Description
CRYPT_DEFAULT	5	Default password encryption algorithm
CRYPT_ALGORITHMS_ALLOW	1, 2a, md5, 5, 6	Algorithms permitted for new passwords
CRYPT_ALGORITHMS_DEPRECATE	None (setting commented)	Retired algorithms still in use
LOCK_AFTER_RETRIES	NO (setting commented)	Lock account after failed number of retries (set in /etc/default/login file)
AUTHS_GRANTED	None	Authorizations granted to all
PROFS_GRANTED	Basic Solaris User	Profiles granted to all
CONSOLE_USER	Console User	Profiles granted to console
PRIV_DEFAULT, PRIV_LIMIT	basic, all (settings commented)	Privileges granted to all

Authorizations, profiles, and privileges are all aspects of the security model that are integrated into the Solaris operating system. An *authorization* is a kernel-based mechanism that governs access to some fundamental system behavior, such as writing to a device or scheduling a process for future execution.

A profile, also called a *rights profile*, lists a set of rights or permissions (in the form of authorizations) that can be applied to a user or a role. A profile can grant a normal user, among other things, the right to execute one or more programs with the effective permissions of another user, usually the root user. Every user is assigned the Basic Solaris User profile by default, which grants users permission to conduct normal system operations. With this approach, all users start out with a profile; the Basic profile just includes the rights a default user should have. The administrator can extend those rights by adding other profiles to their account configuration. The values for the keys PROFS_GRANTED and CONSOLE_USER each define a list of such programs.

Privileges are fine-grained permissions. They govern the low-level operations every program uses to work with system resources, such as the ability to modify a file or access a directory that you do not own. All three types are elements you will study in detail to prepare for the OCP exam.

When set to YES, the key LOCK_AFTER_RETRIES locks any user's account after a consecutive number of failed login attempts against it. By default, the mechanism is set to NO and commented out. It's a good idea to leave this key alone until you have more than one login account available on the system. If you lock yourself out of your only non-root account, it takes quite a bit more knowledge and guidance to restore access.

The CRYPT_DEFAULT key, as you can see, is set to a value that stands in for the actual algorithm. The number 5 is a placeholder for the code that supports the SHA256 algorithm. The same holds true for each value listed with the CRYPT_ALGORITHMS_ALLOW key. Each code represents an algorithm currently supported by Solaris in the form of a body of code called a *shared-object library*. The code definitions and the libraries they represent are stored in the crypt.conf file, which I review next.

The key CRYPT_ALGORITHMS_DEPRECATE, which is both set to a value (__unix__) and commented out, deserves special attention. In prior versions of Solaris, this key made it easier to migrate users from the traditional encryption scheme to more rigorous ones. *Deprecation* is the act of identifying software as obsolete but still in use. If you wanted to migrate accounts on a Solaris 10 box case by case, for example, you could use this configuration to allow for old passwords until they are changed. This process tells the system to tolerate accounts that use the deprecated scheme, for whatever reason, and push them forward when they make a change. On a Solaris 11 system, unless you want to retire a newer algorithm without disrupting users, you can leave this setting as it is.

The crypt.conf file maintains links between the shorthand codes that represent the encryption algorithms in the policy.conf file and the code libraries that implement them. This file is said to support a *pluggable* architecture. That is, an administrator could incorporate new code libraries as they become available by installing the code library on a system, assigning it a short code, and then including the code in the list supported by the CRYPT_ALGORITHMS_ALLOW key.

Because it is just a list of pluggable modules, the crypt.conf file has no keys or configuration comments. In its default form, in fact, none of the entries use all three fields that are available, which include:

- Code (applied in the policy.conf file)
- Path (location of the code library)
- Options (values applicable to the specific module's operations)

Each code is associated with a file that begins with the string "crypt_" and ends with an .so.1 extension. The default location for these files is either the /usr/lib/ security directory or one of the subdirectories that contain code compiled to the run on your particular hardware. So long as the file you're using is placed in a location your system considers the default, you don't have to add a path in the record. If you plan to install a new code library someplace else, you must give the full path to it for the second field.

The third field can contain values understood by the module that will modify the way it works. These values behave like command-line arguments in a way, but are read in by the framework and passed in to the appropriate code module. There's nothing for an administrator to do in such a case except to add them as directed and expect them to work. This file is a thin layer between the details of each code library and its integration into the password-encryption framework, but it's sufficient to do the job. If you review the man page for this file, you'll see its notes are suitable for programmers and administrators with a code-level understanding of how this scheme works. Table 5-2 lists a description the algorithm represented by each shorthand code.

Code	Algorithm	File
1	Message Digest 5 (BSD, Linux compatible)	crypt_bsdmd5.so.1
2a	Blowfish	crypt_bsdbf.so.1
md5	Message Digest 5 (Sun version)	crypt_sunmd5.so.1
5	SHA256	crypt_sha256.so.1
6	SHA512	crypt_sha512.so.1

TABLE 5-2   Password Encryption Algorithms Supported in Solaris 11

The name __unix__ represents code that is built in to a standard programming library and has no file of its own. The crpypt.conf file comments state that this name is reserved, which it is, meaning only that you cannot use it to name another library. To maintain backward compatibility, this code is still available for use in Solaris 11, probably to support any legacy applications that won't work properly without it.

on the Job

Each of these code libraries is supported by a man page that details specifics you may be interested in. To locate them, use the library filename without the extension portion (for example, man crypt_sha256).

Monitoring and Disabling User Accounts

Strengthening password encryption is, of course, one line of defense only. Once a user is logged in, most remaining defenses boil down to *monitoring* the system for unwelcome activity and *auditing* the authentication process to make sure it hasn't been compromised by subsequent configuration work. How you do this work is, again, a question of tradeoffs: Typically, the more thorough and detailed the security processes are, the more knowledge required to maintain them and overhead required to run them. You can conduct some basic monitoring by checking each user account for the following:

- Login status
- Failed login attempts
- No password
- Attempts to gain root access

You will need root access for these operations because you will be reviewing the account information of each user.

When you're working with a lab system or one only you use, it's a simple matter to review the files that manage the configuration of your user accounts (/etc/passwd and /etc/shadow). As the number of accounts grows on a system, however, this approach gets cumbersome. The logins utility is the preferred tool for all cases because it combines key fields from both files, as well as information showing current activity, for a simple, one-stop view. Teach yourself to use it in lieu of the old-school method of examining file content directly.

For extended information on a specific account, use the -x switch, as shown:

```
$ sudo logins -x -l mfernest
mfernest          60004   staff               10      Michael Ernest
                          /home/mfernest
                          /usr/bin/bash
                          PS 082512 -1 -1 -1
```

This output includes the given account's name and numeric identifier, the group name and numeric identifier, and a comment field that describes the account on the first line. The next three lines include the home directory for the account's files, the program shell that runs when the user logs in, and several fields of password information, respectively. The first field in the last line is a two-letter code that indicates the password status. Table 5-3 lists the documented codes for the password field and their meanings.

TABLE 5-3	Code	Meaning
	NP	No password (empty field)
Password Codes	LK	Locked account
Used in the	NL	Logging in disabled
logins Command	UP	Deactivated account
Output	PS	Password appears valid
	UN	Unknown

If an account has a password (or used to have one), the second field on the last line reports the date it was last set; the preceding account shows a date of August 25, 2012. If the account's password status is UP, the date field will report 000000, indicating a password has not been set.

Your first concern should be any account that has an empty password field. If the PASSREQ key in the /etc/default/login file is set to NO, then any account without a password can be accessed with weak authentication alone (that is, just the username). This setup may be suitable for a machine intended for general access, but it's important to overall security that you allow this *explicitly*—that is, only when the purpose is documented and well known. Without that awareness as a hedge, you're leaving the back door open and merely assuming the right people will use it, and no one else.

You could, of course, scan the /etc/shadow yourself, but using the logins -p command is cleaner and simpler:

```
$ sudo logins -p
toby            70000    staff          10       Toby
```

Here, I created an account with the username toby and left the password blank, as shown by the second field in the account's /etc/shadow file entry:

```
$ sudo grep toby /etc/shadow
toby::15605:200:5000:10::15705:
```

The meanings of the remaining fields of an /etc/shadow file record are described in Chapter 6.

Your system can also record failed login attempts to an account if you like. The key SYSLOG_FAILED_LOGINS is kept in the /etc/default/login file. The default value is 5, but the setting itself is commented out as a safety measure. If you deem it necessary to monitor even one or two failed attempts to access an account, you can uncomment this parameter and set it to a lower number.

Nothing will actually happen, however, until you also create the file that receives these notifications. Messages of this sort are written through the kernel's logging facility, which is covered in detail in Chapter 13. In short, when the system accumulates enough failed logins on one account to meet the threshold set by the SYSLOG_FAILED_LOGINS key, all the failed attempts are sent to the system logging facility for recording. The logging facility has its own configuration to determine which file receives log messages from any particular source. The default file for these messages is the /var/adm/loginlog file.

This file, however, does not exist on a default Solaris system. If you want to capture these messages, you have to create it and set it up with the right ownership. To do that, you need to apply some tools I discuss in the following section. For now, you can just follow these steps on your own system if you wish:

```
$ sudo touch /var/adm/loginlog
$ ls -l /var/adm/loginlog
-rw-r--r--   1 root     root              0 Nov 16 09:44 /var/adm/loginlog
$ sudo chmod 600 /var/adm/loginlog
$ sudo chgrp sys /var/adm/loginlog
$ ls -l /var/adm/loginlog
-rw-------   1 root     sys               0 Nov 16 09:47 /var/adm/loginlog
$ sudo svcadm restart system/system-log
<Fail at login five times>
$ sudo cat /var/adm/loginlog
mfernest:/dev/pts/1:Fri Nov 16 09:46:43 2012
mfernest:/dev/pts/1:Fri Nov 16 09:46:54 2012
mfernest:/dev/pts/1:Fri Nov 16 09:47:01 2012
mfernest:/dev/pts/1:Fri Nov 16 09:47:10 2012
mfernest:/dev/pts/1:Fri Nov 16 09:47:19 2012
```

The touch utility will create a file without adding any content to it—a handy tool to keep in mind. Because I used the sudo utility to create the file, it is owned by the root account, which is a necessary part of its setup. This file should also belong to the sys group as well as be readable and writable by the root account only, as shown by the second ls -l command's output. All these facets of configuring a file are covered in the next section of this chapter.

If you have already mangled a healthy number of login attempts before this point, rest assured the system tried to write the messages to this file. Because the file didn't exist, the messages were lost to the ether. They will continue to go nowhere until you restart the logging service itself, which allows the logging process, syslogd, to locate the file, open it, and start writing to it.

The threshold set by the SYSLOG_FAILED_LOGINS key ensures you don't have a lot of attempts getting written to this file all the time because your users may well mis-key their passwords a lot. If you view these events as routine and not worth recording, allowing up to five failures is a tolerant figure.

You may also want to track users who raise their own privileges on the system using the su utility. This utility lets you "switch users" to another account (assuming you have the password for it). Without an argument, it is assumed you want to access the root account. Although it's not a good practice, in my view, you can use the su utility to switch to the root account indefinitely, as follows:

```
$ su
Password: root_password
root@orca:/var/adm# exit
exit
$ su -
Password: root_password
Oracle Corporation        SunOS 5.11    11.0    November 2011
You have new mail.
root@orca:~# exit
$
```

Two ways are shown here. If you invoke the su command without an argument, the system spawns a new shell process for the user with some environment variables updated to reflect the change. If you add a dash, it initializes the new shell environment as if you had logged in directly. You can decide then if you just need root privilege for a few commands or a complete shell environment for more extensive work.

e x a m

ⓦa t c h *The sudo utility lets you switch to the root user, execute a command, and revert back to your own account, all in one command. I use the sudo* *command throughout this book, in fact, to emphasize the importance of making my root-enabled actions easier to audit.*

As more people get root privileges to a given system, you need monitoring so you can track back to the original user any actions that may have had consequences beyond their intended scope. Given enough users with root access, these actions become effectively anonymous, at which point there's no way to directly trace incorrect practices, let alone malicious behavior, back to the user. The /var/adm/ sulogin file is your first defense, and even then it's only effective if you require users to use the su utility. In Solaris 11, it's recommended you maintain the root account as a role for this reason.

The /var/adm/sulogin file records switch-user events starting with the first login, so no setup is required. Here is a brief excerpt of my file (notice that each record captures the general action, the time of the switch, the controlling device for the terminal window, the account switched from, and the account switched to):

```
$ sudo tail -5 /var/adm/sulog
SU 11/13 04:50 + ??? root-mfernest
SU 11/13 04:50 + ??? root-mfernest
SU 11/14 07:34 + ??? root-mfernest
SU 11/14 07:34 + ??? root-mfernest
SU 11/16 07:03 - pts/3 mfernest-root
```

Notice the root user can also switch into other accounts. I did this repeatedly to test a bug I introduced into my own shell environment that made direct login a bit of a hassle. Everyday users may not be so happy to know a root user can do this at will; all the more reason to log these events!

To disable an account, for security concerns or some other reason, you have two fronts to consider: both current and future access to the account. Locking an account is simple; use the passwd -l command and name the account in question:

```
$ sudo passwd -l toby
passwd: password information changed for toby
$ sudo grep toby /etc/shadow
toby:*LK*:15662:200:5000:10::15705:
```

The formerly empty field in the toby account now contains the string *LK*. The user will not have access until the administrator clears the account using the passwd -d command. If the PASSREQ key is set to yes, the user can then establish a new password. It's a common practice today to set a temporary password for such accounts, ensuring no one else is able to jump in before the user has a chance. You can research this technique by searching online if you're interested in implementing it.

Removing active users from your system can be more difficult than it sounds, but in the simple cases, you can kill the process that represents a user's login shell if you have to. It's an abrupt action, so you should be very careful to identify the correct process. Identifying and killing processes are both covered in Chapter 7.

On a more general note, if you need to disable all user logins while you refine or add in new security measures, you can change the run state of the system to prevent anyone from logging in remotely. The init utility, which allows you to change the overall running state of your system, lets you declare a single-user state only a root-privileged user may access with the init S command. This action will disable the desktop login too, because part of its function is to allow remote graphical access. When you launch this command, you wind up at a text screen similar to Figure 5-1.

FIGURE 5-1 Solaris system display after the init S command

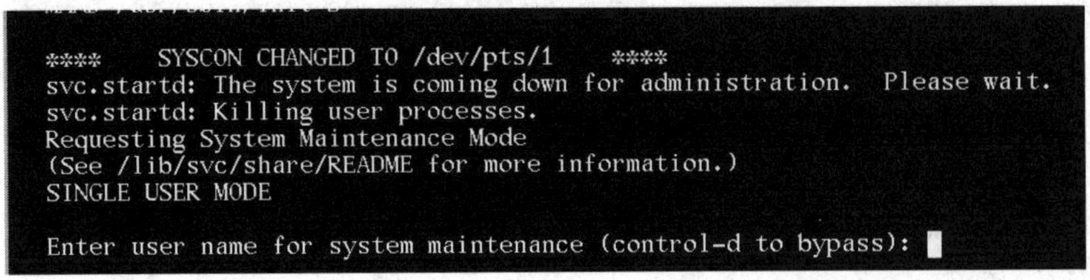

```
****     SYSCON CHANGED TO /dev/pts/1     ****
svc.startd: The system is coming down for administration.  Please wait.
svc.startd: Killing user processes.
Requesting System Maintenance Mode
(See /lib/svc/share/README for more information.)
SINGLE USER MODE

Enter user name for system maintenance (control-d to bypass): █
```

You can log in to the system as the console user; the system is not accessible by
a remote client over the network because the system does not run any network
services from this run state. To resume normal operation, run the svcadm milestone
all command and wait for the system to restore the graphical login service.

CERTIFICATION OBJECTIVE 5.02

Controlling File Access

The core objects of your system, from a user's perspective, are processes and files.
All processes perform some function, but the files contain the instructions needed
to start a process. Files store data and provide the fundamental interface to every
device you can access on a system. In fact, in Solaris, a file even acts as the interface
between a process and a network connection. It is a simple and versatile interface. It
provides a name and a location for every user-accessible thing on a running system.

In Solaris, the base security model for files is called *discretionary access control*
(DAC). This model has two principles:

- The *authorization* to use a file is defined by the account that owns it.
- A file's owner may permanently confer authorization to another account.

Ownership is also defined by a group account. The members of that group may read,
modify (write), or execute the contents of the file.

Finally, there is the idea of a file's *mode*, which defines how the user, group, or
anyone else may use it. So between the fundamental type of a file (code, data, device
access), its ownership, and its mode, there's plenty to think about when learning

all the aspects that go into controlling a file and using it properly. In this section, I break down these elements one at a time. If you're truly new to managing files this way, it takes a little time to get accustomed to managing all these elements at once. It's not hard—administrators deal with them every day on every system—but it takes some appreciation of all these aspects to keep a large number of files in good working order.

Understanding File Types and Permission Modes

The ls utility is the primary tool for reporting a file's settings, which include its type, its access mode, and its user and group owners. These values are all reported when you use the ls -l command. The files listed below are some of the many metadata variations you can find attached to a file:

```
drwxrwxr-x   9 root      sys              17 Nov 16 09:44 /var/adm
-r-xr-xr-x   1 root      bin           46752 Oct 20  2011 /usr/bin/ls
brw-r-----   1 root      sys            126,  0 Nov 18 14:36
/devices/pci@0,0/pci8086,2829@d/disk@0,0:a
lrwxrwxrwx   1 root      root             47 May 27 17:52 /dev/dsk/c3t0d0s0 ->
../../devices/pci@0,0/pci8086,2829@d/disk@0,0:a
-rw-r--r--   1 root      sys            1419 Sep 22 10:00 /etc/passwd
drwxr-xr-x  26 mfernest  staff            38 Nov 18 07:39 /export/home/mfernest
```

For the files shown here, I used the ls -l command and the full file path as the argument. For the directories, I used the ls -ld command to view the attributes of each directory instead of its contents. I've also included in the list two types you may not be familiar with. They're signified by the value given in the first column of the output. The next nine columns express the access mode of the file. There are three sets of the same mode values—one each for the user owner, group owner, and all others on the system. I'll go into more detail further in the chapter.

The second field shown is called the *link count*. For files other than a directory, the link count reflects the number of times a file object on disk is represented by a directory entry. For a directory, this field reports all the subdirectories that link to it. Because all directories refer to themselves in a general form (the dot) and their parent (two dots), a directory's link count is always two more than its number of subdirectories.

The third and fourth fields report the user and group owner of the file. For file types other than devices, the fifth field is the size in bytes of the file. The following field shows the last-modified data associated with the file, followed by the filename.

All the possible values for the first column (file type) are given in Table 5-4.

TABLE 5-4	File Mnemonic	Type Description
File Type Symbols	-	Regular file (text, data, program code)
	b	Block device file
	c	Character device file
	d	Directory
	l	Symbolic link
	s	Socket
	D	Door
	p	Named pipe

A regular file is any file that is not a specialized type. It may contain executable code (compiled or scripted), any type or format of data, or it may contain nothing. As long as it has no purpose that requires specific operating system handling, it's considered a regular file.

A directory is a file with a special purpose. It names and lists all files that can be located by the directory—and that's it. The directory structure used to be pretty simple; at one time you could dump the contents of a directory with a dissembler and show its raw structure. The contemporary internal structure is more opaque, but the function is the same. Files on disk are identified by some index number that organizes one or more disk blocks to hold one sort of data. Directories provide a lookup to these disk locations. They *link* these objects on disk to the file system, giving each file a user-accessible name and location.

Block and character device files, also known as *device interfaces,* provide a similar kind of linkage. Instead of on-disk data, however, the path to a device reflects in a directory-oriented manner the attachments from one device bus to the next that terminate at the device itself. In the preceding example, the path extends from a PCI controller chip to a PCI sub-bus to the disk itself. Each pseudo-directory supplies information about the device in the form of its type and a logical address that represents its attachment point. Block devices support any device that can host a file system; every other kind of device is supported by a character device.

Because physical device paths are long and cumbersome, Solaris uses symbolic links to refer to them from a logical name that is easier to remember. If you bear in mind that regular files and directories are direct links between a file system and a disk, the term *symbolic link* is a little easier to understand. It's a file that simply points to another file. That's all it does. It's not very often as an administrator that you want to point to the same file on disk by different names in different directories, but when you do, a symbolic link is an easy way to do it.

Sockets, doors, and named pipes are more advanced file types the system uses to support different kinds of interprocess communication. With a socket, the communication occurs over a network protocol, probably between different systems. With doors and named pipes, the communication is always between processes on the same system. You don't need to understand these three file types in any depth for the exam, but you should be able to identify them by their character code in ls command output.

The mode of a file refers to whether it is readable, writable, or executable. Columns 2–10 of ls -l output show these values in *symbolic mode,* with a single letter to represent each of these attributes. If all these attributes were enabled for the user and group owner as well as all others on a file, you'd see the string rwxrwxrwx used. If any of these attributes are turned off, the file listing will show a dash instead.

If the file in question is a directory, the meaning of each mode varies accordingly. Table 5-5 lists a brief description for each.

If a regular file is readable, its contents can be read in some fashion: dumped to the screen, printed, or viewed in an appropriate editor. If a directory is readable, it also means the user can view its contents, but in this case the contents are a list of contained files. The same kind of thinking holds true for writability. The permission allows modification in both cases: the data the file contains on one hand, the list of files the directory contains on the other.

TABLE 5-5   Permission Symbols and Meanings

Symbol	File Permission	Directory Permission
-	Disabled	Disabled
r	Read contents	List files
w	Add/remove content	Add/remove files
x	Execute as process	Access inodes

The tricky one is the executable bit. For a file to be practically executable, there must be some kind of interpreter to read its content and treat it as a program. You can enable the execute bit on any file you are authorized to modify, but that doesn't mean it will run like a program. At best, it may fail like a badly written program. But for a directory, the execute bit is quite different; it allows the authorized user to see the *inode data* associated with each file. That is, the user will be able to see the index number that relates the file to the on-disk data structure that points to the file's content. It also allows any user to navigate into the directory itself.

Understanding Special File Permissions

A few other special mode types elaborate on this foundation of readability, writability, and executability of a file. These three types are known as the setuid bit, the setgid bit, and the sticky bit. All of them assign the user a permission or capability it doesn't otherwise have for the purpose of executing that file. That is, each file with one of these bits turned on "sticks" to the invoking user for the duration of the file's use.

The setuid and setgid bits are only useful when applied to an executable program or script. When enabled, they assign authorizations of the file's owner or group, respectively, to the user, in order to run the program. If, for example, the user calls a program file that is owned by root and it has the setuid bit enabled, the user then executes the program with root permission.

This feature comes in handy for special cases such as changing your own password. As you know, your current password is stored in encrypted form in the /etc/shadow file. The permissions on the /etc/shadow file are shown here:

```
$ ls -l /etc/shadow
-r--------    1 root        root         784 Nov 18 07:06 /etc/shadow
```

This data file is owned by the root account. Only the user's read bit is enabled, meaning the root user has to override the normal mode just to update the contents. No one else can see the file's content, much less modify it. The question, then, is how can anyone change their password at all? The answer is the passwd utility, which has the following mode:

```
$ ls -l /usr/bin/passwd
-r-sr-sr-x   1 root      sys        31508 Oct 20  2011 /usr/bin/passwd
```

This program file is owned by root. If the setuid or setgid bits are turned on, the execute bits are also on. When you invoke this program—possible because the execute bit is also on for all other users—you acquire root user and sys group authorizations for the duration of the passwd program. Thus, when you attempt to change your password using this program, it is the root's authorization you are using to modify the /etc/shadow file's content. This authorization goes away once the program terminates; it does not affect any other programs you are running at the same time.

The setuid and setgid bits help solve a difficult problem—namely, how to safely modify a sensitive file that does not belong to a certain user who nonetheless has some important content in the file. There are other interesting uses for these special permissions, too, perhaps as many as there are interesting abuses of them. You'll find most sites discourage any additional use of these bits because of the risks that may follow from applying them too loosely, or incorrectly.

The permission that is just called "the sticky bit" pertains to directories and files, but has a distinct effect on each. When enabled on a directory, the sticky bit lets users share content in a directory. A user with access to the directory can add files that are usable by others with access to it—the /var/tmp directory is a well-known example. The sticky bit ensures only the owner of a file may delete it (unlink it) from the directory. Another user could change the content of the file, but cannot remove evidence of the file's existence. When you create a file with the mkfile command, caching of the file's content is disabled. It can then be used by the kernel as a swap space. This feature has no meaning on a ZFS file system, however, so even though the capability is still supported and documented, you can't use it unless you choose to include other file system types, such as ufs, as part of your system's other storage.

Setting File Permissions and Ownership

Two properties in the user environment help ensure the files you create are properly configured. First, the DAC model asserts the creator of a file is its owner by assigning the account and its primary group to the file. A shell variable known as the umask establishes the default mode for new files (I'll say more about this shortly):

```
$ touch newfile
$ ls -l newfile
-rw-r--r--   1 mfernest staff         0 Nov 18 16:20 newfile
```

My user account and primary group appear in the attributes of this newfile file. The mode, which shows read and write authorizations for me and read authorization only for all others, is the system's default umask for any file. This default means you will have to enable the execute bits by hand when you write scripts, if you want to be able to invoke the script by calling the filename as a program.

Using Symbolic Mode

The single characters that represent the file's mode are referred to collectively as *symbolic mode*. Each character is intended as a one-letter mnemonic, and includes the regular and special modes, all the user types, and a few operator symbols that are used when changing a file's permissions. Table 5-6 lists each of the symbols and its purpose.

The chmod utility lets you use symbolic mode to express changes to a file's permissions in a recognizable but shorthand manner. To use this mode, you need to specify a combination of a user, operator, and permission. For example, if you wanted to turn on the execute bit of a file for the user as well as turn off the read bit for all users, you could invoke the following:

```
$ chmod u+x newfile
$ ls -l newfile
-rwxr--r--    1 mfernest staff          0 Nov 18 16:20 newfile
$ chmod a-r newfile
$ ls -l newfile
--wx------    1 mfernest staff          0 Nov 18 16:20 newfile
```

You can experiment with other combinations as you see fit. Several permutations, such as the end result here, are legal but academic. There isn't much call for a file you can't see but can modify. There also isn't much value in an executable file that has no instructions.

Using Absolute Mode

Absolute mode represents these file modes in the numeric form used for machine storage. In this scheme, each permission (read, write, execute) is given a separate order-of-two value (4, 2, 1) so that any sum of these numbers makes it clear which values were added together. If the user permissions show rwx as the symbolic value, the absolute value is then 7, or 4 + 2 + 1. If the write and execute bits are disabled, the symbolic result is r-- and the absolute value is 4. Table 5-7 lists a few examples to compare the two modes.

TABLE 5-6	Character/ Operator	Description
Table of Symbolic Mode Characters and Operators	u	File user
	g	File group
	o	Other users
	a	All users
	+	Enable
	-	Disable
	l	Locking
	s	Sticky user or group (underlying execute bit on)
	t	Sticky other (directories and files)

You can use the chmod command with any of the absolute values in this table to create a corresponding symbolic representation. To express the setuid and setgid in absolute terms requires a fourth column, which is prepended to the normal mode set. The value 4550, for example, would change the first example in Table 5-7 to the symbolic equivalent r-sr-x---. The value 2666 on the second entry, however, would result in the symbolic equivalent rw-rwlrw-, where the l symbolizes mandatory locking, as noted in Table 5-6. This occurs because the setgid was not declared at the same time. You're not required to know all the implications of these special modes for the OCA exam, but it's worth reading the man page for the chmod utility to understand what mandatory locking is and why it comes into play.

TABLE 5-7	Comparison of Symbolic and Absolute File Modes

Symbolic	Absolute	Description
r-xr-x---	550	Owner/group may read and execute the file.
rw-rw-rw	666	All may read and modify file.
rw--r--r--	644	All may read the file; owner may modify.

Changing File Ownership

In the discretionary access model, the file owner is supposed to have the prerogative to transfer file ownership to another user. The receiving user does not have to be active on the system and cannot refuse the file. The target user can, however, exercise the same prerogative and transfer ownership to another user. The chown and chgrp utilities provide the means to change file ownership by providing a valid username or UID.

There are several potential abuses with these utilities. You could change a file's ownership so it appears to belong to someone who shouldn't have it, for example. You could also assign a file to a UID that's not in use, so it is appears to be owned by no one. In Solaris, this kind of activity is restricted, by default, at the file system level. It's done by enforcing a *privilege*, called file_chown_self. A user can change file ownership only if they have this privilege at the time they call the chown utility. Otherwise, the file system prohibits it.

In the following example, I try assigning a file I own to the root account. The chown utility appears to respond that I don't own the file. To dig a little deeper, I can use the ppriv utility as a wrapper around the same command and invoke its debug mode. The response from the second attempt gives me clearer information.

```
$ ls -l there
-rw-r--r--   1 mfernest staff          6 Sep  9 03:24 there
$ chown root there
chown: there: Not owner
$ ppriv -D -e chown root there
chown[1518]: missing privilege "file_chown_self" (euid = 60004, syscall = 56)
needed at zfs_setattr+0xac5
chown: there: Not owner
```

Non-root users don't have this privilege by default, so chown only works for the root user. This restriction is actually enforced through the ZFS file system property rstchown. It can be turned off, allowing users to change ownership of their files. To demonstrate this, I used the ppriv utility with a debug option to show why I cannot transfer the ownership of the mydata file to the root account:

```
$ touch mydata
$ chown root mydata
chown: mydata: Not owner
$ ppriv -D -e chown root mydata
chown[7088]: missing privilege "file_chown_self" (euid = 60004, syscall = 56)
needed at zfs_setattr+0xac5
chown: mydata: Not owner
```

```
$ ppriv -D -e chgrp sys mydata
chgrp[7090]: missing privilege "file_chown_self" (euid = 60004, syscall = 56)
needed at zfs_setattr+0xac5
chgrp: mydata: Not owner
$ sudo chown root mydata
$
```

I created the myfile file under my own account, but I can't transfer ownership to the root user, or even assign it to a group I don't belong to. As a root user, it's not a problem. To confer this facility to non-root users, you'd have to give each one the file_chown_self privilege. On a file-system basis, you could allow this behavior by setting the rstchown attribute to off, but you still could not change the ownership to the root account.

Disabling Security Risks

Using the chown and chgrp utilities as examples, it doesn't take long to see that certain powerful tools in your repertoire can become *exploits* when put in the wrong hands. In UNIX security in particular, there's only one viable cure for misapplication of knowledge, and that's more knowledge. Now that you know how to add a setuid bit to a file, for example, you also have the information you need to find such files and remove unwanted ones from your system.

Using the find command, you can track down any program that has a mode set you don't like. Using the -perm argument, you can search for all programs in your file system that have a setuid bit turned on, as shown here:

```
$ sudo find /usr -type f -perm -4000 > /var/tmp/setuid_files
```

This command will search the /usr directory for regular files that have the setuid bit set and write them to a file for review. Once these files are discovered, you can determine for each one whether the setting is appropriate and change the mode if not. The find utility, while an I/O-intensive consumer, has a variety of options for locating files by specific attributes that interest you. Be sure to spend some time with its documentation and test multiple ways of using it.

It's often the case in security that you need to implement defenses against attacks you don't understand as well as you'd like. One example that is likely to make most junior administrators scratch their heads has to do with *executable stacks*. A stack in a process is normally where the process keeps running program data, but it has other capabilities that an expert programmer (or hacker) can exploit without making the system administrator any wiser.

To disable the system's allowance for stack data that can also run as code, add the following lines at the end of your /etc/system file:

```
set noexec_user_stack=1
set noexec_user_stack_log=0
```

These controls disable the ability to run code in the stack space and the logging facility that records such events when they occur. It's well beyond the boundaries of this book to explain how executable stacks can pose a problem, but put simply, executable code can allocate and consume memory. If you allow code in a process's stack space to do this, you risk allowing it to consume as much memory as it can, which could lead to performance degradation or even bigger problems if it goes unchecked. Disabling this feature could be viewed as an exercise in turning off a facility you've learned about because you don't understand it. For my money, that's not such a bad idea.

CERTIFICATION OBJECTIVE 5.03

Securing the Authentication Process

So far, you've learned the basics of the authentication scheme, including steps for making user passwords stronger. You've also learned how to identify files by their type, their access modes, and how file ownership determines who is authorized to use a given file. You've also learned the foundation tools for changing file modes and authorizations as you see fit. There's one more thing you need in host security, and that's to protect communications with the system from a remote machine.

Remote communication is, again, another chicken-and-egg problem. If you're logging in to one system from another, your authentication credentials go out over the network. Your username and password would normally go across in clear text— easy pickings for anyone who knows how to monitor the network itself for traffic and sift out just this kind of communication.

For this case, you have to protect the communication session itself from the start, even before logging in. To do that, you need to set up specific parameters by which the two systems can identify and decide to trust each other. That is, unless you're going to accept new connections to new systems unconditionally, you need to know something about that new system you can count as a sign of trustworthiness.

Understanding Solaris Authentication Services

Securing data over the network is, of course, everyone's problem, and it is easiest to solve when there is an agreement on the protocols and services all network users will employ to communicate with each other. A framework called the Solaris Authentication Services supplies implementations of these well-known protocols that apply to different needs. Table 5-8 lists all of them.

The Secure Shell is a popular protocol that allows users to protect all the data that passes over a remote connection, including the authentication process. On many large networks, it is a required protocol for encrypting all communication, just in case. PAM is also a popular toolset that allows administrators to change the core authentication process through configuration files instead of modifying authentication program code. SASL is, as the name mentions, a layer. It's designed to complement an existing network-oriented application, such as e-mail and a few instant messaging protocols, so that security customization can be managed separately from handling communication data.

Secure RPC and Kerberos both serve to automate encrypted authentication services between applications and host machines, respectively. The Network File System (NFS) can be run using Secure RPC so that the credentials needed to access file content are passed in a safe manner over the wire.

The Kerberos system relies on an external agent, called a *domain controller*, that verifies the authenticity of other machines on a network. This approach defends against the possibility of a foreign machine, once connected to a network, from posing as a friendly participant.

TABLE 5-8	Solaris Authentication Services

Service	Description
Secure Shell	Encrypts user communications between hosts
Pluggable Authentication Modules (PAM)	Allows customization of the authentication scheme
Simple Authentication & Security Layer (SASL)	Supports security for network protocols
Secure RPC	Encrypts authentication for Remote Procedure Protocol (RPC) applications
Kerberos	Host-to-host authentication/encryption services

Understanding the Secure Shell

As the name implies, you can use Secure Shell to log in to a remote system and issue commands as if you had opened a local terminal session. The commands are executed on the remote machine; all output to the screen appears local. You use Secure Shell when the underlying is considered unsecured, which applies to any network that does not have a security scheme in place at the machine level (such as Kerberos). Once a secure session is initiated between two systems, all further communication, including user authentication, is encrypted.

This works by having two systems exchange what are called *public keys*. These keys are encryption tools backed by private keys on each system. The exchange of public keys is used to securely create an asymmetric common key. This key is used, in turn, to create and use a symmetric key, with an agreed-upon encryption protocol, that can encrypt data of an arbitrary size. Symmetric keys can only encrypt data as big as the key itself, so this sequence of exchanges is necessary to get to the right tool in a secure manner than both systems can trust.

The encryption scheme is not decipherable by the same key. Instead, the machine's private key, which is not intended for sharing with anyone, is required. This public key–private key scheme is sometimes called a *fingerprint*, because each public key effectively identifies the system that keeps its private key complement. Naturally, this scheme is only as safe as the private key itself.

on the job *The Secure Shell (SSH) keys for a Solaris machine are stored in the /etc/ssh directory.*

Secure Shell interaction is itself a type of *client-server* interaction. The client program, which initiates the Secure Shell request, is called ssh. The Solaris implementation of the server program, which manages all incoming requests, is the sshd process. A user who wishes to interact with a remote system therefore initiates an ssh request, which is negotiated by the remote sshd process, which in turn provides access to the remote system, if all goes well. You can verify the sshd process is running on your system by checking for the sshd process. Alternatively, if you want to get an early start on using SMF services, try this command instead:

```
$ svcs -p svc:/network/ssh:default
STATE        STIME    FMRIonline        8:06:36 svc:/network/ssh:default
             8:06:33    1084 sshd
```

The svcs -p command checks the service name given for any running processes that are associated with it. On my system, the sshd process is running under the identifier (PID) 1084.

Once a session is initiated, encryption itself occurs between the client and server processes only. The person (or application) entering commands/data does so in clear-text form; the output/response is generated in clear text on the server side first, then encrypted for transmission back to the client.

The Secure Shell Protocol has two versions: Version 1 and Version 2. Solaris 11 supports clients for both versions. As a server, it only supports clients using Version 2.

Version 1 is available in the event you must connect to remote systems that are not yet "Version 2 aware." You should use Version 2 whenever possible because it provides stronger and finer-grained controls for securing communications.

Version 2 divides the role of Secure Shell into three functional areas:

- **Transfer Protocol** Manages server authentication, encryption scheme selection, and key exchange
- **Authentication Protocol** Uses the Transfer Protocol to authenticate the client user
- **Channel Protocol** Creates logical connections by which the client can establish a shell, or *forwarding session*

The Transfer Protocol should take place transparently to the user, in much the same way a browser switches from the http to the https protocol before accepting sensitive data from a client. Most clients will want the convenience of an expedient negotiation, although it is possible for the client to handle these terms using options that are included with the ssh client program. The default options for client interaction from a Solaris system are maintained in the /etc/ssh/ssh_config file.

The Authentication Protocol is similarly designed. The Solaris implementation has a list of four methods, ordered strongest to weakest, it can use to conduct the authentication process. The security administrator can therefore impose a more stringent or relaxed process, depending on site policy. Those four methods are:

- Generic Security Service (GSS) API, or GSS-API
- Host-based authentication
- Public-key authentication
- Password authentication

The GSS-API is a programming library that gives software providers a way to link their products to the Solaris platform. In this way, the application can use one of a variety of security implementations written by themselves or a third party. This approach is preferred because it provides greater flexibility for the system than a prebuilt system that is only configurable by its properties. It is accordingly more complex and is only used by default when the system is configured to participate in a Kerberos domain.

Host-based authentication requires comparatively less knowledge and setup. When you boot a Solaris host for the first time after installation, it generates keys that are used to authenticate the host itself and establish the encryption facilities available to initiate a session. These keys are kept in the /etc/ssh directory. A Solaris system is therefore "key ready" to provide host-based authentication services; all you have to do is enable the feature, which is covered in the next section. User authentication is possible once these mechanisms are in place.

Identifying a Secure Shell Server's Default Configuration

On Solaris 11, the default configuration for the Secure Shell server is kept in the /etc/ssh/sshd_config file. The key features are as follows:

- Only Version 2 is enabled.
- Port-forwarding is disabled.
- X11-forwarding is permitted for clients.
- All authentication methods are allowed.

Forwarding describes the ability of a system to pass data directed at one location to another location. When port-forwarding is enabled on a Secure Shell server, for example, it means the system may act as a go-between for two users or applications and provide a lane of encryption to protect the pass-through. X11-forwarding allows a system to pass graphical desktop information in support of remote desktop services. This kind of communication can create a lot of overhead in network traffic, and is therefore discouraged at some sites.

on the
job

A number of other configuration options in the sshd_config file are discussed here. Although they are not required knowledge for the OCA exam, a working knowledge of Secure Shell services is essential for anyone who works with multiple systems and unsecured networks.

Configuring and Using Secure Shell

Secure Shell is managed through a large number of keys, not all of which are present in the default file configurations. Man pages document both the ssh_config and sshd_config file format. When you are ready to go beyond the elements described in this chapter, put some time aside to read these pages carefully because some settings interact with others, in either a mutually beneficial or mutually exclusive way.

To provide working, although not robust, user-authentication scheme, you first configure both the client and server to support the method and to recognize each other. If these roles are interchangeable between two Solaris hosts, then both hosts must be configured as client (through the ssh_config file) and server systems (the sshf_config file). Here are the general steps:

1. Add the key HostbasedAuthentication to the client's and server's configuration file and set the value to yes.

2. Create the /etc/ssh/hosts.equiv file on the server and add the client's hostname to it.

3. Restart the server with the svcadm restart ssh command.

The server system now has weak authentication data for the client system.

The strong authentication component is the system's fingerprint. When you try logging in to the client from the server, you'll see the following message:

```
$ ssh remote-client
The authenticity of host 'remote-client (192.168.0.50)' can't be
established. RSA key fingerprint is
2a:d1:8a:be:ba:e4:b8:93:12:7a:b5:99:5d:f7:14:43.
Are you sure you want to continue connecting (yes/no)? Yes
Warning: Permanently added 'remote-client,192.168.0.50' (RSA) to the
list of known hosts.
```

With the fingerprint registered, the server can now test any fingerprint received from the same IP address and determine if it knows that client. About the only way to make this defense stronger is by typing the fingerprint into the server by hand to ensure it is never made available over the network.

You may also want users to maintain their own fingerprints if they will log in to their own accounts from a remote system. They can use the ssh-keygen utility to create a key (using either RSA or DSA encryption) and store it in their home file system. Copying the public key only to safe remote systems can make it harder for anyone else to hack the account. Here is a sample command session:

```
$ ssh-keygen -t rsa
Generating public/private rsa key pair.
Enter file in which to save the key (/export/home/mfernest/.ssh/id_rsa):
Enter passphrase (empty for no passphrase): safety_phrase
Enter same passphrase again:safety_phrase
Your identification has been saved in /export/home/mfernest/.ssh/id_rsa.
Your public key has been saved in /export/home/mfernest/.ssh/id_rsa.pub.
The key fingerprint is:
08:a3:b0:76:ee:48:b9:7a:cd:a3:9e:91:50:1f:7c:fa mfernest@orca
$ ls ~/.ssh
config        id_rsa        id_rsa.pub    known_hosts
```

I accepted the default location to maintain the public and private keys, then entered a passphrase that protects the files from overwriting (an intruder could try running the utility again to overwrite my keys and gain control). A fingerprint is then created that identifies the username and host system it comes from. You can see from the .ssh directory in my home file system that these files are kept along with files that support my use of the ssh client.

If you repeat this process using only DSA encryption for the type, you'll be able to negotiate a remote connection with any system that may understand this type but not the other. The server in this negotiation then must find a key for the user attempting to log in. By default, it will first look in the user's home directory for a public key in the .ssh/authorized_keys file. If this key does not exist, the server can then attempt any other authentication method that has been configured into the system. If all else fails, the client is challenged with entering a password. This fall-through arrangement allows the server to provide as secure a session as the client's setup will support.

Automating Password Prompts

You can use the ssh-agent utility to store various private keys created by your users. When a login session begins, the ssh-agent utility uses the keys it has been given to automate authentication, which adds an additional element of protection if you want to reduce your exposure on an unsecured network. It's also useful when the client wants to maintain a number of keys that pertain to different remote connections.

To use the ssh-agent, you invoke the command with a program, usually a shell, as an argument. All subsequent Secure Shell operations in that program, which could also be a script, are governed by environment variables the agent adds:

```
$ ssh-agent bash
$ env | grep SSH
SSH_AGENT_PID=2183
SSH_AUTH_SOCK=/tmp/ssh-XXXX8EaWqe/agent.2182
```

Once the program terminates, these environment variables are lost. The user can take advantage of this agency whenever it is convenient to do so. To make it useful, the user must add keys to automate the authentication process. You do this by running the ssh-add utility and giving it access to your keys by supplying your passphrase:

```
$ ssh-add
Enter passphrase for /export/home/mfernest/.ssh/id_rsa: safety_phrase
Identity added: /export/home/mfernest/.ssh/id_rsa
(/export/home/mfernest/.ssh/id_rsa)
$ ssh-add -l
2048 08:a3:b0:76:ee:48:b9:7a:cd:a3:9e:91:50:1f:7c:fa
/export/home/mfernest/.ssh/id_rsa (RSA)
```

When you connect to a known remote system using this shell—assuming you haven't changed your fingerprints, too—the key negotiation will take place silently, and you can get straight to work. This approach may be a nice convenience for a human user, but for scripts that rely on remote systems with secure connections, an automated exchange is the difference between having to attend the program and manage these interactions letting the script complete without supervision.

CERTIFICATION SUMMARY

Security administration is a broad topic in its own right. One big challenge I see for beginners is appreciating the objectives that various technologies help you achieve. Indeed, if you search the Internet with many of the terms introduced in this chapter, I bet you'll find a dozen how-to sites for every one "why-use-it site" on any given technology. Secure Shell is a particularly fine example. It's easy to imagine that the rest of the world magically knows why all this technology is important and what it does.

The exam will test your understanding of these technologies and to what area of security they are meant to apply. When preparing, be sure you know first what the appropriate application is for protecting passwords, securing files, and securing the authentication process itself. This chapter has quite a few tables; this information is something you should memorize. Although you won't find an exam question that asks you to identify a file type by its listing, it is assumed you'll recognize a symbolic link, character device interface, or directory on sight, and can answer any question that includes such information.

TWO-MINUTE DRILL

Controlling System Access

❑ Typical authentication processes rely on a combination of weak data, such as a self-identifying user, and strong data, such as a password that will only match its encrypted counterpart.

❑ The files that control the password encryption schemes available on a Solaris 11 system reside in the /etc/security directory. The policy.conf file determines which schemes are enabled; the crypt.conf file lists the schemes available.

❑ Changing the password status for an account does not affect a user's current session; it only affects the next attempt to log in.

Controlling File Access

❑ The authorization to use a file is determined by its type, ownership, and access modes.

❑ Access mode can be addressed in either of two modes: symbolic and absolute.

❑ All the special file modes are "sticky" in one sense or another. The setuid and setgid bits share the authorizations of the file's owner with the user for the duration of the program the file contains. The sticky bit itself on a directory allows users to share a file without the risk of having it deleted.

Securing the Authentication Process

❑ The Solaris Authentication Services framework supports four methods: Secure Shell, Pluggable Authentication Modules (PAM), Simple Authentication and Security Layer (SASL), Secure RPC, and Kerberos.

❑ The configuration details for Solaris Secure Shell clients and servers are kept in the /etc/ssh directory.

❑ The users on a system can establish their own fingerprints and key vaults in their home directories, and can automate password negotiation using the ssh-agent utility.

❑ Secure Shell Version 2 is composed of three parts: the Transfer Protocol, the Authentication Protocol, and the Channel Protocol.

SELF TEST

Use the following questions to test your recall and understanding of the chapter's material.

Controlling System Access

1. Which two terms define an authorization facility in the Solaris operating system?
   A. Privileges
   B. Secure Shell
   C. Profiles
   D. Encryption

2. What statement identifies a difference between the su and the su – commands?
   A. The su command requires a password.
   B. The su – command can only switch to the root account.
   C. The su command logs the original user out.
   D. The su – reads in the switched-to user's environment.

3. Identify the true statement regarding password encryption in Solaris 11.
   A. Only the first eight characters of any password are encrypted.
   B. SHA512 is twice as strong an encryption form as SHA256.
   C. You can copy encrypted passwords from one Solaris system to another.
   D. You can use any listed encryption scheme at any time.

Controlling File Access

4. Given the following file listing, identify the statement about it that must be true:

   ```
   -r-xr-xr-x   1 root     bin         46752 Oct 20  2011 spoof
   ```

   A. The file spoof cannot be a symbolic link.
   B. No one on the system can read this file's content.
   C. Only the root user can execute this file.
   D. The file spoof is a program you can run.

5. Which option is not a valid invocation of the chmod command? Assume the file foo exists.
   A. chmod a-x foo
   B. chmod 001 foo

    C. chmod u+a foo

    D. chmod 2555 foo

6. Identify the true statement regarding the chown command on Solaris 11.
- A. The root user can always change the ownership of a file.
- B. A file owner can always change the ownership of a file.
- C. The root user must use su or sudo to change a file's ownership.
- D. A file owner can no longer change the ownership of a file.

7. What kind of risk does a program or script file with the setuid/setgid permissions enabled pose?
- A. A setuid program can change the mode of the /etc/shadow file.
- B. The program may contain exploits that could be used to gain root access.
- C. A setuid program can change any account's /etc/passwd information.
- D. The program lets a non-root user change the modes of other files.

Securing the Authentication Process

8. What is a Secure Shell fingerprint?
- A. It's the informal name for the Version 2 Transfer Protocol.
- B. It's a system's or user's private key.
- C. It's a system's or user's public key.
- D. It's the IP/name combination that identifies a host.

9. Identify the correct statement regarding Secure Shell and host-based authentication.
- A. It is stronger than the default authentication method.
- B. It is weaker than the default authentication method.
- C. It is the default authentication method.
- D. It will be disabled if the GSS-API method is in use.

10. Identify the correct statement regarding user keys and automatic Secure Shell logins.
- A. The ssh-agent program requires dedicated keys each time it runs.
- B. The ssh-addkey program cannot be run more than once per user session.
- C. The ssh-addkey program transmits public keys to all hosts known to the client.
- D. The shh-agent program runs until the shell in which it was invoked exits.

SELF TEST ANSWERS

Controlling System Access

1. ☑ **A and C.** A privilege is a granular control that permits a process to carry out some security-sensitive operation. A profile, or rights profile, includes authorizations and possibly the right to execute certain commands as another user, usually the root user.

☒ **B and D** are incorrect. B is incorrect because the Secure Shell does not itself confer any authorizations to a user. Neither does encryption **(D)**; encryption obfuscates data but is not itself a form of authorization.

2. ☑ **D.** The su – command differs from the su command by creating a subshell that reads in the entirety of the switched-to user's environment. The su command reads in the authorizations of the switched-to user, but does not fully replace the shell environment.

☒ **A, B, and C** are incorrect. A is incorrect because both commands require a password. B is incorrect because either command can switch to any account, provided the user knows its password. C is incorrect because neither version of the command logs out the user's starting account.

3. ☑ **C.** The algorithms used for encrypting passwords do not use host or account information for encoding. If you copy a password for one Solaris account into another account, on the same system or a different one, it will still work.

☒ **A, B, and D** are incorrect. A is incorrect because the eight-character limit only applies to the __unix__ encryption scheme, which is disabled by default in Solaris 11. B is incorrect because the number in the encryption scheme refers to the bit-strength of the algorithm. Twice as many bits goes much, much further than one doubling of the strength. D is incorrect because you can configure Solaris 11 to use one encryption scheme at one time; any one of its algorithms may be used, but you can't switch schemes on a whim.

Controlling File Access

4. ☑ **A.** The first column in the output identifies the file's system. A symbolic link must have an "l" in this column.

☒ **B, C, and D** are incorrect. B is incorrect because, although the file's mode does not enable the read permission, the root user and the file's owner can override (or change) the mode. C is incorrect because the execute bit is access for the user owner, the group owner, and all others. **D** is incorrect because you can set the execute bit on any file; it does not have to be a program.

5. ☑ **C.** In symbolic mode, the u stands for user, the a stands for all users. For the command to be valid, the symbol that follows the operator must be r, w, or x.
   ☒ **A, B,** and **D** are incorrect. These are all valid uses of the chmod command.

6. ☑ **A.** The root user can override the access mode of any file at any time.
   ☒ **B, C,** and **D** are incorrect. **B** is incorrect because on Solaris 11, a file owner must have the file_chown_self privilege in order to assign the file to another owner. **C** is incorrect because the root user does not have to assume the owner's identity to change file ownership. **D** is incorrect because although the file owner cannot give away a file with default privileges, the user's account can be reconfigured to allow it.

7. ☑ **B.** The setuid/setgid permissions are not expressly dangerous, but they should only be applied to program code that has been tested against exploits that would give the user more access to the system than intended.
   ☒ **A, C,** and **D** are incorrect, all for the same reason. There is no explicit operation that is conferred upon setuid/setgid-enabled programs. They pose instead a potential vulnerability to system security.

Securing the Authentication Process

8. ☑ **C.** The fingerprint, or public key, is the value a Secure Shell client provides to encrypt messages intended for that client.
   ☒ **A, B,** and **D** are incorrect. **A** is incorrect because there is no colloquial name for the Transfer Protocol. **B** is incorrect because clients use their private keys to decrypt their messages. Private keys should never be shared. **D** is incorrect because the IP address and name of a system are used to identify the fingerprint's owner, but are not part of the public key itself.

9. ☑ **A.** By default, all the authentication methods for Secure Shell are allowed on Solaris 11, but are not configured for immediate use. Without some setup, your Solaris system will use public-key authentication.
   ☒ **B, C,** and **D** are incorrect. **B** and **C** are incorrect because they are mutually exclusive with the A option. **D** is incorrect because all methods are available regardless of how many are implemented. In addition, it is possible that some clients will not work with GSS-API authentication; having a next-best method on hand provides greater flexibility to the abilities of the clients.

10.   ☑   **D.** The ssh-agent program is a per-session utility. It can be used to call any program that calls a remote system and authenticates using the Secure Shell protocol. It terminates when the shell it was invoked in exits.

☒   **A, B,** and **C** are incorrect. **A** is incorrect because the agent program merely stores the keys it is given. It does not limit the number of keys that may be added. **B** is incorrect because there may be no need to run the ssh-addkey program more than once, but you can run it as often as you like. **C** is incorrect because the ssh-addkey program has no role in propagating keys.

6
Managing Users and Groups

W e tend of think of users as the people who can log in to a system. To the system, however, users aren't necessarily human beings attending a running process. A user is really just a small bit of data that defines the credentials, or authorizations, a running process has to acquire before it can perform its work. As people, we tend to think of our login account as our identity on a system. And it is an identity, of a sort, but one that may be far simpler than you'd expect.

The key thing that separates a machine account on the system, such as adm and lpr, from a human user is the login process. Human users have to authenticate themselves to the system before they can run processes. Once they get access to the system, most want to know what they can accomplish and how quickly they can do it. To that end, configuring environments that suit them and make their tasks easier to manage is also important work. In this chapter, I address both issues: how to create, configure, and maintain user accounts on your system, and how to simplify command-line access once you're logged in.

CERTIFICATION OBJECTIVE 6.01

Understanding Users and Groups

User information spells the difference between an executable program file and a running process; that's the heart of the matter. In Chapter 5, you learned how permissions applied to an executable file can prevent unauthorized users from starting it. Solaris 11 goes deeper than that, and in some cases prohibits specific operations in a program from executing. That is, some programs in Solaris can be run by anyone, but they may not operate as expected unless the user has the right privileges. The format command provides a case in point. You'll notice by the executable file's permissions that any user can invoke the command. For it to produce a list of disks the user can then configure, however, they need superuser privileges:

```
$ ls -l /usr/sbin/format
-r-xr-xr-x   1 root      bin           250340 Oct 20  2011 /usr/sbin/format
$ format
Searching for disks...done
```

```
No permission (or no disks found)!

$ sudo format
Searching for disks...done

AVAILABLE DISK SELECTIONS:
       0. c3t0d0 <ATA-VBOX HARDDISK-1.0 cyl 4093 alt 2 hd 128 sec 32>
          /pci@0,0/pci8086,2829@d/disk@0,0
Specify disk (enter its number):
```

The safeguard is embedded in the code, not the file permissions. The program code checks the credentials of the running process to determine whether the user has the rights to access and configure disks. In this way, the focus changes from the executable file's permissions to whether the *user* has all the necessary privileges.

on the **Job**

Testing a running program's permissions is known as process rights *and is governed by a facility called Least Privilege. It takes the security model well beyond file permissions for Solaris administrators. It also ties into a facility known as role-based access control (RBAC). You don't need to understand RBAC or Least Privilege for the OCA exam, but your understanding of the security features Solaris offers is incomplete without them.*

If nothing else, the format command example tells you there is more to security than file-based permissions. User-based information, also called *credentials*, provide the difference. Before exploring how user information influences a process, however, you need to understand how a user first becomes the agent for one or more processes running on a Solaris system.

Understanding Account Types

First, let's distinguish between plain *user* accounts, which you can use to log in to a Solaris system, and *role* accounts, which you can't. That's the only operational difference between them. If you've installed the Live Media version of Solaris 11, your root account is configured as a role by default. To assume root privileges, you must first log in with a user account and then use a command, such as sudo, to switch your user identity. This way, the system can record the time of the switch, which may be useful in determining who might have changed system configuration for the worse. In general, however, roles prevent users from automatically assuming special privileges as they log in.

Your account name, whether a user or a role, is tied to a numeric identifier called the *UID*. The operating system uses this number to determine your current authorizations on the system. (The number 0 is always the superuser's UID.) Accounts that are designed to run root-sensitive processes have a low UID number attached to them. Other accounts begin at a higher default number to highlight the separation in purpose. The first predefined, non-privileged account in Solaris 11 has the name "nobody." By default, it has the UID 60001. Unless you assign a UID explicitly when creating accounts, new users will receive a UID above this one.

You can check the number of your user account with the pcred utility. Pass in the number of a process you're running, such as your shell program, which you can retrieve with the variable expression $$:

```
$ ps
  PID TTY          TIME CMD
 1499 pts/1        0:00 bash
 1588 pts/1        0:00 ps
$ pcred $$
1499:      e/r/suid=60004  e/r/sgid=10
```

I ran the ps command to show the processes running in my shell. The ps process is, of course, already gone by the time the command prompt returns. The $$ expression evaluates to the process identifier, or PID, of the bash shell. The pcred output then that shows my shell runs under the UID 60004 and the group number 10. This output might also be telling you that the full picture is just a bit more complicated. What you're seeing here are three versions of the UID, respectively called the effective, real, and set UIDs of this process. The effective UID represents the number of an account the user has switched to, if any, after logging in. The set UID represents the number of an account the user assumed by running a program file with special permissions assigned to it.

exam
ⓦ**atch** *You do not have to be familiar with the meaning and purpose of effective or set UIDs for the OCA exam.*

A group is *not* an account type. It's a named association that can include zero, one, or multiple users and roles. As discussed in Chapter 5, groups factor into every file's permission set. It allows any defined users and roles to share access to a file that may be owned by someone else. Users and roles have a primary group used to set group permissions on any files they create.

They can also belong to secondary groups to give them broader access to files owned by other users or roles.

Understanding System Databases

Historically, the files that govern user account configuration have been called *system databases*—not because the files you're about to review have sophisticated formats or storage needs (they don't), but rather because there are ways to capture account data for all the machines in a network, store them on a central system, and distribute them from the central system to all the other machines. This kind of system is generally called a *name service*, and it does rely on a storage format that is more like a database. To keep terms simple, however, the term *system database* applies even when we use local files to keep these records.

Table 6-1 lists the local file version of these system databases and provides an overview of their contents.

Each one of these tables could be overruled by a name service if one is used. Solaris is designed in such a way that it's easy for the administrator to change from a local to a remote-based name service when it makes more sense to centralize that information.

Defining a User

The /etc/passwd file stores each user account as a single-line entry of seven fields, separated by colons. The /etc/shadow file stores each account's password, in encrypted form, and provides fields for expiration and change policies. Every

TABLE 6-1	User-Related Configuration Files

System Database (Local File)	Description
/etc/passwd	Holds account login information
/etc/shadow	Holds the password and related information
/etc/group	Holds groups and their account members
/etc/user_attr	Defines roles and other account-specific attributes

/etc/passwd entry has seven fields, beginning with the account name, also separated by colons. The first field in both files stores the account name, so it's easy to cross-reference one account.

A default Solaris 11 /etc/passwd file has 28 entries. I've cherry-picked a few entries here for the sake of a brief example:

```
root:x:0:0:Super-User:/root:/usr/bin/bash
daemon:x:1:1::/:
gdm:x:50:50:GDM Reserved UID:/var/lib/gdm:
pkg5srv:x:97:97:pkg(5) server UID:/:
mfernest:x:60004:10:Michael Ernest:/home/mfernest:/usr/bin/bash
```

The entries here include four so-called system users. Each of these accounts is given a UID below 100 to signify it has been specified as a system account and should never be deleted. My user account has the UID 60004. The daemon account is used to run a few network-based services. The gdm account stands for Gnome Desktop Manager; it runs a process called dbus-launch, which is used to run your main window session. The pkg5srv account will come into play in Chapter 12. In each of these cases, the account is designed so that the processes it runs do not require full superuser access. A key aspect of good security is making sure even obscure system accounts don't have more system access than they require to do their jobs.

Although the root account on my system is configured as a role, there is nothing in the /etc/passwd file to reflect it. The idea of a role was developed long after this file's format was set. Because there is no room in the format for additional attributes, role status is defined in the /etc/user_attr file, which I describe later in this chapter. The absence of role information in this file shows, in a way, that accounts are the same—a role appears to be an additional attribute that disables login capability.

The structure of an account entry is the same across many UNIX variants. Table 6-2 lists the informal name and description for each field.

In Solaris, a lowercase x in the second field is a placeholder that indicates the password resides in the file /etc/shadow. The GECOS, or comment field, is by convention a name. It should tell you who owns, or which system process uses, the account. If you want this field just to reflect the account name, put a lone ampersand

TABLE 6-2   Fields of an /etc/passwd Entry

/etc/passwd Field	Description/Value	Valid Range
Username	User/role name	1 to 8 characters
Password	x (entry delegated to the /etc/shadow file)	N/A
UID	Unique numeric identifier for user/role	100 to 2147483647
GID	Unique numeric identifier for primary group	100 to 2147483647
GCOS/Comment	User's real name (or comment)	Not defined
Home Directory	Initial location upon login or switch	Not defined
Login Shell	Initial process (usually a shell program)	Not defined

(&) in it. The length of the last three fields is not defined. The tools I cover later in this chapter are limited by the maximum length of a command line (2,048 characters altogether). In practice, any entry that exceeds 80 columns should be accompanied by some very persuasive justification.

When you log in to an account (or switch to one using the su - command), your current working directory is set to the home directory specified by the sixth field. It's especially important to get this right for human users because they will likely have additional files they use to configure their environment. This value is used as well to set a variable for the user called HOME. This variable gives the user a reference they can always use to return to their login location.

The seventh field is empty for system account. For users logging in, it is the first process that runs with the users credentials. Usually, it's a shell program that will support a command-line interface, but it can be any executable program you like. There aren't too many ways to get creative with this fact, however. If you changed this field to some short-lived command, such as the ls program, you won't see anything and you'll be logged out as soon as the program terminates. Don't try this before you set up a separate account you can use to log in and change things back! Shell programs are useful in part because they keep you logged in until you want to quit.

The /etc/shadow account stores the user's password in an encrypted form. It also uses a file permission set that prevents anyone but the superuser from even reading the file:

```
$ ls -l /etc/shadow
-r--------   1 root      root          667 Sep 20 06:13 /etc/shadow
```

You can't make file access much more restrictive than that! This permission set requires the root user just to read the file as well as to override the permissions to make changes. The superuser can always force this action, of course, but the request has to be explicit, whether in a program's code or through a command-line option. The five /etc/shadow file entries that correspond with the /etc/passwd file entries I listed earlier are shown here:

```
root:$5$AwkFjRW7$8xsVzEPtH5WIUydm.utz1eVapzqrofBdyDSQ0c805/8:15592::::::
daemon:NP:6445::::::
gdm:*LK*::::::::
pkg5srv:*LK*:15267::::::
mfernest:$5$aACbGoRO$4LooNUrOfKG2zmA61M6AcvhEAe17SZnXEhMLmyqUUE4:15577::::::
```

The second field is literally more cryptic than any other field; it is the account password kept in three parts, each separated with a $ delimiter. The first number refers to the encrypting library used. The second field contains a salt that is used to produce the third field, which is the password itself in hashed form. The full entry tells you what scheme and which salt were used to encrypt the password so that no one can read it, not even the root user. Furthermore, the hash is calculated in such a way that you cannot map back to an unambiguous or correct original value. All you can do, given enough computing power and time, is guess the original value and see if you can produce the same result as the /etc/shadow file content. This technique is the reason your security people want you to have a string of mixed with letters (upper- and lowercase), numbers, and special characters. If you do, a hacker has to go through a much, much larger dictionary of wild guesses to crack your account.

The NP in the daemon account's second field means no password is set for the account. It is not a formally documented value for this field in Solaris. Its purpose is to prevent anyone from logging in or switching to that account, excepting the root user. The accounts that show *LK* in the second field are locked; they have no password and cannot be logged in to.

| TABLE 6-3 | Fields of an /etc/shadow Entry |

/etc/shadow Field	Description/Value
Username	Match to an /etc/passwd entry
Password	Encrypted password, lock string (*LK*), the string NP, or empty
Last Changed	Number of days after 01/01/1970 the password was changed
Minimum	Number of days to pass before changing the password again
Maximum	Number of days the current password is valid
Warning	Number of days before password expiration to warn the user
Inactivity	Number of days the account may remain inactive
Expiration	Number of days after 01/01/1970 that the account will expire
Flags (Attempts)	Number of consecutive failed login attempts

Table 6-3 lists all the fields of an /etc/shadow entry and what they're used for.

The fields represented as a "number of days" use an obscure unit of measure, to say the least. For example, the value 6445, which appears for many system accounts in the last changed field, evaluates to August 25, 1987. It was in 1987 that AT&T and Sun Microsystems created the SVR4 standard and Sun purchased the AT&T source code. It may be that this date correlates to those events.

It's more than reasonable to infer you just need to know what these fields represent and that they each count a whole number, either a number of days passed since January 1, 1970 (also known as an *epoch* in UNIX lore) or just a number of days, period.

As you can imagine, any entry that uses all of these fields will be nearly impossible to manage, requiring the memorization of each field's meaning and having some conversion tool at hand. The conversion is built in to Solaris programs such as the passwd utility, but it doesn't offer human-readable values you can examine. The various options the passwd utility has to change these fields are listed in its man page documentation.

The /etc/group file is far simpler: just four fields, one of which is rarely used anymore. These are shown in Table 6-4.

TABLE 6-4	/etc/group Field	Description/Value
Fields of an /etc/ group Entry	Name	Group name
	Password	Group password (working but rarely used)
	GID	Unique numeric identifier
	User list	Accounts in the group (comma-separated)

A group is defined by a name, its numeric identifier, and the user accounts associated with it. A group password, in principle, adds a layer of protection by requiring a password from any member when relying on the group credential. In practice, I can't remember the last time I have seen it used. It remains part of the file's format so as not to break time-honored programs and scripts that depend on the standard field count.

The /etc/user_attr file first appeared in Solaris 8 as a way to extend user attributes without disrupting the file formats we have covered so far. The entry format is also simple: five fields, separated by colons. The first field is a user that is specified in the /etc/passwd file. The second, third, and fourth fields are not yet in use. The fifth field, however, supports an indefinite list of subfields separated by semicolons. Each subfield is a key-value pair that defines one of several additional attributes.

The attribute that concerns us at the moment has a key named "type." You can use it to set an account to normal (for a regular user account) or role. This file only has to include the accounts to which you want to specify additional attributes. My current /etc/user_attr file looks like this:

```
$ cat /etc/user_attr
#
# The system provided entries are stored in different files
# under "/etc/user_attr.d".  They should not be copied to this file.
#
# Only local changes should be stored in this file.
# This line should be kept in this file or it will be overwritten.
#
root::::type=role
mfernest::::type=normal;lock_after_retries=no;profiles=System
Administrator;roles=root
```

Notice the root account is declared as a role. The mfernest account is a regular account that can access the root role. The second attribute, lock_after_retries, explains itself. The third attribute, profiles, may include a list of rights profiles. Each rights profile may include programs the user can run with an *effective* UID (EUID) or GID (EGID) of another user. These programs may also be configured to run with additional process privileges. Profiles provide one way to designate a list of specific, additional privileges by a functional name, such as System Administrator.

The comment area in the file explains that additional files are kept in the directory /etc/user_attr.d. This arrangement is change in Solaris 11 from how it was organized in Solaris 10. Maintaining system user entries separately simplifies the /etc/user_attr file and stores special-purpose entries where they are less likely to be disturbed.

Changing Standard Login Requirements

The /etc/default/passwd file documents a list of 16 parameters an administrator can use to relax or tighten the rules for user authentication, password requirements, and password aging. It even provides a way to enable password checking, so a user can be warned their new password is easy to guess. These are values that will stand in for any user account with corresponding blank fields in their /etc/shadow file entries. If the individual accounts have a local configuration, it overrides the default values given here. These changes take effect immediately and can be observed on the next login.

The MINWEEKS and MAXWEEKS parameters correspond to the fourth and fifth fields of the entries in the /etc/shadow file. You can only define these values as a number of weeks in the /etc/default/passwd file, even though the /etc/shadow file keeps the value as a number of days. Both parameters are blank by default; you can assign either or both a value if you wish. The PASSLENGTH parameter, which is grouped with these two parameters, lets you set a minimum character length for any password; the default length is 6.

You can use the NAMECHECK parameter to make sure the user's password isn't the same as their login name, a common tactic among users who find authentication a distraction from their tasks. If you don't mind matching account names and passwords, you can un-comment this parameter.

The HISTORY parameter requires the user to rotate through some number of passwords before reusing a previous one. It's typically used in conjunction with the MAXWEEKS parameter to ensure regular password changes. Recycling the same password repeatedly isn't a practice you want to encourage, but few users will thank you for making them invent 26 different passwords, the maximum value the HISTORY parameter supports, before using one again. If the HISTORY parameter is absent from this file, is commented out, or set to zero, its function is disabled. If it is set back to 0, every user with a password history will have it erased the next time they log in.

The next block of parameters described in the /etc/default/passwd file are called *complexity tunables*. Each one allows you to decorate the current password requirements with conditions (or restrictions) to promote harder-to-guess character combinations. Table 6-5 lists these tunables and describes the rules they impose.

By enabling one or more of these parameters, you're setting the rules for all passwords that are created after the fact. Current passwords remain unaffected because they are already hashed and stored in the /etc/shadow file. These policies do not apply to the root account, however. Any time the root user sets or resets a password on any account, these tunables are ignored. Also bear in mind that Solaris 11 requires a password to contain at least one numeric or special character, even with these parameters commented out. You cannot disable this requirement using the /etc/default/passwd file.

You can also defend your system against easily guessed passwords by checking them against a dictionary of common words. The parameters DICTIONLIST and DICTIONBDIR help you do this. The DICTIONLIST parameter accepts a comma-separated list of files, each addressed by its absolute path, that contain dictionary words. The DICTIONBDIR parameter identifies the directory you keep the files in. The given location, /var/passwd, does not exist by default.

TABLE 6-5   Password Complexity Tunables Listed in the /etc/default/passwd File

Complexity Tunable	Effect on Password
MINDIFF	How many characters in a new password must differ from the old
MINALPHA	How many characters must fall in the ranges a–z and A–Z
MINNONALPHA	How many characters must not fall in the ranges a–z and A–Z
MINUPPER	How many characters must fall in the range A–Z
MINLOWER	How many characters must fall in the range a–z
MAXREPEATS	How many times a character may repeat in sequence
MINSPECIAL	How many characters must fall outside the ranges a–z, A–Z, and 0–9
MINDIGIT	How many characters must fall in the range 0–9
WHITESPACE	Blanks allowed in the password string (YES or NO)

If a user changes their password to one that begins or ends with a dictionary word, such as orange5 or 5orange, the system will reject it. The password 5orange5, however, would be allowed. Dictionary checks are a good deterrent against naive attempts at using a weak password, but they won't do much to stop people who know how to get around them.

SCENARIO & SOLUTION

To enable this feature, uncomment the DICTIONLIST and DICTIONBDIR parameters and specify at least one file of words in the DICTIONLIST parameter. The mkpwdict command uses these parameters to create a database in the directory specified by the DICTIONBDIR parameter.

```
$ ls /var/passwd
/var/passwd: No such file or directory
$ tail -2 /etc/default/passwd
DICTIONLIST=/usr/dict/words
DICTIONDBDIR=/var/passwd
$ sudo mkpwdict
mkpwdict: using default database location: /var/passwd.
mkpwdict: using default dictionary list: /usr/dict/words.
$ ls /var/passwd
authtok_check.lock   pw_dict.hwm        pw_dict.pwd        pw_dict.pwi
```

You can test this feature by trying a dictionary word along with one numeric or special character:

```
$ sudo passwd toby
New Password: orange
passwd: The password must contain at least 1 numeric or special character(s).

Please try again
New Password: orange5
passwd: password is based on a dictionary word.

Please try again
New Password: 5orange5
Re-enter new Password: 5orange5
passwd: password successfully changed for toby
```

You get three chances with one invocation of the passwd utility. After that, the utility terminates and you'll have to try again.

Using the passwd Utility

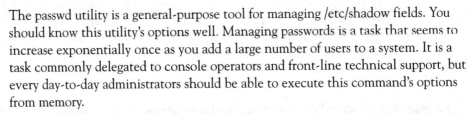

The passwd utility is a general-purpose tool for managing /etc/shadow fields. You should know this utility's options well. Managing passwords is a task that seems to increase exponentially once as you add a large number of users to a system. It is a task commonly delegated to console operators and front-line technical support, but every day-to-day administrators should be able to execute this command's options from memory.

on the

ⓘob

Let's say you need to know if any users have not set a password. You could search the /etc/shadow file yourself, but it's easier to check the password field for all accounts and filter the ones labeled UP (unset password), like this:

```
$ sudo passwd -sa | grep UP
toby      UP
```

That's it. This approach provides better focus than using the grep utility. It's also more flexible. If you have to manage a password repository on an LDAP server, this approach is designed to do the job.

Table 6-6 lists the letter options you'll use repeatedly when managing account passwords. Consult the man page for a complete list of interactions and conditions that follow from these options. Not included in this table are values you can use to disable password properties, such as minimum and maximum password change intervals, when you need to.

It is recommended that you always set the minimum and maximum values at the same time to avoid confusion. Setting the minimum higher than the maximum renders the account password unchangeable until you correct this setting. These and other consequences of conflicting settings are described in the documentation and can take a while to absorb. It's worth your time to walk through them carefully and know what a bad entry looks like.

TABLE 6-6	Options to the passwd Utility	

passwd Option	Field Change	Description
-f *username*	3	Expires the password and forces a change on the next login
-l *username*	2	Locks the account
-u *username*	2	Unlocks the account (field blanked)
-n *days username*	4,5	Minimum days between password changes
-w *days username*	6	Days before the user is warned about password expiration
-x *days username*	4,5	Maximum days the current password remains valid
-d *username*	2	Disables password requirement (field blanked)

CERTIFICATION OBJECTIVE 6.02

Creating and Managing Accounts

Thinking about password policy before creating new users is, for me, a cart-and-horse issue. If you create a lot of user accounts and then make your password policy stringent, you then have to force a password change among all your users before you can claim the new policy is in full effect. That situation is unavoidable in some cases, but no less inconvenient to users. If you've had an online account you rarely use, and the password policy changed in the meantime, you know it can be a hassle.

Now that you've learned the different ways you can improve password strength without much effort, it's a simple matter of creating accounts with the right information to support your users. Remember that a user isn't necessarily a person. It could be an application that uses an account as a way to identify the processes it starts and to apply a set of privileges that aren't as strong as root access but are stronger than what you'd grant to a human user.

Setting Account Defaults

The information you need for a new account will vary with your site requirements. A site may require a specific form for the username, such as the person's initials and employee ID number. If the user is an application, the software vendor may require a certain name to match what's in the code. Other requirements may include a specific shell program, a common location for home directories, and so on.

The easiest way to start is with common defaults (you can change them to suit your needs). In Solaris 11, you can see those defaults using the useradd -D command:

```
$ sudo useradd -D
group=staff,10  project=default,3  basedir=/export/home
skel=/etc/skel  shell=/usr/bin/bash  inactive=0
expire=  auths=  profiles=  roles=  limitpriv=
defaultpriv=  lock_after_retries=
```

We haven't covered some of these properties yet, and some aren't covered in the OCA exam in any depth. Table 6-7 lists each one, provides a default value or explanation, and states where in the book the property is covered, if at all.

TABLE 6-7   User Property Defaults That Can Be Set

User Default	Value	Chapter
Group	Default name, gid	6
Project	Default name, projid	8
Basedir	Default location for home directories	6
Skel	Directory containing shell initialization files	6
Shell	Default login program	6
Inactive	Days dormant before disabling account (off by default)	6
Expire	Total days before disabling account (off)	6
Profiles	Profiles granted	N/A
Roles	Role accounts granted	6
Limitpriv	Operational privileges excluded	N/A
default_priv	Operational privileges granted	N/A
lock_after_retries	Failed attempts before disabling account	6

You can write one or more of these properties to the file /usr/sadm/defadduser, which the useradd command looks for before it creates a new account. If you apply the useradd command option that indicates a specific property along with the -D option, the useradd command will either create the file and fill in your choice, or add it if the file's already been made. If you want to set the default shell to /usr/bin/ksh, for example, you'd do it like this:

```
$ ls /usr/sadm/defadduser
/usr/sadm/defadduser: No such file or directory
$ sudo useradd -s /usr/bin/ksh -D
-D output omitted
$ cat /usr/sadm/defadduser
#Default values for useradd.  Changed Fri Sep 21 07:08:19 2012

defgroup=10
defgname=staff
defparent=/export/home
defskel=/etc/skel
defshell=/usr/bin/ksh
definact=0
defexpire=
defauthorization=
defrole=
defprofile=
defproj=3
defprojname=default
deflimitpriv=
defdefaultpriv=
deflock_after_retries=
```

The -s option covers the first login program, which for human users should be a shell program. As I mentioned before, it could be any program, but it's rarely documented that way because there aren't many useful alternatives. The resulting file, as you can see, covers all the properties printed with the -D option and fills in values. Easy as it looks to change this file by hand, it's better to let the useradd utility do it. It includes validation checks that you might miss if you edit it yourself.

Creating User, Role, and Group Accounts

Solaris supplies separate commands for adding, deleting, and modifying the user, role, and group types. They're easy to remember, too:

- useradd, userdel, and usermod
- roleadd, roledel, and rolemod
- groupadd, groupdel, and groupmod

Each of the "del" commands removes the named type. The groupdel command just removes the named group's entry from the /etc/group file. The roledel and userdel commands go a bit further. A role may have been assigned to one or more user accounts, so the roledel command will check these assignments (in the /etc/user_attr file) and remove them too. If you use the userdel -r command, it will remove the named user's home directory and files as well as the account entry. That option makes it easy to clear disk space of the files and the ZFS file system that was created to contain them.

The "mod" commands are recommended for changing entries in these files instead of using an editor. As you'll discover, the "add" commands fail if you name an entry that already exists, so you can't use them to overwrite current values. It may take an exercise or two to learn the option letters that match each field in an entry, particularly for the useradd utility. Fortunately, the same option letters that apply to the add command are used with the corresponding mod command.

The "add" commands are tools that create the entries you need. Their key benefit is ensuring the entry format is correct. The groupadd command is the simplest of them. Simply name a group, specify a GID and member users if you want, and observe the results in the file:

```
$ sudo groupadd -g 105 -U mfernest specials
$ grep specials /etc/group
specials::105:mfernest
$ sudo groupmod -g 115 -U+toby specials
Found group in files repository.
$ grep specials /etc/group
specials::115:mfernest,toby
$ sudo groupdel specials
Found group in files repository.
$ grep specials /etc/group
$
```

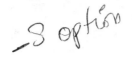
-S option

Here, you can see it's possible to create a group, change it, and delete it. Learning the command options and syntax is all takes. Do be careful about changing UIDs and GIDs on a whim, however. When you create a file or directory, your UID and GID are assigned to the permission set of that file. If you change these values for the account later on, the file permissions are *not* automatically updated. In fact, if you change your UID without taking a careful inventory of all the files you own on a system, you could lose access to them altogether. If you're going to experiment, do so with files and accounts you can throw away if something goes wrong.

e x a m

w a t c h

The response message "Found group in files repository" is vague, but it points to a condition you're not expected to understand for the exam. The documentation shows that you can use the -S option to name an alternate repository. In Solaris 11, the account-based commands can operate on the files you've learned, or on a directory server that uses the Lightweight Directory Access Protocol (LDAP). You don't need to worry about that option for now.

Why the response does not give the name of the group you're working on is anyone's guess. It doesn't seem like a hardship to make the utility report that value.

Because user and role accounts are alike in most respects, you might wonder why a separate set of commands for each type is necessary. The differences in field data are few, but they are also important and complex. You can assign roles to a user account, for example, but not the reverse. A role account requires an entry in the /etc/user_attr file; a user account that has no roles assigned does not. Also, you'll generally set up user accounts for people and just role accounts for the authorizations an administrative user needs from time to time. These and other differences suggest that it's better to keep separate utilities for each type. They use the same letter options for the fields they have in common, so the amount of extra detail you need to remember is minimal.

There is a downside to these per-field options to consider as well. If you have to call out a lot of the fields to create an account—perhaps none of the defaults are suitable—then writing a command to do it can be tedious and error-prone. Here's an example:

```
$ sudo useradd -b /export/home -c "Toby" -g other\
-e "12/31/2012" -s/usr/bin/csh -u 66666 toby
$ grep toby /etc/passwd
toby:x:66666:1:Toby:/home/toby:/usr/bin/csh
$ sudo grep toby /etc/shadow
toby:UP::::::15705:
```

In this example, I specified the UID, the primary GID, the comment, the location for the home directory, the shell program, and the account expiration date. This command does not create the /home/toby directory. To do that, I have to add the -m option, which will create a new ZFS file system for the user, not just a directory.

That's a lot of typing for one command. One well-placed mistake and it will all fail. Worse, it could result in an account you then have to modify to make it right. Adding multiple accounts this way can get tiresome in a hurry. The usermod command, however, does come in handy for quick changes:

```
$ sudo usermod -g staff -s /usr/bin/bash -R+root toby
Found user in files repository.
$ grep toby /etc/passwd
toby:x:66666:10:Toby:/home/toby:/usr/bin/bash
$ grep toby /etc/user_attr
toby::::type=normal;roles=root
```

Everything you need to know about the role-based commands follows from the user-based commands. You cannot assign one role to another role.

The rest is up to you: Experiment with the options and make sure you feel comfortable with the kinds of changes you are likely to make to an account. As always, don't experiment with an account you rely on, just in case. Also keep a backup account handy that has the privileges you need. Nothing is worse than losing access to your own system without an alternate way of getting in.

CERTIFICATION OBJECTIVE 6.03

Configuring Login Initialization

Long before there ever was a browser war, UNIX users amused themselves by arguing over the best screen-based editor (vi and emacs were the top contenders) and the best shell program, of which there were a handful. Some people still go on about their preferred, and therefore best, editor, but the bash shell seems to have choked off that topic for friendly debate. The shells installed by default with Solaris include the following:

- Bourne shell (/usr/bin/sh)
- POSIX-compliant Bourne shell (/usr/xpg4/bin/sh)
- Bourne-again shell (/usr/bin/bash)
- C shell (/usr/bin/csh)
- Korn shell (/usr/bin/ksh)

There are a few others that have specialized uses and are available to install, once you know how to add software to the system. I cover that topic in Chapter 12.

exam
watch

You may be asked to identify the Z shell (/usr/bin/zsh) or the enhanced C shell (/usr/bin/tcsh). They are also installed by default and referenced in Solaris 11 documentation. For the exam, you just need to know they are available options.

These programs are intended as the first program you'll use upon login. It's a system and administrative responsibility to prepare the shell's *environment* with information that tells the shell how to run and who is using it. The system passes this information, via the login command, by defining a number of variables for the shell. You can see some of these variables and their assigned values by using the env command:

```
$ env
SHELL=/usr/bin/bash
USERNAME=mfernest
PATH=/usr/bin:/usr/sbin
DESKTOP_SESSION=gnome
PWD=/home/mfernest
HOME=/home/mfernest
```

If you try this command yourself, you'll get three dozen or so lines of output. I'm showing selected lines here you can identify based on the discussion so far. The SHELL variable tells any program you run what your desired environment happens to be. The PATH variable is a list of directories you allow the shell to search once you name a program to run. When you type **ls**, for example, your shell will check each directory path listed in your PATH variable in order until it finds a matching program file. The PWD variable reports your present working directory (that is, the directory your shell is using for its base of operation). The other environment variables listed here explain themselves.

The set and setenv commands also report a list of variables that inform your shell, some of which also appear in output from the env command. The variables reported by the set/setenv commands are passed along to any program you start from the command line, similar to how the login program does this for the shell. In that sense, every program that can launch another program has a local environment, some of which it can *export* to the new program.

Other environment variables you should be aware of are listed in Table 6-8. Use the setenv command, if you are using the C shell or its enhanced version, to determine which of these variables are exported to new programs. For the remaining shells, use the set command.

TABLE 6-8	Environment Variables to Note

Environment variable	Description
LANG	Reports the language/locale you're currently using
LOGNAME	Your login name (fixed by the login utility)
MAIL	Location of your system mailbox
MANPATH	List of paths to man page files
PS1	Defines the command prompt (excluding csh and tcsh)
TERM	Reports the terminal type you're using

To report the value of a single variable of this kind, use the echo command. Provide the variable as an argument with a $ character for a prefix:

```
$ echo $LANG
en_US.UTF-8
$ echo $LOGNAME
mfernest
$ echo $TERM
xterm
```

The login program passes these values into the program specified by your /etc/ passwd entry, once authentication succeeds. An administrator can add to this work using initialization files that are stored in the /etc directory. The user, however, gets a final say. Using initialization files stored in the home directory, the user can override some of the variables provided, add additional ones, and export them as desired.

on the **job**

See the login utility man page for a complete list of the files the utility reads when preparing an account for access. Understanding the extensive responsibilities this program has will, over time, give you a deep appreciation for the complexity of this process.

There are two fundamentally different shell types: those that derive from the Bourne shell and those that derive from the C shell. The login program will select the appropriate global initialization file depending on the shell type: the /etc/ profile file for the Bourne shell family and the /etc/.login file for the C shell family.

Although it's not a bad idea to examine the text of these two files, interpreting them requires a foundation in reading shell code. At this level, you're expected to know that these files participate in setting up a user account on login as well as which file services which shells. Use the cat or more command to view the contents of either one.

One more detail needs to be added here because the terminology is peculiar. When the login command reads an initialization file to prepare the shell, it is called *sourcing*. Strictly speaking, this term provides an important distinction. An initialization file is written using the same language as a script, which executes one or more commands. A proper initialization file should change the shell environment, which does not require running additional programs. The word *sourcing* gives us a term for keeping separate these two ways of using the shell.

Each shell also has a way to let you source it after you've logged in. Without the feature, you'd have to log out of your system and log back in to see any changes you've made to the shell environment itself. In the Bourne shell family, you source an initialization file using a dot command. For the C shell family, you use the source command. If a senior administrator tells you the global initialization files have changed and you should source your current sessions, it's a quick-and-easy task:

```
$ . /etc/profile
% source /etc/.login
```

The dollar sign ($) is a common prompt for signifying a Korn shell. The percent sign (%) does the same for the C shell. Both global initialization files have permissions that allow any user to source them.

Customizing User Shells

In principle, any user can set up their initialization files without any help from an administrator. All a user has to do is create the shell-appropriate files in their home directory and then source them. That's fine for knowledgeable users, in particular ones who like performing such tasks by hand and without assistance. In practice, the administrator can make this work a little easier by setting up new accounts with the right starter files.

One option to the useradd command I did not cover yet does exactly that. If you make a home directory for a user (using the -m option) as you create the account, you supplement it with the -k option to name a directory of starter files. Solaris also provides the default directory /etc/skel and some starter files, which an experienced administrator can modify as desired:

```
$ ls /etc/skel
local.cshrc     local.login     local.profile
```

If you want your shell of choice to source the appropriate file, you have to remove the prepended "local" from the name. Solaris uses this string so that the files are reported by the ls command without the use of the -a option. Here is an example:

```
$ sudo useradd -s /usr/bin/ksh -u 65555 -c "Test Account" \
> -m -k /etc/skel testing
80 blocks
$ grep testing /etc/passwd
testing:x:65555:10:Test Account:/home/testing:/usr/bin/ksh
$ ls /home/testing
local.cshrc     local.login     local.profile
```

Notice that no filtering takes place. The useradd command just dumps the contents of the /etc/skel directory into the new home directory. The user gets to sort it out from there. If you want this process to be a little bit cleaner, you could establish shell-specific directories to use and populate them only with the files appropriate to each. You may be surprised how far a little extra attention goes for users who don't already know which of these files are useful to them and which files aren't.

Some users may not be as excited about their default environment as the administrator is. Many command-line users like to customize their prompt to reflect a changing element in their environment, such as the time or the current working directory. Doing this correctly requires a foundation in shell language syntax, but you can get a quick lesson just by looking at your current prompt, which is stored in the PS1 variable:

```
mfernest@orca$ echo $PS1
\u@\h:\w\$
```

Up to this point, I've left my own prompt out of most examples, and will do that to save line space from now on. Each shell has a programmable environment that may produce the same or similar result but use different instructions to create it. Here's another version of the same thing, or close to it, using the Korn shell:

```
mfernest@orca:~$ PS1="${LOGNAME}@orca-> "
mfernest@orca->
```

I got the value of LOGNAME using the $ character to read it each time the prompt is produced. The braces around the value separate the variable from the following part of the string, which is literal. I changed the end to make an arrow just for the sake of example. Notice also I included a blank space so that whatever I type doesn't look attached to the prompt. The change is immediate because the shell reads the PS1 value to form the next prompt.

You can share any variable in your local environment with the programs you run by using the shell's export command (or setenv for the C shell family). In a generic shell environment there isn't a need for this, but let's say you want to define a new variable and share it. All you have to do is name a new variable, assign it a value, and then export it:

```
mfernest@orca -> MYVAR=25 ; export MYVAR
mfernest@orca -> echo $MYVAR
25
```

That's all there is to it. To dig deeper, you can look for resources that explain how to take full advantage of the resources your preferred shell has to offer. You will find the most recent literature covers bash, but shell information doesn't really get old; instead, shells just fall out of favor. If you like the Korn shell or C shell, any decent book of any age will help you learn more about it.

CERTIFICATION OBJECTIVE 6.04

Using Shell Metacharacters

You should know something about globbing before leaving this topic. *Globbing* is the term for using special characters to match filenames on the command line. Unlike *regular expressions*, which use special characters to match values in an arbitrary string of text, globbing only operates on the files in the directory you apply them to, usually the current directory.

To appreciate the service globbing provides, it's helpful to imagine a directory with a few dozen files or more in it. Now say you want a long listing (ls -l) of just six of the files, which have some common element in their names. With globbing, it's possible to winnow out the filenames you don't want without having to type in each of the six files you do want. It seems like a very basic skill once you've got the hang of it, but it can seem awkward and even counterproductive until then.

Three globbing elements are formally called *metacharacters*. They're called that because the shell interprets these elements as operators instead of their literal character values. Table 6-9 describes how each globbing metacharacter operates.

By itself, the asterisk (or *splat*) will match all the contents in a directory. It's normally paired with a partial string you want to complete, such as files that start with the same letter:

```
$ ls -ld /etc/z*
drwxr-xr-x  2 root    sys        3 Oct 20  2011 /etc/zfs
drwxr-xr-x  2 root    sys        9 May 27 17:53 /etc/zones
lrwxrwxrwx  1 root    root       7 May 27 17:53 /etc/zprofile -> profile
-rw-r--r--  1 root    bin      177 Oct 20  2011 /etc/zshrc
```

I'm using the -d option here so the command will list the directories matched without reading their contents. Notice also there is an /etc/zprofile file that supports the Z shell, but it's just an alias for the /etc/profile file. The /etc/zshrc file acts as a global initializer for all Z shell users, wherever they may be.

If you want to make a wildcard match for a select number of characters, you can use one or more question marks throughout a string. This metacharacter also gives you a way to pose a requirement, such as matching all files with exactly four characters. Here's an example:

```
$ ls -d /etc/????
/etc/acct  /etc/dhcp  /etc/krb5  /etc/motd  /etc/sasl  /etc/slsh
/etc/bash  /etc/ftpd  /etc/mach  /etc/nwam  /etc/sgml
/etc/cups  /etc/inet  /etc/mail  /etc/odbc  /etc/skel
```

Using braces, you can list the characters you want to match:

```
$ ls -d /etc/f[ot]*
/etc/fonts      /etc/format.dat   /etc/ftpusers
/etc/foomatic   /etc/ftpd
```

TABLE 6-9	Globbing Element	Function
Globbing Metacharacters	*	Matches any number of characters, including none, to complete a filename
	?	Matches one and only one character
	[]	Matches a list or range of characters inside the brackets

Here, I've doubled up, looking for all files in the /etc directory that start with the letter *f*, has the letter *o* or *t* for the second character, and has zero or more characters in the name. You can also express a range of characters by using a dash and listing the first and last characters in the range. You can even list multiple ranges in one brace if you want. Here are some examples:

- [a-z]   Match any lowercase character
- [5-9]   Match any digit from 5 to 9
- [0-3A-C]   Match a digit from 0 to 3 or a character from A to C

As you get comfortable with globbing, you'll find ways to combine these elements for useful combinations. A lot of administrators these days rely heavily on filename completion, a very popular and powerful feature in the bash shell. Globbing may not be as exciting a feature as it was before filename completion came on the scene, but it still has many day-to-day uses.

Using Shell Metacharacters

It may not have occurred to you just yet, but the $ character is also a metacharacter. When I am teaching, I call it the "value of" character because that's what it amounts to. Put it in front of an assigned variable in your shell, and it returns the value held by the variable. In fact, a variety of expressions in your shell can save you a lot of typing. The expression $$, for example, will tell you the process ID (or PID) of the current shell:

```
$ ps
  PID TTY       TIME CMD
 1499 pts/1     0:01 ksh
 3890 pts/1     0:00 ps
$ echo $$
1499
```

The ps command returns the names and numeric IDs of processes your shell is currently running. The echo $$ command shows that the ksh process is the one you're using right now. You can use quite a few more of these shorthand references, but that topic goes further into learning the shell itself.

The metacharacters you should know for the Solaris 11 OCA exam include the tilde (~) and the dash (-). Both are directory navigation aids. The tilde is a shorthand reference for your home directory. The dash refers to the directory you were previously in. It's very short work to go to your home directory and return to the previous directory whenever you like:

```
$ pwd
/etc/zones
$ cd ~
$ pwd
/home/mfernest
$ cd -
/etc/zones
$ pwd
/etc/zones
```

Notice the cd command will report the directory name when you use the dash option, so the last pwd command I used here isn't necessary. The cd command doesn't do the same for the home directory—it assumes you know what that is. But just in case, there's no harm in in refreshing your memory with the pwd command.

CERTIFICATION SUMMARY

To prepare for this topic on the OCA exam, you should understand the premise for user and role accounts, the function of the group type, and the structure of the files (also referred to as *system databases*) that contain this data. In addition, you should know the nine commands used to manage these types and be able to differentiate a valid command from a clearly false one. There's less emphasis on this exam on memorizing options but greater emphasis on knowing the right tool for a task and when to apply it.

As an administrator, you should know very well how to manage passwords. In addition, you should understand the basic initialization process that occurs when a user performs a login successfully, how to add initialization starter files to a user's home directory, and the basics of environment setup and customization. Shells are designed to interpret some characters as operators instead of literal values. This is a rich and deep topic all by itself, but for certification you only need to remember the ones mentioned in this chapter, along with some simple examples that demonstrate your ability to use them correctly.

✓ TWO-MINUTE DRILL

Understanding Users and Groups

❑ A user account is any valid entry that exists in the /etc/passwd file. The password for each entry is kept in the /etc/shadow file. If the user account is a role, that information is stored in the /etc/user_attr file.

❑ Group data is stored in the /etc/group file. The GID extends a user's permissions to files that belong to any group that user is a member of.

❑ The format of each account-based file is defined by a series of colon-separated fields. An administrator is expected to know each format by heart.

Creating and Managing Accounts

❑ Altogether, nine commands are used to manage the user, role, and group types. Each type has three commands to create, modify, and delete entries for that type.

❑ The passwd command manages content in the /etc/shadow file for both normal and role-based users.

Configuring Login Initialization

❑ The two global initialization files are /etc/profile, used for all shells in the Bourne family, and /etc/.login, used for all shells in the C shell family.

❑ Solaris provides three starter initialization files in the /etc/skel/directory. You can copy them into a new user's home directory automatically when you create the account.

❑ Per-user initialization files can be stored in each user's home directory. Users can override any environment variable that is not fixed by the system. Users can also create and export new variables to share with any programs they run.

Using Shell Metacharacters

❑ The asterisk (*), question mark (?), and brackets ([]) are *globbing* operators. They can be used to match filenames in a directory in lieu of typing them out.

❑ The tilde (~) and dash (-) characters are navigation metacharacters. They are shorthand references for the user's home directory and the user's previous directory location, respectively.

SELF TEST

Use the following questions to test your recall and understanding of the chapter's material.

Understanding Users and Groups

1. Which of the following is an illegal username?
    A. Q7
    B. bl00man
    C. 9lives
    D. mitchell5

2. Choose the correct statement for the meaning of the third and fourth fields in the /etc/passwd entry fred:x:50:50:System Fred:/home/fred:/usr/bin/csh.
    A. The account UID is 50; the GID is ignored.
    B. The account GID is 50; the UID is ignored.
    C. The account UID and GID are both 50, but are not related.
    D. The account UID and GID are both 50 and must remain equal.

3. Which statement correctly describes a function of the /etc/group file?
    A. It lists one or more users and roles that are members of each named group.
    B. It lists zero or more users and roles that are members of each named group.
    C. It maintains a password field that no longer works.
    D. It allows virtually any integer as a GID.

Creating and Managing Accounts

4. Which statement is correct?
    A. The /usr/sadm/defadduser file is required for creating new user accounts.
    B. You cannot assign a user to a role.
    C. The useradd command can set an account password; the roleadd command cannot.
    D. Password expiration is disabled for any account that is locked.

5. Which three functions can the passwd command perform?
    A. It can force users to reset their passwords on the next login.
    B. It can prevent users from changing their passwords.
    C. It can warn logged-in users their password is about to expire.
    D. It can set a later expiration date for the account.

6. Which of the following functions can the usermod utility perform? (Pick all the apply.)

   A. It can change the shell program of the account.

   B. It can change the group membership of the account.

   C. It can create a new home directory for the account.

   D. It can change the expiration date on the account.

Configuring Login Initialization

7. Select the correct statement.

   A. The user cannot change their shell program after they log in.

   B. The administrator cannot modify the /etc/profile file.

   C. The administrator cannot run the login program except to log in.

   D. The user cannot modify the /etc/.login file.

8. Which command invocation will create the /home/user5 directory and copy the contents of the /etc/localinit directory into it?

   A. cp /etc/localinit /home/user5

   B. sudo useradd -k -m /etc/localinit/user5

   C. sudo useradd -m -k /etc/localinit user5

   D. sudo useradd -d /etc/localinit user5

9. Select the statement that correctly describes the result of the command-line invocation ". ~/.profile".

   A. It will print the contents of the .profile file from the user's home directory to the screen, if the user if using a Korn shell.

   B. It will print the contents of the .profile file from the previous directory to the screen, if the user if using a C shell.

   C. It will read the contents of the .profile file from the user's home directory into the shell environment, if the user is using a Korn shell.

   D. It will export all variables in the user's Korn shell environment to the home directory.

Using Shell Metacharacters

10. The globbing expression *?[5Za] will match which two filenames?

   A. Z7

   B. B_a

   C. G5Z

   D. Z

SELF TEST ANSWERS

Understanding Users and Groups

1. ☑ **D.** A username cannot exceed eight characters.
    ☒ **A, B,** and **C** are incorrect. These are all legal usernames. As long as a username has a letter character along with at least one character of the opposite case, or a number, the useradd utility will accept it. It will complain if you start the username with a number, but it will still accept the entry. Take some time to experiment with other poor naming choices to see how the utility responds.

2. ☑ **C.** The UID and GID are separate numeric identifiers. There is no system-defined relationship that results if the numbers are the same for one entry.
    ☒ **A, B,** and **D** are incorrect. These are all incorrect inferences from this relationship. It's a popular convention for system accounts to have the same number for the UID and GID, particularly for accounts that should not have members in their group and do not belong to other groups. The system makes no use of this arrangement.

3. ☑ **B.** Each entry in the /etc/group file has four fields for the name, password, GID, and member list of a group. Some groups have only one member: a user account with a primary relationship to that group. Because the /etc/group file only lists secondary group memberships, many of them have zero additional members.
    ☒ **A, C,** and **D** are incorrect. **A** is incorrect because a group entry does not have to specify. **C** is incorrect because the group password is not often used. In Solaris, direct support for it has also been removed, but you can still apply passwords to groups. **D** is incorrect because although a legal GID has a very wide integer range, it cannot be negative. Unused numbers between 0 and 100 are documented as reserved for system use but can be used by the superuser.

Creating and Managing Accounts

4. ☑ **B.** You can assign a role to a user, but not vice versa.
    ☒ **A, C,** and **D** are incorrect. **A** is incorrect because the /usr/sadm/defadduser file is useful for overriding the defaults built in to the useradd command, but it is not required to create new accounts. **C** is incorrect because you can only set passwords with the passwd utility. **D** is incorrect because password expiration is a moot point once an account is locked, but the fields don't change. If the account is unlocked after the expiration date, the user will not be able to log in.

5. ☑ **A, B,** and **D.** You can force a user to change the password with the passwd -f command, and you can set the expiration date later (or sooner) with the passwd -x command. You can prevent a password change by locking the account. Setting the minimum duration for a password to a value greater than the maximum duration will also prevent the user from changing the password.
   ☒ **C** is incorrect. The passwd utility only changes the fields in the /etc/shadow. Users are not notified of any change until the next login attempt.

6. ☑ **A, B, C,** and **D.** The usermod utility has extensive options, including password expiration, you can apply to an existing user account. With the -d and -m options, the administrator can move the user's existing directory to the location specified. This option was not mentioned in this chapter; however, this book is not an exhaustive review of the actual question bank for the exam. You may not be expected to memorize the letter options for these commands, but you should know the operations each one of them can perform.

Configuring Login Initialization

7. ☑ **D.** Any non-root user can read or source the /etc/.login file. Only a user with root privileges can edit the contents.
   ☒ **A, B,** and **C** are incorrect. **A** is incorrect because to change the shell program, the user can simply invoke another one. Shell programs are also commands. **B** is incorrect because a user with root privileges can modify any system file. **C** is incorrect because the login program is also just a command. You can consult the man page documentation to better understand its behavior for a user who is already logged in.

8. ☑ **C.** I've mentioned before that you're not expected to memorize letter options for the exam. That said, you should know that the -k option only works when the -m option is included to create the user directory. If the directory does not exist, the attempt to copy files to that location fails.
   ☒ **A, B,** and **D** are incorrect. **A** is incorrect because the copy attempt will fail due to the target directory not having been created. **B** is incorrect because the options are listed in the wrong order. **D** is incorrect because the -d option specifies a different home directory location. In this case, the user account will see the files in this directory because they are already there.

9. ☑ **C.** In the Korn shell (a Bourne shell family member), the dot operator sources the file that follows, if it contains the proper instructions to modify the current shell.
   ☒ **A, B,** and **D** are incorrect. **A** and **B** are incorrect because sourcing does not print the contents of the sourced file. If the sourcing file contains errors or commands that do print, those results may of course appear. **D** is incorrect because a source file can include instructions to export variables, but exporting all variables is not automatic.

Using Shell Metacharacters

10. ☑ **B** and **C.** You can break down the globbing expression as "zero or more of any characters, followed by one character, followed by one character that is 5, Z or a." Option B contains one optional character (B), one required character (_), and the character a. Option C has one optional character (G), one required character (5), and character Z.

☒ **A** and **D** are incorrect. **A** is incorrect because a correct match has to end with the character 5, Z, or A. **D** is incorrect because a correct match has to have at least two characters.

7

Managing
Processes

T wo concepts comprise the heart and soul of any UNIX-based operating system: files, which establish the names and locations of your data, and processes, which operate on and produce that data. There are, of course, many types of files and processes. If you meditate on this idea for too long, it may not seem like it reveals very much. Just because you know the file and process are important concepts, and they represent the only way a user can interact with the operating system doesn't mean the technical details are somehow trivial, self-evident, or easy to master.

But if you ever feel lost in tracking all the tasks a system is executing, you can almost always step back and ask, "What is the process I'm interested in doing right now? What files does it read from and write to? What code does it rely on? Who started it? How else can I track its behavior?" The concepts you will learn in this chapter, and the tools you'll use to observe those concepts in action, will guide you through the management of any application that runs on Solaris—from scripts to complex relational database management systems. Every application runs as a process, and every process works by the same rules. You can count on that.

CERTIFICATION OBJECTIVE 7.01

Understanding Processes

The kernel will execute code located in a file if the file has the execute bit set and the contents can be interpreted as other process commands or machine instructions. At a fundamental level, that code operates by requesting system resources through functions known as *system calls*. Through system calls, any process may allocate memory, read from or write to files, access a system device, or access other logical resources (such as a network connection) that are managed by the operating system. The operating system determines when the process may start and run, when it has to wait, and when it shuts down. The program code that drives the process, from the user perspective, could be anything: an HTTP browser, a text editor, a database, or even the windowing system is composed of one or more processes that, at their core, all operate according to the same principles.

The events that lead from booting an operating system, to managing your hardware, to creating an interactive user environment, to running programs is a long and complex chain. We can reduce the steps in this buildup, however, to a few observable concepts. First, we should note that all processes are uniquely identified by a number called the *process ID*, or *PID*.

The kernel starts off by spawning processes it needs to manage user processes. In the Solaris operating system, PID 0 is always assigned to sched, which is actually a kernel service; it is exposed as a process so you can observe it, but even a privileged administrator with complete machine privileges has no direct control over its operation.

The sched process gets things rolling by invoking the init command, which is always assigned PID 1 and is the first true userland process. An administrator can use the init utility to change the state of the system: reboot it, shut it down, and so on. As a *daemon process*—one that is designed to run in perpetuity—the init process reads the configuration file /etc/inittab, which stores its marching orders as a series of one-line entries. Beginning with Solaris 10, the key instruction in this file executes the svc.startd process, sometimes called the *delegated restarter*, which takes over the system's initialization process.

If you want to list the order in which processes are started, you can use a command like this one:

```
$ ps -ef | sort +1 | head -9
    root     0     0    0 06:10:04 ?         0:05 sched
    root     1     0    0 06:10:07 ?         0:00 /usr/sbin/init
    root     2     0    0 06:10:07 ?         0:00 pageout
    root     3     0    0 06:10:07 ?         0:32 fsflush
    root     5     0    0 06:10:00 ?         0:05 zpool-rpool
    root     6     0    0 06:10:06 ?         0:00 kmem_task
    root     7     0    0 06:10:07 ?         0:00 intrd
    root     8     0    0 06:10:07 ?         0:00 vmtasks
    root    11     1    0 06:10:09 ?         0:13 /lib/svc/bin/svc.startd
```

The ps -ef command prints all the current processes. The sort +1 command organizes the output according to the PID, which appears in the second column. The responsible party for starting each process, called the *parent process*, is listed in the third column. The last column reports the program name for easier user identification. The head command in this example limits the output to the first nine lines. You can increase this number to see more processes, or omit the head command to list all of them.

The sched and init processes are followed by the pageout and fsflush processes, which are always the third and fourth processes to start. Many UNIX variants reserve the first five PID slots to ensure these fundamental services, also called *system processes*, start up the same way and receive the same numeric identifiers. The Solaris 11 implementation leaves PID 4 open for historical reasons, but uses PIDs 5–8 for additional system processes. Although the init process invokes the svc.startd process early in its life—it is the first process to claim the init process as its parent—it receives the PID 11. You could say that user process initialization truly begins once the svc.startd process gets a chance to run.

PID numbers are assigned in sequence, but you'll always see gaps in ps output. Some processes are short lived and difficult to capture in the snapshots of live processes that a ps command captures. The kernel continues to assign PIDs sequentially until it reaches the highest number the system may assign. When that number is reached, the PID counter reverts to the lowest available PID number and starts over, skipping past any numbers still in use. A PID assignment is not unique over the duration of one operating session unless it never quits. In most cases, however, enough time passes between two uses of, say, PID 15000 that there's no cause for confusion. For systems that cycle through a very high number of process IDs, it's a different matter.

Understanding Process Spawning

Every new process added to the system requires an existing process to spawn it. To create a new process, an existing process *forks*; that is, it asks the operating system to duplicate its program map and assign the copy a new PID. Following that act, the new process issues an exec call, a holdover instruction from the parent, that tells it which program code to use to replace the parent's code. Figure 7-1 illustrates this two-step process.

What isn't replaced in this process includes environment variables and other resources, such as input and output files, that the child process initially inherits from the parent. The new program code may discard some or all of these resources, but chances are it will need fundamental resources, such as a valid working directory, access to keyboard input if it is an interactive process, and so on. Using this model, it's possible for each parent process to instruct the child process how to operate in the current environment. The new program code uses this base to execute its operations in what's called a *sane* manner.

FIGURE 7-1

Spawning a new
process

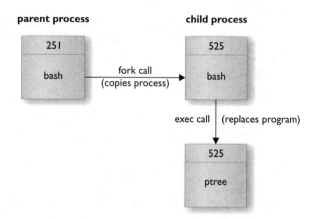

You don't have to think too hard about this process, but you use it all the time on the command line. The shell you use is the parent process to many of the commands you execute, and many commands you execute may spawn their own processes, too. Utilities such as the ps and ls commands are short-lived processes, however. They execute your request, return a result, and restore control back to the shell program, which then awaits another command.

To observe this relationship easily, you can spawn one long-lived command from another. That is, you can execute one shell on top of your current shell, like this:

```
$ ps
   PID TTY          TIME CMD
  1476 pts/2        0:00 bash
  2090 pts/2        0:00 ps
$ ksh
$ ps
   PID TTY          TIME CMD
  1476 pts/2        0:00 bash
  2091 pts/2        0:00 ksh
  2094 pts/2        0:00 ps
```

In this example, I am using the bash shell to execute the ps command. The ps command shows up in the output of its own execution. It uses the TTY device pts/2 because it inherited that value from the shell during the fork process. When I create a Korn shell process, the device pts/2 also shows up for it. The bash shell is still there, but is waiting while the Korn shell uses the I/O resources it inherited from the bash shell to run another ps command.

You can take this observation one step further using a tool called ptree. When given a PID, the ptree command examines that PID to report its parent, and the parent of the parent, and so on. It works up the parent tree as far as it can, and down the child tree, too. If I supply the PID of my bash shell (1476), I'll get the following output:

```
$ ptree 1476
1468  gnome-terminal
  1476  bash
    2091  ksh
      2096  ptree 1476
```

Now I can see my Korn shell is a child of my bash shell. I can also see that my bash shell has a parent process, its terminal window. When a terminal window opens, it spawns a shell in part so it will stay open. If you type **exit** in this window, it will cause the shell program to terminate, in turn causing the window process itself to terminate. With this example, you'd have to type **exit** twice—once to terminate the Korn shell process, and again to terminate the bash shell process.

Every process that is not a system process works this way, and therefore every non-system process has a parent process. Sometimes a parent process dies while the child process continues to operate. When that happens, the process management subsystem will reassign the orphaned process to a new parent—usually the sched process—just so it has one. There is no particular benefit to having one parent process over another.

Understanding Process States

Most program code in a process just wants to execute one instruction after another until it's time to quit. Most processes have no notion of asking nicely to do their work; they just execute instructions and await a result that tells them they can execute another instruction. It's up to the operating system, through the sched system process, to decide when a process may use the CPU to execute code.

When the process requests some system resource, such as memory or file access, the operating system also has to mark the process to show it is waiting on that request. To regulate both kinds of transitions—that is, becoming eligible to execute or waiting on system resources—and others, the operating system updates the process' metadata to record its *state*. The process management subsystem is responsible for managing the state transitions of all processes. Table 7-1 lists the different states a process may enter and what they mean.

TABLE 7-1	Process State	Description
	Idle	Initial state (while forking)
List of Process States	Run	Eligible to execute on a CPU
	Onproc	Currently executing
	Stop	Execution (temporarily) halted
	Sleep	Waiting on an event or timer to expire
	Zombie	Terminal state (not yet closed down)

The entire process model is a bit more complex, but this list of states is sufficient for a first look (and for the OCA exam). Figure 7-2 is a transition diagram that shows how a process can move from one state to the next. Any process must follow this prescribed set of transitions. Having these details at hand will help you form more complete expectations of a process's possible behavior.

The figure shows, for example, that it is never possible to revive a process once it begins termination. You can halt a process and restart it, but you can't bring it back from the dead. It may hang around a while in a zombie state until it is reaped by the system, but that's not something you want either.

FIGURE 7-2

State transition diagram for a process

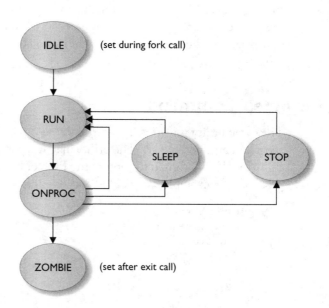

Observing Processes

The Solaris operating system offers a state-of-the-art array of process analysis tools. Introduced initially with the Solaris 8 release, they are collectively dubbed "p-tools" because they all start with the letter p. The p-tools all use the /proc file system to report on or manage the various aspects of any live process; most of them require a PID as an argument. When a p-tool executes, it reads (or changes) data in the process's own data structure. The actions it performs may therefore require superuser or process owner privileges to complete.

The p-tools reside in the /usr/bin directory along with many other utilities that begin with p. It's not easy to pick them out visually, so Table 7-2 lists them all along with a brief description. Some of these utilities are detailed in this chapter. Those that fall outside the scope of the OCA exam are provided for the sake of a complete table only.

Each of these commands has options you will want to research to make full use of it. You can see from the entire table, however, that there isn't much left to imagination for observing or managing a running process, assuming you have the privileges necessary for a given process you're interested in. In the remainder of this section, I cover the p-tools that let you observe useful aspects of a running process.

Using the pgrep Command

The pgrep utility is a good first start because it produces matching PIDs to the program name you specify. The utility matches partial strings to all matching PIDs, too. If you wanted to capture the PIDs of both the svc.startd and svc.configs processes, for example, you could do it like this:

```
$ pgrep -l svc
   11 svc.startd
   13 svc.configd
```

TABLE 7-2   Solaris Tools That Observe or Manage Running Processes

Command Name	Description
pargs *PID*	Lists the command-line arguments the program was started with
pcred *PID*	Reports or changes a process's user/group owner attributes
pfiles *PID*	Lists files opened by the process
pflags *PID*	Reports key status flags, including signals and tracing data
pgrep *pattern*	Returns PIDs matching the given pattern
pkill *pattern*	Sends a signal to processes matching the pattern
pmap *PID*	Lists the segments of the process's virtual memory space
pldd *PID*	Lists code libraries the process is using
preap *PID*	Forces the process to be closed down by its parent
prun *PID*	Resumes the process (if halted)
psig *PID*	Lists the process's signal actions and handlers
pstack *PID*	Prints stack traces for each of the process's lightweight processes (LWPs)
pstop *PID*	Halts the process without terminating
ptime *PID*	Times the process
ptree *PID*	Lists the process's parent and child relationships
pwait *PID*	Waits until the specified process terminates
pwdx *PID*	Reports the current working directory of the process

The -l option gives the long form (that is, the name of the matched process as well as the PID). If you want to see what you get by matching, this feedback is useful. The pgrep tool has far too many options to explore here. From now on, I'll most often use it to return the PID I want to supply to another p-tool. For example, if I wanted to see the process tree for the gnome-session program, I'd invoke it like this:

```
$ ptree `pgrep gnome-session`
730   /usr/sbin/gdm-binary
  746   /usr/lib/gdm-simple-slave --display-id <truncated>
    1222   /usr/lib/gdm-session-worker
      1310   gnome-session
        1351   /usr/bin/ssh-agent -- gnome-session
  ...
```

The back-ticks surrounding the pgrep invocation are a form of *command substitution*. The shell will replace the invocation inside the back-ticks with its result—in this case, the value 1310—and then pass it to the ptree command. I've truncated the output here because the GNOME session spawns a lot of helper applications. If you want to see all the desktop processes started by the session manager, you can review them on your own system.

Using the pargs Command

Some commands have text lines because they include many options or a few verbose ones. PID 746 (the gdm-simple-slave process) is one such example. If you want to see the full command used to start a process, use the pargs command. By default, it prints both a single line and lists the elements that make up the process's *argument vector*, shown in the following output as the argv array:

```
$ sudo pargs 746
746: /usr/lib/gdm-simple-slave --display-id <truncated>
argv[0]: /usr/lib/gdm-simple-slave
argv[1]: <NULL>
argv[2]: <NULL>
```

This output shows we didn't lose much in the ptree command—just two characters. Also, for some reason, the argument vector shows null values for its two elements. It's not helpful output, but it doesn't indicate a problem either. If you've used other UNIX tools that clip command lines after eight characters or so, or don't reveal the arguments supplied, the pargs command is a welcome relief.

Using the pcred Command

The pcred command (short for *process credentials*) can tell you the user and group identity a program is using to run. The privileges are associated with the instance of the program you are running, not just the user or the program file. Consider the passwd program. If you wanted to change your password by hand, you'd have to edit the /etc/ shadow file. Non-root users don't have the authorization to do that (which is good). When you run the passwd program, however, the permissions that are part of the executable file are combined with your permissions so you can change your password, and your password only. The pcred command reveals, in part, how this works.

In a terminal window, run the passwd program but don't answer the prompt. Just leave it like this:

```
$ passwd
passwd: Changing password for mfernest
New Password:
```

In another terminal window, run this command and observe the result:

```
$ pcred `pgrep passwd`
pcred: cannot examine 1490: permission denied
$ sudo pcred `pgrep passwd`
1490:       euid=0 ruid=60004 suid=0  egid=3 rgid=10 sgid=3
```

First, note that I can't examine the passwd process I started! That's because the passwd program raises the privileges required beyond the ones I have. I can, however, examine it if I use sudo, at which point I see process 1490 has an *effective* UID of 0 (root) and a *real* UID of 60004 (mfernest).

Using the pfiles Command

The pfiles command is one of my personal favorites; it reports all the files *and network connections* that a process has open. With one command, you can determine all the files a process is reading from or writing to at any one time; that information goes a very long way to understanding the responsibilities of that process. You can ignore the technical data and just look at filenames to start. Here, for example, is a list of files opened by a Korn shell process:

```
$ pfiles $$
1489:           ksh
  Current rlimit: 256 file descriptors
    0: S_IFCHR mode:0620 dev:541,0 ino:729131539 uid:60004 gid:7 rdev:133,2
       O_RDWR
       /dev/pts/2
       offset:70925
    1: S_IFCHR mode:0620 dev:541,0 ino:729131539 uid:60004 gid:7 rdev:133,2
       O_RDWR
       /dev/pts/2
       offset:70925
    2: S_IFCHR mode:0620 dev:541,0 ino:729131539 uid:60004 gid:7 rdev:133,2
       O_RDWR
       /dev/pts/2
       offset:70925
    3: S_IFREG mode:0600 dev:195,65544 ino:432 uid:60004 gid:10 size:838
       O_RDWR|O_APPEND|O_CREAT|O_LARGEFILE FD_CLOEXEC
       /home/mfernest/.sh_history
       offset:838
```

The file descriptors 0, 1, and 2 are default resources for all Solaris processes, and are some of the resources a child process inherits from its parent. These represent channels for standard input, standard output, and standard error (secondary output). In UNIX parlance, they are referred to as *stdin, stdout,* and *stderr.* All three channels point to the device /dev/pts/2 but are used for different purposes (even a terminal window can be treated like a file). The file descriptor 3 is used by the shell to journal command-line entries.

Using the prstat Command

Before moving on the p-tools that let you alter the state of a process, I should mention one more tool that isn't listed in Table 7-2. It's called prstat, and it is the preferred program for continuous process monitoring on the Solaris platform. The top utility is a popular, cross-platform tool you may have heard of that performs the same role. It has also been ported to Solaris 11, so if you're already familiar with it, like it, and prefer a tool that you also use on other UNIX platforms, you can use it right away.

The prstat utility is, however, specifically designed to do the same job more efficiently on Solaris, and to take advantage of the extensive observability features built in to Solaris's /proc file system. It has an extensive set of options to produce a variety of reports in different formats (which I cannot list fully here). Here instead is a list of highlights of what the prstat utility can do:

- List as many processes as the screen will allow
- Sort processes by size, CPU usage, priority, or execution time
- Break down processes by lightweight processes (LWPs) or threads
- Report latency values affecting each process's performance
- Report specific lists of processes only
- Produce output on a configurable interval and number of iterations

For starters, try each of the prstat commands listed next, one at a time. The first command will terminate on its own. For the others, type **q** when you've seen enough:

```
prstat 5 5
prstat -a
prstat -s size
prstat -L -p `pgrep svc.startd`
```

Read the prstat man page for more details. The prstat utility can provide a wealth of information to anyone who takes the time to learn its ins and outs.

CERTIFICATION OBJECTIVE 7.03

Managing Process States

A few p-tools allow you to change a process's state. The utilities I cover in this section include pkill, prun, pstop, and pwait.

Like some of the observation p-tools you've tried already, some of these tools require appropriate privileges. Tools such as pgrep have no authorization restrictions because Solaris does not hide running processes from the view of any logged-in user (or rather it doesn't hide them by default). Tools such as pcred may require additional privileges because the process information is considered sensitive.

 on the Job

You'll learn these requirements as you go, but if you take note of the sudo command when I use it, you'll know which commands are privilege-sensitive.

Using the pkill Command

The pkill command is an unusual one for a couple of reasons. One, the Solaris operating system already supports the kill command, so it may seem redundant. Two, the pkill command matches patterns instead of PIDs. It operates more like pgrep than the other p-tools, and this makes matters confusing if you try to use the kill command, which requires a PID (or a job ID), and the pkill command interchangeably. With the pkill command, you can bypass using pgrep to get a PID and just name the process you want to signal.

Using these commands, you don't necessarily kill the target process. You send a message, called a *signal*, which is an out-of-flow instruction that can affect the process's state. Every process, regardless of the program code it runs, has facilities to receive and process signals, including the capacity to ignore certain ones if the programmer desires. The kernel uses signals to manage state transitions for every user process. When you use the pkill or kill command, you're asking the kernel to send a signal to the target process for you. The process then *handles* the signal in some way.

TABLE 7-3	Signals Commonly Used by Administrators	

Signal name	Number	Description
HUP	1	Hang up
INT	2	Interrupt (same as Ctrl-C)
KILL	9	Abort
TERM	15	Terminate

Solaris 11 supports 72 different signals; a handful of them have an administrative use. Table 7-3 lists the most commonly used ones.

The HUP signal has the effect of telling a process that its owner is leaving the system; the expected result is that the process terminates because there is no one around to observe its results. It is also used to tell a daemon process to restart. The INT signal instructs programs to quit where they are; for interactive programs, this is equivalent to pressing Ctrl-C in the window of the process you want to interrupt. The KILL signal, also known as a *graceless shutdown*, tells the process to stop whatever it's doing and quit immediately. The receiving process may not defer or ignore this signal. The TERM signal is graceful, in that the receiving process can defer handling it long enough to save files.

Both the kill and pkill commands will accept a mnemonic or numeric value for an option. Both commands will send the TERM signal if one isn't specified. To kill the passwd command I left open in a terminal window from a previous exercise, I can use one of the two listed examples:

```
$ pkill passwd
$ kill `pgrep passwd`
```

Typing Ctrl-C in the same window would also work. Or, if I want to be nasty about it:

```
$ pkill -9 passwd
$ kill -KILL `pgrep passwd`
```

on the job

Sometimes you want to run a process so that it won't terminate as you log out. The nohup command helps with this. If you invoke a command using nohup to control it, the process will ignore HUP signals and keep running. Consult the nohup man page for instructions on its use and some sample invocations.

Using the prun and pstop Commands

If you've ever seen a kind of application called a debugger before, you might have seen it used to stop a program at key points to observe changes to the program's state at a granular level. This is a common method for understanding why and how a buggy program fails the way it does. The debugger works by establishing locations called *breakpoints*, running the program until it reaches one, stopping, and then running until the next breakpoint.

The pstop and prun commands work on this same principle, except instead of setting breakpoints, the user just issues either command to halt or resume the target process. Used responsibly, the pstop and prun commands can provide a form of *job control* that lets you stall a process long enough to gather information on it or complete some other work (if the target process is a CPU hog). Unlike customary job control, these commands don't turn a running process into a background process, one that runs without holding on to a terminal window's resources. They just keep processes from running until you let them resume.

You want to be careful about stopping processes you need, especially if you have root privileges when you use the command. Once you stop a process that supports your desktop, for example, you'll have a deuce of a time getting system control back without rebooting. You should also be careful about calling the pstop command on processes that interact with remote users or communicate on a time-based protocol with other processes.

Using the pwait Command

The pwait utility lets you name a process you want to let finish (or terminate) before the waiting program (such as a shell) may continue. This utility is particularly handy in a script that sets off some jobs as background processes, then needs to wait for them to finish before starting more work. Any shell that calls the pwait command on a running process suspends its own activity until the identified process completes. At that point, control is restored to the shell and it can call a subsequent command.

If you are running a browser, for example, you can retrieve the PID of the browser process with the pgrep utility. In another window, you can enter a subsequent statement to the pwait command so it can run as soon as the browser session terminates:

```
$ pwait browser_PID ; echo "Browser session is done"
```

The pwait command can help manage an uncommon but difficult problem: how to resolve a *race condition* between two processes. This term more commonly applies to multithreaded programming, but it pertains to processes, too. A race condition occurs when there is an assumption that one process will always finish before another, but there is nothing in the system that ensures or enforces that order. Usually a race condition is a product of flawed design or assumptions that should be solved in the program code. The pwait tool provides an immediate workaround, at the process level anyway, until a more elegant solution is available. More generally, if you want to interrupt a program's execution for any reason, the pwait tool gives you the means to do it.

CERTIFICATION OBJECTIVE 7.04

Scheduling System Administration Tasks

The first summit in automating system administration tasks is starting one without being present. All UNIX variants provide two process-scheduling tools, called at and cron, to support this work. Using the at utility, you can schedule a job to execute at some point in the future whether you are logged in or not. Using cron, you can set up a script or process to execute on a recurring interval—every hour, day, week, or month—so you can manage routine jobs without having to think about them.

You do have to think a bit more carefully about the command, scripts, or programs you use with these facilities. For one, there necessarily isn't a command path or environment variables to supplement the job. This usually means you have to provide them, or give each command with its absolute path. Also, the at and cron facilities that fork the processes you specify will share fewer niceties than you would with a customized shell environment. It's rather like a "mission-to-Mars" exercise: You need to make sure the job will have all the information it needs to run correctly.

Some programs are designed with this kind of work in mind, and maintain their own configuration files to read when they start up. The logadm command is one such utility; I'll have more to say more about how it works in Chapter 13.

Using the at Command

The at command supports a one-time invocation of some command "at" some point in the future. To use it, you specify a file that contains the instructions you want to run and a time in the future. The file could be an executable program, but scripts are more common. You can specify time a variety of ways: as a number, as a date, or even using certain mnemonics such as "midnight," "noon," "tomorrow," and a few others.

If you want to enter a variety of instructions from the command, you can specify the time first, and then let the at utility open a secondary prompt to enter commands:

```
$ at 3pm
at> ls
at> <EOT>
commands will be executed using /usr/bin/bash
job 1347400800.a at Tue Sep 11 15:00:00 2012
$ at 2pm tomorrow
at> banner Howdy!
at> <EOT>
commands will be executed using /usr/bin/bash
job 1347483600.a at Wed Sep 12 14:00:00 2012
```

Once I enter a valid time and press ENTER, the utility opens an at> prompt to show it is listening for further instructions. The <EOT> is written out for me when I press Ctrl-D to signify I have nothing more to enter. The at command reads the environment variable SHELL to determine which shell program will handle the job. You can reassign SHELL if you wish; don't forget to export the variable after you change it, so it will get passed on.

Although the job specified will run with resources defined by the given shell, it does not receive a terminal assignment. An at job has no notion of being logged in, and therefore has no standard output device to pass to processes it spawns. The output for the jobs I specified will go to system e-mail. The following example creates a simple job—list the files in the current directory—using the at utility's interactive shell. The system notifies the user that mail has arrived, which contains the results of the action. The mailx utility is a simple e-mail reader suitable for reviewing text messages:

```
$ at 10:45 today
at> ls
at> <EOT>
```

```
commands will be executed using /usr/bin/bash
job 1348073100.a at Wed Sep 19 10:45:00 2012
$ rm nohup.out
You have mail in /var/mail/tim
$ mailx
mailx version 5.0  Type ? for help.
"/var/mail/tim": 1 message 1 new
>N  1 Administrator        Wed Sep 19 10:45    30                            /856
Output from "at" job
? 1
Message  1:
From tim@mayhem Wed Sep 19 10:45:00 2012
Date: Wed, 19 Sep 2012 10:45:00 -0600 (MDT)
From: Administrator <tim@mayhem>
To: tim@mayhem
Subject: Output from "at" job
MIME-Version: 1.0

Your "at" job on mayhem
"/var/spool/cron/atjobs/1348073100.a"
produced the following output:

Desktop
Documents
Downloads
Public
nohup.out
zonetext
```

You'll need the job ID that comes with the response to track the job until it runs, or to remove it if you want to abort. The at -l and at -r commands, followed by the job ID, will perform those tasks for you. Examine the examples section of the at man page to get more ideas on how to use this tool.

Understanding Scheduling Intervals

The cron system defines recurring jobs. It describes each entry with six fields—five that define the interval and one that defines the program to run. Each of the first five fields represents a specific unit of time: minutes, hours, days (of the week or month), and months. The value of each field can be covered by a single number, a continuous range expressed with a hyphen, individual numbers separated by commas, or an asterisk to signify the entire range of values. Table 7-4 lists each field and the range of values acceptable for it.

TABLE 7-4	Cron Entry Fields and Their Values	
Field Position	**Unit of Time**	**Value**
1	Minute	0 to 59, or * for every second
2	Hour	0 to 23, or * for every hour
3	Day of the month	1 to 31, or * for every day
4	Month	1 to 12, or * for every month
5	Day of the week	0 (Sunday) to 6, or * for every day
6	N/A	Full path to command with arguments, if any

Here are a few sample entries:

```
15 3 1 * * /usr/local/bin/somejob
0,15,30,45 * * * * /usr/local/bin/cleanup
0 16 1-10 12 1-5 /usr/local/bin/writecards
```

The first entry runs the somejob command at 3:15 A.M. on the first day of every month. The second entry runs the cleanup command every 15 minutes. The third entry runs the writecards command at 4 P.M., Monday through Friday, for the first 10 days in December. It's worth experimenting with a script that writes a short test message to a known location, such as the /var/tmp directory, and make sure it works as you expect. With these examples and a little practice on your own, you'll find you can configure any recurring interval you need.

Managing Cron Job Tables

Cron jobs are maintained in files, one per user, that are stored in the /var/spool/cron/ crontab directory:

```
$ ls /var/spool/cron/crontabs
adm          root          sys
```

On a fresh installation, you'll see files for these three users only: adm, sys, and root. By default, only the root user has a job that is set up ahead of time. The entries given are meant to run with the privileges of the given user. In that way, you can limit the privileges any scheduled job may run with by adding it to the table of the user with the most appropriate level of permissions.

To review the jobs a user has listed, you can run the crontab -l command with the username as an argument. Without a username, the command will list your job entries if you have any:

```
$ crontab -l mfernest
crontab: can't open your crontab file.
$ sudo crontab -l root
30 0,9,12,18,21 * * * /usr/lib/update-manager/update-refresh.sh
```

The first command attempts to open a file that doesn't exist; the user mfernest has not yet created one. The root user has one job that invokes an update script at the half-hour mark five times a day. Although the adm and sys users have files already set up, they don't have any active jobs; they're commented out. An administrator can edit these files to activate the entries, which saves the trouble of typing them in. Each of these files also has some comments that explain the purpose of the commented entries.

You could also remove these files if you wanted, using the command crontab -r and the username. Turning active entries into comments is a preferred first step, because it's an easy way to track jobs and schedules you might use later. You can also prevent a user from running cron jobs altogether. I'll show you how to do that in just a bit.

Editing Cron Jobs

The cron entry format isn't friendly to the untrained eye, and it's easy to make a mistake with the interval when writing a new one. In order to alert the user to an entry mistake as early as possible, the crontab utility provides an option to open a crontab for the user and then verify the contents as they are saved. If the entry added is rubbish, the crontab utility can complain and refuse to create the file.

This facility requires two steps. When you invoke the crontab -e command, it searches the value of your EDITOR environment setting. The default is the vi editor, but you can change it to a tool you prefer, such as gedit. If the user crontab file already exists, its contents will appear in the editor; otherwise, you get to start from scratch. As long as you define a correct interval, the crontab utility has no need to complain. You can make all sorts of mistakes specifying the program you want to run; crontab does not check whether the file exists, whether it has the right permissions, whether the options or arguments make sense, or anything to verify a valid invocation.

Using crontab -e and the default EDITOR setting, I can enter the following job and verify it with the crontab -l command:

```
$ crontab -e
<edit>
$ crontab -l
1 * * * *  echo "Howdy" > /var/tmp/mfe
```

This job writes a short string to the file on the first minute of every hour, which I can verify once it has had a chance to run:

```
$ ls -l /var/tmp/mfe
-rw-r--r--   1 mfernest staff          6 Sep 11 14:01 /var/tmp/mfe
$ cat /var/tmp/mfe
Howdy
```

Permitting Users to Use Cron

You might be thinking twice about letting any user schedule jobs. They can be run as often as once a minute, and there's nothing in the cron facility to check a job from using too many resources. What you can do is allow or deny access to the service by username. Decide first how you want to set policy. Allowing all users access to cron, except for a few, is one way. Denying all users access, except for a few, is another way. Ideally, you want the approach that will have you writing the fewest possible exceptions.

The inclusive policy works one of two ways. You can add users to the file /etc/cron.d/cron.allow for an explicit inclusion policy. Or, you can have no cron.allow file, which opens access to everyone implicitly; you can then use an /etc/cron.d/cron.deny file to make exceptions to the rule.

Because the system always checks for the cron.allow file first, the exclusion policy works by omitting both files. In that case, only users who have the authorization solaris.jobs.user as part of their makeup can then schedule cron jobs. Assigning this attribute to a user falls outside the scope of this book, but you can do it with the usermod command you learned about in Chapter 6.

By default, the Solaris 11 setup provides a cron.deny file that lists the user's daemon, bin, and nuucp. These entries exist to prevent someone from trying to sneak crontabs into the system that you wouldn't normally think to look for. You can institute similar controls on the at command using the files at.allow and at.deny. The at.deny file exists by default, also in the /etc/cron.d directory.

CERTIFICATION SUMMARY

The process is one of two key concepts that define the heart of any UNIX operating system; Solaris is no exception. The tools Solaris provides to observe and manage processes, however, are a first-class set that most UNIX variants can't fully match. It is well worth your time to commit them to memory, use them regularly, and explore the options a lot of them provide. Although the entire suite of p-tools isn't covered in the OCA exam, using them regularly in practice will pay off time and again.

You also learned two ways to schedule processes for future execution, both one at a time and on a recurring basis. These are staple tools on virtually every UNIX platform. You'll want to study the Solaris implementation of cron carefully, however. The location, purpose, and format of the key files is fair game for the exam, as is your ability to correctly interpret a cron-legal interval configuration.

TWO-MINUTE DRILL

Understanding Processes

❑ Every user process is created by a parent process that forks a copy of itself under a new PID assignment and then replaces the parent's program code with the new program. This is sometimes called the *fork-and-exec model* of process creation and referred to as *spawning*.

❑ You can distinguish a true user process from a so-called system process using the pfiles command. A system process doesn't keep a list of open files.

Observing Processes

❑ The prstat command is Solaris's answer to top. It allows for continuous monitoring of all processes on the system and provides a wide variety of report styles to work with.

❑ You can retrieve the PID of a command using pgrep and a string pattern to match one or more processes.

❑ Some of the p-tools that let you observe various aspects of a process include the pargs, ptree, pfiles, and pcred commands. Remember that different permission rules may apply if the command can return sensitive information about the process.

Managing Process States

❑ The pstop and prun commands let you halt and resume an active process. Be careful about using these tools on an interactive process or one that serves remote users.

❑ The pwait command lets you pause a script or shell until the specified process has terminated.

Scheduling Administrative Tasks

❑ Use the at command to schedule a job to run one time in the future. There are numerous ways to specify the time: numerically, using a calendar date, or even with mnemonics such as "tomorrow."

❑ Use the crontab command to view, add, modify, or delete a job for some recurring interval. Cron entries are kept in per-user files in the /var/spool/cron/crontabs directory and consist of a six-field definition. Access to the cron facility can be set by policy files kept in the /etc/cron.d directory.

SELF TEST

Use the following questions to test your recall and understanding of the chapter's material.

Understanding Processes

1. Which of the processes listed is not a Solaris 11 system process?
    A. sched
    B. init
    C. pageout
    D. fsflush

2. Which two options are valid process states?
    A. phantom
    B. sleep
    C. idle
    D. wait

3. Which action can cause a process to fork?
    A. Running the ls program from the command line
    B. Logging in
    C. Using the Print Screen button on the keyboard
    D. All of the above

Observing Processes

4. What does the pgrep command return?
    A. The first PID that matches the pattern given
    B. The first PID that matches the program name given
    C. All PIDs that match the pattern given
    D. All PIDs that match the program name given

5. Which of the following is not an actual p-tool?
    A. pcred
    B. pargs
    C. puser
    D. pfiles

Managing Process States

6. What would the command pstop $$ do if entered in a terminal window?

    A. Freeze the system

    B. Nothing

    C. Freeze the window it was entered in

    D. Freeze all other windows that are open

7. What does the command prun $$ do if entered in a terminal window?

    A. Resume the system

    B. Nothing

    C. Resume the window it was entered in

    D. Resume any other window that was stopped

Scheduling Administrative Tasks

8. Which option is a valid cron entry that will run a program called /usr/bin/bump every Thursday at 2:35 PM?

    A. 0-34,36-59 2 * * 4 *   /usr/bin/bump

    B. 35 14 5 * *   /usr/bin/bump

    C. 35 2 * 4 *   /usr/bin/bump

    D. 35 14 * * 4   /usr/bin/bump

9. Which statement identifies a key benefit of the crontab -e command?

    A. It lists the contents of the effective user's cron jobs.

    B. It will correct erroneous entries in the user's cron table.

    C. It will not save incorrect entries to the user's cron table.

    D. It will make sure the vi editor is used to edit the user's cron table.

10. What's the greatest frequency at which a cron job can execute?

    A. Every second

    B. Every minute

    C. Every 15 minutes

    D. Every other minute

SELF TEST ANSWERS

Understanding Processes

1. ☑ **B.** The init process is always assigned PID 1. Unlike other low-numbered processes, such as pageout and fsflush, that are completely system-controlled, the init processes opens files and is responsible for spawning the svc.startd process.

    ☒ **A, C,** and **D** are incorrect. These are all system processes. You can verify this fact by running the pfiles command on each one.

2. ☑ **B** and **C.** The possible states a process can have during its lifetime include idle, run(nable), onproc, stop, sleep, and zombie.

    ☒ **A** and **D** are incorrect. These names do not describe a valid process state.

3. ☑ **D.** Any action that requires a new process to execute requires a fork action from a parent process to initiate it. Even when you press the PRINT SCREEN button on your keyboard, you're invoking a program that can take a picture of your desktop (the Solaris program that manages this is called metacity).

    ☒ **A, B,** and **C** are incorrect. Although each is individually correct, it would be incorrect to pick only one of the listed choices.

Observing Processes

4. ☑ **C.** If you have multiple windows open and each is running a bash shell, the command pgrep bash would return a list of PIDs, one for each shell. If there were any additional programs that matched the string bash, their PIDs would be returned as well. It's important to remember the pgrep command does not require a program name, nor does it just match the beginning of a string only.

    ☒ **A, B,** and **D** are incorrect. **A** is incorrect because pgrep will return as many matches as it finds. **B** and **D** are incorrect because the pgrep command does not require the exact name of a running program to return a result.

5. ☑ **C.** There is no puser utility in the standard Solaris complement of executables.
☒ **A, B,** and **D** are incorrect. These are all p-tools reviewed in this chapter.

Managing Process States

6. ☑ **C.** The variable $$ returns the PID of the current process. In a terminal window, it returns the PID of the shell that's running. It's a good idea to run this command one time, if only to understand why running it in a working environment isn't such a good idea.
☒ **A, B,** and **D** are incorrect. **A** is incorrect because it is in fact possible to hang a whole system using the pstop command, but stopping a shell isn't sufficient. **B** is incorrect because the command will render the current terminal window inoperable. That's definitely something, just not something you can do much with. **D** is incorrect because the pstop utility doesn't affect processes you don't specify, unless they depend on the stopped process for some resource.

7. ☑ **B.** If you run pstop $$ in a terminal window and then type in prun $$, you will see what you've typed in the window. That's because the window itself is fine. Only the shell that's using it has been stopped. Still, the shell controls the terminal window, and because it won't accept subsequent commands, the prun $$ command just sits there.
☒ **A, C** and **D** are incorrect, all for variations on the reason just given. Because there's no way for the stopped shell to receive and process the prun $$ invocation, there cannot be any effect on any other part of the system either.

Scheduling Administrative Tasks

8. ☑ **D.** This question requires that you read carefully and remember which fields in a cron entry govern which units of time. Field 1 governs the minutes in an hour. Field 2 governs the hours in a day using the range 0–23. Hence, 2 P.M. is represented by the integer 14. The fifth field governs days of the week, starting with Sunday, which is 0. Thursday is expressed as 4. Any day of the month is okay (as long as it falls on a Thursday), as is every month of the year.
☒ **A, B,** and **C** are incorrect. **A** is incorrect for several reasons, the most noticeable is that it will run on every minute of an allowed hour except for the 35th minute. **B** is incorrect because the 5 is in the wrong field; this entry will run the job on the fifth day of the month only. **C** is incorrect because it will run the job only in May.

9. ☑ **C.** When the crontab utility is allowed to provide the editor, it can read the new table once the editor is dismissed and verify the schedule settings. If they violate the rules for a correct interval, the crontab utility tosses the proposed edits and reverts back to the original file. If there wasn't a file to start with, it doesn't create one.

   ☒ **A, B,** and **D** are incorrect. **A** is incorrect because cron tables for effective users don't exist. **B** is incorrect because crontab does not try to fix an invalid interval setting; it only restores the content of the original (valid) file. **D** is incorrect because the vi editor is the default choice for crontab, but this can be changed by changing the value of the EDITOR environment variable.

10. ☑ **B.** The most granular unit of time the cron facility understands is the minute (the first field of a valid cron entry). Therefore, a scheduled job cannot be run by cron more often than once a minute.

    ☒ **A, C,** and **D** are incorrect, by definition.

8

Administering the Services Management Facility (SMF)

You're learning that an operating system is composed of many different subsystems: device drivers, file systems, user management, process management, and host security are just some of them. Each one of these subsystems, as you've seen, relies on files to hold configuration data and processes to interact with users and other subsystems. Indeed, a lot of early systems administration training boils down to learning the names of processes and the locations and formats of their supporting files.

The Service Management Facility (SMF), introduced for the first time with Solaris 10, provides a way to observe and manage all these subsystems through a common set of utilities. It addresses a time-consuming challenge in systems management—acquiring knowledge of the system's details—and inverts it by creating a comprehensive system for reporting those details. It also solves a leading problem in day-to-day administration: how to restore a system resource that has crashed, as quickly as possible, even without administrator intervention.

In this chapter, you'll learn why SMF was added to Solaris as well as how to use the tools that make it easier for you to monitor a Solaris host and keep the uptime of its services as high as possible.

CERTIFICATION OBJECTIVE 8.01

Understanding the Role of SMF

SMF can be a difficult thing to appreciate on first sight. It replaces a system for managing kernel services and long-running processes, sometimes just called *run control*, that UNIX administrators have used for decades. SMF implementation is quite different from run-control implementation, and requires not just new skills but a different way of thinking about system management. These changes not only take time to learn, they diverge from a well-known model that remains on other UNIX variants. Some experienced admins want to know if they can work around this new system or at least minimize its intrusion on their daily work. The answer is no, which doesn't make anyone happy.

The best answer I can offer to an experienced admin is this: Once you learn what SMF does and what you can get from it, you might be a lot happier than you thought. For up-and-coming admins, there's this answer: You'll wonder why some people want to hang on to the old way of managing their system's services. SMF is a far more comprehensive approach to system management. It offers an easier way to learn the details of each facility your system supports. There's a bit of learning to go through first, but it's worth it.

Understanding Legacy Run Control

If you talk to other admins about what you're learning, odds are most of them will know more about the traditional run-control system than SMF. With that in mind, a bit of history can go a long way to making sense of and appreciating what SMF does to lighten the load of your administrative tasks.

As you learned in Chapter 7, the kernel finishes the boot process by exposing certain system services as user processes. The first four of those processes are sched (PID 0), init (PID 1), pageout (PID 2), and fsflush (PID 3). The init process reads the /etc/inittab file, which contains a list of entries that execute programs to correspond with a particular state of system initialization called a *run level*. Each level establishes an operational level, such as multi-user mode, to imply a set of services needed to support it. Each level is also associated with a number or letter the kernel uses for an identifier (multi-user is run level 2).

Most of the entries in the old /etc/inittab file ran a script in the /sbin directory with a name in the form rc#. The rc stands for *run control*, and the number indicates the run level covered by the script. Each one assigns host-specific information to variables it can use to launch other scripts in the /etc directory. This approach has been a good-enough plan for decades, and is still happily used in other Unix variants. Parts of its infrastructure remain in place today in Solaris 11. You can find its scripts in the /sbin directory, all three-letter file names that start with rc#, and related directories in the /etc directory. They are shown below:

```
$ file /sbin/rc[S0-6]
/sbin/rc0:  executable /usr/sbin/sh script
/sbin/rc1:  executable /usr/sbin/sh script
/sbin/rc2:  executable /usr/sbin/sh script
/sbin/rc3:  executable /usr/sbin/sh script
/sbin/rc5:  executable /usr/sbin/sh script
/sbin/rc6:  executable /usr/sbin/sh script
/sbin/rcS:  executable /usr/sbin/sh script
$ ls -d /etc/rc*d
/etc/rc0.d  /etc/rc1.d  /etc/rc2.d  /etc/rc3.d  /etc/rcS.d
```

I've used globbing expressions here to narrow the output. Notice when using brackets that you don't need to separate one character from another, or even one character from a range of characters. Brackets signify a range of values, any one of which may be used to form a match. Notice that some scripts in the /sbin directory don't have a corresponding /etc subdirectory. That's because run states 5 and 6 represent transition states, not running states, and have no additional actions that can be added to them.

This chain of delegation may seem overdone when you consider it; the files I've shown here aren't even the whole story. This implementation, however, gives you a way to customize the initialization process by adding scripts to an appropriate run-control directory. You might integrate third-party applications into your startup routine by interposing scripts at a certain run-control level or just modify the existing scripts to alter your system's operations.

The run levels themselves are hard-coded into the kernel's initialization scheme. The administrator can change which scripts are called for each run level, but the meaning for each run level is considered well defined and not open to change. The init command, as I will show later, uses these numbers as arguments to change the current run level of the system. Table 8-1 lists the run levels and their system meanings.

In practice, the values you are likely to use with the init command are 0, 5, and 6. These values still work as arguments to the init command, although their effect is no longer derived from reading entries in the /etc/inittab file.

TABLE 8-1	Description of System Run Levels

Run Level	Description
0	Indicates the system is ready to boot or is safe to shut down
S	Administrative mode (single user)
1	System accessible to console (local) user only
2	System accessible to remote users (multi-user)
3	Initializes network services such as NFS (multi-user with network services)
4	Unused
5	Shuts down and powers off the system
6	Reboots the system

The limitations of this system aren't obvious on first blush. It's a simple, sufficient, and flexible framework for initializing the subsystems that support the user environment. There is instead an absence of features that, once you think about them, you might wish you also had.

For example, let's say your e-mail service dies. Under traditional run control, how would you first learn about it? Chances are you (or an expectant user) will notice no new messages have come in for a while. You might verify the problem by checking the sendmail daemon process using the ps or pgrep command. If it doesn't show up in a search, you know it's not running. How do you fix it? Assuming there's no persistent cause for its failure, you can restart the process, send a test message, and announce the all-clear that e-mail service has been restored.

If the problem is deeper, however—let's say another admin botched the configuration file, or another process that e-mail depends on failed first—then you have to work up the dependency chain (assuming you know how), identify the cause, fix it, and restart any other dependent processes that were also affected. This repair routine takes as long as you need to isolate the cause, learn what you didn't already know about the dependency chain, and walk back the repairs to the original problem. The time to restore the service, in short, depends on you and your current knowledge. And, in a busy environment, the time to repair is a key factor in a system's overall availability.

on the **job** *It's worth remembering that users don't judge system availability by its actual uptime. They judge by the results they get for the requests they make.*

SMF addresses time-to-repair factors in several ways. For starters, it moves responsibility for knowledge of the systems' details from the administrator's brain to a set of tools anyone can use. As an example, let's say someone believes your system's e-mail service, run by the sendmail process, has died. You'd probably check it like so:

```
$ ps -ef | grep sendmail
  smmsp  1428    1   0 02:27:25 ?       0:00 /usr/lib/sendmail -Ac -q15m
   root  1435    1   0 02:27:26 ?       0:00 /usr/lib/sendmail -bd -q15m
$ pgrep sendmail
1428
1435
```

What would you look for if it had died? Nothing. The absence of the process in this kind of search tells you it's not running—and that's all there is to learn. With SMF tools, on the other hand, you don't have to interpret the absence of a process:

```
$ svcs -x sendmail
svc:/network/smtp:sendmail (sendmail SMTP mail transfer agent)
 State: online since October 12, 2012 02:26:24 AM PDT
   See: sendmail(1M)
   See: /var/svc/log/network-smtp:sendmail.log
Impact: None.
```

The svcs -x command is a debug report that shows the current state of a service (not the process), includes references to documentation, and describes the impact of the service in its current state; it's healthy, so there's no impact. But with SMF, you'd also know *how* a service is broken:

```
$ svcs -x sendmail
svc:/network/smtp:sendmail (sendmail SMTP mail transfer agent)
 State: disabled since October 12, 2012 07:23:47 AM PDT
Reason: Disabled by an administrator.
   See: http://sun.com/msg/SMF-8000-05
   See: sendmail(1M)
   See: /var/svc/log/network-smtp:sendmail.log
Impact: This service is not running.
```

This output also tells you when the service stopped. You can use the documentation references to learn more about the service, including the specific error at hand, and refer to the service's log file to see if there's more information. That's one command and no guesswork (provided you know the service's name). This difference may not matter much to a Solaris expert, but for anyone who manages multiple system platforms or hasn't yet mastered the details of a Solaris system, it's a big timesaver.

Understanding What SMF Adds to Run Control

SMF isn't merely a rewrite for traditional run control. Although it relies on different processes and configuration files, it is actually a wrapper for all the subsystems that make up the Solaris environment. It doesn't just launch daemon processes or execute scripts for services like file system mounting and network card setup. Here are some of the additional features SMF includes:

- **Registration**   Every service is named and defined in a standardized form. SMF provides a namespace to ensure each service name is unique.
- **Monitoring**   Each service operates under a predefined set of state changes.
- **Management**   The administrator can disable a service without moving or changing its scripts or configuration files.
- **Dependency tracking**   A service can define other services as *dependencies*, making it easier to find indirect causes of failure. A service may also define *dependents*, which are other services that will rely on it.
- **Configuration repository**   The service definition and the run-time information of its instances are maintained in a single database you can read and modify.

Under SMF, every element that contributes to the user environment is managed by a service. This scheme provides a uniform system that applies equally well to kernel subsystems, daemon processes, and even milestones (the SMF equivalent of run levels). I'll discuss each of these aspects in detail throughout the chapter.

Understanding the Role of a Service

An SMF service defines and manages one system resource. It supplies the definition, the configuration details, and the means to hold the run-time state of a process, kernel subsystem, or other facility that adds to the system environment. It is not an actual resource, such as a file system, security auditing process, or e-mail service. It is a kind of common descriptor that can be applied to any system resource, regardless of its type or how it operates.

A service relates to other services by declaring *dependencies*. That is, each service can name other services it depends on and specify how it depends on them. This information makes it possible for SMF to do the following:

- Graph a start order for services from dependencies to dependents
- Determine which graph lines are separate and can be started concurrently
- Notify dependent services when their dependencies fail or restart

In traditional run control, startup scripts are prefixed with an *S* (for start) or *K* (for kill) and then numbered to produce an order. You can observe this arrangement by listing the contents of one of the /etc/rc#.d directories:

```
$ ls -l /etc/rc2.d
total 12
-rw-r--r--   1 root       sys            1587 Oct 20   2011 README
-rwxr--r--   5 root       sys            1836 Oct 20   2011 S47pppd
-rwxr--r--   2 root       sys             230 Oct 20   2011 S89PRESERVE
```

This start order could *imply* a dependency between the scripts, but without comments in the scripts themselves or other documentation, appreciating such relationships is a matter of administrator knowledge—or finding out by trial and error. We have to assume the default sequence is appropriate, if not optimal, but also it could change in a future Solaris release. That fact means a customized scheme is subject to review every time there's an upgrade.

Because all services are registered and stored in a single database (the *configuration repository*), SMF processes can determine which services are related to each other and which aren't. The result graph reveals separate startup paths that can be run concurrently during startup, which promotes faster booting. You'll find documentation that says these paths are started in parallel, but that only holds if there are multiple cores to run on. These paths always run concurrently, and they can run in parallel if there are sufficient CPU resources to allow it. Unfortunately, there's no easy way to observe these graphs.

The dependency graph also adds a feature you might not notice on your own. SMF can *restart* services when they fail—either from process termination or because a dependency failed first. It does this by monitoring the services and checking their current state. If a service isn't online and should be, the service's startup routine gets called. If restarting suffices, all is well; the repair is made as quickly as one can expect. Even better, any dependents affected by the loss will be restarted, too. This feature all but eliminates the task of identifying failed processes and restarting them.

Bear in mind, a service failure's effect may not be completely transparent to users. If your httpd server goes down, for example, any browser client with an active keep-alive session may be interrupted. You'd need to manage client session information so it can be restored once the service resumes. Still, with automated restarts, the server downtime turns into a blink instead of a long nap.

Here's an example in which I observe my Apache HTTP server is running by noting the PIDs. After I kill each PID, I look again:

```
<find lowest PID running the httpd process>
$ ptree 709
709   /usr/apache2/2.2/bin/httpd -k start
   745   /usr/apache2/2.2/bin/httpd -k start
   765   /usr/apache2/2.2/bin/httpd -k start
   782   /usr/apache2/2.2/bin/httpd -k start
   793   /usr/apache2/2.2/bin/httpd -k start
   830   /usr/apache2/2.2/bin/httpd -k start
<kill each PID>
$ pgrep http
1726
1730
1729
1725
1728
1727
```

What happened? The *restarter service* noticed the change in service state—that is, there were no processes left to monitor—and restarted the service. SMF doesn't actually protect processes from failure; it just restores them. Some Solaris documentation refers to this as *predictive self-healing*. In my opinion, the term *predictive* is a bit much; *reactive* is more appropriate, and to my mind completely adequate.

It might escape your immediate notice that SMF treats all Solaris resources the same. Whether it's a daemon process, a mounted file system, a device tree manager, or even SMF facilities themselves, everything is a service. Once you learn the system, you learn a uniform method for casting every existing and new operating system feature the same way. The tools we discuss in the next section (the svcs and svcadm commands), in particular, make it possible to analyze virtually any feature Solaris offers through a single point of control.

Identifying a Service and its Instances

All service names take the form of a Fault Management Resource Identifier (FMRI). The FMRI format borrows from the Uniform Resource Indicator (URI) format defined in the Internet Engineering Task Force (IETF) document RFC 3986. This is the same format used to define Uniform Resource Locator strings (URLs). It has two required components for any URI string: a *scheme* and a *path*. A scheme is a mnemonic prefix followed by a colon. For SMF, the primary scheme is svc:. The path for a service includes one or more *categories* and a *service name*, separated by forward slashes (/). The string terminates with an *instance name*, separated from the service name by another colon. The following are all examples of FMRI strings:

```
svc:/application/graphical-login/gdm:default
svc:/system/filesystem/root:default
svc:/network/http:apache22
svc:/milestone/single-user:default
```

Each of these services represents a system feature with a different purpose: supporting graphical login, maintaining the root file system, supporting an HTTP server, and observing the operational state of the system, respectively. The naming convention makes it easier to address the feature regardless of how it operates.

An alternative scheme SMF uses, lrc:, denotes system facilities that remain under legacy run control. SMF does not control these scripts, but it does observe them. It assigns each of them an FMRI in the form of a mangled directory path. Underscores replace any periods that occur in the file path; the period is a reserved character in the FMRI convention On a default Solaris 11 installation, there are only two of these:

```
$ svcs | grep lrc
legacy_run     2:26:25 lrc:/etc/rc2_d/S47pppd
legacy_run     2:26:25 lrc:/etc/rc2_d/S89PRESERVE
```

Service categories provide a logical directory scheme. They signify a location (as well as the domain) of each service. They also make it easy to reuse appropriate but generic service names, such as "server" and "client." Whoever writes a service manifest can assign arbitrary subcategories to their service, but the top-level categories, described in Table 8-2, are established by the SMF framework.

These top-level categories are self-evident and not otherwise defined. The milestone category and its services, however, deserve a special mention. A milestone is sometimes called a *synthetic* or *aggregate service*. A milestone service doesn't monitor a system facility, but is a checkpoint in the startup process similar to a traditional run level. It can be referred to by other SMF services as either a *dependency* or a *dependent*, which establishes its place in the boot order.

Some milestones are direct counterparts of well-known run levels and are named accordingly; I cover these later in the chapter. Other milestones capture states in the boot process. There's not a compelling reason to mark these states as run levels,

TABLE 8-2 SMF Service Categories

Service Category	Description
application	Services based on user processes
device	Services supporting individual devices and the device tree
legacy	Monitors for traditional run-control scripts
milestone	Services that track other services via a checkpoint
network	Services that support remote client and host access
platform	Services specific to hardware features
site	Services for third-party software
system	Services representing kernel facilities

but they can be handy in low-level debugging and analysis of the boot process. You should know these milestones exist and examine them once you become familiar with the tools. Table 8-3 lists these other milestones and describes them.

Service names come in a variety of styles because there is no established convention for naming them. Generic service names, you may notice, tend to supplement their categorical path. Others are namesakes of the kernel service or daemon process they monitor. Still others have no obvious pattern or meaning to them—or at least to me. The one convention that seems to hold is separating words in a service name with dashes. This mix of styles means you have to pay

TABLE 8-3 Milestones Not Associated with a Traditional Run Level

Milestone FMRI	Description
svc:/milestone/unconfig:default	Framework for removing system config data
svc:/milestone/devices:default	Devices-configured checkpoint
svc:/milestone/config:default	System-configured checkpoint
svc:/milestone/network:default	Ready to open network resources safely
svc:/milestone/name-services:default	Able to resolve name lookups
svc:/milestone/self-assembly-complete:default	First boot after install configuration complete

more attention to cryptic service names. Otherwise, you'll have to search through the entire listing of services to find the ones you need but forgot. Here are a few examples of the different types I've described:

```
svc:/network/smb/client:default
svc:/system/fmd:default
svc:/network/socket-config:default
svc:/system/devchassis:cleanstart
```

These examples are a service with a generic name, a service named after the process it monitors, a service with a dashed name, and a service you probably would not guess existed on your system, respectively. In the next section, you'll learn how to examine these services using the svcs command. In the meantime, remember that service names, not process names, index the SMF environment.

The last piece of an FMRI is the *instance*. A service's instance can override or complement its configuration with values that only have meaning at run time, such as the PID of a monitored process. Most services have one instance, which by convention is named "default." Some services have multiple instances, such as the console-login service. It maintains eight instances, one for a physically attached console (screen), two for serial connectors, and five virtual screens you can switch to from the default console:

```
svc:/system/console-login:terma
svc:/system/console-login:termb
svc:/system/console-login:default
svc:/system/console-login:vt2
svc:/system/console-login:vt3
svc:/system/console-login:vt4
svc:/system/console-login:vt5
svc:/system/console-login:vt6
```

You can list all non-default service instances, if you want, using this command:

```
# svcs -a | grep -v default$
```

The grep -v command filters lines that do not match the given string. The $ used here matches the end-of-line marker, so only the lines that don't end with the string "default" will remain. The result is 44 lines of output on my system, so I won't show them here. You should try it on your system and look over the results.

Understanding Service States

Every service has an initial binary state: It is either disabled or enabled. If it is disabled, that term will appear in the output to a svcs command:

```
$ svcs ntp
disabled        2:24:53 svc:/network/ntp:default
```

This service represents the Network Time Protocol (NTP), which a host can use to synchronize its clock with another system. It's disabled by default because the administrator has to configure which remote systems will be used as a time server. The SMF framework is especially handy because it's possible to register such a service with the system without activating it at every boot.

The term *enabled* does not appear in this command's output unless the -l or -x switch is used. An enabled service has instead a full lifecycle state that reflects transitions into and out of the online state. That is, every state description you'll see in a default svcs command listing, other than disabled, is a consequence of being enabled. The enabled states are listed in Table 8-4.

An enabled non-legacy service has five possible states, four of which you are ever likely to observe: offline, online, degraded, and maintenance. You can fairly say that "online" is good, and "offline" is not necessarily bad. "Degraded" is not good; "maintenance" is just bad. If you see a service in offline mode for a long time, it could be that a dependency is in a confused or latent state. If you see a service in degraded mode, which is rare in my experience, it means the service consists of multiple parts, enough of which are running to keep the service going. If your service is in maintenance mode, SMF has tried to restart it several times without success. It is then up to the administrator to deduce the cause and correct it. Figure 8-1 illustrates the transitions among these states.

TABLE 8-4   States for Enabled Services

Service State	Description
legacy_run	Observed only; script was run, no state information.
uninitialized	Named but not yet configured.
offline	Not yet in service (checking dependencies).
online	Operating normally.
degraded	Partially running.
maintenance	Restart attempts exhausted; administrator required.

FIGURE 8-1

State transition
diagram of an
enabled service

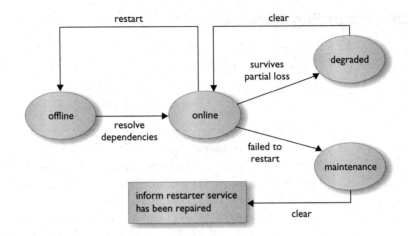

The degraded and maintenance modes are two cases in SMF where the framework cannot determine a restorative course of action. These are the two modes you'd like to hear about as soon as possible, if you're not monitoring services continuously. In the next section, I show you how you can add software to your system that can notify you of these service state transitions by e-mail.

Comparing Run Levels to Service Milestones

The run-level idea is still important to the Solaris system. SMF milestones improve on it by using names that make the purpose of each service's state more apparent. The explicit dependencies attached to each milestone make it possible to order the startup of services in a way that doesn't sacrifice the flexibility of the traditional model.

In the traditional model of numbered scripts, you insert one script between two others by assigning an interposing number to the filename. If you have an S14dothis script and an S29dothat script, the new script can be named S17whatever to achieve the desired order. In the milestone system, however, you don't have to hard-code the proper placement like this. By specifying your dependencies in a service description, you allow the configuration repository to calculate the right placement, thus removing the need for careful research and the risk of guesswork.

Some run levels listed in Table 8-1 have corresponding milestones, as shown in Table 8-5.

TABLE 8-5	Run Level	Milestone
	S	svc:/milestone/single-user:default
Milestones	2	svc:/milestone/multi-user:default
Associated with	3	svc:/milestone/multi-user-server:default
Run Levels	3	svc:/milestone/all:default (by default, an alias for multi-user-server)

There are no milestone equivalents for run levels that reboot or shut down the operating system session or power off the machine. It is still common practice to use the init command with a run-level argument, or to use one of the namesake utilities, such as halt, poweroff, reboot, or shutdown, to perform these tasks.

You can also use these milestones to boot your system, in the event you don't want the system to get all the way to the multi-user-server milestone. Just name the appropriate one. On SPARC systems, you can use the boot PROM command at the ok prompt with the -m switch to introduce a milestone. On X86 systems, you can modify an existing GRUB directive to do the same.

The all milestone represents the default run level for your system. It establishes services up to the multi-user-server milestone, but can be modified by the administrator. It's useful, on one hand, for rebooting frequently to a milestone of choice. The all milestone can be set to match any other bootable milestone, so the system boots up to the single-user milestone and doesn't call any subsequent services, for example, even if they are enabled.

The all milestone is also responsible for starting services with no declared dependencies or dependents—services you would otherwise miss by changing your service's state to a more explicit milestone.

Understanding the Configuration Repository

All service definitions start out in a file called a *manifest*, an XML-formatted document that configures all the elements a service associates with the facility it covers. These manifests are stored in two locations on your system: the /etc/svc/ manifest directory, which contains so-called *early imports*, and the /lib/svc/manifest directory, which contain the rest. Manifests kept in the early-import directory are loaded first in order to avoid certain dependency issues with other services. The manifest files in both locations are sorted into subdirectories that mirror their category path.

When you boot a newly installed system for the first time, these manifest files are read one by one, sorted into a dependency graph, and then added to the file /etc/svc/repository.db, also known as the *configuration repository*. This process repeats for any new or modified manifest files that are discovered in these directories on subsequent boots.

Unlike other flat text files—called databases *in the system's documentation—the repository file has a database-specific format that is not readable with a text editor. You can use the file command to show the format is not regular text:*

```
$ sudo file /etc/svc/repository.db
/etc/svc/repository.db: data
```

The traditional form of managing a process's configuration and run-time data is via well-known and transient files, respectively. In Solaris 11, some core services have replaced one or both kinds of files with *property groups* maintained in the database instead. Other services may use a repository property just to point to their configuration files. Either way, the repository is a central location for getting more information on a service of interest.

The svc.configd process is the repository's gatekeeper. It manages all requests made to read, update, or add its entries. The svc.startd process and users of other SMF tools such as the svcadm and svccfg utilities are three such clients that could access the database at the same time. By moderating among them, the svc.configd process ensures each record is touched by one request at a time. Figure 8-2 illustrates the relationship svc.configd maintains between the repository and client requests.

You can use the pfiles command to see the open descriptors maintained by both the svc.configd and svc.startd processes. I've summarized a look at the svc.startd process here by just counting the number of connections (doors) it has to the svc.configd process:

```
$ sudo pfiles `pgrep svc.startd` | grep "door to svc.configd" | wc -l
      5
```

This information isn't particularly insightful, but it does imply a robust communication between the two processes. If you analyze the svc.configd process this way as well, you may notice it talks to itself a lot, too.

Client
relationships with
the svc.configd
process

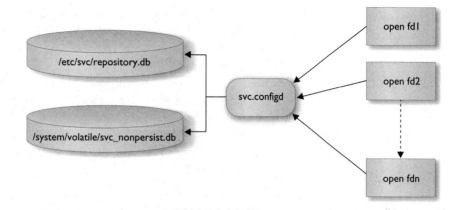

Understanding the Restarter Daemon

The init process still reads the /etc/inittab file. Now, however, there is one key entry
for it to execute that invokes the svc.startd process. Because this process picks up
the job the init process used to do, it is sometimes called the *delegated restarter*. It's
called a restarter because once system initialization reaches the "all" milestone, that's
the remaining job: to restart any service that has stopped for any reason (other than
being disabled by an administrator).

During bootup, the svc.startd process relies entirely on the contents of the
configuration repository to launch each dependency graph of services, to observe the
state of each service, and to monitor services once they become active. The restarter
has to manage different kinds of dependencies—some are stricter than others—and
it has to monitor different kinds of services according to their type. For example, a
service that represents a daemon process uses an abstraction called a *contract*, which
links the restarter to the PID of the process. If the PID goes away, the restarter is
informed by the change in the contract (the PID is now invalid) and goes about the
business of calling the program again. Other services are represented by a script that
runs and exits; in this case, a contract won't do any good.

If you read your documentation carefully, you may note that any service can
configure a restarter other than the svc.startd process to operate on its behalf. The
Solaris operating system, in fact, has a second restarter: the inetd process. The svc.
startd process delegates responsibility for all network-based services to this process,

which acts as a utility and de facto delegate in traditional run control. Because it is managed directly by the svc.startd process, the inetd process no longer operates as a command utility. This work has been assumed by the inetadm utility, which is discussed in the next section.

The svc.startd process has other tasks it performs as well. Without going into details outside the scope of the OCA exam, it's worth a few moments of your time to examine the process using the p-tools outlined in Chapter 7. Pay particular attention to the number of LWPs spawned by this process, as well as the number of open file descriptors. The restarter's health is essential to the health of your entire system; take some time to learn it well.

CERTIFICATION OBJECTIVE 8.02

Administering SMF Services

The Service Management Facility is a complex framework of files, services, and interacting processes. There's even more to learn, such as how to write a manifest and observe how property groups are kept in the configuration repository. These are considered advanced skills you don't need to know for the OCA exam. However, the tools you'll use to manage individual services and explore the repository are the same ones you'll use for more advanced operations later on. Thanks to some thoughtful design, there are just a few key tools to learn.

The svcs utility is your primary tool for observation. It has options to investigate the various aspects of a service. Because it is a read-only tool, anyone can use it to observe the services available on the system (unless an administrator has removed the privileges necessary). Both the svcadm and inetadm utilities let you modify a service's state; the inetadm utility also lets you modify network-specific properties. To modify properties of a non-network service, you'd use the svccfg utility. Details on each command follow.

Using the svcs Command

By default, the svcs command lists the current time, the time started, and the full FMRI of enabled services. Using the -a switch, it will also report disabled services. The output for either command is too long to reproduce here, as shown by line count:

```
$ svcs | wc -l
     148
$ svcs -a | wc -l
     217
```

To get started, you can filter this output with string matches, using the grep utility or a similar tool. Using a category for matching may reduce output to a manageable level. When you don't know specific services by their names, sifting the output of these commands is about all you can do. It may also help you to see how services are categorized.

If you do know a service by name, you can save a bit of effort. The svcs utility will match the string you supply against all listed service and instance names. (The string "default" isn't useful; most service instances share that name.) You can often match a single service using its service name alone; it's rarely necessary to type the full FMRI:

```
$ svcs gdm
STATE          STIME    FMRI
online         2:26:29  svc:/application/graphical-login/gdm:default
$ svcs cron
STATE          STIME    FMRI
online         2:26:16  svc:/system/cron:default
$ svcs apache22
STATE          STIME    FMRI
online         7:38:32  svc:/network/http:apache22
```

For more general service names such as "server" and "client," you'll get multiple matches. You can then use the category to narrow your results, like this:

```
$ svcs server
STATE          STIME    FMRI
disabled       2:24:53  svc:/application/pkg/server:default
disabled       2:25:02  svc:/network/ldap/server:openldap_24
disabled       2:26:25  svc:/network/nfs/server:default
$ svcs nfs/server
STATE          STIME    FMRI
disabled       2:26:25  svc:/network/nfs/server:default
```

The svcs command also provides switches for reporting specific details. I recommend using the svcs -xv command, without a service parameter, when first logging in to a recently booted system. This command reports all services that were transitioned to a degraded or maintenance state during the boot (or remain that way after reboot). It also reports disabled services with dependents that cannot operate without it. It's an easy way to determine if you are starting with a healthy system:

```
$ svcs -vx
svc:/system/dumpadm:default (system crash dump configuration)
 State: disabled since October 12, 2012 02:25:06 AM PDT
Reason: Disabled by an administrator.
   See: http://sun.com/msg/SMF-8000-05
   See: man -M /usr/share/man -s 1M dumpadm
Impact: 4 dependent services are not running:
        svc:/system/fmd:default
        svc:/system/fm/asr-notify:default
        svc:/system/fm/smtp-notify:default
        svc:/system/devchassis:daemon
```

You will occasionally find hyperlinks to an online message resource that, as of this writing, is no longer supported. Do, however, note the list of dependents affected by the loss of service. I doubt even well-versed Solaris admins know the full impact of their essential services going offline. With SMF, there's no need at all to keep this information in your head; you only have to remember how to ask.

If you want more detailed information on a service, use the -l option and name the service that interests you. This option lists several attributes in long form (as opposed to the columnar form the -v option includes). Among these attributes are:

- Full FMRI
- Service description
- Enabled (true or false)
- Current state
- Next state (if the service is currently in transition)
- Time the current state was established
- File path to the service's log file
- FMRI of the service's restarter
- Contract ID (if the service manages processes)
- Manifest files that define or refer to the service
- Dependencies defined and their current state

As you become more familiar with the meaning of these fields, you may find yourself consulting the svcs -v command output more frequently. Until then, it's just about everything you might want to know at first glance about a service. The manifest files are included because changes made to these files will affect the configuration at the next reboot. (You can also push changes from a manifest file to the repository with the svccfg import subcommand. See the man page for details and a sample invocation.)

The dependency information includes a grouping, such as this excerpt from the name-services service:

```
$ svcs -l name-services
fmri          svc:/milestone/name-services:default
name          name services milestone
...
dependency    require_all/refresh svc:/system/name-service/switch (online)
dependency    optional_all/refresh svc:/network/dns/client (online)
dependency    optional_all/refresh svc:/network/ldap/client (disabled)
dependency    optional_all/refresh svc:/network/nis/client (disabled)
```

Grouping refers to the qualifier and directive pair, such as optional_all/refresh, given just before the FMRI. There are four qualifiers altogether, including the terms require_any and exclude_any. These terms define the coupling between the dependency and the target service. These terms are documented in the man page for smf.

Listing the dependents or dependencies of a service by themselves is simple. Use the -d switch to list just the services your chosen service depends on. Use the -D switch to list the services that depend on the one you've named. If you're picking services at random to play with, chances are you won't see a listing with the -D option. It is not as common for one service to declare other services that depend on it, but it can play an important role in helping to optimize service initialization order. Here are examples of both:

```
$ svcs -d cron
STATE          STIME     FMRI
online         2:25:53   svc:/system/filesystem/local:default
online         2:26:18   svc:/milestone/name-services:default
$ svcs -D cron
STATE          STIME     FMRI
online         2:26:25   svc:/milestone/multi-user:default
```

The cron facility relies on the local file system and the name services milestone to operate. It declares the multi-user milestone service as a dependent. This declaration ensures the milestone will be notified if the cron service fails, restarts, or is disabled by an administrator.

Not all services monitor running processes, but you can use the svcs -p command to retrieve PIDs for the ones that do. The examples here show services with no PID, one PID, and multiple PIDs attached to the service, respectively:

```
$ svcs -p filesystem/local
STATE          STIME      FMRI
online         2:25:53    svc:/system/filesystem/local:default
$ svcs -vp cron
STATE          NSTATE         STIME     CTID    FMRI
online         -              2:26:16   90      svc:/system/cron:default
               2:26:16        549 cron
$ svcs -vp apache22
STATE          NSTATE         STIME     CTID    FMRI
online         -              7:38:32   155     svc:/network/http:apache22
               7:38:32        1725 httpd
               7:38:33        1726 httpd
               7:38:33        1727 httpd
               7:38:33        1728 httpd
               7:38:33        1729 httpd
               7:38:33        1730 httpd
```

Notice that I used the -v switch as well in two of these examples, which includes the column CTID (short for contract ID). SMF observes every process-driven service through a contract, which includes a contract holder. Usually, the holder is the restarter itself (the svc.startd process).

For more information on the primary attributes of a service, use the svcs -l command. This "long" listing expands the values reported with the -v switch and includes some advanced terms. Notice, for example, that each dependency is detailed by an additional term (require_all, require_any, or optional_all). This term specifies how a dependency influences a service. Consult the man page on smf for more information on these terms.

Using the svcadm Command

You can use the svcadm utility to change the state of a service. There are seven subcommands altogether, which are summarized in Table 8-6.

TABLE 8-6	Subcommands for the svcadm Utility

Subcommand for svcadm	Description
disable *FMRI*	Terminates service (current and future sessions)
enable *FMRI*	Starts service (current and future sessions)
refresh *FMRI*	Updates service configuration from repository (does not restart)
restart *FMRI*	Restarts service (online or degraded mode)
clear *FMRI*	Tries to change state (from degraded to online, maintenance to offline)
mark *FMRI*	Matches service state to instance state (degraded or maintenance mode)
milestone *milestone_FMRI*	Used to enable/disable services as necessary to reach the specified milestone

One thing SMF provides that traditional run control does not is a way to turn a service on or off *and* maintain that preference across reboots. That is, once you disable a service, that information goes to the repository and is applied to subsequent sessions until you change it back. To do the same thing in traditional run control, you could remove a script from its directory or change its name (so it won't be read on startup). With SMF, you can make this change without modifying any underlying objects:

```
$ sudo svcadm disable cron
$ svcs -p cron
STATE        STIME   FMRI
disabled     23:23:35 svc:/system/cron:default
```

When you change a service's property setting, the configuration repository creates a snapshot of the change, making it possible to roll back to the original settings if needed. You can therefore edit a repository entry without immediate consequences on a running service, similar to the way you edit some configuration files without affecting the processes that read them. The refresh subcommand lets you push changes to the service from the repository when you're ready. If the underlying service is a process, however, a refresh won't affect the service until the next reboot or the service is restarted.

Restarting a service is a process equivalent to sending a hang-up signal to an underlying process. For a daemon process, a restart interrupts the process so that it will re-read its configuration file. You can think of this as a "hard refresh" if you like, because sometimes configuration changes come from the repository. For services that don't monitor a process, the restart subcommand may be undefined, in which case it is ignored, or it may be the same as a refresh. Each service may define what occurs with a refresh and restart directive as it suits the supported facility.

The clear subcommand attempts to place a service maintenance mode into offline mode, assuming the administrator has made repairs and the service is ready to run properly. In SMF terms, placing a service offline prompts the restarter to start it again. To avoid a vicious cycle, the restarter will place a service back to maintenance mode if starting fails after three tries. The service configuration may also include a timeout value so the restarter can stop trying if the service doesn't respond within that interval. If a service is in degraded mode, the clear subcommand attempts to place it back in online mode.

on the Job

The mark command is an advanced facility that supports testing new services and overall SMF operations. It allows a service or SMF tester to match the state of a service with an instance that is in degraded or maintenance mode.

The milestone subcommand lets you temporarily enable or disable services according to the milestone you want to set. Any reboot following this subcommand will restore the milestone level to all. Many veteran administrators assume this subcommand is similar to using the init command with a run-level argument, but it does not change the run level of the system. Run level is still controlled only by the init process and init-related namesake utilities, such as the halt, shutdown, reboot, and poweroff commands.

Adding Notifications to SMF

The restarter makes the job of restoring services almost as transparent to the administrator as to users. The actual task is often trivial; it's the time needed to identify and isolate the problem that accounts for most of the downtime. If a service falls into maintenance mode, however, you're back to the original problem. Without an immediate way to restart, someone has to identify the problem (by noticing a lack of service) before you can repair it. For a process with many users, such as an HTTP server, getting quick notification is a top concern. For some sites, knowing that a service was restarted automatically is also important information.

SMF in Solaris 11 addresses this concern with an e-mail notification scheme you can apply to any service state transition you want to monitor. To enable it, you need to make sure the smtp-notify package is installed on your system. Enable the smtp-notify service and observe it with the svcs -vp command:

```
$ pkg list smtp-notify
NAME (PUBLISHER)                          VERSION                IFO
system/fault-management/smtp-notify       0.5.11-0.175.0.0.0.2.1 i--
$ sudo svcadm enable system/fm/smtp-notify:default
$ svcs -vp smtp-notify
STATE      NSTATE        STIME    CTID   FMRI
online     -             0:02:38  182    svc:/system/fm/smtp-notify:default
                         0:02:37  2464   smtp-notify
```

Once this service is in place, you can raise notifications for all changes on all services or for a specific change and service. You may want to know immediately, for example, if any service transitions into maintenance or degraded mode. You might also want to know if your HTTP server changes to or from online mode. You can add these directives by setting properties in the configuration repository. Refer to Table 8-4 for a list of all the states you can specify, along with a from- or to- prefix.

Here, the first example configures e-mail notification to my account (mfernest) if any service transitions to maintenance mode. The second example configures the http:apache22 service to notify me if it changes to or from the online state. You can use the svcprop command, as shown, to verify the changes. Restart any named services to pick up the notification property.

```
# sudo svccfg -s system/svc/global:default setnotify -g to-maintenance
mailto:mfernest@localhost
# sudo svccfg -s http:apache22 setnotify to-online,from-online mailto:mfernest@
localhost
$ svcprop -p to-online apache22
to-online/smtp,active boolean true
to-online/smtp,to astring mfernest@localhost
$ svcprop -p from-online apache22
from-online/smtp,active boolean true
from-online/smtp,to astring mfernest@localhost
$ sudo svcadm restart apache22
```

Once you've set up notifications, use the svcadm utility to change the state of a service you've assigned notifications to. Use the mail utility to check for messages. It takes a bit more knowledge to push a service into maintenance or degraded mode, so stick to testing with the svcadm utility unless you're confident you can safely add bugs to (and remove them from) your system.

Using the Namesake Commands

As I've said throughout this chapter, SMF replaces the run-control method of executing enumerated scripts to bring the system, one run level at a time, up to its full capabilities. SMF does not, however, remove well-known methods for changing the run levels themselves. Table 8-5 lists the values for run levels that can also be used as arguments to the init command to change the run level.

There are also what I have called *namesake* commands: shutdown, reboot, halt, and poweroff. The last three are the near-equivalents to the commands init 6, init 0, and init 5, respectively, except that the halt and poweroff commands do not walk through a graceful shutdown of services. Their job in life is to flush any updated content to disk and shut down the system quickly. They're useful commands to explore when you're working alone on a system.

on the job

Using the reboot command, you can also invoke a fast reboot. On an X86 system, calling a fast reboot will bypass firmware checking and the boot loader (GRUB) and transfer control immediately to a newly loaded kernel program. On a SPARC system, a set of power-on self-tests (POSTs) are bypassed to achieve the same effect. You can do this with the reboot command by invoking the -f switch.

CERTIFICATION SUMMARY

The Solaris OCA exam states two requirements for SMF: Explain its role and administer its services. With that general view in mind, understanding how SMF improves upon the traditional UNIX run-control model is key: It names all system facilities as services, defines them by a list of common attributes (including dependencies on other services), and establishes a database for storing those attributes. This arrangement is governed by a process that will automatically restart any service. The fundamentals of SMF administration boil down to learning the details of a handful of utilities. Each one has a short list of options and/or subcommands to remember.

TWO-MINUTE DRILL

Understanding the Role of SMF

❑ The Service Management Facility supercedes the traditional UNIX run-control system that has remained in wide use for decades.

❑ The svc.startd process, which is called by the init process, is also known as the *delegated restarter*. Its primary job, following service initialization, is to monitor and restart failed services.

❑ The svc.configd process manages access to the configuration repository (/etc/svc/repository.db), which stores service attributes as property groups.

❑ SMF service names follow the Fault Management Resource Identifier (FMRI) scheme, which is related to the URI convention also used for Internet URLs.

❑ Services declare other services as dependencies and dependents. This information is used to establish a boot-order graph that helps to optimize the startup process.

Administering SMF Services

❑ The svcs command reads the public attributes of any process. It includes options to show more verbose information as well as list dependencies and dependents, the PIDs of any observed processes, and any services that are currently broken.

❑ The svcadm command changes the current state of a service. Once enabled, a service may transition through several states in its lifetime, including offline, online, maintenance, and degraded.

❑ The svccfg command allows you to examine and modify the contents of the configuration repository.

❑ Although you can use the svcadm command with a milestone to enable or disable a number of services at once, only the init command manages the current run level of the system.

❑ You can set notifications for service state transitions by enabling the smtp-notify service and configuring its repository properties.

SELF TEST

Use the following questions to test your recall and understanding of the chapter's material.

Understanding the Role of SMF

1. Which two options are valid SMF top-level categories?

A. site

B. arch

C. kernel

D. system

2. Which feature does the SMF framework support that traditional run control does not?

A. It allows for dependents between services/processes.

B. It lets you start up services/processes in a predetermined order.

C. It provides a way to report the system's operational state.

D. It lets you determine if a process is not running.

3. What does a service in an offline state signify?

A. It's transitioning to a disabled state.

B. It's about to go online.

C. It's waiting on a dependency.

D. It has been restarted more than once.

4. Which statement identifies a capability of a run level or milestone that is not supported by the other?

A. Milestones signify the system's current level of operability.

B. You can use a run level to bring the system to maintenance mode.

C. You can use a run level to reboot the system.

D. You can use a milestone to disable remote login capability.

5. Which of the following strings is not a legal FMRI?

A. svc:/system/global:default

B. lrc:/etc/rc2_d/S99Install

C. svc:/application/thirdpartysvc:instance

D. svc:/milestone/single-user

Administering SMF Services

6. Which three commands will report the PID of the sendmail process?

   A. svcs -p smtp

   B. svcs -l sendmail

   C. pgrep sendmail

   D. svcs -p sendmail

7. Which two statements are correct?

   A. Only the refresh subcommand can update the configuration repository.

   B. Only the restart subcommand can update the configuration repository.

   C. Only the refresh subcommand can update the process ID.

   D. Only the restart subcommand can update the process ID.

8. What is the run level of a Solaris 11 system after the command svcadm milestone single-user has been executed?

   A. S

   B. 1

   C. 3

   D. Undefined

9. What does the init 5 command do?

   A. It halts the system.

   B. It suspends the operating system.

   C. It powers off the system.

   D. It reboots the system.

10. Which option identifies information the svcs -x command reports that the svcs -l command does not?

   A. Reference documentation

   B. Service description

   C. The full FMRI of the service

   D. The service log file

SELF TEST ANSWERS

Understanding the Role of SMF

1. ☑ **A** and **D**. Although a service writer can establish subcategories as part of the service FMRI, the top-level categories are fixed.
   ☒ **B** and **C** are incorrect. These names appear in the paths of device drivers but are not service categories.

2. ☑ **A**. Whereas traditional run control has an implicit scheme for dependencies, it has no method for letting one process declare itself as a prerequisite to another process's operation.
   ☒ **B, C,** and **D** are incorrect. **B** is incorrect because traditional run control has a startup order that is implied by numbering the scripts and separating them by numbered run levels. **C** is incorrect because milestones reflect and can be used to alter the operational state of the system. **D** is incorrect because with traditional run control, you determine a process is not running by its absence from a report.

3. ☑ **C**. A service in the offline state is waiting for its dependencies to resolve; the next state of the service may depend on the success or failure of those dependencies to come online.
   ☒ **A, B,** and **D** are incorrect. Services do not transition from online to offline on their way to being disabled, nor is the transition from offline to online state guaranteed. Also, there is no state in SMF that tracks a number of starts or restarts attempted.

4. ☑ **C**. There is no milestone you can change to that reboots the system.
   ☒ **A, B,** and **D** are incorrect. **A** is incorrect because both systems have a way to signify the current level of operation. **B** is incorrect because you can use the svcadm milestone none command to bring the system into maintenance mode. **D** is incorrect because you can use the command svcadm milestone single-user to disable the services that are part of the multi-user milestone, which include network capability.

5. ☑ **D**. In this case, there is no instance name, so the FMRI is incomplete.
   ☒ **A, B,** and **C** are incorrect. These are all legal FMRIs, although **C** is not a service that ships with Solaris 11. Note that **D** is legal without an instance name because all lrc:-based FMRIs are just modified file paths.

Administering SMF Services

6. ☑ **A, C,** and **D.** Any one of these invocations will return the PID of the sendmail process. Both **A** and **D** work because one names the service and the other names the service instance; either will match the full FMRI.
☒ **B** is incorrect. The svcs -l command will report the contract ID of a service but not the PID.

7. ☑ **D.** Most process-based services just send the HUP signal to the process, forcing it to terminate and restart. This action changes the PID.
☒ **A, B,** and **C** are incorrect. **A** and **B** are incorrect because either subcommand may update the repository, just in different ways. **C** is incorrect because the refresh action can only update the repository configuration; it cannot affect running processes managed by the service.

8. ☑ **C.** Milestones and run levels are not correlated.
☒ **A, B,** and **D** are incorrect. **A** and **B** are incorrect because if you change the operational milestone using the svcadm utility, the current run level does not change with it. **D** is incorrect because the current milestone level and run level may stay in sync, but the system does not get confused.

9. ☑ **C.** After bringing the system down to a quiescent state, the init 5 command instructs the machine to turn power off.
☒ **A, B,** and **D** are incorrect. **A** is incorrect because halting the machine means flushing updated data to disk and does not power off the system. **B** is incorrect because the init 5 command transitions the operating system through each run level down to 0 before issuing the power-off instruction. **D** is incorrect because the init 6 command reboots the system.

10. ☑ **A.** There is a great deal of overlap between the svcs -x and svcs -l reports, but the former aims at helping the administrator understand the cause of any problems and their impact as well as where to find more information.
☒ **B, C,** and **D** are incorrect. All three options describe information that both commands report.

9
Understanding Projects and Tasks

A mong the objectives for the Solaris 11 OCA exam, you'll notice nothing listed for Solaris projects. There is also nothing listed for resource management, the subject of Chapter 10, other than a brief mention as part of Solaris Zones, the subject of Chapter 17. And yet the next two chapters, as well as part of Chapter 16, offer foundation material that isn't directly relevant to the exam.

I do know this book is just a certification prep guide, and such books typically promise to stick to just what you need to take the exam. I hope you'll read these extra chapters anyway. I think you'll understand why I think a) this material is important for you to know, and b) it will better prepare you for the exam anyway.

The degree of integration among the new and different technologies introduced in Solaris 10, and now Solaris 11, is especially strong. It may have occurred to you, for example, that without ZFS technology, you can't have boot environments that share storage space. Without IPS, it wouldn't be as simple to install SMF services alongside the software it monitors. Without SMF, it wouldn't be as easy to modify the network services you'd like running for each boot session. You get the idea; a lot of design work has been put into each technology leveraging the others.

Solaris Zones represents the epitome of that work. As you'll see when you read Chapter 17, zones configuration draws from nearly every technology Solaris 11 has to offer, including two we haven't covered yet: resource management and virtualized networking. I've given these topics extended treatment because without them it's very easy to believe they are integral parts of Solaris Zones technology, but it's the other way around. Without all the developments made in networking and resource management since Solaris 8, you would not have the extensive feature set you have for zones.

The reason for a separate chapter on projects is less apparent. In short, a project shares many characteristics with a zone. Once you understand how to use a project to manage a group of processes, you'll see how zones apply the same concepts. Once you see how resource management controls and virtual networking are used without zones, it will be easier to see how all three concepts come together to make a Solaris 11 Zone such a powerful tool. When you get to Chapter 17, you'll have learned enough about these supporting technologies that focusing on zones by themselves will be far easier work.

CERTIFICATION OBJECTIVE 9.01

Understanding Projects

A *project*, in the simplest sense, identifies and relates a collection of processes. Starting with Solaris 8, every single process has a project identifier, called projid, as part of its metadata. You can observe this value by specifying it when you want to examine one or more processes. You can also retrieve the project name with the same utility:

```
$ ps -o project,projid -p $$
PROJID  PROJECT
   10  group.staff
$
```

In this example, I report the project name and the ID of my shell process (the value of the $$ expression). Using that result, I can locate the record for it in the /etc/project file. It's no coincidence that the number 10 is the same as the GID for the staff group, but it's not shared data between the two fields. There is also significance to this name format that I'll cover in a moment. The /etc/project records don't have much else to look at—just four empty fields you can use to refine the project's details, who can access one, and what resource limits they have. I'll also cover these shortly.

Projects were introduced in Solaris 8 as a means to define a workload, a collection of processes for which the administrator may want a unified view and control. A workload may take several forms. A project could be defined as some number of processes that interact with each other, or perform the same work in parallel. It could be defined as all the programs executed with the same credentials. It could be defined as all processes run by users who belong to one group. However you define one, a project gives you a way to observe and manage something more than a single process and something less than all the processes running on your system at once.

In my experience teaching this topic to Sun and Oracle customers around the country, this benefit sounds less intriguing than it is, or perhaps it sounds like a small solution to a big problem (enterprise management). It's hard to say, because many students who haven't been told projects are useful decide to check their e-mail when I introduce this topic. But for my money, they're a very simple solution to a set of challenges in administration whose magnitude is more apparent than real.

Here's a simple illustration. Using the prstat –J command, you can get a report that shows the resource demands made on your system, broken down by project ID. In the following example, you see three active projects reported (the aforementioned group.staff entry along with the system and default projects):

```
 1412 mfernest     57M    31M sleep   12   19   0:00:00 0.4% updatemanagerno/1
 1396 mfernest    130M    16M sleep   59    0   0:00:00 0.4% gnome-settings-/1
PROJID    NPROC  SWAP   RSS MEMORY      TIME  CPU PROJECT
   10      33 1748M  384M   25%   0:00:05 13%  group.staff
    0      70  498M  181M   11%   0:00:58 7.8% system
    3       1 3848K 2800K  0.2%   0:00:00 0.2% default
```

To get this output, I used the command prstat –c –J 1 1. The –c option provides scrolling output instead of refreshing the screen. The numeric arguments ask for a one-second interval report (the default is 5) one time. The project breakdown takes up a fixed amount of space at the bottom of the screen. The remaining space above displays as many processes as the terminal window allows. I have truncated the report to show the last two processes displayed.

For the next example, I added the entry user.mfernest to the /etc/project file and gave my UID (60004) for my project ID. I then rebooted the session so all processes that are otherwise charged to the group.staff project would be charged to the user. mfernest project instead. No other changes were necessary. Using the same prstat command, I got the following output:

```
 1439 mfernest     57M    31M sleep   12   19   0:00:00 0.6% updatemanagerno/1
 1420 mfernest    130M    16M sleep   59    0   0:00:00 0.6% gnome-settings-/1
PROJID    NPROC  SWAP   RSS MEMORY      TIME  CPU PROJECT
 60004     36 1854M  444M   28%   0:00:08 23%  user.mfernest
     0     68  478M  178M   11%   0:00:57 9.2% system
     3      1 3848K 2800K  0.2%   0:00:00 0.3% default
```

Both reports were taken a minute or so after booting up to obtain similar resource numbers. Once I have defined projects in this way, it's clear who's demanding the most CPU and memory resources at the moment: me. That's not surprising for a small Solaris environment (1GB RAM) with one user logged in to the graphic console. Of course, the percentages will vary according to the resources available. The hard numbers—number of processes (NPROC), virtual memory (SWAP), and physical memory (RSS) required—should stay the same despite the number of CPUs and RAM available, so you should be sure to consider these percentages against the physical resources available.

All it took here was an additional entry to the /etc/project file, and I have reported that's a bit more specific. If you defined a project for the most demanding users on a system this same way, you'd have a quick and convenient view on the relative demands they make from a Solaris system.

Understanding Default Projects

Projects can be defined by the credentials of the process owner: the system, no particular user (default), a login or role account, or a group. They can also be defined by an arbitrary name and project number with a supplied list of users and groups. How you do it depends on what workload you want to account for and how. Of course, you don't have to apply projects to your work at all; the default projects exist so each process can be associated with a project identifier. These five projects are described in Table 9-1.

The default and group.staff projects are backstops for any non-root process that does not have a more specific project available. Following this scheme, projects themselves remain unobtrusive if you're not interested in applying them. At the same time, you can add a more specific default project for any user or group by declaring them. In the preceding example, the resource demand charged to the group.staff project was accordingly assigned to the user.mfernest project. If you find this progression of default projects useful—from default to group to user-based project assignments—it is built in and ready to use.

TABLE 9-1   Standard Project Accounts

Project Name	Projid	Description
System	0	All system processes and daemons
user.root	1	All processes running as root
noproject	2	Reserved
default	3	All users not in the staff group
group.staff	4	All users in the staff group

You can also define any project as a user's or role's default project by updating the last field of the account's /etc/user_attr entry. First, however, define the project in the /etc/project file. You can list members of it by adding them to the fourth field of the project record. It should look like this:

```
ocademo:105::mfernest::
```

Details for doing this without editing by hand are in the following section. Next, to change an account's default project to this one, you need to modify the last field of the account's /etc/user_attr entry, as follows:

```
mfernest:::type=normal;lock_after_retries=no;profiles=System
Administrator;roles=root;project=ocademo
```

This change overrides the default scheme that relies on project names and allows you to associate any user, role, or group with any project you like. After a reboot, the last few lines of output from the prstat command should look like this:

```
 1502 mfernest    10M 2312K sleep   53   0   0:00:00 0.1% bash/1
 1474 mfernest    34M  16M sleep    59   0   0:00:00 0.1% notification-da/1
PROJID    NPROC  SWAP   RSS MEMORY     TIME  CPU PROJECT
  105       35 1842M  443M    28%  0:00:09 7.6% ocademo
    0       68  478M  178M    11%  0:00:59 1.0% system
    3        1 3848K 2800K   0.2%  0:00:00 0.0% default
```

All I have done in these examples is reassign the project for the resource demands I make when I log in. Without a variety of different workloads running under different non-root accounts on the system, it takes a bit of setup to show a bit of variety. But don't get hung up on the idea of viewing workloads solely by who runs them; it's just a scheme for naming the collection of processes you'd like to observe. Projects get more interesting once you decide to limit the resources you make available to them. That discussion is coming shortly.

The default project is important because it determines the project ID assigned to any incidental processes you may execute while you are logged in. From the command line, you can identify your default project using the id -p command:

```
$ id -p
uid=60004(mfernest) gid=10(staff) projid=105(ocademo)
```

Note that the projid isn't just additional information that has been added to a process's metadata. It's considered a primary part of the credentials, along with the UID and GID. It's not included in the default output for the id command because there's no knowing who has written a script that might break if the default output changes. The projid value is nonetheless inherited by children processes. In the upcoming section on tasks, you'll see how to start new processes in another project, provided you have permission to use it.

You can use the projects utility to see which projects are configured on your system and which ones you can access. In the following example, I've made a number of projects available to the mfernest account. I can review them by name with the projects command, use the -v option to read the project description, and use the -l option to see all project information. I can also supply another user/role name to see which projects they have access to:

```
$ projects
default group.staff user.mfernest gnome ocademo
$ projects -d
user.mfernest
$ projects -l gnome
gnome
     projid : 11111
     comment: "Desktop"
     users  : (none)
     groups : staff
     attribs:
$ projects toby
default group.staff gnome
```

In this configuration, my account can access five projects; the user.mfernest project is my account's default. I'll discuss the format of each entry, although you can see from the detailed listing that a project record has five fields. The account toby, which I created in a previous chapter, has access to the gnome project by way of belonging to the staff group. The -v option, not shown here, will display all project names along with their comment fields.

This utility may seem unnecessary; a simple grep invocation can print any record in its native form, of course. But the projects utility isn't just for reading the /etc/ projects file. It can also read a database of project entries. The next section explains the motivation for thinking beyond a local file for keeping project definitions.

Projects are not the only changes to standard Solaris services that are built in this way. Authorizations, privileges, and CPU pools, to name three more, were all added to Solaris 8 to preserve compatibility with the tools customers have written using them. You don't have to modify your work if you don't intend to use these facilities. At the same time, you can incorporate them whenever you like, and create custom configurations using them (to varying degrees) to meet your needs.

Understanding Project Integration in Solaris

The design for projects goes beyond using it on one system. The /etc/projects file is sometimes called a database, as other lookup tables in the /etc/ directory are, because its information can also be stored in and retrieved from a Name Information Service (NIS) or Lightweight Directory Access Protocol (LDAP) server. The Solaris operating system includes a name resolver service that historically has been configured using the /etc/nsswitch.conf file. For each lookup table, this file declares the lookup method: a local file or some remote service.

Using this approach, an end user doesn't have to wonder how the system handles lookups. The syntax of each entry allows the administrator to configure more than one resolver service, such that lookups of purely local interest can be handled with a file (such as /etc/project), while site-wide identities are available from a centralized server.

The default entry for the project database refers to the local file only:

```
$ grep project /etc/nsswitch.conf
project:    files
```

As a primary process attribute, however, it makes sense to define a global project table if host, user, group, and other tables are maintained the same way. Figure 9-1 illustrates with solid lines the idea of retrieving project attributes either from a file or from an NIS server. The name resolver also allows a configuration by which the local service can return an error message, such as NOTFOUND, and pass control to the remote service, which may contain project names that are not locally defined.

This scheme is one reason projects are given a large range of numeric identifiers, as many as are allowed for UIDs. You probably don't want to manage tens of thousands of different workloads as unique projects. You do, however, want it to be easy to identify your projects with a unique number. One way to do so is by matching project IDs to the users or groups who own them (as the group.staff project does).

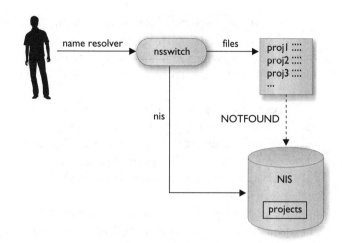

FIGURE 9-1

Project lookup
using a file or
remote name
service

Another way might be to assign ranges of numbers to different groups in a large environment. In either case, project numbers should start above 100—all two-digit numbers are considered reserved for system definitions.

Understanding the /etc/project File Format

A project record has six fields altogether. The first five fields define the project and its members and provide room for a comment. The remaining field will contain a list of key-value pairs, or attributes, that define any resource constraints you might place on the project. The meaning of each field is given in Table 9-2.

TABLE 9-2   Fields in an /etc/project Record

/etc/project Field	Use	Description
1	String	Project name
2	ID	Numeric identifier
3	String	Comment field
4	List	User members
5	List	Group members
6	List	Attributes

The fourth and fifth fields are useful when the user.*username* and group.*groupname* naming scheme doesn't suit your needs. You can name a project with a valid string; the rules that apply to user and group names also apply to projects. The numeric identifier should be greater than 100 and less than the maximum on your system for a UID.

You can add users and groups to a project with a comma-separated list. You can also use wildcards to include everyone (*), exclude someone by name (!*name*), or explicitly exclude all (!*) who are not listed. By applying inclusion measures, you allow users and groups to assign their processes to a project. Exclusion measures may be useful when you want to ensure a workload will have no additional processes assigned to it.

Here are three examples and accompanying descriptions you can use to better understand the meaning of each wildcard, used in conjunction with literal user and group names:

```
punjab:201:Diamond:larry,curly,!moe::
newhart:1000:Hospitality::staff,!darryl:
solitude:5555:Fortress:superman,!*::
```

The punjab project allows the users larry and curly to use it, but excludes moe. Strictly speaking, excluding moe is merely an explicit designation. Users who are not named also cannot use this project. The newhart project allows anyone belonging to the staff group to use it, but no one from the darryl group. The solitude project defines superman as the exclusive user of the project. You don't have to make elaborate use of wildcard syntax for effective lists, but they can be helpful to document the scope of a project's utility. As with most configurations, the simplest arrangement that fits your needs is best.

Managing Project Entries

One thing you should avoid is creating these records with a text editor. In support of that advice, Solaris provides the same utilities for projects—projadd, projdel, and projmod—as it does for managing users and groups. These tools help you avoid problems by validating field values and safeguarding your database against typos that might cause project-oriented code to throw errors. Adding and modifying project entries this way may seem tedious at first; you need to use a separate switch to refer to each field. However, should you end up scripting this work to apply to multiple systems, using tools that make your intentions clearer and validate your work is never bad.

In this example, I use the projadd utility to create a punjab project, as shown previously. It shouldn't work on my system, as the users larry, curly, and moe haven't been created:

```
$ sudo projadd -p 201 -c Diamond -U larry,curly,'!moe' punjab
projadd: User "moe" does not exist
projadd: User "curly" does not exist
projadd: User "larry" does not exist
$ grep punjab /etc/project
$
```

The command syntax is fine; the wildcard has to be quoted to keep the shell from interpreting the bang as a negation operator. The projadd utility, however, couldn't validate the usernames supplied and therefore rejected the request. To see this command succeed, you can replace the account names shown with ones that exist on your system. Or you can remove the -U switch and its parameters to make the project and then add users or groups later with the projmod utility.

All the options available with the projadd utility are listed in Table 9-3. The project name is always the final parameter. In addition to options for setting up each field, the projadd utility lets you write entries to an alternate file (-f) and verify the syntax of existing records (-n). Note that the -n option does not look for bogus values in an existing record, only an incorrect record.

The attributes you can add to a project are best treated as a separate subject; I'll discuss those later in the chapter. A project's attributes are a list of key-value pairs, where the values themselves also take a special form. Most project keys are resource controls you use to limit the demands a workload can make on your system. As you'll see in the upcoming section, there are controls you can use to limit the number of CPUs, the amount of RAM, and even the number of lightweight processes (LWPs) a workload may allocate.

TABLE 9-3	Option to projadd	Description
	-p	Project ID
Options to the projadd Utility	-c	Comment string
	-U	User list
	-G	Group list
	-K	Attribute list
	-f	Alternate file to use
	-n	Check entries (syntax only)

Deleting a project has the same effect as deleting a user account. It removes the name and description from the file (or database), but any active processes using the project ID are not affected. The name goes away, but the projid is still attached. In the following example, I deleted my account's default project and checked the project ID:

```
$ sudo projdel ocademo
$ id -p
uid=60004(mfernest) gid=10(staff) projid=105
```

If I add the project back as it was, the name reappears. If you want to experiment with project entries, it's a good idea to use an alternate file for testing. If you intend to edit the file by hand, bear in mind the -n option does not validate data, just the record syntax.

For managing existing projects, the projmod command has many of the same options as the projadd command (including options to check syntax and use an alternate file). It also includes options for specifying the kind of change you want to make to a user, group, or attribute list. You can remove an existing value, replace existing values, or add to them. These additional options are described in Table 9-4.

It's a good idea to test these new options carefully. Replacing existing users when you meant to add news ones can quickly upset an active project. Changing a project name has no direct effect on a running process because the process data structure only stores the project ID. It could, however, affect any scripts that check project names as part of their work. Notice also that it's possible to address the same project ID with different names.

TABLE 9-4	projmod Option	Description
Additional Options Available with the projmod Utility	-A	Apply specified data to active projects
	-a	Add data to the field listed
	-s	Switch fields with the data provided
	-r	Remove data from the fields
	-l	Change the project name
	-o	Allow duplicate project IDs (used with -p)

To demonstrate each of these options, I've created a file called /testproj and added in the following records, using existing accounts on my system:

```
$ cat /testproj
punjab:201:Diamond:mfernest,toby,testing::
newhart:1000:Hospitality:toby:!staff:
solitude:5555:Fortress:testing,!*::
```

I use a different option on each record to show adding, switching, and removing a field, as follows:

```
$ sudo projmod -f /testproj -s -U '!*' punjab
$ sudo projmod -f /testproj -a -G adm newhart
$ sudo projmod -f /testproj -r -U testing solitude
```

With these commands, I expect to have replaced the users in the punjab project with no one allowed, added the group adm to the newhart project, and removed the user testing from the solitude project:

```
$ cat /testproj
punjab:201:Diamond:!*::
newhart:1000:Hospitality:toby:!staff,adm:
solitude:5555:Fortress:!*::
```

Finally, because I've excluded everyone from the solitude project, I'll rename it:

```
$ sudo projmod -f /testproj -l empty solitude
$ grep empty /testproj
empty:5555:Fortress:!*::
```

The practices you develop in managing project records this way, along with the utilities you've learned for managing user and group records, will hold you in good stead as you learn more Solaris command interfaces. The trend has been moving away for a long time from hand-editing these simple but important files to using tools that validate their syntax and content. Some configuration files, such as the manifest used for services and IPS packages, use XML grammars to standardize syntax. Others are moving into the SMF configuration repository for the sake of a centralized location and to allow a service to manage startups for you. It has all been done in the name of reducing the trouble that can arise from typos and other errors that are easier for a machine to spot than the human eye.

Understanding Tasks

Some workloads consist of many parts. When you log in to your Solaris 11 system with a user.*username* project in effect, that project is charged with every process that runs under your account name, including all the programs that comprise your windowing system. Even though you want to know the total resource demand of that login session, you might also like to see how it breaks down between windowing system and shell program demand.

On a larger scale, you might have multiple services that work together in a loose fashion, such as a database that various processes all use, acting as proxies for remote clients. Let's say some of those clients represent customers, vendors, database administrators, and business managers. Each group has a different level of authorization and needs a different view of the data. As a systems administrator, you want to account for all this activity as one workload, but you also want to distinguish between types of use.

Tasks are directly associated with a number of related processes. It takes a little more work to observe them because they do not have a command interface like projects do. In the following example, I sort through all the processes by project and task ID. I filter the results to display only tasks associated with my default project (ocademo):

```
$ ps -o project,taskid -e | sort -u | grep ocademo
  ocademo    133
  ocademo    134
  ocademo    139
  ocademo    256
```

As it turns out, most of the processes I am running fall under the same task (133). The last three task IDs each cover one process. You can see which ones are using the ps command again and filtering the task ID:

```
$ ps -o fname,taskid -e | grep 256
/usr/bin/xscreensaver 256
```

A project of any complexity, especially one composed of different processes spawned by different users, will create a hierarchy of tasks and processes. Figure 9-2 illustrates the breakdown of processes currently running in my default project. The illustration includes a detail of ptree command output, indicating the usual way processes will add up under a single task.

If you have some technical background in UNIX fundamentals, you may be asking why have tasks, when you could possibly use process groups, sessions, or a similar abstraction that has been around for a while and is well known, at least by experienced administrators. The idea is the same, which is to relate some number of processes together with an abstraction to view them as a whole. The intended goal is to make sure each task can be assigned specific resource limits that affect all process-level demands under that task. Without going into full detail, it appears the task abstraction avoids certain limits or complications that leveraging one of these existing mechanisms would leave unanswered.

FIGURE 9-2

Project ocademo with tasks and process names or counts

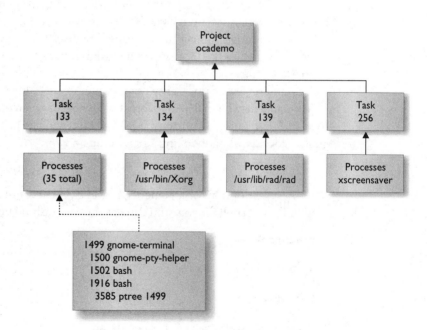

Managing Tasks at Run Time

The projects you may access are defined in the /etc/project file (or centralized name service). To use a project other than a default one, you need a way to assign a command (or running process) to it. Alternatively, you may want to create new tasks in order to have a separate accounting for the processes that are generated by it. The newtask utility provides the following capabilities:

- Run a command as a separate task
- Run a command in an assigned project
- Move a process from one project to another
- Refuse subsequent newtask commands when starting a process
- Emulate the login process before starting a process

You cannot choose the numeric task identifier or join a process to a current task. It can only be inherited from the parent process or generated by using the newtask utility. You therefore cannot assign an arbitrary collection of processes to a single task, only to a single project. If you wanted to do this, however, you could write a script that launches the processes you have in mind and then place that script in the appropriate project.

A careful review of this utility's syntax reveals these limits. Notice an assigned project name may be included before any process or command. A separate invocation is required for either case. Note also you may only finalize a task or emulate logging when invoking a new command:

```
newtask [-p project] [-v] [-c pid | [-Fl] [command...]]
```

Without any options or arguments, however, the newtask command will create another default shell for you. You can get the new task ID by using the -v option:

```
$ newtask -v
168
$ newtask -v
169
$ newtask -v
170
$ ps -o fname,taskid | grep bash
bash      168
bash      169
bash      170
bash      131
```

Executing these commands in the same window doesn't do much, however. In this case, the active task is the last one created. Creating a new task in each terminal session means all the work performed in each one can be accounted for differently, which can be helpful when you want to observe several long-running tasks you start by hand or by calling a script.

To demonstrate the newtask utility fully, you need an account with access to at least two projects. To that end, I have included the entries in my /etc/project file, shown here. I've also changed my /etc/user_attr configuration so the ocademo project is no longer my account's default. After a reboot, all processes associated with my login should be charged to the user.mfernest project:

```
user.mfernest:60004::::
gnome:11111:Desktop::staff:
ocademo:105::mfernest::
```

You can refer to the examples of the preceding prstat output and remind yourself what the report looks like with the -J option. As before, the user.mfernest project is now accountable for about 40 processes, and about 28% of RAM (that is, of the memory I've configured for the virtual machine I'm using). The graphic desktop system is fairly expensive on my limited resources—or seems to be.

I can verify this by tracing the processes associated with my desktop display and assigning them to the gnome project. Using the prstat -J command, I can then assess the relative demand those processes make. The approach I will take here isn't elegant, but it is easy to follow if you want to try as well. I started by using the ptree utility on my screensaver process, figuring it would show me a root process for some, if not all, of my desktop-related processes:

```
$ ptree `pgrep xscreensaver`
835    /usr/sbin/gdm-binary
  858    /usr/lib/gdm-simple-slave --display-id /org/gnome/DisplayManager/Displa
    1249   /usr/lib/gdm-session-worker
      1330   gnome-session
        1440   /usr/bin/xscreensaver -nosplash
```

It also occurred to me that PID 1330, the gnome-session process, might be running more than the screen saver, and perhaps other parent processes had other children, too. I ran the ptree utility using PID 835 and discovered 18 processes altogether, each of which I assigned to the gnome project with the following invocation:

```
$ sudo newtask -p gnome -c PID
```

The sudo invocation is necessary for any process not executed with my account's credentials. Unfortunately, the ptree command does not have an option to list just the PIDs; otherwise, I could write a brief script to loop through a newtask invocation for each one. The simplest approach starts the gdm-binary process in the gnome project; its children processes will naturally follow. Configuring that approach is beyond the scope of this book. Nonetheless, the prstat report now gives us a single line to report the resource demands of the gdm-binary process and all its children:

```
      13 root       20M    19M sleep   59     0    0:00:39 0.0% svc.configd/28
    1431 mfernest   32M    15M sleep   59     0    0:00:00 0.0% clock-applet/1
  PROJID    NPROC   SWAP   RSS MEMORY      TIME  CPU PROJECT
   11111       16  1011M  299M    19%  0:00:53 2.2% gnome
   60004       22   879M  166M    11%  0:00:12 1.0% user.mfernest
       0       65   440M  168M    11%  0:01:09 0.2% system
       3        1  3848K 2800K   0.2%  0:00:00 0.0% default
```

The gnome project does not yet include all processes that can be properly charged to the desktop. Also, each process will get its own task identifier. Use the -v option to receive this value. Having one task for each process in a project is fine for general reporting, but if you intend to configure resource limits as well, managing every process through its task will be tedious. Nonetheless, this exercise shows that you can separate the cost of processes that support your use of the system from the cost of processes you need to produce some direct result.

Finalizing a task means the command you invoke cannot create a new task. You can use this option to prevent spawned processes from charging their own processes to other projects or new tasks. To test this behavior, invoke a new shell process in a finalized task and then try to create another task in that session. Notice that using the root privilege to escape this setup won't work:

```
$ newtask -F ksh
$ newtask ksh
newtask: settaskid failed: Permission denied
$ sudo newtask ksh
Could not join default project
sudo: the invoking task is final
sudo: no resource pool accepting default bindings exists for project "user.root"
newtask: settaskid failed: Permission denied
```

A finalized setting is not an access-oriented attribute the root user may override. Rather, it is an immutable setting that limits how the current task may operate. It is not therefore suitable for the following examples in the chapter. If you are following along on your own system, dismiss this terminal window or put it aside and use a different one.

How to use the -l option to your advantage may appear simple or tricky, depending on how you use it. If you apply it as intended, it lets you start a session fresh in another project:

```
$ newtask -p ocademo -l
Oracle Corporation     SunOS 5.11     11.0     November 2011
You have new mail.
$ id -p
uid=60004(mfernest) gid=10(staff) projid=105(ocademo)
```

You can invoke a different shell if you wish. You can also invoke some other command, but if the new process depends on the environment of your original login, it may not function properly. A graphical program, such as a browser, will not work because it cannot receive the same environment context—GNOME processes are assigned to the same user, but there is also session information that distinguishes one user's login with the desktop session from one without it. It's helpful to think of a newtask -l invocation as if you were logging in from another machine:

```
$ newtask -p ocademo -l firefox
Error: no display specified $
$ newtask -p group.staff -l xterm
xterm Xt error: Can't open display:
xterm:   DISPLAY is not set
$ newtask -p group.staff -l man projects
...
```

You can now create projects as you wish and assign existing and new processes to them. If you already know how to write scripts to start long-running processes, you can add the newtask utility to assign them to separate projects and account for them accordingly. You don't even have to reboot after configuring if you don't want to. The newtask -c option lets you reassign a running process to your project of choice. You'll end up with a different task identifier for each moved process. If that's better than rebooting in the near future, so be it.

Managing Projects, Tasks, and Resource Controls

As I've said throughout the chapter, measuring resource demand by project, although useful, is also just a beginning. A project also gives you the means to apply resource limits by workload rather than by user or individual processes.

Chapter 10 covers the general concept of resource management as it applies to the whole system, in particular CPU resources (known as pools), process scheduling, and physical memory resources (known as resource caps). You can refer to the discussion in Chapter 11 for details on establishing file system quotas. Resource controls themselves (rctls, for short) apply to the project database and therefore affect only projects and the tasks and processes they govern.

Understanding Resource Controls

Resource controls are named by their type and the resource they apply to. All process-level controls, for example, begin with a "process." prefix. Each control declares an upper bound on a system resource, assuming the user has the proper authorization and the system has an available supply. Some of these controls rely on application-specific knowledge because they limit (or maximize) a specialized resource. All the process-level controls are listed and described in Table 9-5.

Some of these controls you may recognize based on the discussion regarding process utilities in Chapter 7. You can use the pmap utility, for example, to determine the heap, stack, and segment sizes currently allocated by a process. You can use the pfiles utility to see how many open descriptors a process has. Other controls listed here are specific resources used by relational databases—sharing memory, interprocess communication, and so on. You would normally apply these controls following the guidance of the product's vendor.

There are only three controls for tasks, all meant to control the aggregate demands of the processes they oversee. Table 9-6 lists and describes these controls.

Task controls are limiting agents, by and large. You would most likely use them to ensure an included process doesn't run away. These limits act as ceilings for their process-level counterparts. That is, a process control setting cannot override a task

TABLE 9-5   Project Resource Controls for Processes

Process Control	Description	Type/Unit
process.max-address-space	Total segment size allowed	Bytes
process.max-core-size	Core file size allowed	Bytes
process.max-cpu-time	CPU time allowed	Seconds
process.max-data-size	Heap size allowed	Bytes
process.max-file-descriptor	Open files allowed at one time	Integer
process.max-file-size	Largest writable range for a file	Bytes
process.max-msg-messages	Total queued messages allowed	Integer
process.max-msq-qbytes	Total size of messages allowed	Integer
process.max-port-events	Total events allowed per port	Integer
process.max-sem-nsems	Total semaphores allowed per set	Integer
process.max-sem-ops	Total operations allowed per call	Integer
process.max-stack-size	Stack space limit	Bytes

control setting. This condition also means it is possible for a task to reduce, without explicitly allocating resources itself, the limits that may be set at the project level. Thus, different tasks can express different tolerances for process resource demands.

Some project-level controls are redundant as a result, but also applicable as overrides to process or task settings. Rather than include them in a table with redundant descriptions, I'll list them here:

- project.max-lwps
- project.max-processes

TABLE 9-6   Project Resource Controls for Tasks

Task Control	Description	Type/Size
task.max-cpu-time	Total CPU time for processes	Seconds
task.max-lwps	Total LWPs allowed	Integer
task.max-processes	Total processes allowed	Integer

These two aside, project controls take an aggregate view of the resources that processes will demand. Table 9-7 lists and describes the project-level controls.

The CPU controls (cpu-caps, cpu-shares, pool) can establish a fractional amount of CPU time in a couple of forms. You can also assign a project to work from a specific pool of CPUs; I detail the meaning of these settings in the next chapter. All the controls regarding identifiers limit the instances of a resource type a process can use; the project provides a limit on all its processes using them. The memory resource controls how much kernel memory or RAM the project's processes may try to reserve. Although you can limit processes by their map size, that amount relates to virtual memory (RAM and swap space combined). At the project level, you want to make sure the workload does not demand more RAM than you want to allow.

TABLE 9-7   Project Resource Controls for Projects

Project Control	Description	Size/Type
project.cpu-caps	Available percentage of one CPU	Integer
project.cpu-shares	Used with Fair Share Scheduler	Integer
project.max-contracts	Total system contracts available	Integer
project.max-crypto-memory	Kernel memory for crypto operations	Bytes
project.max-locked-memory	Total RAM that can be locked	Bytes
project.max-msg-ids	Total message queue identifiers	Integer
project.max-port-ids	Total event port identifiers	Integer
project.max-sem-ids	Total semaphore identifiers	Integer
project.max-shm-ids	Total share memory identifiers	Integer
project.max-shm-memory	Total shared memory	Bytes
project.max-tasks	Total tasks allowed	Integer
project.pool	Assigned CPU pool	String

exam

watch

Specific knowledge of all resource controls is not required for the exam. As mentioned at the top of the chapter, however, understanding how resource controls work with projects will deepen your understanding of resource controls as they apply to Solaris Zones.

Eleven resource controls are dedicated to zones. As you will see in Chapter 17, every operating system instance in Solaris 10 or Solaris 11 is a zone. There is a distinction between the global zone, which contains the kernel, and local zones, which isolate their operating environment from other local zones. There's some potential for confusion because projects in the global zone are not, strictly speaking, on par with projects in a local zone. Except, that is, that all projects are subordinate to the zones that host them.

All but two zone controls are redundant controls found at the process, task, or project level. These controls can be used by themselves, or to establish an upper bound for controls applied at these lower levels:

- zone.cpu-cap
- zone.cpu-shares
- zone.max-locked-memory
- zone.max-lwps
- zone.max-msg-ids
- zone.max-processes
- zone.max-sem-ids
- zone.max-shm-ids
- zone.max-shm-memory

The two remaining controls affect resource behavior for a zone only and bear no direct relationship to any project. I list them here so this chapter presents a full record, but I detail their meaning and use in Chapter 17:

- zone.max-lofi
- zone.max-swap

One last control, named rcap.max-rss, is not tied directly to these abstractions. This control lets you limit the total memory, in the form of resident set size (RSS), that all processes in a project may accumulate. Remember that you can observe both the virtual size and RSS of a process through the default output of the prstat command. As you will learn in Chapter 17, you can also apply this control to a zone.

For the moment, think of a zone as a kind of project that can isolate a number of processes as well as manage resources for them. There's more to a zone than that, of course, but for the moment you don't need the whole conceptual model. A zone, as an isolated operating environment, may also contain projects. When that's done, zone controls take precedence over project controls, just as project controls take precedence over task controls, and so on, with process controls. Figure 9-3 illustrates all the resource boxing at work using all these facilities.

FIGURE 9-3

Resource controls applied to zones, projects, task and processes

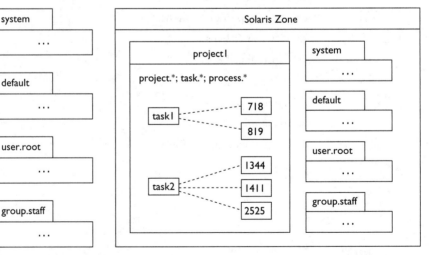

Figure 9-3 doesn't reflect it for lack of space, but you can also apply resource controls to system-defined projects. Be thoughtful when applying controls to a default project; processes that are not tied to named projects end up in one of these groups. If you have a lot of incidental workload and tight constraints applied to your default projects, you could see a lot of unwanted behavior when these projects reach their limits.

Defining Resource Controls as Attributes

At long last, you are ready to apply resource controls to a project. Now that you understand how to manage a project, assign processes, and identify the controls available, you need one more piece: how to specify a control with the proper format. If you already tried adding an attribute with the projmod or projadd utility, you might have seen this result, which doesn't do anything:

```
$ sudo projmod -a -K project.max-tasks ocademo
$ projects -l ocademo
ocademo
     projid : 105
     comment: ""
     users  : mfernest
     groups : (none)
     attribs: project.max-tasks
```

It's legal syntax to name a resource control without specifying a value. The documentation I have reviewed does not say what purpose it serves to allow this, but there it is. You may also have discovered it's insufficient to supply a value:

```
$ sudo projmod -s -K project.max-tasks=128 ocademo
projmod: rctl "project.max-tasks" value "128" should be in ()'s
$ sudo projmod -s -K "project.max-tasks=(128)" ocademo
projmod: rctl "project.max-tasks" value missing action "(128)"
projmod: rctl "project.max-tasks" unknown privilege "128"
projmod: rctl "project.max-tasks" missing value
```

It's not just a matter of naming a resource and a limit for it. Three elements are required to specify a resource control:

■ **Privilege**   Defines who can modify the resource setting (at run time)

■ **Value**   Establishes the resource limit

■ **Action**   Defines what happens if you reach the limit

The privilege value can be set to basic or priv (for privileged); the default is basic. There is also a system privilege, which means the value given for the resource cannot be changed during the operating system session; this setting is not applied by a project, but exists for all resource controls as a hard limit. When an attribute is set to basic privilege, you can use the prctl utility (discussed later) to modify the limit. You might do this when you feel the constraint has been improperly set or needs to be raised without interrupting the system. The privileged setting also allows a run-time change, but only if the calling process has the sys_resource privilege enabled.

on the Job

See the man page for privileges. The privilege model is discussed briefly in Chapter 5.

The value is understood as the unit specified in the resource control tables shown earlier. There are also suffixes you can use to signify a larger unit of measure for bytes, seconds, and integers. For example, you can use 5K to mean 5MB, 5,000 seconds, or 5,000 units, depending on the base unit of the control. The man page for resource_controls provides a complete table.

The actions that apply to project attributes are known as *local actions*, in contrast to global actions, which are covered in Chapter 10. When a resource limit is met or exceeded—whether it is set at the process, task, project, or zone level—the violation is assigned to the process responsible for inducing it. Should a violation occur, you can execute one of three actions:

- **none** Take no action.
- **deny** Refuse the request.
- **signal=*signal*** Send the defined signal to the assigned process.

In each case, the action should reflect a desired outcome for the process that is subject to it. Let's say you set a limit of the number of file descriptors a project's processes may have. If one process happens to exceed that limit, is it better to observe the condition and take a later action, or to return an error for the process, indicating a refused request, or to issue a valid signal to the process, which may cause the process to terminate?

Some resource control violations cannot be caused by a process request. CPU controls other than process.cpu-time and task.cpu-time fall into this category. In such cases, process-level actions have no meaning. Also, some actions can be thwarted by the actions allowed at a global level. These details are also included with Chapter 10.

To apply a control as a project attribute, you specify a privilege, a value, and an action as a comma-separated list in parentheses. Let's say I want to limit the number of file descriptors any one process can have in project ocademo to 128. Any process that attempts to open more should be refused. I want to restrict changing this limit to users with the sys_resource privilege. The following incantation will set the control:

```
$ sudo projmod -s -K process.max-file-descriptors="(priv,128,deny)" ocademo
$ projects -l ocademo
ocademo
     projid : 105
     comment: ""
     users  : mfernest
     groups : (none)
     attribs: process.max-file-descriptors=(priv,128,deny)
```

Let's add a few more controls to see what the record entry will look like:

```
$ sudo projmod -s -K project.max-tasks="(priv,32,signal=SIGHUP)" ocademo
$ sudo projmod -s -K process.max-tasks="(priv,128,deny)" ocademo
$ sudo projmod -s -K task.max-lwps="(basic,128,none)" ocademo
$ projects -l ocademo
ocademo
     projid : 105
     comment: ""
     users  : mfernest
     groups : (none)
     attribs: process.max-file-descriptors=(priv,128.deny)
              process.max-tasks=(priv,128,deny)
              project.max-tasks=(priv,32,signal=SIGHUP)
              project.max-tasks
              task.max-lwps=(basic,128,none)
```

Notice that the value for any key can have multiple parts. Each value can specify one privilege level, one limit, and one action. This arrangement, however, does not prevent you from applying more than one action or threshold, or even one value per privilege level.

Managing Resource Controls at Run Time

In order to establish hard limits, the system applies a global hard limit to every resource control. Even if you don't set these controls yourself, they apply to every active process, task, and project. When you do apply these controls as project attributes, you are setting limits equal to or lower than the system limit using the privileged and basic privileges. Following this model, you might think of the privileged setting as a firm limit—where you tend to deny requests for more resources—and the basic setting as a soft limit—where you tend to observe demands for more resources.

The controls associated with a process include all process, task, project, and zone controls, for a total of 39 controls. For a task, the process controls are removed from view, leaving 27. For a project, all task and process controls are removed from view, leaving 24. For zones there are 11 controls. You can obtain these results yourself using the prctl command. This example uses the -P option to report each control on a single line. The -i option introduces the type of abstraction you're seeking followed by an identifier for that type:

```
$ prctl -P -i process $$ | grep system | wc -l
      39
$ ps -o taskid= -p $$
   131
$ prctl -P -i task 131 | grep system | wc -l
      27
$ ps -o projid= -p $$
60004
$ prctl -P -i project 60004 | grep system | wc -l
      24
$ prctl -P -i zone 0 | grep system | wc -l
      11
```

Each control may report up to four lines, one for usage information and one for each privilege level, if set. By filtering the system lines out and taking a count, I get the number of controls displayed for each type. Notice I added an equal sign to the process fields I wanted to report; this symbol eliminates the column header. Your operating system is also known as the global zone, which always has the identifier 0.

The prctl utility has two functions: to get or set the value of a resource control for one or more types. With no options applied, the default behavior assumes a process ID has been supplied and returns all controls at all privilege levels for that process. You can test this with the command prctl $$ if you want; you'll receive about 115 lines of output, depending on the number of non-system privilege controls that are in effect.

To get filtered output, you specify the privilege level and name for the control you want. The -P option strips the spaces out and renders all values to their lowest unit of measure:

```
$ prctl -n project.max-lwps -i project 60004
project: 60004: user.mfernest
NAME       PRIVILEGE        VALUE    FLAG   ACTION              RECIPIENT
project.max-lwps
       usage            102
       system           2.15G    max    deny                    -
$ prctl -P -n project.max-lwps -i project 60004
project: 60004: user.mfernest
project.max-lwps usage 102 - - -
project.max-lwps system 2147483647 max deny -
```

The usage line shows the project currently uses 102 LWPs. You can sometimes corroborate these usage numbers with other tools; the prctl utility just saves you the trouble. In this case, you could list all processes by LWP that belong to the user. mfernest project and count them:

```
$ ps -o project -Le | grep user.mfernest | wc -l
   102
```

The system setting is not a hardware limit. It's the limit of the data type (a 32-bit signed integer) the kernel uses to count LWPs—far more than you'd be able to use, even on a very large system. Many system limits reflect the range of the storage type in the code, not the hardware.

The syntax gets a bit more involved when you want to modify an active control. Table 9-8 gives a brief rundown of the modify options.

TABLE 9-8	prtcl Modify Option	Description
Modify Operation Options for the prctl Utility	-t	Privilege level (basic or privileged)
	-p	Recipient PID
	-r	Replace first matching control with -v value
	-s	Set new resource control with -v value
	-x	Delete specified control
	-v	Value
	-e/-d	Enable/disable action

Using the -t option, you can specify the basic or privileged level of the control to modify. The system level is only valid for getting the value. If you are changing a control for a task, project, or zone, you must address the change to a member PID using the -p option. Similar to the way you modify a project entry, you must also specify if you are setting, replacing, or removing a control. The -v option is only necessary for setting or replacing operations. The conditions for enabling or disabling actions is a bit more involved; consult the prctl man page for full details.

This example shows the number of file descriptors permitted for the Firefox browser running on my system. Although the action for the basic and privileged levels is the same, the basic level is lower. Presumably it's intended as a soft limit.

```
$ prctl -n process.max-file-descriptor `pgrep firefox`
process: 1647: /usr/lib/firefox/firefox-bin
NAME     PRIVILEGE         VALUE     FLAG   ACTION              RECIPIENT
process.max-file-descriptor
         basic              800       -     deny                   1647
         privileged        65.5K      -     deny                    -
         system            2.15G     max    deny
```

I don't need the sys_resource privilege to raise the basic level value. I also don't need to specify basic with the -t option to set the value because it is the default. I can just use prctl to replace 800 with 1K. To confirm the change, I include the -t option to limit the output:

```
$ prctl -n process.max-file-descriptor -v 1K -r 1647
$ prctl -n process.max-file-descriptor -t basic 1647
process: 1647: /usr/lib/firefox/firefox-bin
NAME     PRIVILEGE         VALUE     FLAG   ACTION              RECIPIENT
process.max-file-descriptor
         basic             1.00K      -     deny                   1647
```

The prctl man page has a few more examples. The rules for matching controls may seem complex, but naming the control, level, and type of resource control will help you avoid having to observe all of them on every query. In the next chapter, you'll learn to use the rctladm utility, which gives you the means to observe these thresholds and integrate them with the logging services covered in Chapter 13.

CERTIFICATION SUMMARY

The primary goal of this overview on projects and resource controls is to give you a better foundation for understanding zones, both for the OCA exam and for systems administration practice. Without this foundation knowledge, it's easy to assume resource management "just works" for zones. All it takes, however, is one hand-edited zone configuration with a typo in it to create errors or failures you may not be skilled or knowledgeable enough to correct. Without knowing how resource controls are implemented or where to look them up, it could be a long time before you identify the trouble. For example, I once fixed an rctl that was written as (basic,1K. deny). The customer, a big user of zones, had tried to isolate the symptoms back to this cause for weeks. I am sure they simply glossed over this typo several times.

The next chapter, on resource management, is also a run-up to zones. It's not material you must have for the OCA exam, but I hope you'll take me at my word that it's important to learn now: As a practicing systems administrator, some understanding of resource management can save you a lot of grief. Waiting until you prepare for the OCP exam to learn it is, in my view, just a bad idea.

✓ TWO-MINUTE DRILL

Understanding Projects

❑ All Solaris processes have a project identifier as part of their metadata.

❑ The five predefined projects are system, user.root, noproject, default, and group.staff.

❑ Project definitions can be configured in a local file (/etc/project) or stored in a database served by a lookup service such as NIS or an LDAP server.

❑ The default project for any user/role account can be set in the /etc/user_attr file.

Understanding Tasks

❑ A task is one collection of processes that belong to a project.

❑ Parent processes pass their project and task identifiers to their child processes.

❑ You can retrieve the task ID of a process with the ps -o command option.

Managing Project, Task, and Process Resources

❑ Only the system can generate task identifiers.

❑ The newtask utility lets you assign an active process or new command to a project, or just a new task group.

❑ The prctl utility lets you get or set the resource controls of active processes, tasks, and projects.

SELF TEST

Use the following questions to test your recall and understanding of the chapter's material.

Understanding Projects

1. You just added a new end-user account, robert, to a Solaris system. Which project will his processes be charged to by default?
A.   group.staff
B.   user.root
C.   default
D.   user.robert

2. Which project is accessible by users joe and sally and the group blossom?
A.   blossom:155:joe:sally:blossom:
B.   bloom:201:Blossom:joe,sally:blossom:
C.   blossom:333::joe:sally,blossom:
D.   bloom:102::joe,sally:all:

3. What does the projects command do if invoked with no options or parameters?
A.   Lists all projects in the database
B.   Lists projects only in the /etc/project file
C.   Lists all default projects
D.   Lists all projects the current process can access

Understanding Tasks

4. Identify the correct statement regarding the newtask command's features.
A.   You can finalize any process's task.
B.   You can change your default project.
C.   You can change the project of your current shell.
D.   You can join any project.

5. What is the minimum number of tasks an active project can have?
- **A.** Zero
- **B.** One
- **C.** Two
- **D.** Three

Managing Project, Task, and Process Resources

6. Select the option that is not a valid resource control.
- **A.** process.max-lwps
- **B.** task.max-lwps
- **C.** project.max-lwps
- **D.** zone.max-lwps

7. Which two commands can you use to assign resource controls to a project?
- **A.** projadd
- **B.** newtask
- **C.** prctl
- **D.** rctladm

8. Which one of these attribute values could be valid?
- **A.** (basic, 5, none)
- **B.** (100, basic, deny)
- **C.** (deny, 25K, priv)
- **D.** (priv, 25, signal=)

9. What is the resource limit for projects?
- **A.** No limit
- **B.** The system level value of zone.max-projects
- **C.** The system level value of project.max-processes
- **D.** The system level value of zone.max-tasks

10. How many attributes can you assign to a single process control?
- **A.** One
- **B.** Two
- **C.** Three
- **D.** More than three

SELF TEST ANSWERS

Understanding Projects

1. ☑ **A.** The default group for a new user is staff (10).

   ☒ **B, C,** and **D** are incorrect. **B** is incorrect because only processes run from a root-owned shell will be charged to this project. **C** is incorrect because this project covers users who do not belong to the staff group. **D** is incorrect because user.*username* projects are not created by default.

2. ☑ **B.** There are six fields in a project record, and these hold the project name, project ID, comment, users, groups, and attributes. Multiple users or groups are separated by a comma.

   ☒ **A, C,** and **D** are incorrect. **A** is incorrect because user joe is listed in the comment field. **C** is incorrect because the group blossom is listed in the user field. **D** is incorrect because "all" is not a predefined group or a wildcard.

3. ☑ **D.** By default, the projects command lists the projects accessible to the current user.

   ☒ **A, B,** and **C** are incorrect. **A** is incorrect because you can accomplish this with the projects -l or projects -v command. **B** is incorrect because the projects command does not determine if it reads the local file or something else. That decision is configured in the /etc/nsswitch.conf file. **C** is incorrect because there is no option for listing all projects that serve as defaults.

Understanding Tasks

4. ☑ **C.** The newtask -p *otherproject* -c $$ command will change the project of your current shell.

   ☒ **A, B,** and **D** are incorrect. **A** is incorrect because you can only finalize tasks for a new command, not a running process. **B** is incorrect because you can only change your default project by configuring the /etc/project file and/or the /etc/user_attr file. **D** is incorrect because you can only join projects that include you as a user or as part of a group.

5. ☑ **B.** For a project to be active, it must have at least one process. Every process must have a task identifier.

   ☒ **A, C,** and **D** are incorrect. **A** is incorrect because a project with no active processes is not in use. **C** and **D** are incorrect because a single process is sufficient to put a project in play.

Managing Project, Task, and Process Resources

6. ☑ **A.** You can control the number of LWPs available at every level except per process.
   ☒ **B, C,** and **D** are incorrect. These are all valid resource controls.

7. ☑ **A** and **C.** You can use the projadd utility to include attributes when you create a project. You can use prctl to set new attributes on an active process, task, or project.
   ☒ **B** and **D** are incorrect. **B** is incorrect because the newtask utility cannot modify resource control limits. **D** is incorrect because the rctladm command does not affect project-level (local) attributes.

8. ☑ **A.** The order for resource control attribute is privilege level, value, action.
   ☒ **B, C,** and **D** are incorrect. **B** and **C** have their attributes out of place. **D** is incomplete; a signal action must be declared because there is no default.

9. ☑ **A.** There is a practical upper limit for active projects, which is the number of processes running if each one runs in its own project. There is, however, no set limit for active projects.
   ☒ **B, C,** and **D** are incorrect. **B** is not a valid resource control. **C** and **D** could be inferred limits for active projects, assuming again every process ran in its own project, but they do not establish an expressed limit on the number of projects.

10. ☑ **D.** You can assign an attribute for each value you want to use as a limit. The following key-value pair is valid: process.max-cpu-time=(priv,30,signal=SIGXCPU),(priv,40,signal=SIGTERM),(priv,50,signal=SIGKILL).
    ☒ **A, B,** and **C** are incorrect. You are not limited to one privilege level, or to the number of changeable privilege levels, or even to the number of listed privilege levels.

10
Applying Resource Thresholds

I n Chapter 9, you learned how Solaris projects can help isolate a group of processes, collectively called a *workload*. Using a project, you can more easily observe the resource demands a workload makes and place limits on its consumption at the process, task, project, and zone levels using resource controls. It takes a while to appreciate the meaning and best use of all the controls, but that learning can come over time as your need for these tools dictates. The key objective for now is that you know Solaris provides this capability and using it can make monitoring Solaris systems a lot easier.

But wait, there's more! In addition to the process-oriented controls I detailed in the last chapter, Solaris also provides facilities that extend merely setting and observing thresholds into creating a fully virtualized environment of resources. An administrator can also do the following:

- Incorporate system logging into resource controls
- Control physical memory demand
- Change the process-scheduling rules
- Manage CPU availability in a fine-grained and coarse-grained way

There's another feature that belongs to this list, too, but it isn't covered until Chapter 16: creating virtualized network components. These can be controlled using what are called *flows*. But I'm getting a bit ahead of myself: The reason for introducing these subjects now is to prepare foundation knowledge for what Solaris Zones are and how they work. These foundation topics come up as subjects for the Oracle Certified Professional exam, and for that exam you'll need to understand them in greater detail than I am presenting here. For now, it's all about building up to zones, which are presented in Chapter 17, in a more careful and gradual manner.

CERTIFICATION OBJECTIVE 10.01

Logging Resource Thresholds

In Chapter 9, I described the utilities you can use to set and observe various resource thresholds at various levels of privilege. The /etc/project file gives you the means to manage these settings statically, whereas the prctl command lets you manage them on the fly. I reserved from that discussion any mention of the rctladm command for one reason: It integrates resource monitoring with the system logging facility, and the book doesn't cover how logging works until Chapter 13.

Here's the short course on logging: In order to notify administrators of various events in the course of operation, many processes write to a file in a process generally called *logging*. The administrator can refer to these files, or *logs*, to understand behavior that relates to the process's current state or actions. Many applications, such as databases and HTTP servers, maintain their own logs because their information is specialized and targeted toward an administrator with specific knowledge of that software.

For kernel-based service and system-oriented processes, however, a centralized logging system is a more efficient use of resources. On the Solaris platform, the syslogd process is responsible for reading these notices. Each service or process, generally called a *facility*, can issue a message describing some event. The message includes a *severity* to suggest how important the message is to the facility's state. The syslogd process reads these messages and, based on its configuration, may write them to a file for later reference or just ignore them.

With resource attributes, the actions you can invoke when exceeding a threshold include doing nothing, refusing the extra allocation, and sending a signal to the requesting process. The rctladm utility lets you go one step further by issuing notices to the system logging facility. This utility manages the *global state* of each resource control, which includes:

- Whether system logging is enabled
- The level of severity at which notices are sent
- The flags that pertain to each attribute

Executing the rctladm command without arguments will list every resource control (39 altogether), along with its logging state, and global flags. The default for logging is off, excepting a few resource controls for which logging is unavailable; these are marked "n/a" in the output:

```
$ rctladm | grep n\/a
project.cpu-cap          syslog=n/a...
project.cpu-shares       syslog=n/a...
zone.cpu-cap             syslog=n/a...
zone.cpu-shares          syslog=n/a...
```

The records produced by the rctladm command are wide. For the sake of the book's format, I've removed the third column from this output. Also note that I've used a backslash to interpret the forward slash as a literal character. The output shows two properties: cpu-cap and cpu-shares. These values, once set, are hard limits. There is no call a process can make to increase CPU resources. The sched process selects processes for execution and assigns them to an eligible CPU, and cannot request more CPUs to handle a workload that saturates the current allocation. Because there is no way to exceed established caps or shares, logging a violation is irrelevant.

Each resource control also has a list of global flags to describe attribute qualities that cannot be modified, including:

- A control's unit of measure (count, bytes, seconds)
- Valid or required signals
- Valid or required actions

For example, the output for the process.max-cpu-time control will show the following global flags:

```
$ rctladm process.max-cpu-time
process.max-cpu-time   ...   [ lowerable no-deny cpu-time inf seconds ]
```

These values are described in Table 10-1.

Each flag describes a condition established by the nature of the resource. Similar to a task that has been finalized, as discussed in Chapter 9, these are immutable settings that cannot be overridden by privileged users. Every resource control has at least one global flag that documents the unit of measure it uses (count, bytes, seconds).

TABLE 10-1	Global flag	Description
Global Flags for the process. max-cpu-time Resource Control	lowerable	Non-privileged callers may lower this control's value.
	no-deny	The deny action is disallowed.
	cpu-time	The SIGXCPU signal is valid.
	inf	Resource is considered virtually infinite.
	seconds	Allocation is measured in seconds.

on the **job** *The full list is documented in the man page for the rctblk_set_value library function. This page also documents local resource flags. There's no need to memorize these flags. Just knowing where to look if you see an unfamiliar one in rctladm output will save you a bit of time.*

The rctladm utility supports four switch options, which are described in Table 10-2. Using the -l option, you can name any controls you want to print using a space-delimited list. With or without the -l option, if you name no controls, the command prints out all 39 of them:

```
rctladm -l process.max-data-size project.max-tasks
process.max-data-size      syslog=off...
project.max-tasks          syslog=off...
```

Again I have truncated the output because a full listing is too wide for the page.

Using the -e option, you can enable logging for one or more controls. You can also establish a higher level of severity than the default, called notice. Here are two examples—one relies on the default severity, the other establishes a higher level:

```
$ sudo rctladm -e syslog zone.max-lofi
$ sudo rctladm -e syslog=info project.max-lwps
$ rctladm -l zone.max-lofi project.max-lwps
zone.max-lofi              syslog=notice...
project.max-lwps           syslog=info...
```

Once you have changed the action for a single control, the system creates the file /etc/rctladm.conf and writes the settings for all controls to it. You can then use the -u option to read in settings from this file as you like. It is also read by the SMF service svc:/system/resource-controls:default when it starts up, so the settings can be

TABLE 10-2	rctladm Switch	Description
Switches for the rctladm Utility	-l [names]	List all (or selected) resource control information
	-u	Read settings from the /etc/rctladm.conf file
	-d [all | name]	Disable logging for one or all resource controls
	-e syslog[=severity] name	Enable logging (at an explicit level of severity)

applied at boot time. The -u switch only reads the whole file; any named controls after the switch are ignored. Here is an excerpt of the file to show the format of the records:

```
$ cat /etc/rctladm.conf | grep -v none
#
# rctladm.conf
#
# Parameters for resource controls configuration.
# Do NOT edit this file by hand -- use rctladm(1m) instead.
#
project.max-lwps=syslog=info
zone.max-lofi=syslog=notice
```

I've used grep -v command to strip all lines containing the string "none." The result preserves the file's preamble, which reminds you to prefer using the tool over manually editing the contents (good advice). Remember that the kernel doesn't save configuration changes to itself. If you're changing the default configuration of a service, the changes have to go somewhere: either in a file or in the service configuration repository, as discussed in Chapter 8.

You can disable global logging for a control with the -d option and the control's name. So long as you name any valid control, regardless of its current configuration, the command will not return an error. Disabling a disabled control will return quietly. You can observe the effect either by running the rctladm command again or by reviewing the contents of the /etc/rctladm.conf file.

To see what such notices look like and how the information works its way from a threshold violation to a system log file, see Chapter 13.

CERTIFICATION OBJECTIVE 10.02

Capping Memory

Take a look at the resource controls that refer to memory:

```
$ rctladm | cut -f1 -d ' ' | grep memory
project.max-locked-memory
project.max-shm-memory
project.max-crypto-memory
zone.max-locked-memory
zone.max-shm-memory
```

Each of these controls constrains a specific attribute for memory (locked, shared, used by cryptographic operations) that be may be included in a process's overall allocation. None of them can limit the total memory that is visible to a process. A *memory cap* does that work; by definition, it has to operate as a supervisory control. That is, when the process's total memory allocation is taken into account, a supervisory control asks whether this amount, regardless of how it is specified or put to use, falls within bounds established by the administrator. To better understand how a memory cap works, a review of what we've learned about the pmap utility will help.

You may remember that a pmap command will output two kinds of memory allocation for a process: the resident set size (RSS) and the virtual size, reported as SIZE by the ps and prstat utilities and the column Kbytes in pmap output. The Kbytes refers to how much memory the process wants guaranteed by the system to support a segment. The RSS refers to how much physical memory the process currently occupies. Here are the first few lines of output for my shell program:

```
$ pmap -x $$ | head -6
1963:   ksh
             Address      Kbytes      RSS      Anon   Locked Mode   Mapped File
0000000000400000             4          4        -        - r-x--   ksh93
0000000000411000             4          4        -        - rw---   ksh93
0000000000412000            48         36        -        - rw---   [ heap ]
FFFFFD7FFE600000          6756        212        -        - r-x--   en_US.UTF-8.so.3
```

Notice the RSS value can be the same or smaller than the virtual size. The process segment gets a discount if some portion of its guaranteed size has already been mapped into memory by another process. This size is guaranteed by charging the total amount from *virtual memory*, or the sum of physical memory and swap space the system has available. The RSS is charged against actual RAM.

Let's say you have 16GB of RAM, and it's more than enough for your current workload. You'd still like to limit how much physical memory is made available to some project or zone. Maybe you're worried about memory leaks from a long-running process, or too many spurious memory-hungry processes being raised at once. Or maybe you'd just like to know when the physical memory demand of some workload exceeds an expected amount. What's the most effective way to impose a limit?

In Solaris the answer is a *memory cap*. A cap constrains just the physical (resident) memory a project or zone consumes. It is still a threshold in one sense. When the cap is exceeded, there is an action-oriented result. It is a predetermined action, or rather reaction, and although you can control the reaction by degree, through parameter settings, you cannot change what it does: move pages of memory from RAM to swap space until the offending project or zone's RAM consumption falls below the cap.

It's impractical to gauge memory demand after each allocation request. Instead, Solaris monitors capped memory controls with the rcapd daemon process, which responds when the total memory demand by a project or zone exceeds its configured limit. The rcapd daemon will *page out* sections of the RSS that are accessed infrequently (the specifics of paging are not documented). This action continues until the total RSS consumption falls below the assigned threshold. For a project, you can only set this attribute in its /etc/project entry. The prctl command does not operate on this key.

The control is rcap.max-rss; its base unit of measure is in bytes, although you can use the same suffixes as other controls to express larger units. You can also manage this control using the projadd and projmod utilities covered in Chapter 9. You cannot, however, put this control into effect on a currently active project. As noted earlier, the prctl utility does not work with this control. You can, however, add the control to an idle project, use the newtask utility to assign work to it, and then observe the behavior.

I created a project for the Firefox browser to cap its RSS demand and see what happens as I open more browser tabs. Once this is in place, I can launch my browser using the newtask utility and assign the process to its namesake project:

```
$ sudo projmod -K rcap.max-rss=150M firefox
$ projects -l firefox
firefox
     projid : 2222
     comment: "Browser"
     users  : mfernest
     groups : (none)
     attribs: rcap.max-rss=157286400
$ newtask -p firefox firefox &
$
```

The Firefox version I'm using launches its own process called plugin-container. It's a bit less noise on the screen if I show just these two processes in a prstat report. I can look up the PIDs for each process and pass them in by hand, which is easy enough to do, but I like to write command lines that are as expressive as I can make them:

```
$ prstat -J -c -p `pgrep firefox`,`pgrep plugin` 1 1
Please wait...
   PID USERNAME  SIZE   RSS STATE  PRI NICE      TIME  CPU PROCESS/NLWP
  5631 mfernest   98M   35M run     57    4   0:00:25 2.6% plugin-containe/3
  5614 mfernest  262M  101M sleep   37    4   0:00:05 0.0% firefox-bin/18
PROJID    NPROC  SWAP   RSS MEMORY      TIME  CPU PROJECT
  2222        2  360M  136M  8.7%   0:00:30 2.7% firefox
Total: 2 processes, 21 lwps, load averages: 0.06, 0.07, 0.07
```

At the moment, my browser has three tabs open to various sites and uses 136MB of my system's RAM. It turns out that the browser in normal operation can provide a dynamic workload, especially if the sites you visit run a lot of JavaScript and issue many callbacks to the site.

By default, the rcap service that initiates and monitors your memory caps is disabled. You can either reboot your system with at least one cap in place, and the service will start on its own, or enable it yourself. Once it's enabled, you can use the rcapstat utility to monitor the cap:

```
$ sudo svcadm enable rcap
$ svcs -p rcap
STATE        STIME    FMRI
online       8:27:27  svc:/system/rcap:default
             8:27:27     5705 rcapd
$ rcapstat
   id project        nproc    vm   rss   cap    at avgat    pg avgpg
 2222 firefox            2  182M  265M  150M  254M    0K   96M    0K
 2222 firefox            2  182M   14M  150M   73M   73M   19M   19M
 2222 firefox            -  182M   14M  150M    0K    0K    0K    0K
```

In the time I took to enable the service, the browser processes apparently increased their RSS demand. The rcapstat report, which repeats every five seconds by default, shows the reduction in size from 265MB to 14MB. The remaining statistics show what amount of *paging* took place to get the process under—well under—the 150MB cap. Each column for rcapstat output is described in Table 10-3.

The report breaks down paging activity into two sections: attempted paging and estimated successful paging. The rcapd process can't actually page memory out of another process. It can only mark (recommend) areas of memory for paging and ask the system to the do the work. Other factors only the kernel can observe contribute to when and how much paging the system will perform, and even when it does the rcapd process can only estimate the net result.

The paging activity captured previously, dropping RSS from 265MB down to 14MB, seems not only extreme but counterproductive. Indeed, the next time I used the browser it had to page a big part of its program map back into RAM, which caused a noticeable lag. Subsequent tests, in which I visited a few sites I often use, showed a tempered response and brought the RSS to just under the 150MB cap. It appears that rcapd becomes more aggressive (and less discriminating) to the degree the cap is exceeded.

TABLE 10-3   Output Columns of the rcapstat Utility

rcapstat Column	Description
id	Numeric identifier for the project (or zone)
project	Assigned name
nproc	Number of processes last observed
vm	Total program size (backed by memory or swap)
rss	Total resident size
cap	RSS cap
at	Total memory paging attempted by rcapd
avgat	Average paging attempt during interval
pg	Estimate of memory paged out
avgpg	Average estimated memory paged out

You can adjust this behavior with the rcapadm utility. Along with enabling or disabling the rcap SMF service for you, via the -E and -D switches, it can also adjust how often the rcapd process scans, samples, reports, and checks for new projects' caps. It can also assign memory caps to zones on the fly, as you'll learn in Chapter 17.

Use the rcapadm -c command to relax the enforcement of memory caps based on the availability of physical memory itself. The default is 0, meaning a cap is always enforced. The higher this number is set, the more physical memory must be consumed before enforcement starts. This setting allows you to set limits for monitoring but hold off on enforcement until it's necessary for keeping physical memory available to future demand.

All the interval-based parameters—scan, sample, report, and config—are set as key-value pairs following the -i switch. Remember, these settings are global and apply to any and all memory caps at once. By default, the rcapd process scans every 15 seconds, samples and reports every five seconds, and checks for new capping definitions every 60 seconds. The command to enable the service and declare the default settings would be as follows:

```
$ sudo rcapadm -E -i scan=15,sample=5,report=5,config=60 -c 0
```

It's not a good idea to apply a memory cap as a tight lid unless you are going to relax enforcement to some degree. Otherwise, the rcapd process will induce paging at every detected violation, and all processes may feel some collateral effect of frequent or heavy disk activity. Setting some kind of cap, however, also makes it easier to monitor consumption by the projects (or zones) that use them.

CERTIFICATION OBJECTIVE 10.03

Scheduling Processes

Using the rctladm command, you won't see any resource controls that relate to process scheduling. As with memory caps, scheduling is an aspect of system control that manages the environment in which processes operate. Although current process state and behavior have some influence on how it is scheduled, these forms (other than tweaking a process's priority) are indirect. It's the system's job to moderate the needs of all user processes and make sure every process gets time to execute.

That said, user process scheduling itself is open to configuration. You can apply several scheduling systems to one or more processes to establish the rules you think are a good fit for them. The process-scheduling systems you can use in Solaris 11 are listed in Table 10-4.

You'll learn more about these schedulers when you prepare for the OCP exam. The Fair-Share scheduler is important to us because it is designed specifically with projects (and zones) in mind. The project.cpu-caps resource control, when set, assumes the Fair-Share scheduler controls the project.

on the
job

You may come across two other scheduling classes that are not available for administrative use. One is called SYS and is used for threads that manage kernel services. Any thread in the SYS class can preempt a user thread for as long as it wants. The other is called SDC, short for System Duty Cycle. This scheduler uses the user and kernel priority ranges but is dedicated to ZFS.

Imagine for a moment you have several projects running, all with workloads you consider important to varying degrees, at least with respect to the compute power you have available. If you put all of your projects under the control of a Fair-Share scheduler, you can allot a relative amount of available computing resources to each one using a model based on shares. If you have five projects, each with the same number of shares, it's the same as saying you want each project to receive the same *minimum* of resources to process their workloads. Regardless of the number used to

TABLE 10-4   Process Schedulers Available in Solaris 11

Process Scheduler	Mnemonic	Description
Real-Time	RT	Fixed priority, deterministic response time
Time-Sharing	TS	Adjustable priority, good response time
Inter-Active	IA	Similar to TS (used with graphical desktop)
Fair-Share	FSS	Project-based CPU allocation
Fixed-Priority	FX	Fixed priority, some user control

express shares, if five projects all have an equal share, each project is assured at least 20 percent of the available compute resources to do its work.

Chances are, however, you'd use the Fair-Share scheduler to provide more compute resources to some projects than others. You can configure this by changing the number of shares associated with each project and using a Fair-Share scheduler to distribute resources accordingly. Let's say you wanted projects A and B to get at least 35 percent each of the compute time available, while projects C, D, and E each get at least 10 percent. Setting the project.cpu-shares value for each project to 35, 35, 10, 10, and 10, respectively, would do the trick.

I've used a total of 100 shares in this example to keep things simple. Shares are not percentages, however; they are ratios. Had I assigned the values 5, 5, 2, 2, and 2, all other things being the same, I'd have the same ratios and therefore the same configuration. The scale of the values I choose could play some role in the numbering. Shares are expressed in whole numbers, so if you want three-and-a-half times more CPU power for one project over another, you can use 7 and 2, 35 and 10, or another combination.

Had I assigned the values as 5, 17, 11, 19, and 23, I'd have some other equally valid ratios using a total of 75 shares. Each number of shares is weighed against the total shares allocated by all projects. The minimum compute time each assignee can expect, assuming all projects are active and are demanding their full share, will range between one-fifteenth and just under one-third.

Bear in mind, however, that no workload simply consumes some percentage of CPU resources because it's available. It can only request what it needs by way of its processes executing instructions to process data. Therefore, it may be that one project, given a 35-percent share, has nothing to do but wait for more data to process. The time it could consume is made available to the other projects, some of which might need extra compute time. Shares do not represent a cap, therefore, but a floor.

To institute shares among your projects requires three steps:

- Apply the cpu-shares resource control to each project.
- Make the Fair-Share scheduler your default process scheduler.
- Reboot the system.

First, consider what kind of resource control project.cpu-shares is. You can use the rctladm command to observe the control's global traits:

```
$ rctladm -l project.cpu-shares
project.cpu-shares    …   [ no-basic no-deny no-signal no-syslog count ]
```

You can research these bracketed attributes in the man page for the rctlblk_set_value library call if you wish. The no-basic and no-deny attributes effectively disable privilege level and action for this control. You're nonetheless required to specify a full triplet of values when adding this control to a project.

Let's say I wanted to give twice as many shares to my user.mfernest project as to my firefox project. I'll include group.staff and ocademo, a holdover project from the last chapter, into this mix. I want them to have as much attention as the user.mfernest project, assuming they have any workload. My projmod commands are:

```
$ sudo projmod -K "project.cpu-shares=(privileged,6,none)" user.mfernest
$ sudo projmod -K "project.cpu-shares=(privileged,6,none)" group.staff
$ sudo projmod -K "project.cpu-shares=(privileged,6,none)" ocademo
$ sudo projmod -K "project.cpu-shares=(privileged,3,none)" firefox
```

The dispadmin -d command lets you change the default process-scheduling system to Fair-Share. It requires the scheduler's mnemonic code, listed in Table 10-4, as a parameter. Although you can move all processes from one scheduling system to another (not covered in this book), at this point it requires less foundation to reboot and let the system do the work. Changing the default on a fresh system will create and populate the /etc/dispadmin.conf file with values to be used for subsequent system sessions.

```
$ sudo dispadmin -d FSS
$ cat /etc/dispadmin.conf
#
# /etc/dispadmin.conf
#
# Do NOT edit this file by hand -- use dispadmin(1m) instead.
#
DEFAULT_SCHEDULER=FSS
```

It's worth your while from now on to also ask whether an SMF service is involved in a low-level configuration option like this one—and indeed there is:

```
$ svcs -p system/scheduler
STATE            STIME     FMRI
online           Jan_21    svc:/system/scheduler:default
```

On reboot, this service will read the value recorded in the /etc/dispadmin.conf file and apply it. To see whether processes are now operating under the FSS scheduling class, use the -c switch of the ps command to report it:

```
$ ps -c
  PID  CLS PRI TTY          TIME CMD
 1607  FSS  59 pts/1        0:00 bash
 1627  FSS   1 pts/1        1:16 plugin-c
 1610  FSS   1 pts/1        0:06 firefox-
```

Isolating and measuring the effects of Fair-Share scheduling is trickier. One thing you might do is execute an infinite loop under a given project to raise their demands past their allocation and watch CPU utilization with the prstat -J command. Be aware, however, that observing the effect is not as simple as expecting CPU utilization to match share allocation under any workload. Scheduling is never that simple. You now know how to change the default scheduling system to favor a project-oriented approach to managing your processes.

More importantly, you have one more key piece that adds to the way Solaris Zones are configured. If you take some time now to experiment with the Fair-Share scheduler, you will have one less detail to ponder when you are ready to learn zones. Zones, if anything, are built on a sizable mass of subsystems like this one. It's far easier to see what a zone is, and what it isn't, by examining these pieces in isolation.

CERTIFICATION OBJECTIVE 10.04

Pooling CPUs

The last topic I'll review with a better understanding of zones in mind is CPU configuration. Over the years, operating systems have developed more sophisticated and flexible tools that allow administrators to configure certain processes to run on certain CPUs. Often the objective was to improve overall system utilization, but nowadays there may be additional goals as well, such as improving the system's resilience to hardware failures and configuring a large complement of physical resources into a collection of smaller logical computing resources.

The project control managing CPUs is called project.cpu-cap. It's an odd control on a couple of fronts. For one, it values a single CPU as 100 units. By assigning a value such as 250 to this control, you allot 2.5 virtual CPUs to the project. It is up to the system to calculate and support this allocation from the pool of available CPUs. The administrator only has to specify a value within the means of the CPUs available, and then let the system apply the limits to the workloads defined by each project. Figure 10-1 illustrates how a four-CPU system might be divided among four projects with various needs in mind.

Like the project.cpu-shares resource control, the project.cpu-cap control only operates at the privileged level, does not log, and does not accept signals. In other words, all but the action component of its declaration does anything meaningful. Because you can treat a CPU as 100 units, however, you can divide your available CPUs in a share model that bears resemblance to shares in the Fair-Share scheduling model. With caps, however, the numbers used have a hard meaning. If I wanted to dedicate a fourth of a CPU to my user.mfernest project, I'd change the project accordingly:

```
$ sudo projmod -K "project.cpu-caps=(privileged,25,none)" user.mfernest
```

If you can treat an eight-CPU system as having 800 "caps" you can assign to your projects, you can make some clear distinctions between workloads and the relative horsepower you want to assign to each. Using CPU caps is considered a *fine-grained* approach to distributing those resources. It doesn't conflict with other approaches, including Fair-Share scheduling as described earlier and the techniques to follow, which apply CPUs as discrete (*coarse-grained*) resources.

One of the early techniques developed along these lines is called *process binding*. By binding a process, or process LWPs, to a specific CPU, the administrator ensures

FIGURE 10-1

A four-CPU system allocated to projects using cpu-caps

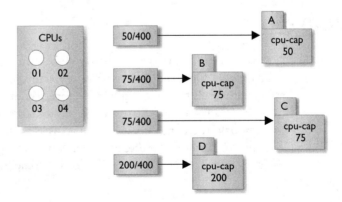

those execution entities only run on the specified CPU. In the same way a process spawns new processes in the same task by default, a bound process spawns child processes that run on the CPU it is bound to. Process binding is one way to restrict a process from dominating more than one CPU. In Solaris, the pbind utility supports this technique.

Another technique, called *processor fencing*, lets the administrator remove some CPUs from a system's complement and assign them to a logical group. Processes can be assigned to the group so they only execute in that group. Whereas process binding assigns a process to a specific CPU, but does not prevent other processes from using it as well, processor groups only run the processes assigned to them. This technique might be appropriate to a mission-critical workload, or just to keep one workload separate from another for ease of observation and clarifying performance statistics. In Solaris, the psrinfo, psradm, and psrset utilities govern this use of fencing processors into groups and assigning processes to them.

Small sets of processors can be easier to observe than all the CPUs in a system with many cores. For one, the mpstat command, used to report processor activity, provides a way to look at set activity instead of individual CPUs, similar in concept to the prstat -J command. If the processes assigned to a processor set can be treated as a single workload, the process of understanding the demands of that workload can be significantly reduced. Sometimes certain workloads prove to operate more efficiently on a small set of cores as well. Figure 10-2 illustrates an ad hoc relationship between some workloads and a processor set. In this illustration, each folder represents a number of processes that have been assigned to each set by an administrator.

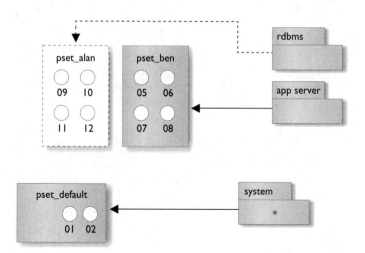

FIGURE 10-2

Workloads assigned to different processor sets

The most recent concept in this area is called *CPU pooling*. Processor sets and CPU pooling both manage the assignment of processors to groups and processes to execute in a specific group. A CPU pool is an abstraction that operates between processes and processor sets, making it possible for the system to alter the members of a processor set over time. CPU pools, then, offer automated handling of processor sets. They use configuration policies and workload assessment to determine, for example, when it might be better to move a CPU from one set to another to balance resources against demand. The primary tools for this work are the pooladm and poolcfg utilities.

By assigning a project to a pool, it becomes possible to move processors from one pool (which contains at least one pset) to another. This movement occurs when the system is enabled to detect the following:

- Saturation of demand on one pset
- CPUs that can be moved from another pset

Administrators can also perform this task manually (using the poolcfg utility), but automating the resource shift according to policy is a lot more attractive when you have many machines to monitor. Figure 10-3 illustrates a potential migration from one pool to another.

FIGURE 10-3

Projects using pools with transferring CPUs

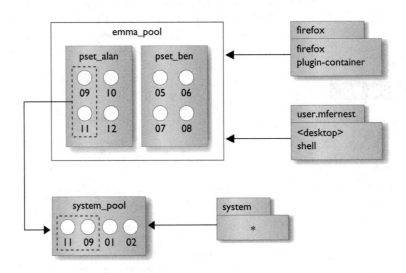

The difference between managing processor sets, using the psradm and psrset utilities, and configuring their use, using the pooladm and poolcfg utilities, is the difference between managing processor sets by hand and turning over their control to a policy-driven automated system. You can assign several processes to one pset, and you can assign several projects to the same pool; you cannot, however, do the reverse.

This trade-off between more control and efficiency through automation may seem imbalanced, but it depends on what you want to accomplish on a system. Creating processor sets by hand is simpler, but it is harder to use observation data to indicate when a change in processor set balance might be appropriate. Creating robust pool configurations has a steep learning curve, but the payoff in setting one correctly increases in proportion to the system's configuration complexity.

Putting all the processes that belong to one project in a processor set could be more trouble than it's worth. It's not a complicated task, just a tedious one. Assigning a project to a pool, however, rivals the rcap.max-rss control for simplicity. You can simply declare the pool you want a project to draw its CPU resources from:

```
$ sudo projmod -K pool.project=jones user.mfernest
$ projects -l user.mfernest
user.mfernest
...
        attribs:  pool.project=jones
```

If you reboot and this pool does not exist, the system will revert the pool assignment to the system's default pool. There's no potential for sending a project into space with a bad pool name. There is, however, the possibility of creating a bottleneck with a pool configuration that lacks the resources to manage its workload efficiently.

CERTIFICATION SUMMARY

This chapter helps you understand how the resource demands of a project can be managed with controls that limit the view of each resource as an administrator sees fit. By defining projects and imposing controls over their resource demands, you can create a system of workloads that are easier to isolate, monitor, and adjust for better use of the system. Although memory caps, process scheduling, and CPU controls are considered proper subjects for the OCP exam, learning about them now will make it easier to understand what a zone really is: a project workload that can be fully isolated from other project workloads on the same system.

✓ TWO-MINUTE DRILL

Logging Resource Thresholds

- ❑ Resource controls may log messages when their thresholds are violated.
- ❑ The rctladm utility lists each control along with its logging state and global traits.
- ❑ rcap.max-rss and project.pool are not counted as resource controls but are applied to projects in the same general manner.

Capping Memory

- ❑ Memory caps apply to the resident memory (RSS) consumed by processes in a project.
- ❑ The rcapadm utility lets you configure the interval for scanning, sampling, reporting, and checking for project caps configurations. You can also relax paging by tying enforcement of memory caps to how much physical memory the system has to spare.
- ❑ The rcapstat utility reports the amount of paging attempted to reduce a project's memory consumption below its RSS threshold.

Scheduling Processes

- ❑ You can change the default process scheduler on your system with the dispadmin -d command, which stores non-default values in the /etc/dispadmin.conf file.

Pooling CPUs

- ❑ The project.cpu-caps control lets you distribute CPU resources in units of 100 per CPU.
- ❑ If you want to manage processor sets by hand, use the psrinfo, psradm, and psrset utilities.
- ❑ If you hope to run projects and zones on top of policy-managed pools, you'll need to learn the poolcfg and pooladm utilities.

SELF TEST

Use the following questions to test your recall and understanding of the chapter's material.

Logging Resource Thresholds

1. What does the resource control trait "inf" define?
   A. An informational control setting
   B. An informal control setting
   C. An infinite control setting
   D. An infinitesimal control setting

2. How many cpu-shares resource controls are there?
   A. Zero
   B. One
   C. Two
   D. Three

Capping Memory

3. What is the maximum resident size any one process segment can achieve?
   A. Half of its virtual size
   B. All of its virtual size
   C. Half of its total process size
   D. All of its total process size

4. What is the rcapd default policy for enforcing memory caps?
   A. Enforce any cap immediately
   B. Enforce caps if physical memory falls below a certain level
   C. Enforce caps if virtual memory falls below a certain level
   D. Enforce caps if the swap device is empty

5. Which aspect of memory capping cannot be tuned using rcapadm?
   A. Configuration update checking
   B. Paging interval
   C. Scanning interval
   D. Reporting interval

Scheduling Processes

6. Which three options are valid user scheduling classes?

   A. Real-Time

   B. Fair-Share

   C. Time-Share

   D. Fixed-Share

7. Assume you have three projects with assigned shares of 50, 100, and 150, respectively. If all three projects are busy, what percentage of CPU time would you expect the 150-share project to receive?

   A. 33 percent

   B. 50 percent

   C. 150 percent

   D. 100 percent

8. What is the default process-scheduling class on a Solaris system?

   A. Real-Time

   B. Time-Share

   C. Fixed-Priority

   D. Fair-Share

Pooling CPUs

9. Pick the two correct statements regarding pools.

   A. You can assign more than one project to a pool.

   B. You can assign more than one pool to a project

   C. You can assign more than one processor to a pset.

   D. You can assign more than one pool to a pset.

10. Which statement identifies a difference between a pset and a pool?

   A. You can set a process's pool with the prctl command.

   B. You can set a project's pool with the rctladm command.

   C. You can observe a pool's utilization with the mpstat -a command.

   D. You can observe pset utilization with the mpstat -a command.

SELF TEST ANSWERS

Logging Resource Thresholds

1. ☑ **C.** The inf trait means the resource is considered virtually infinite when taking its upper limit into consideration. Time spent on CPU, for example, is constrained by the 64-bit-wide variable that holds it, but this value is unreachable by any practical measure.
    ☒ **A, B,** and **D** are incorrect. All are incorrect interpretations of the shorthand term "inf."

2. ☑ **C.** The cpu-shares control is available for projects and for zones.
    ☒ **A, B,** and **D** are incorrect. These are not the correct counts for the number of cpu-shares resource controls supported.

Capping Memory

3. ☑ **B.** The resident size of any segment in a process map is some or all of the space guaranteed to the segment upon allocation.
    ☒ **A, C,** and **D** are incorrect. **A** is incorrect because there is no rule that says resident size must consume a fixed ratio of virtual size. **C** and **D** are incorrect because the resident size of a segment bears no direct relation to the overall process size.

4. ☑ **A.** By default, all memory caps are enforced at the moment the resident size of a capped project is recognized.
    ☒ **B, C,** and **D** are incorrect. **B** and **C** are incorrect because when setting the enforcement policy for caps with the rcapadm command, you can only select a number from 0 to 100. You cannot set it according to a ration of available memory. **D** is incorrect because rcapd policy does not take swap device status into account.

5. ☑ **B.** The paging algorithm is a function of the kernel and cannot be set using the rcapadm utility.
    ☒ **A, C,** and **D** are incorrect. All of them can be set using the rcapadm utility.

Scheduling Processes

6. ☑ **A, B,** and **C.** You can refer to Table 10-4 or review the dispadmin man page for a listing of valid scheduling classes.
    ☒ **D** is incorrect. There is no scheduling class called Fixed-Share.

7. ☑ **B.** As defined, the third project receives 150 of 300 total shares assigned and should therefore be assured of half of the available processing time when all projects are busy.
   ☒ **A, C,** and **D** are incorrect. **A** is incorrect because it assumes share values don't change the balance of shares available. **C** and **D** are incorrect because they are spurious values.

8. ☑ **B.** Time-Share is the de facto default scheduling class on UNIX platforms. You can verify this by using the ps -c command on a system that has not had its default scheduling class reset.
   ☒ **A, C,** and **D** are incorrect. Both **C** and **D** are plausible choices for a default scheduling class and could be put in place with the dispadmin -d command. **A** should not be used as the default scheduler.

Pooling CPUs

9. ☑ **A and C.** Pools are designed to host multiple psets and can be the resource target for more than one project at one time.
   ☒ **B and D** are incorrect. A pset may only belong to one pool at any time. A project may only use one pool at a time.

10. ☑ **D.** The mpstat command is able to gather statistics on the pset level as well as by individual CPUs.
    ☒ **A, B,** and **C** are incorrect. **A** is incorrect because you cannot assign a single process to a pool. **B** is incorrect because you can only assign a project to a pool in the /etc/project database. **C** is incorrect because the mpstat command does not monitor pools, just psets.

11

Configuring Additional Storage

Y ou first learned about ZFS technology in Chapter 4, which showed how Solaris 11
supports a variety of different file systems that may use locally attached storage or
remote storage, or can even be a construct of kernel memory used to simplify access
to certain parts of operating system data such as process-oriented data (procfs) and file-oriented
swap space (tmpfs).

This chapter goes one level deeper into how to manage physically attached
storage. Strictly speaking, managing your local storage on Solaris 11 is just
one aspect of ZFS technology. Practically speaking, however, learning how to
manage storage is fundamentally different from learning to manage file systems. It
incorporates a body of knowledge and skills, traditionally known as *logical volume
management,* that was once considered a realm for experienced administrators who
support large file systems and highly available systems (also known as *clusters*).

It's a simple matter to learn and use the zpool utility, which provides the tooling
for this territory. This chapter is also an excellent opportunity to see just how
much knowledge and skill have been reduced to using this one tool. You may
not ever need to appreciate just how much work it once was to manage a complex
storage configuration—and that's a good thing. However, it will help you in the
long term to learn how much power ZFS technology puts at your fingertips through
the zpool utility.

CERTIFICATION OBJECTIVE 11.01

Understanding Logical Volume Management

Since its introduction in Solaris 10, ZFS technology has reinvented the way
administrators manage all aspects of disk-based storage: allocating storage devices,
creating file systems, tuning them for better combined efficiency, supporting backups
of file system data, allocating disk-based resources for the system (such as swap and
core dump space), and so on. Most operating systems support these tasks with tools
that are not directly related to each other, but produce objects that other tools can
build on. Physical disks, for example, are connected to the operating system through
their device drivers. The operating system's *volume management* subsystem identifies

these disks as storage components and presents them for use by file system utilities. The utilities organize the storage space into some amount of metadata, needed to track the state of the file system itself, reserving the rest for user data storage.

The administrator makes the file system available to user processes by *mounting* it to a location (directory) on the root file system. Once it is mounted, user processes can create, modify, and destroy files on it, given the proper permissions. Just like networking is defined as a stack of independent protocols that work together, disk input/output operations (or I/O for short) can be viewed as an arrangement of independent kernel modules that convert user data into units of storage (called *data blocks*, or sometimes just *blocks)* and channel that data to a specific device. Figure 11-1 presents a logical view of the I/O stack that gets user data from a process to disk storage.

The simplest relationship pairs one disk, or a single *partition* of a disk, to one file system. This arrangement suffices for most small-scale systems. It's when you can't afford the total time it takes to replace a failed disk—identifying the failure, getting the replacement component, effecting repair, and restoring the data from backup— that relying on a single physical storage device becomes risky. It may also be that the logical storage space you require—let's say for a collection of very large and growing files—may exceed the capacity of any one disk you intend on deploying. In either case, you need more than one device to support the file system.

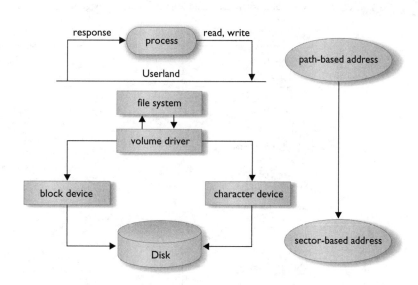

FIGURE 11-1

Logical view of I/O, from process to storage

Using multiple storage devices to support one file system is known as *logical volume management*, which has traditionally been supported two ways. One method employs special hardware that presents multiple physical disks as a single logical volume to the operating system. A second method uses software to configure such an arrangement, using devices that are also independently attached to the system. Which approach is better depends on a number of factors. All other things being equal, however, hardware solutions are typically more expensive and arguably better-performing. Software solutions are typically more flexible, from an administrator's perspective, and arguably more effort to maintain. Figure 11-2 depicts both a hardware- and software-based logical volume management configuration. Notice the software configuration requires an additional kernel-based driver to mediate between the physical disks' drivers and the operating system's volume management facility.

There are several ways to arrange disks in a logical volume to achieve different effects. The simplest of them is called either a *concatenation* or a *stripe*. A concatenation uses the combined space of all disks to create one large logical disk. The file system you make on top of a concatenated volume is said to *span* the disks. The biggest advantage to a concatenation is that it uses all the space of all the disks that belong to it.

FIGURE II-2   Hardware- and software-based logical volume management

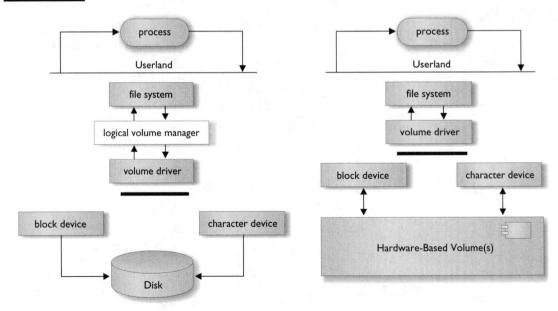

A stripe has the same logical arrangement, but is configured differently. In a stripe, the disks are treated as equal members in the volume. The file system is organized over a stripe in a way that spreads the I/O operations evenly over all members. Because these disks are mechanically independent, they can operate in near-parallel fashion, which improves overall I/O performance by reducing the delay of a single disk's service time. Figure 11-3 shows a concatenation of disks, usually depicted in a vertical arrangement of devices, and a stripe of disks, usually depicted in a horizontal arrangement.

The logical configuration most people understand right away is a *mirror*, a pair of disks that maintain copies of the file system data. The file system sees this redundant arrangement as one storage volume. The component that maintains the mirror's state—whether it is hardware or software based—mediates between the file system and the member disks. In normal operation, the managing component replicates the data (after a write operation) and chooses the disk to retrieve data from in a read operation. If a disk fails, the managing component routes all requests to the surviving disk. From an administrator's viewpoint, the redundancy is lost until the data can be replicated to a replacement disk. From a user's point of view, there's no apparent loss at all.

FIGURE 11-3   Logical view of concatenated and striped volumes

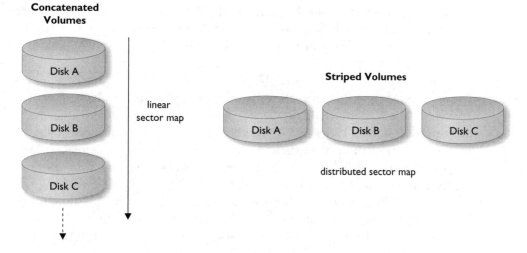

Understanding RAID Levels

It's common in enterprise environments to combine these forms for multiple benefits—specifically, using a stripe for better performance with a mirror for better availability. In environments where the size of a working data set exceeds the size of individual disks, this arrangement is especially important. A traditional stripe spans multiple disks and provides improved performance by sacrificing the flexibility of a concatenated volume, which can be expanded if the demand for space reaches the capacity of the volume. The mirror protects the volume against the loss of a disk. There are two general forms of this type, which you may have heard described as a *redundant array of independent disks*, or *RAID*. The general term for a mirror is RAID 1; for a stripe or concatenation, it is RAID 0.

The order of these layers once mattered quite a bit. At one time, many RAID-compliant devices or software supported only mirrors of stripes (also known as RAID 0+1). In this arrangement, if you lost one disk, you'd have to restore the entire stripe it belonged to before you could restore your mirror. There is also the perceived risk that the other stripe could fail before you completed recovery of the first. If you're the kind to worry about unlikely scenarios with disastrous consequences, it's hard not to worry about that.

A more resilient arrangement, called RAID 10, mirrors the individual disks together first and makes a stripe of the mirrors second. In this arrangement, losing one disk means losing redundancy for just that element of the stripe. Now you can worry about a plausible but much less likely event—that you might lose the surviving sub-mirror before you can recover the first. However, you could lose any other disk in this arrangement during recovery and the stripe would maintain its availability.

It's expensive, of course, to double up on equipment. To hedge against this cost, some sites use a redundancy scheme based on *parity data* instead. Its starts with a stripe that is large enough to hold the data. You then add one more disk to account for parity data storage. Parity data is derived from the data users will write to the volume. If (or when) a stripe member fails, the user data from that member is recalculated using the surviving user and parity data. A variety of these parity arrangements have been devised over time; each one is defined by a different RAID level.

RAID 5 is one such form that was popular and available in both software and hardware implementations. RAID 5 distributes the space reserved for parity data across all the disks in the stripes. Parity regions are staggered on the disks so that each one resides in a different range of disk blocks. Staggering promotes a better distribution of write demand to the disks. Figure 11-4 illustrates such an arrangement.

FIGURE 11-4

RAID 5 user and
parity disk layout

Parity-based redundancy schemes in general have a few disadvantages when compared to mirrored stripes. Calculating parity data, when there's a lot of data to either write or reconstruct, is a significant cost. If you modify data in a way that does not include all blocks on all disks, known as a *full-stripe write*, there's additional time you have to spend on reading the parity information for an entire stripe of data before modifying part of it.

Although RAID 5 is often touted as a cheap alternative to mirroring disks, it can be just as effective as a RAID 0+1 arrangement. RAID 0+1 requires twice the disks; RAID 5 requires one extra disk. Both protect you from one disk failure. RAID 0+1 protects you from a second disk failure only if the second disk is part of the stripe just lost. In that view, there isn't much to separate the two arrangements except cost. RAID 0+1 offers better performance with a single-disk failure than RAID 5 does, but most sites don't think about performance *before* they think about data availability. There are, in short, three virtues to consider: high performance, high availability, and low cost. It's generally held that as you focus on a single virtue as being most important, you sacrifice some measure of the other two to achieve it.

on the
job

RAID levels themselves aren't general descriptions of disk arrangements: they're defined by standards that are maintained by the Storage Networking Industry Association (SNIA). ZFS pools do not adhere to these standards, strictly speaking, so while it's useful to refer to RAID levels as terms, it's only for the sake of comparing them to the arrangements that ZFS applies to pool devices.

You can apply other factors in determining the best disk arrangement for your system or application. You may also find some IT shops prefer one arrangement over others. The reasons may be nontechnical, such as preference for a particular product or vendor. They could also be based on expectations that haven't been tested. Nonetheless, all these implementations take the form of additional software and hardware that has to integrated with the kernel, the file system, and even the application, then configured, and then kept in tune throughout. The result is sometimes a long list of settings that requires multiple training sessions to understand and maintain. When it comes to reliable I/O that performs well, configuration errors that can work in your favor are all but unheard of.

Understanding the Role of Pools in ZFS Technology

When ZFS technology was first introduced, it seemed like the beginning of the end for logical volume management tools dominated by a third-party market. With ZFS, it doesn't matter if you use a Storage Area Network (SAN), a Network-Attached Storage (NAS) appliance, a locally attached disk array, or even a bunch of unrelated storage components. ZFS treats them all the same way: as sources for storage space that can be placed in a pool.

A ZFS *pool*, or *zpool* for short, mediates between a collection of *virtual devices* and a number of *datasets*. Because there is no direct relationship between a dataset and its disk space, which is the traditional arrangement in operating systems, ZFS lets you create as many datasets as you like, as long as the pool has available space. (Remember that ZFS adds little-to-no metadata when creating datasets.) You can also add storage to the pool without disrupting dataset operations. For the administrator, these capabilities result in greater flexibility in maintaining and modifying these resources.

A *virtual device*, or *vdev* for short, plays a specific role inside a pool. Some vdevs are simple storage, such as a whole disk or disk partition. Others are arranged a specific way, such as a mirror of simple storage or what ZFS calls a *raidz group*. ZFS supports three kinds of raidz groups, all of which are parity data arrangements that follow the RAID 5 model reviewed in the previous section. Table 11-1 gives a full list of ZFS vdevs. Those marked with asterisks are not discussed further in this book.

ZFS mirrors do not follow the RAID 0+1 model. Because devices have to be mirrored before they can be added to a pool, there's no means for creating the stripe first. However, as you add multiple mirrored disks to a pool, you end up concatenating them. When writing to disks, ZFS has a built-in mechanism for *dynamic striping*. That is, the read/write performance of the pool is based on the amount of writing committed to disk and to the number of devices in the pool ZFS can use. As a result, in many cases administrators don't even have to tune the pool; ZFS makes that process as transparent as it possibly can.

The raidz groups listed show you one way users try to get multiple benefits where they can—namely, both performance and the availability of their data. Raidz2 and raidz3 configurations allow for two or three disks to fail, respectively, before losing

TABLE 11-1	Virtual Devices Supported in ZFS Pools

vdev Type	Description
disk	Any block device (whole disk or disk partition)
file	A regular file (intended for experimentation)
mirror	Multiple disks (or files) with replicated data
raidz(1)	A stripe of disks/files with single-parity of data
raidz2	A stripe of disks/files with double-parity of data
raidz3	A stripe of disks/files with triple-parity of data
spare*	A device that can replace another device when it fails
log*	A device that accepts synchronous file writes to a pool
cache*	Supports the storage facility layer between the disk and main memory

data integrity itself. These arrangements offer similar resiliency to RAID 10, a stripe of mirrored disks that can tolerate many combinations of multiple disk failures, but at a lower equipment cost and a tolerable drop in performance if or when the disks break.

You cannot make one kind of vdev inside another in a zpool. That is, you cannot make a mirror of mirrors, or a raidz group from other raidz vdevs, or any mix-and-match combination of them. When these devices are added to a pool, the result is a concatenation of their storage (excepting spare, log, and cache devices).

Although you can use a regular file for storage in a ZFS pool, using one is strongly discouraged. On Solaris 10 systems with UFS root file systems, using files for zpool vdevs was a popular workaround for casual experiments, as long as you didn't mind having a pseudo-zpool on a UFS file system that might not survive a reboot. Now that ZFS is better known and supports root file systems, the case for using files isn't as tempting. Also, adding pseudo disks to a VirtualBox machine provides a more stable and realistic way to conduct similar experiments.

Recall the term *dataset* from Chapter 4. Datasets include ZFS file systems, volumes (such as the dump and swap space), and snapshots. These objects rely only on the pool's ability to store and retrieve data. The pool's internal arrangement is irrelevant to a dataset, unless it breaks in such a way that the dataset is no longer whole. With a redundant arrangement in place (mirrors or a raidz group), you can view the pool on two levels: first, by the accessibility of data to its users and second, the pool's ability to tolerate a disk failure.

This view is the point of a logical volume layer between your disks and your file systems. It removes a dependency that otherwise forces your file system drivers to react to loss of a disk. With the addition of a redundant arrangement, the administrator can remove simple disk failure scenarios from the user's view and repair them without affecting the availability of the data. If you can calculate the value of time and opportunity lost when your data becomes unavailable, you can determine if it's worth the cost in planning and extra disks to avoid it. With ZFS, you can reduce the cost down to the disks you need for redundancy and the planning down to assessing the best pool implementation for your needs.

CERTIFICATION OBJECTIVE 11.02

Administering ZFS Pools

Disk management is a practice that becomes more demanding as the number of disks in use grows. If you read the commonly repeated selling points for ZFS, you might get the idea that it was designed to handle some infinitely large array of disks, but that's not really the point. ZFS sets limits that are so far beyond most practical concerns, they're irrelevant to capacity planning. That said, administrators still have to consider the arrangement of storage resources that make sense for their applications, their users, and their own site infrastructure. In this section, I just scratch the surface. I explain what you need to create a pool, how to create different disk arrangements (and destroy them), and how to monitor their status.

You'll learn to do all this work with a single tool, the zpool utility. In order to get a preview of things to come, however, I also refer to specific pool properties that differ from the dataset properties you learned about in Chapter 4.

Understanding ZFS Pool Requirements

The one hard limit ZFS pools have for a simple device, whether it is a disk, a disk partition, or a file, is a minimum size. All devices must have at least 128MB of capacity to offer. Even when ZFS was introduced, this limit was trivial for most interested users because it ruled out early-generation thumb drives and disk partitions that were too small to use for anything else. ZFS can also determine if a device is already in use—by another file system type—and will not use it. ZFS does *not* read or try to save data left behind by prior use.

Given a whole disk, ZFS will label it with an Extensible Firmware Interface (EFI) label. This act may change the original layout of the disk. Any data left on the disk will be overwritten by the new layout, but not erased. ZFS does not perform so-called *secure deletion*, in which remaining data is scrubbed off the disk before reusing it. For a recent disk, all cylinders but one are assigned to a single partition; this space is used for creating datasets. The remaining cylinder is reserved for private use by ZFS.

You can examine a disk's layout using the format command, as follows:

```
$ sudo format
Searching for disks...done

AVAILABLE DISK SELECTIONS:
       0. c3t0d0 <ATA-VBOX HARDDISK-1.0 cyl 4093 alt 2 hd 128 sec 32>
          /pci@0,0/pci8086,2829@d/disk@0,0
       1. c3t1d0 <ATA-VBOX HARDDISK-1.0 cyl 1022 alt 2 hd 128 sec 32>
          /pci@0,0/pci8086,2829@d/disk@1,0
       2. c3t3d0 <ATA-VBOX HARDDISK-1.0 cyl 1022 alt 2 hd 128 sec 32>
          /pci@0,0/pci8086,2829@d/disk@3,0
       3. c3t4d0 <ATA-VBOX HARDDISK-1.0 cyl 1022 alt 2 hd 128 sec 32>
          /pci@0,0/pci8086,2829@d/disk@4,0
Specify disk (enter its number): 1
selecting c3t1d0
[disk formatted]

FORMAT MENU:
        disk       - select a disk
        type       - select (define) a disk type
        partition  - select (define) a partition table
        current    - describe the current disk
        format     - format and analyze the disk
        fdisk      - run the fdisk program
        repair     - repair a defective sector
        label      - write label to the disk
        analyze    - surface analysis
        defect     - defect list management
        backup     - search for backup labels
        verify     - read and display labels
        save       - save new disk/partition definitions
        inquiry    - show disk ID
        volname    - set 8-character volume name
        !<cmd>     - execute <cmd>, then return|
        quit
```

```
format> partition
PARTITION MENU:
        0       - change `0' partition
        1       - change `1' partition
        2       - change `2' partition
        3       - change `3' partition
        4       - change `4' partition
        5       - change `5' partition
        6       - change `6' partition
        7       - change `7' partition
        select - select a predefined table
        modify - modify a predefined partition table
        name   - name the current table
        print  - display the current table
        label  - write partition map and label to the disk
        !<cmd> - execute <cmd>, then return
        quit
partition> print
Current partition table (original):
Total disk cylinders available: 1021 + 2 (reserved cylinders)
```

Part	Tag	Flag	Cylinders	Size	Blocks	
0	unassigned	wm	0	0	(0/0/0)	0
1	unassigned	wm	0	0	(0/0/0)	0
2	backup	wu	0 - 1020	1.99GB	(1021/0/0)	4182016
3	unassigned	wm	0	0	(0/0/0)	0
4	unassigned	wm	0	0	(0/0/0)	0
5	unassigned	wm	0	0	(0/0/0)	0
6	unassigned	wm	0	0	(0/0/0)	0
7	unassigned	wm	0	0	(0/0/0)	0
8	boot	wu	0 - 0	2.00MB	(1/0/0)	4096
9	unassigned	wm	0	0	(0/0/0)	0

As you can see by the long output, the format utility is menu driven and supports a variety of functions. If you run a format command without the right privileges, you won't see a list of disks as you do here. The format program starts first, then determines if the invoking user has the privileges necessary to view and modify the system's disks. If not, the command will terminate after reporting this error.

For this example, I created three 2GB virtual disks and added them to my VirtualBox virtual machine running Solaris. They're identified as disk selections 1, 2, and 3 in the preceding output. You can select a disk by entering the index number, after which you see a menu of options. In this case, I selected disk 1 and called the partition command, followed by its print command to report the layout of the disk. Notice the first cylinder is allocated to partition 8, but is also included in the range covered by partition 2. Solaris uses partition 2 to report the disk's full range of cylinders; standard practice dictates that it is otherwise left alone, so administrators and system applications can use it to report the disk's total size.

To get this report, I first had to use the fdisk command (output not shown) to accept the system's default configuration for this disk because it appeared completely new to the system after booting up. The disk driver that manages these disks uses the cylinder to break down its total capacity. It has been decades since disks were governed by a physical cylinder geometry, but it's still convenient to break a disk down into logical cylinders. In this case, the driver allots about 2MB per cylinder; it then takes 1,021 cylinders to cover the disk's capacity. If you wanted to break the total disk into partitions, you'd assign each partition a range of contiguous cylinders for its space; that's the old method for setting up individual file systems that a ZFS pool makes obsolete.

Understanding the zpool Command

The zpool command has 22 subcommands, including a help subcommand that will list all of them:

```
$ zpool help
The following commands are supported:
add       attach   clear    create   destroy  detach   export   get
help      history  import   iostat   list     offline  online   remove
replace   scrub    set      split    status   upgrade
For more info, run: zpool help <command>
```

Many of these operations have to do with aspects of pool administration an experienced administrator would be expected to handle. You can, of course, experiment with any of them, but you're only expected to know a few for the Solaris OCA exam; Table 11-2 lists those.

TABLE 11-2   zpool Subcommands Covered in Solaris OCA Exam

zpool Subcommand	Description
create	Create a new pool using the named devices
destroy	Destroy an existing pool and release devices
get	List pool properties
set	Modify pool properties
history	List previous zfs and zpool commands
iostat	Report pool I/O statistics
list	List existing pools and key properties
status	Report pool composition and health

The following sections walk you through the proper use of each subcommand.

Creating and Destroying ZFS Pools

To create a zpool, you must supply an unused pool name and a vdev specification. To destroy one, name an existing pool. You can name a device, as shown in the example, using the short listing given by the format command. (If you want, you can interrupt the format command with CTRL-D immediately after it lists the disks on the system.)

```
$ sudo zpool create ocapool c3t1d0 c3t3d0 c3t4d0
'ocapool' successfully created, but with no redundancy; failure of one
device will cause loss of the pool
$ zpool list
NAME       SIZE   ALLOC   FREE   CAP   DEDUP   HEALTH   ALTROOT
ocapool   5.95G   128K   5.95G    0%   1.00x   ONLINE   -
rpool     7.94G   6.72G  1.22G   84%   1.00x   ONLINE   -
$ sudo zpool destroy ocapool; zpool list
NAME      SIZE   ALLOC   FREE   CAP   DEDUP   HEALTH   ALTROOT
rpool    7.94G   6.72G  1.22G   84%   1.00x   ONLINE   -
```

The output will advise you that a simple device concatenation offers no protection against a failure. To create a redundant pool, you add the appropriate vdev term to introduce the list of devices that make it up. For example, to make a raidz1 group, add that term to the command after the pool name, followed by at least three devices, like so:

```
$ sudo zpool create datap raidz1 c3t1d0 c3t3d0 c3t4d0
$ zpool list datap
NAME   SIZE   ALLOC   FREE   CAP   DEDUP   HEALTH   ALTROOT
datap  5.94G  253K    5.94G  0%    1.00x   ONLINE   -
```

Notice the size of the datap zpool shows the total capacity of the disks used. One disk's worth of space, however, will be used for parity data. If you view the size of datap *as a dataset*, you'll see this cost factored in:

```
$ zfs list datap
NAME   USED   AVAIL   REFER   MOUNTPOINT
datap  117K   3.89G   34.6K   /datap
```

The available space for the dataset is 3.89GB. The pool didn't change in the meantime; it just counts all data of any type toward its capacity. The pool size does not factor out parity data as a built-in cost when calculating capacity; the latter does.

Mirrors are reported differently. When you create a mirror, all data you write to a pool is replicated, once per device in the mirrored vdev. Because there is no additional data to store (such as parity information), the zpool utility reports a mirrored pool's capacity and its dataset size as (roughly) the same:

```
$ sudo zpool create mirp mirror c3t3d0 c3t4d0
$ zpool list mirp ; zfs list mirp
NAME   SIZE   ALLOC   FREE   CAP   DEDUP   HEALTH   ALTROOT
mirp   1.98G  126K    1.98G  0%    1.00x   ONLINE   -
NAME   USED   AVAIL   REFER   MOUNTPOINT
mirp   85K    1.95G   31K     /mirp
```

Be mindful of this distinction on reporting with the zpool and zfs utilities. The reasoning I give here does *not* come from documentation. If there is an engineer's document or blog that explains why you'd want a pool to report capacity for parity redundancy data one way and mirrored redundancy data another way, I haven't yet come across it.

To create a pool of multiple mirrors or raidz groups, use the vdev term to introduce each new group of devices. If I had four extra devices available, for example, I could create what amounts to a RAID 10 pool as follows:

```
$ sudo zpool create mirmir mirror c3t3d0 c3t4d0 mirror c3t5d0 c3t6d0
```

In this arrangement, each device is mirrored. The mirrored devices are concatenated together for size. Now my pool could lose up two disks and survive

(if those two disks are not from the same mirror). The same is true for multiple raidz groups in the same pool. There's greater redundancy and therefore greater resiliency to failure. What a site ultimately has to settle on is some justification for redundancy that protects not just the value of the data, but the value of its availability. What do you stand to lose if your data storage becomes unavailable? What degree of protection is justified to avoid or mitigate that loss? These are the questions that system planners must resolve.

Disk for disk, raidz groups require less overall capacity than mirrors to provide redundancy. The zpool utility, however, only enforces the need for one more device than what the parity scheme required. You can create a raidz2 group, for example, using only three devices—even though it's impractical. Table 11-3 lists both the required and recommended minimums for each raidz group type.

If you need good performance, it is recommended that you build a large pool with multiple raidz groups of the same type, rather than one very large raidz group. Doing so cuts down the number of devices you have available for user data. A 10-device raidz group in a pool, for example, will use 1/10 the capacity for parity data. Two five-device raidz groups in a pool will use 1/5 the capacity for parity data. This tradeoff is expected: For better performance, you'll sacrifice cost (in the form of less storage space).

You should also understand that for mirrors and raidz groups, it is assumed you would use devices of equal size to create each vdev. You can mix device sizes, but the capacity of the vdev will be constrained by the smallest device in the group, not the aggregate device capacity.

Setting ZFS Pool Mount Points

ZFS pools are also datasets; it just depends on the utility you use to view them. They have all the properties of a dataset, including a mount point. By default, the pool name serves as the initial mount point. But sometimes you want the pool name to

TABLE 11-3	Minimum Devices For Each raidz Group

vdev Type	Protection	Required Devices (Parity Plus One)	Minimum Recommended
raidz(1)	Single-parity	Two devices	Three devices
raidz2	Double-parity	Three devices	Five devices
raidz3	Triple-parity	Four devices	Eight devices

mean something to administrators (who have to manage many pools) and the mount point to mean something to users (who need application-friendly locations). When that's the case, you can set the pool's mount point to another name at creation time, or change it after the fact:

```
$ sudo zpool create -m /myapp mfedata c3t3d0
$ zpool list mfedata
NAME      SIZE   ALLOC   FREE   CAP   DEDUP   HEALTH   ALTROOT
mfedata   1.98G   167K   1.98G   0%   1.00x   ONLINE   -
$ zfs list mfedata
NAME      USED   AVAIL   REFER   MOUNTPOINT
mfedata   94K    1.95G    31K    /myapp
```

The first command will create the directory you specify if it does not exist, and it will fail if the directory exists but isn't empty. If you can set this mount point when you create the pool, it eliminates any possibility a user (that is, a process) could try to use the pool as its default mount point. Otherwise, use the zfs utility to update the mountpoint property. Remember the storage doesn't have a mount point; the dataset does.

```
$ sudo zfs set mountpoint=/yourapp mfedata
$ zfs list mfedata
NAME      USED   AVAIL   REFER   MOUNTPOINT
mfedata   94K    1.95G    31K    /yourapp
```

Understanding ZFS Pool Properties

Solaris 11 supports 18 different properties for a ZFS pool. Some of them are reported in the default zpool list output. You can get a complete list for a pool with a get subcommand:

```
$ zpool get all mfedata
NAME      PROPERTY      VALUE                  SOURCE
mfedata   size          1.98G                  -
mfedata   capacity      0%                     -
mfedata   altroot       -                      default
mfedata   health        ONLINE                 -
mfedata   guid          11017741863454066485   -
mfedata   version       33                     default
mfedata   bootfs        -                      default
mfedata   delegation    on                     default
mfedata   autoreplace   off                    default
mfedata   cachefile     -                      default
```

```
mfedata   failmode        wait                    default
mfedata   listsnapshots   off                     default
mfedata   autoexpand      off                     default
mfedata   dedupditto      0                       default
mfedata   dedupratio      1.00x                   -
mfedata   free            1.98G                   -
mfedata   allocated       94K                     -
mfedata   readonly        off
```

The properties shown here that are included in the default output of the zpool list command include size, allocated, free, capacity, dedupratio, health, and altroot. With the exception of the altroot property, these properties are reported by ZFS only and cannot be modified by the administrator.

exam

ⓦatch   *Pay particular attention to the properties reported in the zpool list command output, autoreplace, listsnapshots, and autoexpand. The zpool man page provides complete information on each of these properties and is the definitive source for review.*

One property that may be difficult to understand right away is the dedupratio property. It supplies a multiple of the data's real size to its actual storage cost. After a dataset opts in to deduplication, ZFS can replace repeated blocks of data written to that dataset with metadata that refers to a single on-disk location. The more datasets that subscribe to deduplication in a single pool, the greater savings you can realize, but the savings is calculated at the pool level. If your dedupratio is currently 1.10x, for example, it denotes that a mean average of unit storage covers 1.1 times the actual data. The higher the ratio, the more units of data there are that can be represented by a single unit of storage.

It can take some time to see a clear distinction between the pool and dataset properties. The compressratio property, for example, is reported per dataset, and it's reasonable to wonder why. The difference has to do with the object each property has in mind. Although any dataset can have compression set to on, compression does not operate on blocks that are (or could be) shared by two or more unrelated datasets.

Deduplication, however, will operate on any block that is common between any two datasets in the same pool, as long as both datasets have the property set to on.

From time to time, you may need a customized list of properties. Using the zpool list -o command, you can name any properties you want printed in a list. If you want to use these properties in a script program, you can also use the -H option to omit the headers:

```
$ zpool list -o size,free,health,guid mfedata
 SIZE   FREE  HEALTH                  GUID
1.98G  1.98G  ONLINE  11017741863454066485
$ zpool list -H -o guid mfedata
11017741863454066485
```

Reviewing ZFS Pool Command History

The history subcommand reports commands executed on an existing pool—using either the zpool or zfs utility—that modify its state. When you're in doubt about the current state of a pool, you can use this report to inform or refresh your understanding. The -l option, placed after the word "history" on the command line, will include the source of the command:

```
$ sudo zpool history mfedata
History for 'mfedata':
2012-11-06.01:47:04 zpool create -m /myapp mfedata c3t3d0
2012-11-06.01:59:35 zfs set mountpoint=/yourapp mfedata

$ sudo zpool history -l mfedata
History for 'mfedata':
2012-11-06.01:47:04 zpool create -m /myapp mfedata c3t3d0
[user root on orca:global]
2012-11-06.01:59:35 zfs set mountpoint=/yourapp mfedata
[user root on orca:global]
```

Output with the -l switch includes the user, system, and zone type as the command source. The term "global" refers to the operating system as a zone, one that can support so-called non-global zones, which I discuss in Chapter 17. The history subcommand also supports an -i switch that reports changes made by one of ZFS's internal mechanisms. The meaning of that output goes beyond the scope of this book.

Checking ZFS Pool Status and Health

A pool's overall health is one of its properties, and can be reported using either the zpool get command or the zpool list -o health command, or as part of the default zpool list command output. For a mirrored or raidz-type pool, the health of the whole depends on the state of each device (and its role), which can manifest in several ways. To see this detail, use the zpool status command instead. In the following example, I created a pool called dunder with a raidz vdev with three devices:

```
$ zpool status dunder
  pool: dunder
 state: ONLINE
  scan: none requested
config:

        NAME          STATE     READ WRITE CKSUM
        dunder        ONLINE       0     0     0
          raidz1-0    ONLINE       0     0     0
            c3t1d0    ONLINE       0     0     0
            c3t3d0    ONLINE       0     0     0
            c3t4d0    ONLINE       0     0     0

errors: No known data errors
```

After shutting down this virtual machine, I removed the virtual hard disk represented by the device name c3t4d0 to emulate a disk loss. After reboot, the status report showed as follows:

```
$ zpool status dunder
  pool: dunder
 state: DEGRADED
status: One or more devices could not be opened.  Sufficient replicas exist
        for the pool to continue functioning in a degraded state.
action: Attach the missing device and online it using 'zpool online'.
   see: http://www.sun.com/msg/ZFS-8000-2Q
  scan: none requested
config:

        NAME          STATE     READ WRITE CKSUM
        dunder        DEGRADED     0     0     0
          raidz1-0    DEGRADED     0     0     0
            c3t1d0    ONLINE       0     0     0
            c3t3d0    ONLINE       0     0     0
            c3t4d0    UNAVAIL      0     0     0  cannot open

errors: No known data errors
```

The overall health of this pool is marked DEGRADED. It is still usable, but its overall state has been compromised by the loss of a disk. That is, users may not notice the loss unless they perceive a change in I/O performance. The administrator, however, knows that the pool will not survive a subsequent device loss until repairs are made. Notice the zpool status command output includes an explanation of the problem and suggests the necessary actions to effect repair.

You can extrapolate from this output what a pool with multiple vdevs might look like. In this example, the pool is degraded because its raidz group is degraded. The raidz group is degraded because one of its devices is unavailable. The device was present at one time, then it just went away as far as the operating system can tell. Naturally there are different states to report based on the device at hand and its consequences to the virtual objects it belongs to. The outcome would be similar for a mirrored vdev; I will leave the proof of that case as an exercise you can try on your own.

Table 11-4 lists and describes all the device states reported by the zpool status command.

If you have multiple pools you'd like to check for errors without looking through a lot of output, the zpool status -x command will detail only pools that are not in a healthy state. To stay within the scope of this guide, I merely destroyed the dunder pool I had and remade it after restoring the virtual disk and rebooting. Then I checked the status using the -x switch:

```
$ zpool status -x
all pools are healthy
```

Had I used this command with the dunder pool still broken, it would have given the same output as if I had named the pool instead.

TABLE 11-4   Device States Reported by the zpool status Command

Device State	Description
ONLINE	Normal operation
DEGRADED	Partial failure of a virtual device (vdev)
FAULTED	Device made unavailable due to a failure
OFFLINE	Device made unavailable by administrator
REMOVED	Device removed while in use
UNAVAIL	Device inaccessible

Reporting Storage Pool I/O

When determining the performance of a pool, there are two general measures to apply: the number of read and write requests fulfilled by all the pool's datasets, and the total amount of data transferred in either direction. These two measures exist in a balance that is determined by the workload demand. In a given unit of time, the more read and write requests you have to process, the fewer opportunities you have to transfer data. The more data you have to transfer in either direction, the less time you have to take new requests.

The zpool iostat command reports three categories of statistics: capacity, operations, and bandwidth. Capacity is reported by allocated and free space. Operations and bandwidth are divided into read and write categories. To get useful results, you can apply a duration (in seconds) over which you want to average these statistics. You can also apply an interval count if you want a predetermined limit to the number of lines output:

```
$ zpool iostat rpool 3 3
               capacity     operations     bandwidth
rpool        alloc   free   read  write   read   write
----------   -----  -----  -----  -----  -----  -----
rpool        6.72G  1.22G      6      4   220K  74.4K
rpool        6.72G  1.22G      3      0  2.83K      0
rpool        6.72G  1.22G      0      0      0      0
```

This example reports I/O statistics for the rpool pool every three seconds for three intervals. There's not a lot of activity, and the value of studying I/O performance with virtual disks like this is rather academic. Still, you can see for each line there is a per-second calculation for each value over the duration specified. During the second interval, for example, there was an average of three read operations per second, and an average of 2.83KB of data read.

on the
job

Using this output, you can assess the demand on a pool over any given interval. The average of data transferred by the number of operations completed is a useful measure in some respects, but also rather coarse. At best, it can tell you whether you have an efficient balance, and even then only once you have set your own goals for either metric: how many IOPS you need to support or how much data you need to transfer to suit your business.

CERTIFICATION SUMMARY

In this chapter, you first learned why logical volume management, once considered an advanced administration skill, has become something every Solaris administrator should be familiar with. You also learned the basics of the RAID model, and how ZFS storage pools, called *zpools*, integrate this facility into everyday ZFS storage operations. Strictly speaking, you don't need to know the points of this lesson for the exam. To develop practical storage administration skills, however, you do need to know why ZFS includes this technology in its makeup. It is far easier to understand ZFS if you have some appreciation for what it replaces.

For the exam, you need to focus on the operations of the zpool utility and the meaning of the output from the subcommands described in this chapter. There is even more to learn about managing ZFS pools, but you're not expected to understand these operations well until you've acquired a bit more experience.

✓ TWO-MINUTE DRILL

Understanding Logical Volume Management

- ❑ A ZFS pool can use whole or partial disks, or even files for storage space. The minimum capacity requirement per device is 128MB.

- ❑ A vdev defines the arrangement of devices in a pool. The recommended arrangement is one that provides redundancy in the event of failure: either a mirror or a raidz group.

- ❑ All pools concatenate the devices or vdevs that are added to them. ZFS distributes the data you want to write across the devices in the pool, using a feature called *dynamic striping*.

- ❑ Solaris 11 offers three types of parity-data schemes that provide protection for one, two, or three disk failures at a time. Each type requires at least one more disk for user data than are supplied for parity data.

Administering ZFS Storage Pools

- ❑ ZFS pools have storage properties that differ from dataset properties. The ones you should understand for the OCA exam include the default columns reported by the zpool list command (size, allocated, free, capacity, dedupratio, health, and altroot), autoexpand, autoreplace, and listsnapshots.

- ❑ A pool also has dataset properties. By default, it will be mounted to a directory that matches the pool name. Although the mount point is a dataset property, you can set it at pool creation time if you prefer.

- ❑ Remember that a zpool will report the capacity of all disks in a raidz group. For a mirror, it will only report nonreplicated capacity.

- ❑ The compressratio property belongs to a dataset. The dedupratio property belongs to a pool. Unrelated datasets cannot share compressed data, but they can share deduplicated data.

- ❑ Use the zpool status command to determine how a redundant pool may have been degraded.

- ❑ You can review all the commands that have been used to alter a pool's state with the zpool history command.

SELF TEST

Use the following questions to test your recall and understanding of the chapter's material.

Understanding Logical Volume Management

1. Which is the traditional role of logical volume management?
   A. Using one device to support multiple file systems
   B. Replacing physical disks with files
   C. Using multiple devices to support one file system
   D. Naming disks according to site conventions

2. What feature could a RAID 10 model provide that a RAID 0+1 model cannot?
   A. Protection against disk loss
   B. Protection against file corruption
   C. Possible protection against multiple disk losses
   D. Possible protection against multiple file corruptions

3. Which two statements accurately describe parity data?
   A. Data that can be used to help calculate lost data
   B. Data that can be used to help calculate replicated data
   C. Data that can be used to restore a stripe
   D. Data that ensures an equal distribution of data in a disk group

4. Which of the following items is not a valid zpool device or vdev?
   A. cache
   B. stripe
   C. log
   D. raidz3

5. Which of the following two items are considered a dataset?
   A. raidz3
   B. snapshot
   C. mirror
   D. filesystem

Administering ZFS Storage Pools

6. Which of the following is not a valid zpool state?

A. HEALTHY

B. ONLINE

C. UNAVAIL

D. REMOVED

7. What is the result of the command zpool create raidz2 c1t1d0 c1t2d0 c1t3d0, assuming the devices listed are available for use?

A. The pool is created without errors or additional output.

B. The pool is created; the user is told the pool falls below the recommended minimum number of devices.

C. The pool is not created; an error message is generated.

D. The pool is created but immediately shows a DEGRADED state.

8. Assume you have created a pool and turned on deduplication for its dataset. You then copy the same 30MB file into it three times, each time with a different name. Which value is closest to what you'd expect to see for the dedupratio property?

A. 10.00x

B. 1.30x

C. 1.03x

D. 3.00x

9. Which of the following statements is true?

A. You can make a mirror of mirrors in a pool.

B. You can make a mirror of raidz groups in a pool.

C. You can concatenate vdevs and devices in a pool.

D. You can make a raidz group of raidz groups in a pool.

10. What capacity, approximately, would the zpool command report after creating a pool with the command sudo zpool create bloom raidz2 c1t3d0 c3t3d0 c3t3d0? Assume each device has a 4GB capacity.

A. 12GB

B. 8GB

C. 6GB

D. 4GB

SELF TEST ANSWERS

Understanding Logical Volume Management

1. ☑ **C.** Logical volume management originally addressed the problem of hosting growing file systems on a device with limited capacity.

   ☒ **A, B,** and **D** are incorrect. **A** is incorrect because operating systems have supported disk partitions for a long time. **B** is incorrect because this option describes disk virtualization. **D** is incorrect because disk or volume naming, although not a widely used option, has been available on most operating systems for decades.

2. ☑ **C.** A stripe of mirrored disks can survive multiple disk failures, as long as all the submirrors of one group don't fail. In no case will a RAID 0+1 configuration, also known as a mirror of stripes, survive two disk losses.

   ☒ **A, B,** and **D** are incorrect. **A** is incorrect because both configurations protect against the loss of any one disk. **B** and **D** are incorrect because volume protection does not extend to individual files that are deleted or corrupted.

3. ☑ **A** and **C.** Parity data derives from user data once it has been written to a stripe of devices. When a stripe member is lost, the surviving user data and parity data can be used to calculate the missing element. This function serves two purposes: one, to maintain data availability to the user; two, to rewrite the lost data to the replacement device.

   ☒ **B** and **D** are incorrect. **B** is incorrect because replicated (mirrored) data is an alternate approach to redundancy. **D** is also incorrect because parity data plays no role in distributing user data among devices.

4. ☑ **B.** In ZFS, there is no implicit or explicit stripe object. Striping itself is a process that is applied at the time data is written to a pool. You can concatenate devices and vdevs together, but you cannot make a stripe.

   ☒ **A, C,** and **D** are incorrect. These are all examples of valid objects in a ZFS storage pool.

5. ☑ **B** and **D.** Although you can call any object that uses zpool storage a dataset, the documentation is fuzzy on this point. The zfs man does not list a clone as a type of dataset. This fact seems to me like unfair territory for an exam question, but keep it in mind, just in case.

   ☒ **A** and **C** are incorrect. These are vdev types. Any pool you make using a vdev can be treated like a dataset as long as you address it using the zfs utility.

Administering ZFS Storage Pools

6. ☑ **A.** The correct term implied by the false term HEALTHY is ONLINE. The name of the pool property that contains this value is health.
   ☒ **B, C,** and **D** are incorrect. These are all valid states for either a zpool device, vdev, or pool.

7. ☑ **C.** The command does not include a pool name. The command interpreter will assume the term "raidz2" is the desired pool name. It will reject that name because the term is a reserved vdev type.
   ☒ **A, B,** and **D** are incorrect. **A** is incorrect because if a legal pool name is included in the command, this option correctly describes the outcome. **B** is incorrect because the zpool create command only enforces the required minimum number of devices for a vdev. It does not recommend a more practical number. **D** is incorrect because the zpool create command does not support creating a broken pool.

8. ☑ **D.** The dedupratio property is a multiple of the actual storage cost. The higher the multiple, the more user data is represented by a block of storage. Assuming an empty pool, saving the same file content three times under a different name should result in a factor of approximately 3.00x.
   ☒ **A, B,** and **C** are incorrect. These are all distracting values with no particular justification. **B** and **C** might seem plausible, if you focus on the size of the file in the example, but file size is irrelevant. It's a question of how many times ZFS can swap regular data blocks it has seen before with metadata that points to identical blocks it already has on disk.

9. ☑ **C.** You can, in fact, concatenate dissimilar devices and vdevs together. When you first try it, the zpool utility will complain. It will also tell you to use the -f switch if you want to insist. This is not recommended, naturally, but it is not completely prohibited either.
   ☒ **A, B,** and **D** are incorrect. These are all examples of nesting one vdev inside of another. This is forbidden by ZFS (along with every other logical volume solution I have worked with). All ZFS vdevs must be "top-level" devices.

10. ☑ **A.** Recall that the capacity of a zpool is reported as the sum of its devices when creating a raidz group. This rule holds even when the devices reserved for parity outnumber the devices reserved for data. The size of the dataset for this example would be 4GB, minus some overhead for metadata.
   ☒ **B, C,** and **D** are incorrect. These are all incorrect values; they represent 2/3, 1/2, and 1/3 of the total device space, any of which may seem plausible if you forget the rule for raidz group pool capacity.

12

Adding and Updating Solaris Software

I f you are new to systems administration, you will soon learn that updating system software can be a time-consuming process for those who manage production systems. But it's not because package installation is hard. Rather, it's knowing exactly what you have installed on a system and then tracking its effect on system performance and availability that can be tricky.

As home PC users, we're accustomed to thinking most software updates are part of a straightforward and useful maintenance process. Occasionally, you install something that interferes with your use more than it helps, but generally that's not the case. Business enterprise systems, however, may run a complex arrangement of programs that rely on each other. Each one can be sensitive to seemingly innocent changes, in feature updates, communications protocol and data format changes, and even bug fixes and license upgrades. Sometimes software is even designed to stop working if the version numbers of other software it talks to happen to change.

Finding, reviewing, installing, and removing software packages aren't difficult. Ensuring that the interactions among all software components don't break, however, can take a lot of time in planning, in testing, and in timing roll-outs to coincide with other needed changes. There may be changes to consider in hardware and in the operating system, too, as well as in business code. In this chapter, you'll learn how the Solaris 11 environment has evolved to help you meet these challenges head-on.

CERTIFICATION OBJECTIVE 12.01

Understanding the Image Packaging System (IPS)

In this chapter, you'll learn to use a new type of software management tool called the Image Packaging System (IPS). IPS replaces a decades-long utility known to many as System V Release 4 (SVR4) packaging, a software management scheme once held as a standard among several major UNIX vendors, including Sun Microsystem, Hewlett-Packard, and IBM. At one time, the SVR4 standard was a boon to anyone who had to manage packaging on two or more of these platforms in the course of a day's work. These days, it isn't just the motivation for uniform platform software that has waned. The zeal for better tools has inspired lots of innovating. There are today as many popular software installation tools as there are operating systems to support them, each with its own strengths.

IPS is a product of many lessons learned: in managing software files, in stretching the SVR4 system beyond its intended purpose, and by observing what has worked well in other package schemes. It is also designed to take advantage of features specific to a root file system based on ZFS and serve the two platforms on which Solaris runs (SPARC and X86). IPS has a full suite of roles and components that account for these conditions.

Understanding IPS Roles

Before I describe the key roles IPS components play, let's consider the contemporary challenges for getting software in the first place:

- You want to get your software from the network (no physical media to track).
- You need software from several providers (not just Oracle).
- You need to install to desktop systems and servers, which may have different software needs.
- You may need to install software to an inactive boot environment you're not using.
- You want to install to either the X86 or SPARC platform without having to check.

IPS supports all these objectives and more. It does so with roles that let you define your own locations for storing installable objects (including, but not limited to, files and directories), catalog them by their attributes and properties, and install them to targets other than your active operating system session. The role names are given in Table 12-1.

TABLE 12-1	IPS Roles	Description
Roles in the Image Packaging System	Repository	Stores package content and indexing data
	Publisher	A provider of one or more packages
	Package	A list of actions to take on an image
	Image	Any installation target (client)

The repository replaces conventional physical media or ISO files as a bundled form for system software. It is also a collection of directories and files, along with other IPS-specific data, but can be located on any Solaris 11 system and replicated easily. It can support one or more publishers, each of which provides a named source for packages. You can store all the software one site needs in a single repository. You could make several repositories, all with the same content or each with different content. But because you can always establish a named location on the network for each one, you have a much better chance of keeping track of it than physical media or a single file.

A publisher is a software source. The default publisher, solaris, indicates what kind of software it contains. You would expect other IPS publishers to use names that are more specific, such as a company name or Internet site address. From the client's perspective, the publisher is the important handle; the repository location only tells a configured client where to find the publisher. In fact, one client can even list the same publisher in different repositories and define which one to prefer when more than one is available.

A package contains a number of objects, the most common types of which are files and directories. IPS refers to each one as an *action* (that is, by the way it changes the intended target) or *image*. Other actions in a package may augment the system in an indirect way. For example, some post-configurations, such as adding a new account to manage software, can be added as part of an IPS package instead of requiring post-installation work to do the same.

An image describes any environment that can use the IPS tools to process package actions on itself. You may have any number of images on a single system; boot environments and zones (covered in Chapter 17) are both a kind of image, as is your current active environment. Each image has its own configuration files to define what kind of client it is, what package actions it can and can't process, and what actions have been taken on it so far.

Each of these roles gives the administrator a far more flexible view of package management, at the cost of some complexity and perhaps a few features that don't seem important at first blush. In this chapter, we discuss the fundamental purpose of these roles and stick to the primary lesson of managing packages as a client. As a high-level reference, though, Figure 12-1 illustrates these roles and their relationships.

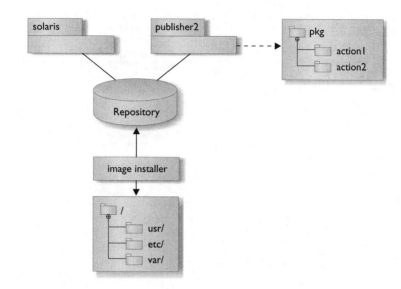

FIGURE 12-1

PS roles and
relationships

Understanding Repositories and Publishers

As a replacement for physical media, the IPS repository acts more like a package exchange than a client resource. There are installer tools, of course, such as the pkg utility and the Package Manager, to help you retrieve packages, but there are also tools to help you create repositories (the pkgrepo utility) and populate them with publishers. You can then add packages, using the pkgsend utility, by associating them with a publisher. A repository is just a store with content produced by publishers and made available to subscribers.

On any system that hosts a repository, an installer tool can access a repository's packages through a file-based URI. The system can also make the repository available to remote systems by configuring and enabling the SMF service svc:// application/pkg/server:default. This service starts the pkg.depotd process, which uses an HTTP server to serve packages in a streamed-file format. Figure 12-2 illustrates the various IPS clients using a repository for storing and retrieving packages.

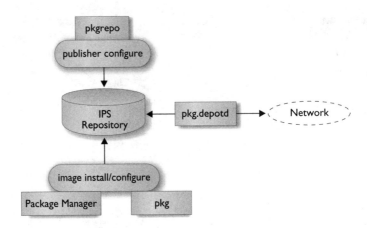

FIGURE 12-2

IPS client tools
that use the IPS
repository

Your Solaris 11 default installation points to the solaris publisher at the repository Oracle supports, available at the URI http://pkg.oracle.com/solaris/release. For the sake of illustration, I've added a repository and my own publisher to a Solaris 11 system, just to show that a client may be aware of multiple sources for packages and to show one repository at a file-based URI:

```
$ pkg publisher
PUBLISHER          TYPE      STATUS    URI
solaris            origin    online    http://pkg.oracle.com/solaris/release/
michael            origin    online    file:///export/repo/
```

Although the command is intended to list the publishers an image is aware of, the TYPE column actually reports the type of the repository. There are two types: origins and mirrors. An origin repository supports an index for its publishers' catalogs and provides a search facility for clients; a mirror will only serve package content. Using the two types together, origins can support all package search requests while the mirror repositories support download requests.

The SMF service that makes a repository remotely accessible has the FMRI svc:/ application/pkg/server:default. It is disabled by default, because a default Solaris installation does not have a repository installed. You can create a simple repository using the pkgrepo command, add a publisher, and connect to it with the pkg utility, which is shown later in this chapter. If you want to add packages and share them with other systems, you'll then need to configure the service before enabling it.

Understanding Packages

The service metaphor used in SMF—naming each entity with an FMRI and using an XML-based manifest for its configuration—also applies to IPS packages. The configuration is stored as a list of properties. There can also be many variations of a single package's contents: its platform type, system limitations, software version, and license agreements can all vary according to the image configuration. SMF uses instance names to distinguish services of the same general type; IPS hides these details, exposing only release information that qualifies the package name. It is up to the image configuration to indicate which other package details, known generally as *facets* and *variants*, apply to it.

Think about it this way: Let's say you want to install a special-purpose code library to an X86 system running Solaris 11. In the SVR4 packaging model, you'd have to locate the X86 version of the package first. If you then need to upgrade or patch the software, you also have to make sure you have upgrade/patch for the right platform. With third-party software, some patches and upgrades might apply to specific releases of the operating system, or other such details may be important. Platform, release number, and license grade could all factor in to locating the proper package to install, and many variations of one package could exist.

In the IPS system, these same factors are submerged in the package name. Major version releases and patch fixes are treated like instance information—details that follow in the full name of any one package. If there is a difference in package files between the SPARC and X86 platform, IPS calls them *variants* (that is, platform-specific differences). These are handled by determining the image's variation. If the target is a SPARC machine, all it will receive from the package collection are any generic files and any SPARC-specific variants. The other general type (facets) deals with optional aspects of an image, such as the language sets it supports. If a package has documentation specific to a language the image doesn't support, there is no need to install it.

Thus, although you have access to all the packages of a solaris publisher, the image determines which actions of each package apply to it. You only act on the package components you can use. For example, here's what happens when I try to install a SPARC-specific network adapter driver:

```
$ sudo pkg install network/eri
Creating Plan
pkg install: The following pattern(s) only matched packages that are
not available for the current image's architecture, zone type, and/or
other variant:
    network/eri
```

This entire driver package includes a SPARC variant in its metadata. The image configuration for my system is stored in the file /var/pkg/pkg5.image. It includes a key, variant.arch, which is set to i386. Once the pkg utility identifies the mismatch between package and image, it stops and reports the error. Under this scheme, it's possible to make packages that supply every object in one collection name, and not worry if the image will install it correctly.

Some packages just serve to describe relationships to other packages. A group package, for example, lists all the packages that belong to one installation setup, similar to the way an SMF milestone lists all the services that make up the milestone. A LiveMedia CD installation, for example, applies a group package called solaris-desktop, containing all the packages a desktop setup requires. You can list these packages out if you like:

```
$ pkg contents -m group/system/solaris-desktop | grep ^depend | wc -l
     511
```

The -m switch reports the raw manifest of a package, which includes any actions other than installing a file or directory. I used the grep command to sift the lines beginning with the word *depend*. The wc -l command reduced that output to the number of packages that make up the group, 511.

An incorporation package constrains an image from changing the packages it lists. Packages that belong to an incorporation are said to be *consolidated*. The incorporation package freezes consolidated packages, usually so they can only be altered with minor changes or patches. This mechanism ensures you don't accidentally upgrade one package and break the way it works with the other members of the consolidation. The packages that make up all the Java components installed on Solaris 11, for example—the Java Development Kit (JDK), the Java Runtime Environment (JRE), and their demo programs—all belong together, even though they are bundled as separate components:

```
$ pkg contents -m java/java-incorporation
$ pkg contents -m java/java-incorporation | grep depend
depend fmri=developer/java/jdk-7@1.7.0.0,5.11-0.173.0.0.0.0.0 type=incorporate
depend fmri=library/java/java-demo-7@1.7.0.0,5.11-0.173.0.0.0.0.0 type=incorporate
depend fmri=runtime/java/jre-7@1.7.0.0,5.11-0.173.0.0.0.0.0 type=incorporate
```

A group ensures you include any prerequisite packages with the one you name. An incorporation ensures you don't change one package that others depend on. With these and other features in IPS, an administrator has a more sophisticated set of controls and a lot of built-in safeguards than were available with SVR4 packaging tools.

Understanding the Package FMRI

One IPS FMRI represents one package and all the ways it can be installed. Recall that an FMRI follows URI syntax, so it must include a scheme and a path. Also, it may define its own separators for distinguishing the elements of a path. The forward slash and period are reserved characters, but any other special marks (such as & or ? or %20%) may be used. An IPS FMRI looks like this:

```
pkg://solaris/system/dtrace@0.5.11,5.11-0.175.0.0.0.2.1:20111019T070941Z
```

The scheme name, pkg, is always followed by a colon. The publisher name is an optional part of a fully qualified FMRI, but if it is included it is preceded by two leading forward slashes. Any single forward slash is part of the package name: It can be a directory, category, or something else. The IPS definition does not specify how these should be interpreted. Table 12-2 lists all the possible elements of a fully qualified FMRI and the punctuation marks that separate them.

TABLE 12-2   Elements of an IPS FMRI

FMRI Element	Preceding Mark	Description
pkg:	N/A	Scheme
solaris	//	Publisher (optional)
system/dtrace	/	Package name
0.5.11	@	Component version
5.11	,	Build version
0.175.0.0.0.2.1	-	Branch version
20111019T070941Z	:	Timestamp

A package's actions are described in a file called a *manifest*. The actions may include files and directories to be installed, but can also include symbolic or hard links to create, driver interfaces to configure, license agreements to accept, and dependency declarations for the image to verify. A package may even add new users and groups associated with software included in the package.

Understanding the IPS Image

In the same way that a repository is just a location for publishers, an image is one location for installing packages. The location is configured to receive packages according to any variants, facets, or other conditions it lists. The three image types are full, partial, and user. A full image, such as a boot environment (BE), acts as a parent to a partial image (such as a zone). User images make it possible to test an installation that differs from the host system. You could define a user image, for example, to test installing SPARC files to an X86 system.

The image abstraction makes each installation location independently configurable. This capability isn't something a new administrator may think about just yet, but it does let package developers establish differences in their software for installing to a boot environment, a zone, or some other target. This approach allows the image to define the correct (or desired) parameters; all package developers have to account for are the variations they care to support.

Understanding the Update Manager

Three tools are supplied to install packages to an image: the command-line pkg utility, the graphical Package Manager utility, and the Update Manager, which can be operated either way. I'll cover the first two utilities through the rest of the chapter. Owing to the way it is put together and made available for use, however, the Update Manager implementation deserves special mention.

First, it is managed by a separate SMF service:

```
$ svcs -p pkg/update
STATE         STIME    FMRI
online        2:25:31  svc:/application/pkg/update:default
```

Recall that the svcs -p command will list any active processes maintained by the service. The Update Manager doesn't have one, as the output shows. As it turns out, however, the Update Manager isn't idle. When the service is enabled, it writes a cron job using the root account's identity. The job is a script that is scheduled to execute five times a day. You can see this entry using the crontab -l command:

```
$ sudo crontab -l
30 0,9,12,18,21 * * * /usr/lib/update-manager/update-refresh.sh
```

In a cron entry, the minutes of the hour appear in the first column. The hours of the day appear in the second column in 24-hour format; multiple entries in any column are comma-separated. The remaining columns, shown here with wildcards for values, represent the day of the month, the month of the year, and the day of the week, respectively. See the man page for the crontab command to get the correct numeric range for each one. The last column lists the command to execute.

As shown, the update-refresh.sh script will execute at 12:30 A.M., 9:30 A.M., 12:30 P.M., 6:30 P.M., and 9:30 P.M. The comments written in that script file fully describe the process it follows. In summary, it will check the image's preferred publishers for updates. A notification icon will appear to the desktop user.

Although intended for use as a desktop tool, you can invoke the Update Manager with the pm-launch command, as follows:

```
$ /usr/lib/pm-launch pm-updatemanager
```

CERTIFICATION OBJECTIVE 12.02

Updating the Solaris 11 Image with IPS

In IPS terminology, *updating* is defined as installing the most recent version of a package or image. This definition includes first-time installations, too, which are listed separately (hence, the two windows shown by calling the Update Manager through the Package Manager). Remember also that any constraints and dependencies built in to packages already installed may prevent the image from adding packages. All the Update Manager does, then, is automate this approach.

When you update a client's full image, you are merging its current state with updated packages components, including packages you may have added after the initial installation. The image's constraints have to be worked out with your publishers' catalogs so only the necessary package actions are downloaded. Unlike SVR4 packaging, in which you have to remove one package version to replace it with a later version, IPS packages can complement its legacy components on an image, possibly reducing the total time needed for the download, installation, and verification process.

Before an image update begins, the image generates a plan that includes the following factors:

- Number of packages to install
- Number of packages to update
- Number of mediators to change
- Estimated space available
- Estimated space to be consumed
- Whether to create a new boot environment
- Whether to activate the new boot environment
- Whether to back up the current boot environment
- Whether to rebuild the boot archive

All the terms listed here, except the term *mediator*, should be familiar. Mediators are used to manage all the links to one file that may have occurred in multiple implementations of the same package (such as different major releases of the same software). If your system has two or more implementations of the same package (for example, Java 6 and Java 7), there may be a common file name and location between them, such as installing a Java executable file in the /usr/bin directory. Mediators determine which version should take precedence when both are installed.

Once all these factors have been evaluated, the full image update process occurs in the following steps:

1. Package download
2. Installation phase
3. Package state update phase
4. Image state update phase

Using the Command-Line Interface

To run an update from the command line, use the pkg update subcommand. This option relies on a long list of default behaviors, so the subcommand supports many switch options to override them. For example, it's usually the case that you want to create and activate a new boot environment after updating the image to see if you like the results, and to provide a way to roll back if you don't. The default behavior also lets you accept any license agreements included automatically if you don't want to attend the update process. Using the option switches available, you can override these safeguards and conveniences as you see fit.

To run through an update without committing to the entire process, you can use the -nv switch to perform a dry run of the process. The result with these options in use is a list of every package affected in the update, which will take some time to generate and may be long enough to overrun the buffer of your terminal screen. On my system, the total line count for the result shows as follows:

```
$ sudo pkg update -nv | wc -l
    548
```

You can instead redirect the results to a file and review the packages that will be affected at a later time. In any event, remember that it takes a while to download and install all the files in an image update. Although the system isn't locked while this process occurs, you probably want to leave the system to complete this process as much as you can.

Using the Package Manager

The Package Manager's toolbar includes an Updates option. When this option is selected, the image will prepare the system by checking currently installed files against each publisher it is aware of. If updates are available, the image gathers the details to prepare for installation. Figure 12-3 shows the preparation phase in process after the Updates toolbar button has been clicked.

Once this preparation process completes, the Update Manager component presents two lists: one for installation details, listing the packages that will be affected, and one for update details, listing packages that will be added. A full image update can take a long time to process, so choosing a window in which you won't need to use the system heavily is a good idea. Figure 12-4 shows the confirmation dialog box that follows a successful preparation phase.

FIGURE 12-3   Preparation panel for updating the image

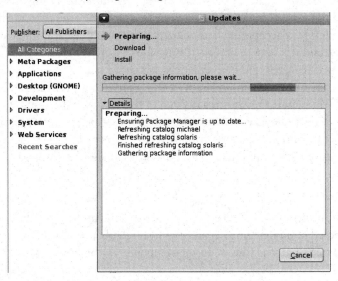

FIGURE 12-4   Confirmation dialog box for updating the image

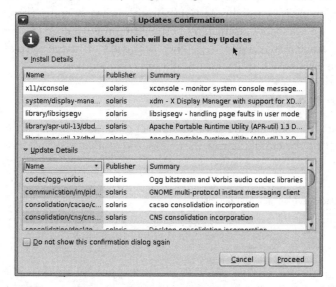

Managing Software Packages

Desktop users who want all the latest changes to software as they become available can make good use of the Update Manager through the Desk Manager interface. Server administrators usually have to take a more systematic approach to software change. When you have to maintain systems for their performance, usability, and availability to many users, you always want to have a short list of likely causes in mind when these qualities degrade. Any change to a system is prime suspect when these factors change noticeably. In such cases, logs and change documentation help the administrator to track potential causes of adverse change and quickly determine how to reverse or mitigate its effects. As a beginning administrator, you need to understand how these conditions may affect the tasks you're asked to perform.

As a sole user of a desktop system, however, you're far less likely to manage each change as carefully. This difference is what separates the pkg utility from the Package Manager graphical tool. You'll find the Package Manager covers the basics of package management well, whereas the pkg utility gives you far more flexibility and power in defining your installation configuration.

Using Package Manager

Figure 12-5 shows the Package Manager graphic interface, which you can invoke by selecting the circular arrow in the desktop toolbar.

FIGURE 12-5   The Package Manager graphic interface

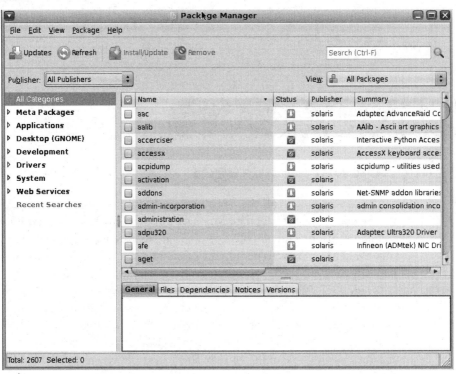

Several views are available that you can use to reduce the package listings currently visible. The View drop-down box to the right of the display includes filters for the following:

- All Packages
- Installed Packages
- Updates
- Not Installed Packages

You can also limit or expand your view of publishers if you have more than one. What's more, you can invoke the Package Manager utility from a terminal session. The command resides in the /usr/bin directory, which is included in your default PATH variable:

```
$ sudo packagemanager &
```

You'll see some error output in your terminal session if you call this utility without using sudo. Writing to the package's log requires root permissions, as does making changes to the image. The Package Manager panel will still appear, but any action requiring root privileges will fail.

Listing Packages and Their Contents

You can select any package from the Package Manager view to get more information about it; it does not have to be installed. Once a package is selected, you can get more details using the tabs located at the bottom of the display. The tabs and the contents they include are as follows:

- **General**   An overview of the package with high-level details
- **Files**   A list of all installable files and directories
- **Dependencies**   A list of packages required to support the selected package
- **Notices**   License agreements and copyright notices
- **Versions**   Installed and available versions of the package

Package Manager dependency information for the nethack package

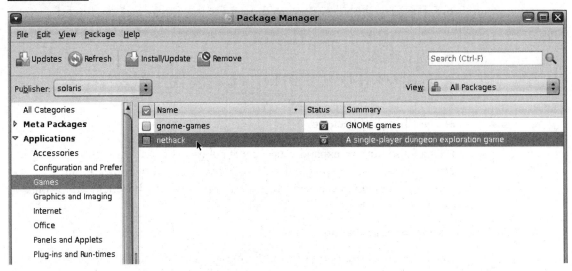

Figure 12-6 shows the Applications | Games category selected in the Category panel, as well as the nethack page selected in the Package panel. The Dependencies tab is also selected and shows the packages needed to properly support the nethack game.

Searching For and Verifying Package Installation

Chances are you won't know the specific names of the packages you want off the top of your head. The Package Manager supports a search facility that is useful for narrowing the field of possibilities with a good keyword or two. Figure 12-7 shows a search using Package Manager with the search term "http," which turns up 14 packages. Using the more specific term "httpd" would reduce the results to one package: Apache Web Server V2.2.

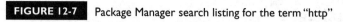

FIGURE 12-7 Package Manager search listing for the term "http"

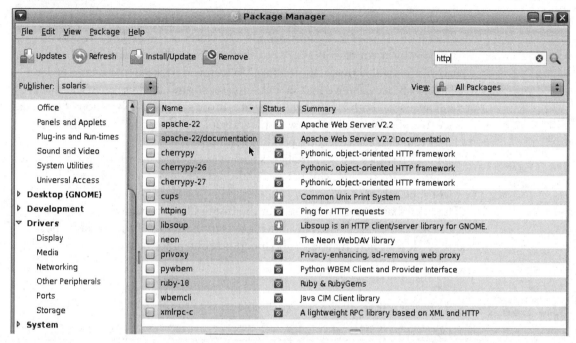

Once you locate a package, you will find it in one of three states, assuming it hasn't been damaged:

- Installed
- Updates Available
- Uninstalled

The information available in the tabs should be the same regardless of its state, as long as the image is up to date with its publishers. You can use the Refresh button to update the package catalogs and make sure the image has the most current package information available.

Installing and Removing Packages

You may have noticed the Install/Update and Remove buttons in the Package Manager toolbar are grayed out by default. The status of the package triggers one or both buttons if you tick its check box. For an uninstalled package, the Install/Update button will activate. If you check an installed package that has no updates available, only the Remove button will activate. For installed packages that have updates available, both buttons will activate. If you select a combination of packages at once, the appropriate buttons will still activate, but their actions will not apply to packages that don't have a corresponding status.

Figure 12-8 shows the gcalctool package has been checked, which in turn enables the Remove button. Once this button is selected, a Remove Confirmation dialog box will appear.

The same dialog box style is used for the Install Confirmation and Update Confirmation messages. The only difference is in the status of the package checked and the following action. There is no functional difference between a fresh install

FIGURE 12-8   Package Manager with an installed package checked

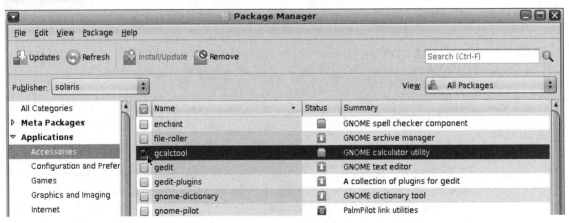

and an update, except that an update always implies the most recent version of a package, and possibly requires fewer files to complete the job.

This isn't all that Package Manager can do. Under the File menu, you'll also find the following choices:

- Add Publisher
- Manage Publishers
- Manage Boot Environments

With the Manage Publishers panel, shown in Figure 12-9, each publisher appears with the attributes Sticky and Enabled. The Enabled attribute is self-evident. When an image configures a publisher as Sticky, it means updates to any package installed from that publisher must come from the same publisher. You cannot turn off these attributes for the system publisher, but you can for any additional publishers you add.

FIGURE 12-9   Manage Publishers panel in the Update Manager desktop application

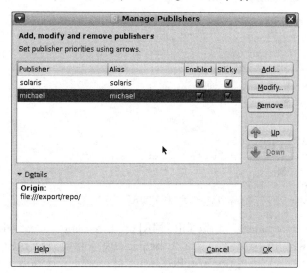

Using the pkg Command

The Package Manager utility is convenient for general use, but it lacks a full range of capabilities. For full control over the image configuration, the pkg utility supports 36 subcommands, some of which reverse the effects of others. The commands you are expected to know for the OCA exam are listed in Table 12-3. Most of the remaining subcommands perform an action, such as setting an image or publisher property.

These subcommands correspond to the same actions you are expected to know in the Package Manager utility. The following sections illustrate the use of each subcommand.

Listing Packages and Their Contents

The list subcommand produces the content you will also find under the General tab of the Package Manager. To use it, supply a package name that is specific enough to match at least one package. Here is an example using the gcalctool package I discovered working with the Package Manager:

```
$ pkg info gcalctool
          Name: desktop/calculator/gcalctool
       Summary: GNOME calculator utility
      Category: Applications/Accessories
         State: Installed
     Publisher: solaris
       Version: 5.30.2
 Build Release: 5.11
        Branch: 0.175.0.0.0.0.0
Packaging Date: September 27, 2011 08:22:14 AM
          Size: 1.54 MB
          FMRI: pkg://solaris/desktop/calculator/gcalctool@5.30.2,5.11-
                0.175.0.0.0.0.0:20110927T082214Z
```

The components of the full FMRI are listed one line per element in this output, along with the state and size of the package, followed by the fully qualified FMRI.

If the package is not installed, you can use the -r option to retrieve package details from the publisher.

TABLE 12-3	pkg Subcommand	Description
Selected Subcommands of the pkg Utility	list	Package name, version and state
	info	Full package description (including licensing)·
	contents	Package manifest information
	update	Install the latest package version
	install	Install new package (can also update)
	verify	Validate package installation
	search	Find package by query pattern (installed or not)
	uninstall	Remove installed package

The pkg list subcommand provides summary information of installed packages. It's a good choice to review summary details or to list several packages at once. In particular, this subcommand reports three different installation attributes by default: whether it is installed, frozen, or obsolete. In this example, I list the pinentry package:

```
$ pkg list pinentry
NAME (PUBLISHER)                    VERSION                  IFO
security/pinentry                   0.7.6-0.175.0.0.0.2.537  i--
```

If a package is frozen, it cannot be upgraded. You can get more information on the reason for the freeze by adding the -c switch to the command. There are several reasons a package might be made obsolete, such as renaming it.

The contents subcommand reports the same information as the Files tab of the Package Manager. Given the name of a package, a listing of the files and directories needed to install the package is given:

```
$ pkg contents pinentry
PATH
usr
usr/lib
usr/lib/pinentry
usr/lib/pinentry-curses
usr/lib/pinentry-gtk-2
usr/share
usr/share/info
usr/share/info/pinentry.info
```

The contents subcommand also supports a -t option that lets you specify the type of objects you wish to see in the output.

Searching For and Verifying Package Installation

The search subcommand lets you find any package available in any active repository configured with your image. Naturally, it depends on an origin repository to work, and does not require that you match terms that are part of the package name. In fact, the pkg search subcommand will also return packages that cannot be installed to the current image, as this example shows:

```
$ pkg search httpd
INDEX       ACTION VALUE                              PACKAGE
basename    file   usr/apache2/2.2/bin/amd64/httpd    pkg:/web/server/apache-
22@2.2.20-0.175.0.0.0.2.537
basename    file   usr/apache2/2.2/bin/httpd          pkg:/web/server/apache-
22@2.2.20-0.175.0.0.0.2.537
basename    file   usr/apache2/2.2/bin/sparcv9/httpd pkg:/web/server/apache-
22@2.2.20-0.175.0.0.0.2.537
```

The search term "httpd" returns one package in the Package Manager utility. Here, you also see one package, but three matches on the term as a filename value. One entry shows the executable file specific to an AMD64 platform, and one to a SPARC platform. The remaining entry that appears is a wrapper program designed to call the platform-specific file installed to the image.

You can determine a package is correctly installed by verifying it. This process compares the installed package to the manifest and determines whether the image objects are the same as when first installed. Naturally, this kind of verification can cause problems with files that will change after installation, such as configuration data. Nonetheless, this subcommand makes it very easy to determine if a package has been compromised:

```
$ pkg verify gcalctool
$ sudo rm /usr/bin/gcalccmd
$ pkg verify gcalctool
PACKAGE                                                  STATUS
pkg://solaris/desktop/calculator/gcalctool               ERROR
        file: usr/bin/gcalccmd
            Missing: regular file does not exist
```

In the first verify command, the package checked out cleanly. After I deleted a file from its content list, I ran verify again: The image reported the missing object.

Fortunately, the IPS system has an answer for this problem. When you find a package in this condition, you can use the pkg fix subcommand to repair the file. This action is somewhat like an update; only the file(s) needed to effect repair are downloaded from the repository and installed:

```
$ sudo pkg fix gcalctool
Verifying: pkg://solaris/desktop/calculator/gcalctool                ERROR
        file: usr/bin/gcalccmd
                Missing: regular file does not exist
Created ZFS snapshot: 2012-12-09-21:48:28
Repairing: pkg://solaris/desktop/calculator/gcalctool

DOWNLOAD                                 PKGS        FILES      XFER (MB)
Completed                                1/1          1/1        0.0/0.0

PHASE                                 ACTIONS
Update Phase                             1/1

PHASE                                   ITEMS
Image State Update Phase                 2/2
```

The fix subcommand verifies the package to identify the damaged component(s). It then creates a snapshot to protect the original image, in case the fix does more harm than good. Then the process operates just like an installation or update: by downloading the needed file, updating the package, and updating the image. Although you're not expected to know the fix subcommand for the OCA exam, it's exactly what you want once you discover a damaged package.

Installing and Removing Packages

As I mentioned previously, the steepest part of the learning curve with IPS at first is probably learning package names. For that, the Package Manager search facility provides a convenient way to explore. In the absence of a desktop, the pkg search command is also effective but clutters the screen a bit more.

Once you know the names of packages, installing and removing (or uninstalling) them is a straightforward process. Remember that each installation requires the phased process described throughout this chapter, and includes updating the image after each action. The install and uninstall subcommands, in that respect, look about the same once you have invoked them. Here is the output from an uninstall of the nethack package:

```
$ sudo pkg uninstall nethack
          Packages to remove:  1
        Create boot environment: No
 Create backup boot environment: No

PHASE                                          ACTIONS
Removal Phase                                  165/165

PHASE                                            ITEMS
Package State Update Phase                         1/1
Package Cache Update Phase                         1/1
Image State Update Phase                           2/2
```

To assess the impact of a package installation or removal without committing the action, use the -nv options. This will perform a dry-run that previews the number of files affected and image-oriented actions. Although this option cannot assess the time required—something you might like to know before updating the entire image—you can get some feel for the duration of the install by the number of actions required to complete the process.

CERTIFICATION SUMMARY

In this chapter you learned the skills you need to apply the Update Manager, Package Manager, and pkg tools to manage and update your Solaris software. You can use these same tools to install third-party software that is bundled using IPS. With a little more exploring, you can make IPS packages yourself, and take advantage of all the careful engineering that has gone into its making.

Remember that a package is not just a collection of files, but a list of actions, two of which are installable directories and files. The remaining actions can help you remember that IPS is more than a way to package programs and data your system needs. It is also a method for protecting and maintaining the elements you need to ensure the health and consistency of your system's configuration.

Commit IPS's key concepts to memory, including the roles and elements discussed in this chapter. That will go a long way to helping you remember why IPS is built the way it is, and how it can help you tackle the challenges that await you in managing software changes in a mission-critical environment.

TWO-MINUTE DRILL

Understanding the Image Packaging System (IPS)

❑ The roles in the IPS system include repositories, publishers, packages, and images.

❑ A repository hosts one or more publishers of software. A host system may include one or more images, or separately configurable install targets.

❑ Packages are lists of actions that can be committed to an image. Not all actions the package contains may apply to all image types.

Updating the Solaris 11 Operating System with IPS

❑ The Update Manager and Package Manager are graphical tools intended for use with a desktop environment.

❑ To update an image means installing the latest version of each package the image contains.

❑ Each update process creates a plan, downloads packages from the repository, executes the actions, and updates the image. The process may include creating boot environments that preserve the original image as well as activating the updated image.

Managing Software Packages

❑ You can get package details through the General tab of the Package Manager or the pkg info subcommand.

❑ The pkg contents subcommand will list the files and directories that a package installs.

❑ The pkg search command is string-based and useful for learning package names associated with a particular file. You can also use the search text field in the Package Manager.

❑ The pkg verify subcommand will tell you if all the installed objects of a package are present and in their original condition. You can use the pkg fix subcommand to effect repairs if you want to package restored.

SELF TEST

Use the following questions to test your recall and understanding of the chapter's material.

Understanding the Image Packaging System (IPS)

1. What does an origin repository do that a mirror repository can't do?
   A. It serves packages to remote systems.
   B. It can be updated with new packages.
   C. It provides a searchable index of packages.
   D. It can be added to an image through the Package Manager.

2. Which option describes an incorporation package?
   A. It contains no actions, just the names of other packages.
   B. It disallows major updates to its member packages.
   C. It bundles other packages together into one installable unit.
   D. It installs dependencies for other packages.

3. Which option describes a possible package variant?
   A. One that will work on SPARC systems only
   B. One that will work on any Solaris system
   C. One that includes support for French and German
   D. One that only supports English

4. Which option is not included in a package's FMRI?
   A. Build Release
   B. Packaging Date
   C. Install Status
   D. Publisher

Updating the Solaris 11 Operating System with IPS

5. Which two tools can you use to update a whole image?
   A. Update Manager
   B. Package Manager
   C. The pkg utility
   D. The pkgrepo utility

6. Which option is the final phase of a package installation, update, or removal?

   A. Package update phase

   B. Package verify phase

   C. Image verify phase

   D. Image update phase

7. Which pkg subcommand can you use to determine if an installed package is frozen?

   A. list

   B. verify

   C. info

   D. contents

Managing Software Packages

8. Which option will not invoke an install plan when used with the pkg utility?

   A. fix

   B. remove

   C. install

   D. update

9. Choose the two correct statements.

   A. A package cannot have two files with the same name.

   B. A repository cannot have two publishers with the same name.

   C. An image cannot have two publishers with the same name.

   D. A publisher cannot have two packages with the same name.

10. Which of the following two options are package actions?

   A. license

   B. fix

   C. verify

   D. depend

SELF TEST ANSWERS

Understanding the Image Packaging System (IPS)

1. ☑   **C.** A mirror repository has no metadata, only package content. It is designed to serve packages only.
   ☒   **A, B,** and **D** are incorrect. These are all actions of properties associated with either repository type.

2. ☑   **B.** An incorporation package is designed to keep other packages consistent with each other. It does this by preventing its member packages from being updated.
   ☒   **A, C,** and **D** are incorrect. **A** is incorrect because all packages contain actions, whether they install files or not. **C** is incorrect because this description comes closest to describing a group package. **D** is incorrect because the installation tool is responsible for installing the dependencies for any desired package.

3. ☑   **A.** Package variants describe some unchanging aspect of the image, such as its supporting hardware type.
   ☒   **B, C,** and **D** are incorrect. **B** is incorrect because an object that works equally well on all Solaris 11 images has no necessary variation. **C** is incorrect because additional language sets are treated as facets or aspects of a system that may or may not be part of its image. **D** describes a system that has no additional language facets.

4. ☑   **C.** The install status of any package is part of the image's data, not the FMRI.
   ☒   **A, B,** and **D** are incorrect. All are components of a package FMRI.

Updating the Solaris 11 Operating System with IPS

5. ☑   **B and C.** Both the Package Manager and the pkg tool provide options to update all packages on the image for which updates are available.
   ☒   **A and D** are incorrect. **A** is incorrect because the Update Manager provides notification of available updates. It doesn't install them. **D** is incorrect because the pkgrepo utility can be used to create repositories and add publishers to them; it does not install software to an image.

6. ☑   **D.** After any package action that changes the image, the image configuration itself is reconciled.
   ☒   **A, B,** and **C** are incorrect. **A** is incorrect because the package update phase occurs immediately before the image update phase. **B** and **C** are incorrect because there is no verification phase in any of these processes.

7. ☑ **A.** The list subcommand pertains to installed packages only. Its default output includes a column for reporting installed, frozen, and obsolete flags on a package.
☒ **B, C,** and **D** are incorrect. **B** is incorrect because the verify subcommand will tell you whether a package has had its files altered since it was installed. **C** is incorrect because the info subcommand reports the high-level details of the package, whether it is installed or not. **D** is incorrect because the contents subcommand reports the files and directories that are included with a package.

Managing Software Packages

8. ☑ **B.** The pkg utility does not have a remove subcommand. The correct term is uninstall.
☒ **A, C,** and **D** are incorrect. All are subcommands that will invoke an install plan if it is necessary to change the current state of the image.

9. ☑ **B and D.** A repository uses the publisher name to distinguish package content from different providers. Because the name of a package encompasses all variations of that package, including version and release changes, there isn't a way to create another package with the same name.
☒ **A and C** are incorrect. **A** is incorrect because a package can host two or more files by the same name, as long as they are in different directories. **C** is incorrect because an image can point to as many publishers by the same name as it wants, as long as they reside in separate repositories.

10. ☑ **A and D.** Package actions describe the effect a package has on an image, including the objects installed (files and directories), users and groups added, properties set, license agreements, and so on.
☒ **B and C** are incorrect. Both are pkg utility subcommands.

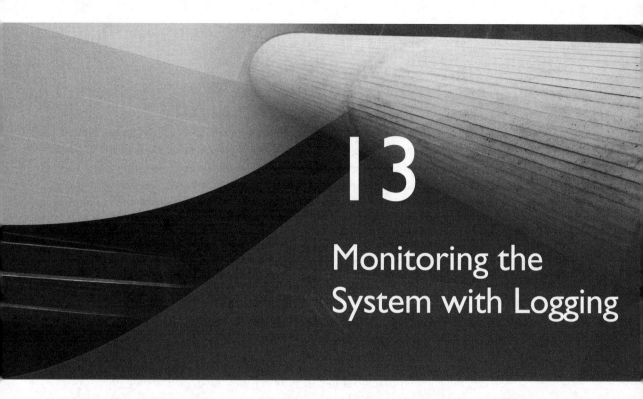

13
Monitoring the
System with Logging

A ny long-running software program needs a way to record events, both expected and unexpected, that help an administrator explain its errors and internal changes worth noting. Although many large applications have their own scheme for doing this, a centralized logging system has many advantages. For one, it lets the administrator integrate and consolidate a wide variety of applications and subsystems to use the same service. For another, it lets administrators decide whether one common log file or several specialized log files make more sense for their site's system management.

Many systems maintainers recognize a need to centralize the service not only for one system, but for a wide variety of systems they have to maintain. Consequently, the Internet Engineering Task Force (IETF) maintains a Request for Comments document called RFC 5425, which describes in full technical detail the syslog protocol. The Solaris operating system, along with several other UNIX-based platforms, use this document as a guide for their logging services.

You don't need to know this document well to prepare for the exam; far from it. You don't even need to understand all the details of the Solaris implementation; you just need to know the basics. In this chapter, I explain they key roles of the logging system, how you can configure it, how you can manage the records it produces, and how you can interact with it with a simple user-level utility.

CERTIFICATION OBJECTIVE 13.01

Understanding System Logging

The process syslogd is the heart of the logging system. It has its own SMF service, svc:/system/system-log:default. When running, the process maintains a file, /var/run/syslog.pid, that stores its current PID; you can also retrieve the PID with the command pgrep syslog. The configuration file, /etc/default/syslog, maintains one setting that lets the syslogd process receive logging messages from remote systems. I'll say more about this setting in the configuration section.

The process's job in life includes reading messages from a list of what you might call *message producers*. A message producer is a known location to which the operating system, its user processes, and possibly remote hosts, can send messages they want the system to write in its log. On Solaris, the key message producer is a logical device known as the STREAMS log driver, represented by the file /dev/log. If you use the file command to examine it, you'll see it is reported as a character device. It is, in fact, a symbolic link to a pseudo device the operating system creates during the boot process:

```
$ file /dev/log
/dev/log:   character special (160/5)
$ ls -l /dev/log
lrwxrwxrwx   1 root      root             27 Oct 20  2011 /dev/log ->
../devices/pseudo/log@0:log
```

You'll see this file in the output of the pfiles command:

```
$ sudo pfiles `pgrep syslogd`
1428:       /usr/sbin/syslogd
...
   6: S_IFCHR mode:0000 dev:540,0 ino:9559 uid:0 gid:0
rdev:160,6
      O_RDONLY
      /devices/pseudo/log@0:log
      offset:0
```

I've omitted the other open descriptors for now, including ones I'll discuss later. As you can see, the syslogd process keeps this device open to read. Once new content arrives at this location, the process will come around, check for a non-empty buffer, and then consume the contents.

on the
Job

I find it helpful to research the implementation details of every process I need to study. Knowing which files each process relies on reinforces for me, time and again, that there's no mystery in how the system is assembled. You may not know how code works, but in Solaris you can always find the files that a process reads from and writes to.

The syslogd process also produces its own messages without using a device interface, but for everyone else it forwards and filters what message producers send and routes those messages to *consumers*, which are described in a bit. The /dev/log file is the staging point for messages issued by user processes and kernel subsystems on the local machine. The syslogd process can also read messages from remote hosts that are accessible through a mechanism called a *transport provider*.

There are three general sources for remote messages that the syslogd process can read. The first is any transport provider defined in the file /etc/netconfig, also known as the system's network configuration database. Looking at the sixth column of each entry in this file, you'll find a list of logical devices similar to /dev/log. Feel free to examine these devices as I did earlier if you're curious about them.

The second source is any transport providers listed in the /etc/net directory:

```
$ ls --classify /etc/net
ticlts/      ticots/      ticotsord/
```

The --classify switch signifies via a familiar symbol the file type in the listing; these three entries are also directories. These names also appear as the last three device types listed in the /etc/netconfig database. As directories, they each hold two files, named hosts and services. If a transport provider is specified in any of these six files, the syslogd process can read the log messages produced by those providers. The syslogd process is not configured to do that by default. I'll show you how to configure that capability later in the chapter.

Sorting Log Messages by Facility

What you've learned so far is that the syslogd process has only two kinds of sources to read from: local and remote. What you need to know, as an administrator, is *who* sent the message. The syslogd process is given a hard-coded list of these names, collectively called *facilities*. Some facilities identify a general group of agents. For example, any part of the operating system that needs to send a log message falls under the facility name "kern." Some facilities are more specific because they point to critical services most users depend on, such as the e-mail and authorization systems, which are covered by the facility names mail and auth, respectively. Table 13-1 has a full list of facilities, along with a brief description of each one.

| TABLE 13-1 | Facilities Recognized by the syslogd Process |

Facility Name	Description
audit	Auditing systems that rely on syslog
auth	Authorization system (login, su, getty, others)
cron	Jobs run by cron and at; not used by Solaris
daemon	Daemon (long-running) processes
kern	Messages from any kernel service
local0-local7	Locally configurable facilities
lpr	Line printer spooling
mail	E-mail system
mark	Timestamp messages generated by syslogd
news	USENET network news system
user	User processes; names any source not defined by another facility
uucp	UNIX-to-UNIX copy facility; does not use Solaris logging
*	Wildcard representing all facilities except mark

Many of these facilities describe services that aren't further explained in this book. This logging framework has been a staple of UNIX systems for a long time and is employed by many variants. The facilities themselves are well known to the whole UNIX community, but are not implemented the same way on all platforms. Solaris, for example, does not integrate job scheduling (via the cron and at services) or system-to-system serial file transfers (via uucp) into the logging facility. Other facilities are used by groups with an important but specific focus, such as security (auth and audit facilities) or terminal-based information sharing (news facility).

The syslogd process uses the mark facility to issue regular timestamps as log messages. You might use this facility to mark time at an interval of your choosing, or just to confirm the syslogd process is active when the facilities are quiet.

Sorting Log Messages by Severity

Along with who sent a given log message, you need to know how important it is, especially when lots of messages are coming in at once. Some messages report milestones you want to note but don't have to do anything about. Others messages report service failures or errors you need to address as soon as you become aware of them. For this purpose, the logging framework includes a list of *severity* labels that separate messages by their urgency.

Severity applies equally to all facilities. Although it is not necessarily documented which facilities use which severities for what reasons, the severity labels themselves are usually taken at face value. That is, if a kern facility message has a severity level of info (indicating it's merely informational), administrators can assume the message content doesn't require their immediate attention. It's up to the programmer to adopt the conventions for assigning the proper severity and applying them consistently. Table 13-2 lists these levels from most to least severe.

TABLE 13-2   List of Severity Levels in Logging

Level of Severity	Description
emerg	A panic condition; broadcast to all logged-in users by default
alert	Requires immediate action
crit	A possible or impending failure, such as a hardware device
err	Errors of a less dire nature
warning	Important to observe; immediate action not necessary
notice	Benign condition that may require special handling
info	Informational; no action required
debug	Normally used when developing or testing program code
none	Ignores all messages from named facility

All told, you have seven practical ways to sort messages from any given facility. The debug severity level is usually applied by programmers only, and then with a form of the code that typically is not deployed into a production environment. If you do enable it, once you learn how to configure for it, you may find some facilities are extremely chatty. Be sure it's okay to reconfigure the system log quickly once you've had enough.

Understanding Selectors

You apply a severity level to a facility name by joining it with a dot (for example, kern.warning). This pairing is called a *selector*. You can use it to tell the syslogd process to filter any facility's messages at the severity level you apply *or higher*. That is, the selector kern.warning will tell the process to ignore any kernel messages of notice, debug, or info severity. The higher the severity, the more messages you want to ignore, leaving fewer (but more important) messages for the process to forward. You can also use a comma to declare multiple facilities at the same severity. The phrase local0,daemon.notice includes both facilities at the notice level.

on the Job

In a modern software messaging system, we'd call the syslogd process a kind of publisher, an agent that decides which messages to make available to its consumers by applying selectors.

You can also chain a list of selectors together with semicolons as well as use the facilities wildcard (*) and the none severity to create compound rules. For example, if you wanted to log all facilities at severity crit or higher, but accept no messages from user processes at all, you could use the following expression:

```
*.crit;user.none
```

If you wanted all facilities to report errors except the kernel and authentication subsystem, which you want to report notices, you could write the following:

```
*.err;kern.notice;auth.notice
```

In this example, the err severity covers all facilities. It is overruled, in a sense, by any subsequent description that applies to the current message. So although the descriptions for the debug and daemon facilities lower the required severity, mail.crit actually raises it. Using this line, the syslogd process will not read mail.err messages because mail.crit, a higher severity, overrules it.

You cannot use the wildcard to *glob* names; that is, you can't use it to expand the names of facilities or severities that have common characters. If you use the facilities local0 through local7, for example, you *cannot* address them all at once like this:

```
local*.warning
```

To address, say, three of them at once, you'd have to write the following:

```
local0.warning;local1.warning;local2.warning
```

Using all local facilities the same way is about the only case where you might have to write a lengthy selector. In most other cases, you won't require an elaborate chain. Each selector is just a filter for log messages you want to forward to one consumer, and you can define as many log consumers as you require. So now the question is, what is a message consumer?

Understanding Actions

What I have called a consumer so far is what the syslogd process considers an *action*. An action is nothing more than the message receiver, of which there are three types: files, users, and hosts. If you've worked with other UNIX logging systems, you've probably seen the contents of the default file ("action") for logging messages. On Solaris, that file is /var/adm/messages. It is by no means the only one. All the selector-action pairs defined for your system are stored in the file /etc/syslog.conf. When the syslogd process starts, it processes this file and associates each selector with the action specified. The first two non-comment lines are:

```
*.err;kern.notice;auth.notice              /dev/sysmsg
*.err;kern.debug;daemon.notice;mail.crit   /var/adm/messages
```

The first selector is used to write to the device /dev/sysmsg. This file acts as a router to so-called *console devices*. A console device is any display that is authorized to receive administrative messages. It's what you are using while the operating system session boots up, before the graphic login display appears, and during shutdown. The other default selector writes to the file /var/adm/messages. Again, these are just default values. You can add more selectors and actions if you like, or change the ones you have. There are four forms you can use to specify a new action, as shown in Table 13-3.

| TABLE 13-3 | Forms for Actions in /etc/syslog.conf File |

Action Form	Description
/path_to_file	Append messages to named file, if it exists
@host	Forward messages to syslogd on named host
user1,user2,user3,Ö	Write messages to terminals of named logged-in users
*	Write messages to terminals of all logged-in users

There is a catch to this otherwise straightforward process. The syslogd process doesn't read the /etc/syslog.conf file as straight text. Instead, it uses a preprocessor tool called m4 to parse the file for macros. One such macro is ifdef, which you see used in the last half of the file:

```
mail.debug                    ifdef(`LOGHOST', /var/log/syslog, @loghost)
```

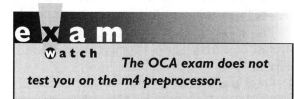

w a t c h *The OCA exam does not test you on the m4 preprocessor.*

This macro gives the syslogd process a way to decide if it should forward log messages to the named file or the machine identified as the *loghost*. If the variable LOGHOST is set in the syslogd process's environment, it will forward messages to the named system; otherwise, it will forward them the file /var/log/syslog.

If you name a file, the syslogd process tries to open that file in order to append messages to it. If the file does not exist, this operation *might* fail silently; it depends on how it is specified. If you've been experimenting along with me, you may have spotted this complaint in the /var/adm/messages file:

```
Sep  8 13:39:09 orca syslogd: /var/log/syslog: No such file or directory
```

When the mail.debug selector is parsed, the syslogd process checks for the file, but only if the LOGHOST environment variable isn't set; otherwise, it has no need. If a log file is deleted after the syslogd process has started, it will forward messages to the bit bucket. The syslogd process keeps the file descriptor open—you can verify this with the pfiles command—but the name of target file is lost. To reestablish the connection, you must create the file *and* restart the syslogd process.

A typo of the filename could result in sending a lot of log data to the bit bucket, so it's well worth your time to ensure the files you name exist as specified in the /etc/syslog.conf file. If you send messages to another system that is not configured to accept them, the action will fail silently. If your system cannot find the IP address for that system, however, the syslogd process will log a warning like this:

```
Sep  8 13:35:05 orca syslogd: line 22: WARNING: server1 could not be resolved
```

The next three entries in the /etc/syslog.conf file forward messages to the users root, operator, and all (*). The operator user isn't defined on a default system, so you should add a user by that name, or change the name operator to a valid user. Forwarding a message to any user depends on their having a window open that can receive terminal-oriented communication.

Understanding Messages

To review what you've learned so far, Figure 13-1 summarizes the logging system's message-forwarding scheme. Reading from the /dev/log device and possibly some remote message producers, the syslogd process applies a selector to each received message. This selector filters the message by its facility and severity for forwarding to a named action, or as I've been calling it, a consumer. If it passes, the message is forwarded to a named file, remote system, or user(s). The message is dropped silently if the consumer is not set up to receive it.

A message is always a single line of text. It can, however, take several forms, depending on a few factors that go beyond the scope of this book. An obvious one

FIGURE 13-1

Flow of messages from producer to consumer through the syslogd process

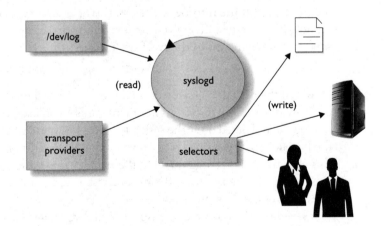

depends on whether the message comes from a kernel subsystem or user process. Here is an example of two local messages:

```
Sep  8 09:52:58 orca pseudo: [ID 129642 kern.info] pseudo-device: fcsm0
Sep  8 09:52:58 orca genunix: [ID 936769 kern.info] fcsm0 is /pseudo/fcsm@0
```

Each message includes a timestamp, the host of record, and the specific facility that is reporting. The information in brackets is called a *message ID*. This identifier is generated by the msgid command, which the log(7D) device uses by default to help sort messages. This number is *not* unique per-message. It is a value based on the content of the message string itself. Messages from the same reporter at the same facility and severity level *should* produce the same message ID. Messages from different reporters using different facilities and severities *can* produce the same message ID. It is not an unlikely event, either; on my system, the message ID 702911 came up repeatedly for a diverse group of messages.

on the **Job**

A technical term with parentheses indicates the man page section of the documentation. These are also a hint to the type of facility under discussion. Section 7D, for example, documents device drivers. Section 2 documents system calls such as fork(2), and so on. Use the command "man intro" to see a complete list of sections.

The remainder of the string is the message itself. In the example, the pseudo device subsystem reported the creation of a device fcsm0, after which the genunix subsystem reported the creation of its file interface. As you can see by reviewing your own messages file after a few reboots, the kern.info selector is fairly chatty.

If the reporter is a user process, it is identified in two parts: the program name and, because any process could in principle run as multiple instances, the PID. The next example shows a successful remote login attempt captured as a log message:

```
Sep  8 10:21:31 orca inetd[14141]: [ID 317013 daemon.notice ] telnet[5125]
from 10.2.0.21 20005
```

The reporting facility in this case is the inetd process, which falls under the category of a daemon facility. The message content shows the process logged a Telnet connection, capturing the host IP of the connecting user and port used to connect. Each message will contain whatever the application programmer deems useful to report. Commercial applications that use logging extensively may provide a documented scheme that makes it easier to map brief messages back to more detailed explanations and, when needed, steps to resolving a problem.

CERTIFICATION OBJECTIVE 13.02

Configuring Logging Services

Managing the logging service is quite straightforward. The syslogd process reads the /etc/syslog.conf file each time it starts up. All you have to do is change the file, as you deem fit, and restart the process. As mentioned earlier, you'll make sure any files, hosts, or users you have specified already exist. For testing, any users you've specified have to be logged in via a session that can receive (and display) log messages.

You could terminate the syslogd process with the kill or pkill command, but that's more force than you need. By design, daemon processes will restart when they receive a signal called HUP (short for hang-up). Upon restart, these processes reread their configuration files, if they have one, and proceed. This interaction ensures the least possible downtime of the process. The following command will restart the syslogd process and make your changes to the /etc/syslog.conf file take effect immediately:

```
$ sudo kill -HUP `pgrep syslogd`
```

Parallel to the brute-force approach, you could disable and enable the service like this:

```
$ svcadm disable system-log
$ svcadm enable system-log
```

But again, this means a little more downtime for the process and isn't necessary. Use the restart subcommand instead; you'll get the same effect as sending a HUP signal.

Reconfiguring Selectors and Actions

There are as many ways to define selectors and actions as you might like to invent. The examples section of the syslog.conf man page offers this sample configuration:

```
*.notice                /var/log/notice
mail.info               /var/log/notice
*.crit                  /var/log/critical
kern,mark.debug         /dev/console
kern.err                @server
*.emerg                 *
*.alert                 root,operator
*.alert;auth.warning    /var/log/auth
```

In this example, log messages are separated by severity in the first three entries. For whatever reason, the administrator thinks the notice file should include informational messages from the mail facility too. When a facility is not qualified by severity, as in the fourth selector, all severities are included (there is no severity wildcard). Any kernel error or more severe message is directed to another system—perhaps as a hedge against a system crash. All logged-in users receive the most severe messages to prompt them to save their work. The last entry appears to be a facility-oriented selector, capturing messages that could indicate attempts to hack the system's authorization setup.

Such a configuration probably derives from experience using the logging system. Without documentation to explain exactly how Solaris implements RFC 5425, an administrator learns over time the kinds of messages each facility produces at each level of severity, how chatty or sparse that pair is, and how informative the messages are. You could invent a scheme or apply one that is recommended by an experienced administrator.

It largely boils down to a few criteria that could arguably be called a matter of taste. You might choose:

- Separate actions for each selector (or selector chain)
- Multiple actions for the same selector (or selector chain)
- Different targets (files, remote hosts, users) for different selectors
- Different targets for the same selectors (for a local and remote record)

User targets make sense when the message calls for an immediate response or promotes ongoing, console-based monitoring. Remote host targets make sense when you'd like to record all log messages to a single machine, creating a central log host, or if you're worried the reporting system may lose the information. Remote hosts also make sense when storage space on the local system is scarce or when the local system is a virtualized instance.

For the sake of testing, I will define a selector for the local0 facility and have it write to a file in my home directory. The entry looks like this:

```
local0.info                           /export/home/mfernest/log
```

Once I restart the syslogd process, it will read this entry and attempt to open the file in append mode. You can observe the result as follows:

```
$ sudo kill -HUP `pgrep syslogd`
$ sudo pfiles `pgrep syslogd`
2142:/usr/sbin/syslogd
...
```

```
 7: S_IFREG mode:0644 dev:195,65539 ino:3884 uid:0 gid:0 size:247265
    O_WRONLY|O_APPEND|O_NOCTTY|O_LARGEFILE
    /var/adm/messages
    offset:247265
 8: S_IFREG mode:0644 dev:195,65544 ino:290 uid:60004 gid:10 size:131
    O_WRONLY|O_APPEND|O_NOCTTY|O_LARGEFILE
    /export/home/mfernest/log
    offset:0
```

I've included in this output the open file descriptor for the /var/adm/messages file just to show the syslogd process does this for each named file. The same holds true if you're writing to a host. If you add an entry like

```
local1.info                           @orca
```

to your /etc/syslog.conf file and restart the process, you'll see a corresponding descriptor in your pfiles output:

```
11: S_IFCHR mode:0000 dev:540,0 ino:20877 uid:0 gid:0 rdev:129,41
    O_RDWR
    sockname: AF_INET6 ::  port: 33233
    /devices/pseudo/udp6@0:udp6
    offset:0
```

The new action directs messages to host orca; the text information is delivered over a network port and received to the remote host's syslogd daemon for processing. In the section on writing log messages, I show you how to test both of these selectors.

Accepting Remote Messages

The remote systems you can receive messages from, as shown earlier, is determined by the transport providers your system understands. Transport providers take the form of a kernel loadable network module (such as tcp and upd) or a device interface file such as /dev/ticotsord. This level of network service operates below the level of system identification, so you don't need to specify the machines from which you will receive log messages. You just need a way to resolve their system names to IP addresses; an entry in your /etc/hosts files suffices for that.

To allow remote logging sources on your system, you can modify the SMF service, svc:/system/system-log:default, which maintains a contract observer for the syslogd process. You can observe this relationship with the following command:

```
$ svcs -p system-log
STATE          STIME    FMRI
online         10:56:17 svc:/system/system-log:default
               10:56:17     2051 syslogd
```

This service stores a property group, called config, that contains the property name log_from_remote. Using the following commands, you can set the property to true and restart the syslogd process:

```
$ svccfg -s system-log setprop config/log_from_remote=true
$ svcadm restart system-log
```

To verify a change has occurred, you can use the pfiles command to see the syslogd process now has more file descriptors open:

```
$ sudo pfiles `pgrep syslogd`
2142:/usr/sbin/syslogd
...
   4: S_IFCHR mode:0000 dev:540,0 ino:32945 uid:0 gid:0 rdev:129,56
      O_RDWR
      sockname: AF_INET6 ::  port: 514
      /devices/pseudo/udp6@0:udp6
      offset:0
   5: S_IFCHR mode:0000 dev:540,0 ino:38818 uid:0 gid:0 rdev:146,55
      O_RDWR
      sockname: AF_INET 0.0.0.0  port: 514
      /devices/pseudo/udp@0:udp
      offset:0
...
```

This portion of the output shows the syslogd process is now listening to the udp and udp6 device interfaces. Solaris supports the two versions of the Internet Protocol: The udp interface represents version 4, the 32-bit system addressing scheme that has been in use nearly since the dawn of UNIX time. Version 6, a 128-bit address scheme that allows far more addresses, is by comparison new, but was first defined by a working specification in 1998. The well-known port address for receiving remote log messages is 514. If you use a firewall on your network, it must be reconfigured to allow this traffic through.

The Solaris operating system maintains a legacy file, /etc/default/syslogd, you can also use to allow remote log messages. Changing the SMF service property is the preferred method, but the file remains for backward compatibility, to support Solaris users who rely on it by way of program code, scripts, established practice, or just force of habit. To use it, simply uncomment the last line of the file and restart the syslogd process as you wish. This file overrides the SMF setting, so if you want to experiment with the setting, you may find it easier to edit the file than invoke the svccfg command multiple times.

CERTIFICATION OBJECTIVE 13.03

Managing Log Files

On-disk storage space is not the precious commodity it once was. Still, a system that runs a lot of chatty processes and logs every facility at a low severity level can consume a lot of space. The default installation parameters for Solaris 11 still configure the /var file system as a separate entity, so you can place whatever limits you want on the disk space you allow for log messages and other variable-size files: print spools, software install manifests, and so on.

With logging systems, disk space is only one issue. Managing the files themselves is another, one that is best served with an explicit plan. Separating records by selector is one possible strategy. It can be easier to manage logs if they are already sorted by content in some fashion.

One common activity associated with log files generally is *rotating* them, the practice of switching the current file for an empty one with minimal disruption to the logging service. In most logging schemes, the administrator sets a file size to indicate when it should be rotated. The administrator can also to set a time interval, so the files are rotated regularly regardless of size. As an built-in defense against consuming a file system's space, rotation utilities will also expire old log files, based on rules for the number of old log files allowed or the combined disk space they consume. Another common log management activity is *archiving*, which can include renaming and compressing old log files.

Rotating Log Files

The rotation tool that is bundled with Solaris 11 is logadm. It has an extensive set of options that allow the administrator to specify rotation criteria for any log file on the system, not just the system logging scheme. When called against an existing log file, the logadm utility renames old log files with a numeric suffix before creating the new one. If you run the logadm utility right now, it will rename your current file messages.0 and create a new messages file. Once you reach 10 of these files, the logadm utility will also delete the oldest (11th) one. These are default rules you can modify.

You don't have to learn these options to use them right away, however. When it is invoked without arguments, the logadm utility reads the file /etc/logadm.conf and applies the rules it contains. The entry for the file /var/adm/messages looks like this:

```
/var/adm/messages -C 8 -a 'kill -HUP `cat /system/volatile/syslog.pid`'
```

The -C option limits the number of old files retained. The -a option specifies a post-rotation command. Here, the maximum number of old files to keep is set to 8. After rotating the file, logadm will send a HUP signal to the syslogd process so it opens the new file. It's beyond our depth in this book to explain why this is necessary; you should know, however, that you can't switch files by name and fool a currently running process into thinking it's the same file as before.

There are numerous other options to the logadm utility. It covers rotation rules by size and time interval, provides a default renaming scheme and expiration policy, and supplies the means to define your own. It does not include a compression utility for reducing old log files, but you can invoke an external command to archive a rotated log file however you like. Use the man pages for the logadm utility and the logadm.conf file to research these options and browse a few small examples.

on the **Job** *The details of the logadm utility aren't called out for the OCA exam, but knowledge of them will go a long way in a working environment. When adding a new application onto a Solaris system, sooner or later you will want to know how to handle logging. If your site administrators prefer to keep to one logging system whenever possible, you'll need the logadm utility to manage files.*

CERTIFICATION OBJECTIVE 13.04

Writing Log Messages

The tail -f command is one way to watch a log file as records are added. This option (short for "follow") copies up to the last 10 lines of the named file, after which it checks the file every second. New lines in the followed file are copied and printed to the tail command's output. It may seem like a primitive tool, but it's still popular among operators who need to watch log messages throughout their shift.

You can also write one-line messages to a log file as a user using the logger command. You might do this to incorporate an ad hoc event scheme to your logs, such as noting when a project milestone has been reached, an operational shift has ended, or perhaps to incorporate other information like building access records. You can write scripts that log their beginning and end of long-running operations, such as storage backup, and so on. A logger command may contain up to four settings, which are listed and described in Table 13-4.

Notice by reading that selectors have an underlying numeric *priority*, which is used to assert precedence when multiple messages are pending. These priority levels are defined in RFC 5425, and they could be used by anyone who doesn't care to use selectors, but there is no technical reason to prefer them.

You can use the tag to replace the reporting facility, which by default will be the user who executes the logger command. A tag name can provide a more helpful identifier as part of the message, possibly the name of a calling script or other keyword agreed upon by site administrators.

Once you have a new selector set up and have restarted the logging daemon, the logger command makes it easy to test. Here are two examples using the local0 and local1 facilities I configured earlier in the chapter:

```
$ logger -i -p local0.info -t SHOWOFF Happy logging!
$ tail -1 /export/home/mfernest/log
Sep  9 03:34:22 orca SHOWOFF[2650]: [ID 702911 local0.info] Happy logging!
$ logger -i -p local1.alert -t Test2 Happy host logging!
$ tail -1 /var/adm/messages
Sep  9 03:37:33 orca Test2[2653]: [ID 702911 local1.alert] Happy host logging!
```

You can use the tail -f command to observe your tests as they mix with other log messages that might be coming in.

TABLE 13-4	logger Option	Description
	-i	Send logger command's PID as part of the message
Options to the logger Command	-f *file*	Read message from the named file
	-p *priority*	Selector or a valid priority number
	-t *tag*	Mark message line with named tag
	Message	Message (overrides file content if -f is also specified)

CERTIFICATION SUMMARY

In this chapter you learned how the Solaris system logging facility works: how different agents report their conditions, how the syslogd daemon reads and processes them, and how it defines local and remote targets to receive them. The system employs a messaging model in principle, but in practice it requires a detailed understanding of the configuration syntax and rules of operation to set it up correctly. For the exam, you can expect questions on correct configuration and valid message recipients to stand out over questions on the model or the expected applications of a logging system.

✓ TWO-MINUTE DRILL

Understanding System Logging

- ❏ The Solaris logging system is an implementation based on the IETF document RFC 5425.
- ❏ The syslogd process collects messages from the /dev/log file interface. It can also receive log messages from a remote host.
- ❏ Messages are categorized and prioritized by selectors, which describe a facility and a minimum level of severity to record. A selector's action describes a target for qualifying messages: a file, a remote system, or one or more logged-in users.

Configuring Logging Services

- ❏ The list of selectors and actions read by the syslogd process are kept in the file /etc/syslog.conf. (You can direct the syslogd command to read instructions from an alternate file. Consult the man page for this option.)
- ❏ Set the property config/log_from_remote to true if you want to receive messages from remote hosts. This property is part of the service svc:/system/system-log:default. You can also enable remote messages in the /etc/default/syslogd file by uncommenting the last line.
- ❏ It is always necessary to restart the syslogd process for configuration changes to take effect. You can send a HUP signal to the syslogd process or use the svcadm restart subcommand on the system-log service.

Managing Log Files

- ❏ The logadm utility is the default Solaris tool for rotating log files. It has options to execute arbitrary pre- and post-rotation commands, as the administrator sees fit.
- ❏ The /etc/logadm.conf file lists the default policies for default Solaris logging applications, including the system logger.

Writing Log Messages

❑ Command-line users or scripts can use the logger utility to write log messages. The user can specify either a selector or a valid priority number to qualify the message, and may also replace the default tag.

❑ The user can supply the message on the command line or read it in from a file, as long as the message is a single line of text.

SELF TEST

Use the following questions to test your recall and understanding of the chapter's material.

Understanding System Logging

1. Which two options are valid selectors?
   A. news.info
   B. lpr.news
   C. local5.*
   D. mail.none

2. Which of these files or commands will reveal the current PID of the syslogd process? (Pick all that apply.)
   A. svcs -p system-log:default
   B. pgrep syslog.conf
   C. cat /var/run/syslog.pid
   D. cat /system/volatile/syslog.pid

3. Which of the following options are valid syslog actions? (Pick all that apply.)
   A. The file messages
   B. The user root
   C. @localhost
   D. *

4. A log message will always contain which two options listed?
   A. Tag
   B. Message
   C. Message ID
   D. Port number

5. Which statement correctly describes the selector chain *.err;kern.warn;user.none?
   A. Errors or higher from all facilities, warnings or higher from the kernel, plus no severity restrictions on messages from user processes.
   B. Errors from any facility except the kernel and users; warnings only from the kernel facility; nothing from the user facility.

C. Errors from all facilities, plus warnings from the kernel, including all higher severities. No messages of any severity from the user facility.

D. All errors except for kernel warnings and user messages that have no severity.

Configuring Logging Services

6. What happens if you disable the svc:/system/system-log:default service?
    A. Only messages of emerg severity are forwarded.
    B. The /var/adm/messages file is rotated.
    C. No log messages are forwarded
    D. The /etc/syslog.conf file is immediately read again.

7. Assume you have configured the system-log service to allow log messages from remote hosts. Which statement is a correct outcome?
    A. Nothing changes.
    B. The inetd process will open UDP port 514.
    C. The syslogd process tries to resolve the IP of any hosts named in the /etc/syslog.conf file.
    D. The syslogd process restarts itself.

8. Which statement correctly describes a requirement to send messages to a remote host?
    A. You must create a transport provider for each remote host.
    B. You must provide an IP address for the remote host.
    C. You must have access to a DNS service.
    D. You must edit the /etc/default/syslogd file.

Managing Log Files

9. How does the logadm utility know which log files to process?
    A. It reads the file descriptors of any logging daemons that are opened in append mode.
    B. It reads the actions written in the /etc/syslog.conf file.
    C. It reads either a log file name or mnemonic description of log files in the /etc/logadm.conf file.
    D. The most important system files are hard-coded in the program.

Writing Log Messages

10. Assuming the syslogd process is running, which option correctly describes an outcome of this command: logger -i -p local0.alert -t fred How it is going?

  A. The message "How it is going" will be written to /var/adm/messages.

  B. The message will include the PID of the logger command.

  C. The tag fred is added to the username that called the logger command.

  D. The syslogd process will restart.

SELF TEST ANSWERS

Understanding System Logging

1. ☑ **A and D.** Each combines a valid facility with a valid severity.
   ☒ **B and C** are incorrect. **B** is incorrect because news is not a valid severity level. **C** is incorrect because the wildcard symbol applies to facilities only.

2. ☑ **A, C, and D.** The svcs -p command outputs any running processes that the named service observes. The syslog.pid file is maintained in two file systems: One is specified by the syslogd process itself, and the other used in the /etc/logadm.conf file to restart the syslogd process following log rotation.
   ☒ **B** is incorrect. The wrong argument is given. The required argument to the pgrep command is the name of the running process; here, the configuration file is used instead.

3. ☑ **B, C, and D.** The root user is of course valid, but remember that the username isn't verified. The syslogd process only checks to see if a user by the name given is currently logged in. The name localhost, even though it is not remote, is a hostname the system can always resolve. The * symbol stands in for all currently logged-in users.
   ☒ **A** is incorrect. All file targets must be specified with an absolute path.

4. ☑ **A and B.** Every log message must have some non-zero string of information to send and is tagged by the reporting facility or by some other relevant string.
   ☒ **C and D** are incorrect. **C** is incorrect because the message ID facility, provided by the log device driver, can be disabled. **D** is incorrect because port numbers will only occur in message strings that choose to include them.

5. ☑ **C.** When a severity is given, it includes all severities of greater urgency. A subsequent selector that includes a lower severity can be added by specifying it. Finally, a whole facility can be disabled by specifying the severity none.
   ☒ **A, B, and D** are incorrect. **A** is incorrect because it suggests the severity none disables the normal interpretation of severities instead of disabling them altogether. **B** is incorrect because you don't override higher severity levels with subsequent lower severity levels in the chain. **D** is incorrect because it states a contrary view of selector interpretation.

Configuring Logging Services

6. ☑   **C.** Disabling the system-log service shuts down the syslogd process. All the syslogd process does is forward messages from the producers, so called, to the consumers, which are described by actions in the /etc/syslog.conf file. Once enabled, the syslogd process will act on any messages that are still pending.

   ☒   **A, B,** and **D** are incorrect. **A** is incorrect because no forwarding can occur while the syslogd process is stopped. **B** is incorrect because log rotation is only handled by invoking the logadm process. **D** is also incorrect; the configuration file is only read as the syslogd process starts up.

7. ☑   **A.** Nothing changes due to reconfiguration until the syslogd process is restarted.

   ☒   **B, C,** and **D** are incorrect. **B** and **C** state actions that will occur, but only after the syslogd process has been restarted. **D** is incorrect because the syslogd process does not have a way to restart itself.

8. ☑   **B.** In order for the syslogd process to send messages to another server, it must be able to resolve the server name provided to an IP address. Name resolution can occur by any means the system is configured to handle, including an entry in the /etc/hosts file or access to a Domain Name Server (DNS) that does the same work. Without a valid IP address, the syslogd process cannot connect to the remote machine.

   ☒   **A, C,** and **D** are incorrect. **A** is incorrect because the transport providers defined cover all normal network address requirements. **C** is incorrect because DNS is just one way to resolve system names to IP addresses. An /etc/hosts entry works just as well. **D** is incorrect because this file has a setting to accept remote log messages, but no help for sending them.

Managing Log Files

9. ☑   **C.** A /etc/logadm.conf file entry can give the name of the file to manage at the beginning or end of the entry line. In the second case, some mnemonic that describes the affected file(s) is fine. The actual file(s) affected can be specified literally or with globbing characters.

   ☒   **A, B,** and **D** are incorrect. Although these options each specify a potentially valid source for information the logadm command could use, it only relies on the logadm.conf file or information provided as a command-line argument.

Writing Log Messages

10.   ☑   **B.** The -i option inserts the PID of the executing logger command into the message string.
   ☒   **A, C,** and **D** are incorrect. **A** is incorrect because the selector has no control over the target it writes to. It depends on the configuration. **C** is incorrect because any tag you specify will replace the default tag, not supplement it. **D** is incorrect because no message issued through the logger command will make the syslogd process restart.

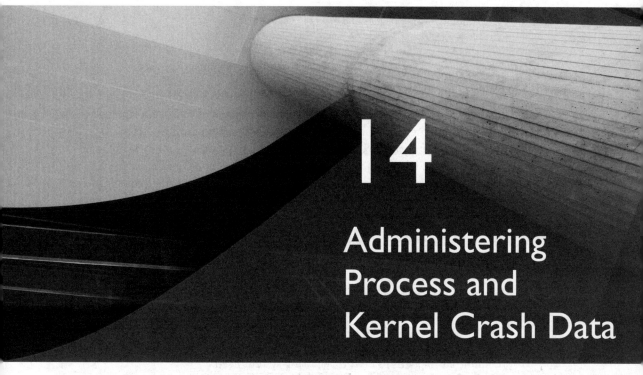

14

Administering
Process and
Kernel Crash Data

A s a new Solaris user, you may come across a file named "core" on your system. Chances are you'll determine how big it is and delete it once you know. Core files can take up a lot of space and there's not much to do with them without quite a bit more training. You could point this file out to a more experienced colleague, who might want it or might tell you just to delete it. Your colleague might tell you it's the result of some program that crashed and leave it at that. And, because you're in the business of keeping programs running, you might be happy to dispose of a program corpse you can't do anything for.

Historically, core files have been interesting to a very small number of Solaris administrators, possibly parallel to the number of doctors who find corpses interesting. That said, they're not particularly mysterious things, unless untimely program death makes you nervous. A core file is just a copy of a running program frozen at the time it failed. It is something a knowledgeable administrator can use to understand the cause of failure, and perhaps use that information to prevent failure in future executions of the same program. A *crash dump* is simply a copy of a failed program that happens to be the operating system itself.

In this chapter, you won't learn how to become a program coroner. That's an advanced skill. Instead, you will learn how and why core files are created. You'll also learn how to configure your Solaris system so you can manage what they are named, where they are stored, and how many you care to keep on your system at one time. You'll also learn how to make a healthy process or operating system write a core dump and keep running, in case an expert user wants you to create one for him or her.

CERTIFICATION OBJECTIVE 14.01

Understanding Core Files

I see no real need for mystery or trepidation concerning a core file. That said, I must admit that most admin students seem to suffer in silence or bury themselves in their e-mail when I say that. But look, it's really not a big deal to understand where they come from and why.

For a process to run on Solaris, it first has to be composed from a number of segments. The segments of any Solaris program will include the following items:

- Its program code, also called its *text*
- Data declared when the program was allocated

- An area to track the program's progress, called the *stack*
- An area to locate additional allocated memory, called the *heap*
- Library code that is referenced by the text
- So-called anonymous memory

When one of these segments is called for, the *dynamic linker* is responsible for adding it to the program map. After these calls are completed, the program can begin execution.

You do not have to take any of this information on faith. The pmap(1) program you learned in Chapter 7 will show you the segment map for any running process you name. Here, for example, is output from the pmap tool for the shell program I'm using:

```
$ pmap $$
1895:     bash
08044000      16K rw---    [ stack ]
08050000    1212K r-x--    /usr/bin/bash
0818F000      24K rw---    /usr/bin/bash
08195000     168K rw---    [ heap ]
FE480000      56K r-x--    /usr/lib/locale/common/methods_unicode.so.3
FE49D000       8K rwx--    /usr/lib/locale/common/methods_unicode.so.3
FE4A0000    6744K r-x--    /usr/lib/locale/en_US.UTF-8/en_US.UTF-8.so.3
FEB46000       4K rw---    /usr/lib/locale/en_US.UTF-8/en_US.UTF-8.so.3
FED40000     184K r-x--    /lib/libcurses.so.1
FED7E000      16K rw---    /lib/libcurses.so.1
FED82000       8K rw---    /lib/libcurses.so.1
FED90000       4K rw---    [ anon ]
FEDA0000      24K r-x--    /lib/libgen.so.1
FEDB6000       4K rw---    /lib/libgen.so.1
FEDC0000      64K rwx--    [ anon ]
FEDD7000       4K rwxs-    [ anon ]
FEDE0000       4K rw---    [ anon ]
FEDF0000      24K rwx--    [ anon ]
FEE00000       4K rw---    [ anon ]
FEE10000    1352K r-x--    /usr/lib/libc/libc_hwcap1.so.1
FEF72000      44K rwx--    /usr/lib/libc/libc_hwcap1.so.1
FEF7D000       4K rwx--    /usr/lib/libc/libc_hwcap1.so.1
FEF80000       4K rw---    [ anon ]
FEF90000       4K rw---    [ anon ]
FEFA0000       4K rw---    [ anon ]
FEFB0000       4K rw---    [ anon ]
FEFB7000     208K r-x--    /lib/ld.so.1
FEFFB000       8K rwx--    /lib/ld.so.1
FEFFD000       4K rwx--    /lib/ld.so.1
 total   10208K
```

Each line that starts with a hexadecimal address is a *segment mapping*. The rightmost column lists the file, also called a *backing store*, from which the segment was mapped. If there is no file, it's because the segment is a data structure that's created and maintained only during the life of the program. It's shown in square brackets and described by one of a few terms, including the heap and the stack. These elements don't have a file to back them, so they are instead backed by swap space. The segments labeled [anon], short for anonymous memory, are so called because no name binds them either to a backing file or to a specific run-time purpose.

We need to note two specific segments before moving on. One, you'll notice the last segments listed are backed by the file /lib/ld.so.1. This library of code and data is called the *dynamic linker*. It's responsible for locating and attaching each required segment to the process map. It loads at the highest available address in the map and loads additional libraries from the top down. The next segment loaded may seem strange, judging by the name, but it's actually libc.so.1, also called the standard C library. If you look up your file system mounts and recall the discussion from Chapter 4, you'll remember this file is mounted with the lofs(7D) driver so it can be aliased to its well-known name and location. Once the dynamic linker maps it in, however, the name gets translated back to its source.

Taken as a whole, these segments include everything the program requires to run: code and data provided by the executable file, code and data provided by shared object libraries, run-time metadata that manage the program's state, and space for more resources as they are called for. Each segment lists an address in the process map, the amount of memory it requires, and a permission set. But this isn't a map drawn up by necessity alone. It is also a *guard* against certain events that could tell the system something has gone wrong.

For example, let's say one of the shell program's instructions tried accessing memory at a location that was computed to be FD880000. Looking at the map, you'll notice nothing's listed at that location. When the operating system sees this, it will decide something has gone wrong and has gone undetected. Because its first concern is protecting program data from corruption, it will raise a signal that tells the program to shut down. By default, the program will respond by dumping these segments into a file called core as it terminates. This file's location is determined by the program's *current working directory*. For many programs, this location will be the same directory in which the executable file resides, but the program can also change it over time.

An analyst who knows the anatomy of a run-time process and the right tools to use can examine the core file and identify the reason for the failure. The stack area is often a key part of this analysis, because it contains the chain of instructions (function calls) that lead up to the point of failure. The analyst can use this or other information contained in the core file to determine the root cause of the failure and then, ideally, determine how to prevent failures from this error in the future. But it's important to remember this process is *good*. Concern for the safety of data has to come before concern for the run-time availability of the program. It makes no sense to admire a process that runs without any failures if you cannot also guarantee the results it produces are correct.

But that's it! A core file is just a snapshot of a process map at one point in time. Although you don't need to know much more than that, one simple thing you can do with any core file is learn which program produced it. Using the file(1) command on any core file, a Solaris system will tell you exactly that:

```
$ ls core
core
$ file core
core:    ELF 32-bit LSB core file 80386 Version 1, from 'bash'
```

The file command examines the first two bytes of the file you name. These two bytes are called the file's *magic number*, which is encoded with the file's key attributes. The file command simply interprets these attributes into human-readable form and prints them. In the case of a core file, it also lists the name of the program.

A skilled analyst can derive a lot of information from a core file, including the mappings of the process. You can do this, too, if you're curious, with the following incantation:

```
$ echo "::mappings" | mdb core
    BASE     LIMIT      SIZE NAME
  8044000   8048000     4000 [ stack ]
  8050000   817f000    12f000 /usr/bin/bash
  818f000   8195000     6000 /usr/bin/bash
  8195000   81bf000    2a000 [ heap ]
...
 fee10000  fef62000   152000 /usr/lib/libc/libc_hwcap1.so.1
 fef72000  fef7d000     b000 /usr/lib/libc/libc_hwcap1.so.1
 fef7d000  fef7e000     1000 /usr/lib/libc/libc_hwcap1.so.1
 fef80000  fef81000     1000
 fef90000  fef91000     1000
```

```
fefa0000 fefa1000    1000
fefb0000 fefb1000    1000
fefb7000 fefeb000   34000 /lib/ld.so.1
feffb000 feffd000    2000 /lib/ld.so.1
feffd000 feffe000    1000 /lib/ld.so.1
```

This output differs a little from pmap command output. It includes the base and limit address for each segment, and size is reported in hexadecimal instead of decimal notation. It does not include the permission set and doesn't give the anonymous memory segments a name. It is nonetheless easy to recognize as the same map of segments and addresses.

CERTIFICATION OBJECTIVE 14.02

Generating Core Files

Creating a core file isn't a mysterious process either. There are two general ways of going about it: the system creates one, based on an event in the process it deems unsafe; or a user creates one, either by providing bad input known to cause core dumps or just by asking for one. Unless the program itself is in an early stage of development, or it's not an important one, someone will (or should) want to analyze it, possibly a support technician. It's usually maintaining developers that want to create these snapshots—without forcing the program to terminate—to better understand the code. Others concerned with troubleshooting or performance analysis may also want these images to help them trace problematic or overly expensive operations within the code.

Several conditions make the OS worry about a process's data and force it to terminate. Most of them refer to cases where the OS thinks the program should know exactly what to do and where to do it, but appears confused. If the program code tries to access memory at a map location that isn't populated, that's one kind of problem. If the program tries to write data to a segment that doesn't contain data (a condition known as a *segmentation fault*), that's another. Executing an instruction that isn't supported by the processor, called an *illegal instruction*, is yet another. Any of these conditions may be raised by errors that exist in the source code, by errors added during the compilation process, or by modifying the code after it has been compiled. There are other more technical causes as well.

You can communicate these conditions to a process yourself to see what happens. Let's say you want to see what happens to a program that receives a segmentation fault message. The kill -l command lists all the signals the kernel can send. Not all of them are fatal or induce core dumps. For the sake of a brief example, I'll focus on segment violation, which is defined as signal 11:

```
$ kill -l 11
SEGV
```

The mnemonic SEGV describes the signal for human readability; to the kernel and process, the number alone is a hard-coded and complete communication. You can also use the kill program to send this signal to a process you own or have the privileges to affect, using the -s switch. The process must generate a core file when it receives this signal, which it will drop in the process's current working directory. For a shell program, that directory is always the one its user last changed it to, as this example shows:

```
$ ksh
$ pgrep ksh
2214
$ pwdx 2214
2214:    /var/tmp
$ kill -s 11 2214
Segmentation Fault (core dumped)
$ ls -l /var/tmp/core
-rw-------   1 oracle staff   13645869 Aug 23 04:38 /var/tmp/core
```

The pwdx command, introduced in Chapter 7, reports the current working directory of a process. In this example, I killed a Korn shell program that I started on top of my bash shell so I could see the confirmation message. The file listing shows the program was recorded in the expected location. You can also determine that the process knows why it stopped using an mdb command, as follows:

```
$ echo "::status" | mdb /var/tmp/core
debugging core file of ksh (64-bit) from orca
file: /usr/bin/amd64/ksh
initial argv: ksh
threading model: native threads
status: process terminated by SIGSEGV (Segmentation Fault), pid=2214 uid=60004
```

The file includes the cause of program failure as well as some other information a core file analyst can use to infer the best approach to analysis and perhaps the most useful understanding of the problem. This particular file might also mislead the analyst in the early going because there's no program-related cause to attribute to this signal. Still, generating core files this way helps you understand what can cause them; the only mystery left is *how* the kernel decides to send such a message. However, learning that process and analyzing the outcomes goes well beyond the scope of this book.

There are kinder and gentler ways to produce core files. Perhaps you just need an image of a process before or after some command-line or GUI input. Although developers typically use the gcore command to study a program, you can use it as an observation tool if you're interested in learning the differences between a healthy process and one that has failed. The gcore program is kinder and gentler in a couple of ways. Through various argument switches as well as default behavior, it lets you do the following:

- Produce a core file without terminating the process
- Attach the PID to the generated file (default)
- Name the file something else
- Locate the file somewhere else
- Choose the segment types you want to record

For simple use cases, just supply the PID as an argument. As you will see in the next example, a core file knows when it has been created with the gcore command:

```
$ ps
  PID TTY          TIME CMD
 1895 pts/1        0:00 bash
 2286 pts/1        0:00 ps
$ ksh
$ pgrep ksh
2287
$ gcore 2287
gcore: core.2287 dumped
$ file core.2287
core.2287:    ELF 64-bit LSB core file AMD64 Version 1, from 'ksh'
$ echo "::status" | mdb core.2287
debugging core file of ksh (64-bit) from orca
file: /usr/bin/amd64/ksh
initial argv: ksh
threading model: native threads
status: process core file generated with gcore(1)
```

Although the gcore command will not cause the process to abort, it does need to grab it long enough to read out the program map. The facility in a process that allows this kind of grabbing is limited by design to one program at a time. Be aware of other users on a shared system who are also interested in a process you want to examine. The gcore command includes an -F switch to evict another grabbing process if it can't be detached by some other means.

CERTIFICATION OBJECTIVE 14.03

Understanding Crash Dumps

A crash dump is also a core dump, but with a few important differences. One, it is a snapshot of the kernel program, the code that is the heart of your operating system. As a result, it will contain not just information about user processes, but also the components that make up the operating system: devices, drivers, file systems, process management. The operating system is not only code that's completely unfamiliar to most users, it's also services many of us rely on without ever knowing what they are or what they do.

Two, when the kernel has to dump core to protect data, it means everything comes to a halt, ergo the name *crash dump*. As a result, a crash dump can't be written directly to a file—which file system is stable if the kernel halts? Thus, the process by which a crash dump is recovered to a file is more elaborate than what you've learned for a process, and has to be studied with a bit more care to support it correctly.

But let's start with elements that have something in common with process core dumps. For one, the kernel program, like a process, relies on a mapping scheme to organize its resources in memory and form a coherent image. Although it's not organized quite the same as a process, we have a corollary tool to the pmap command, called the modinfo command, that reads and reports this mapping. This command lists all the components that make up the kernel's services which, like code libraries, are linked to the base code. You may hear these components called loadable modules, device drivers, or just "drivers," or maybe by some other term. The kernel has a dedicated map-linking process called krtld, otherwise known as the *kernel runtime loader*.

It's also a very long list of services, as this example shows:

```
$ modinfo | wc -l
261
```

On my practice system running in VirtualBox, 260 modules are currently loaded (subtract one for the table header)—far more than I'd care to enumerate here. It's sufficient for now to look at the first four entries:

```
$ modinfo | head -4
 Id Loadaddr          Size   Info Rev Module Name
  0 fffffffffb800000  1ff8ae  -    0  unix ()
  1 fffffffffb95d068  2df7e0  -    0  genunix ()
  3 fffffffffbbe4000    6008  1    1  specfs (filesystem for specfs)
```

Each entry shows an ID number kept by the kernel program, the kernel program address where a module has been mapped, its total size (code and data) in bytes in hexadecimal format, additional information interesting to kernel-oriented users, and a text description. The first two entries, unix() and genunix(), form the core. The first service they link in is specfs, the pseudo file system that only handles certain device files. The rest of the output has some interesting facets to it: For one, you can learn the order in which loadable modules are added and how much memory they require. Beyond that, there's not much for a novice to learn from it.

What is particularly daunting about this program, if you're thinking about taking a closer look, is the sheer wealth of information. Also, it doesn't bear much further resemblance to a process because its concerns include managing many diverse resources, including:

- Processes
- System and peripheral devices
- File systems
- Terminal communications
- Interprocess communications
- Network communications

If that's not enough to dissuade most people, learning to navigate this structure relies on a sometimes cryptic, sometimes archaic set of terms and instructions. A small percentage of users have much interest at this level of system operation. The vocabulary that governs conversations about it tend toward direct use of technical terms that become familiar by repetition and a strong ability to attach meaning to what first seem like an arbitrary list of symbols.

Still, at its heart, a crash dump is a core file. Unlike process dumps, it has one default location. In Solaris 11, the default directory is /var/crash. The dump file itself has to be extracted into two files. One is a symbol table that maps human-readable names to the hexadecimal address scheme of the kernel code. The first part of its filename is simply unix. The other file, which goes by the name vmcore, is the kernel snapshot itself. The files share an extension, a number to show that one file is the right map for the other. In the /var/crash directory, you will also find a file called "bounds" that contains the number assigned to the next file pair generated:

```
# ls -l /var/crash
total 1243279
-rw-r--r--   1 root     root              2 Aug 26 07:00 bounds
-rw-r--r--   1 root     root        3318904 Aug 26 07:03 unix.0
-rw-r--r--   1 root     root      507924480 Aug 26 07:05 vmcore.0
-rw-r--r--   1 root     root      137101312 Aug 26 07:01 vmdump.0
# cat bounds
1
```

Notice the change in prompt for this example. Access to this directory is restricted, so you'll have to assume the root role to view its contents. I created a core dump on my machine for show and tell, which resulted in the vmdump.0 file. The bounds file was then incremented by the system to prepare for the next crash dump. I extracted the files unix.0 and vmcore.0 using a command I'll show you in the next section.

You can also apply the file and mdb commands to these objects if you like. The output from the mdb command doesn't appear useful, at least not until you learn you must feed it both files. The mdb command needs the symbol table to make sense of the core's contents, so a proper invocation looks like this:

```
# echo "::status"| mdb unix.0 vmcore.0
mdb: failed to read panicbuf and panic_reg -- current register set will be
unavailable
debugging crash dump vmcore.0 (64-bit) from orca
operating system: 5.11 11.0 (i86pc)
image uuid: 76d44672-140b-ca60-e0f0-ea84948c0171
panic message:
dump content: kernel pages only
```

```
# echo "::mappings"| mdb unix.0 vmcore.0
mdb: failed to read panicbuf and panic_reg -- current register set will be
unavailable
           BASE             LIMIT              SIZE NAME
fffffe0000000000 fffffe0080000000          80000000 kpmseg
ffffff0000000000 ffffff0003e00000           3e00000 kvalloc
ffffff0003e00000 ffffff0083600000           7f800000 kpseg
ffffff0083600000 ffffff0102e00000           7f800000 kzioseg
ffffff0142e00000 ffffff0146e00000           4000000 kmapseg
ffffff0146e00000 fffffffffc0000000       fe79200000 kvseg
fffffffffc0000000 fffffffffb7fb000          3b7fb000 kvseg_core
fffffffffb800000 fffffffffbd5f000            55f000 ktextseg
fffffffff800000 fffffffffc00000            400000 kdebugseg
```

One element of note in the status output is the panic message. I'll have more to say about that in the next section. The output also tells us what content we're looking at—kernel pages only. That's quite a bit lighter in storage than a dump of all memory, and it's usually sufficient. Unless you need to track down a particular user-kernel interaction in detail, the kernel pages have a lot of information.

The remaining output doesn't mean much without further background information. It's important to see, however, that a crash dump is just another file with its own format. It takes a certain passion for detail and obscure vocabularies to dig in, but the information is available to anyone who needs or wants to learn how to read it.

CERTIFICATION OBJECTIVE 14.04

Generating Crash Dumps

As with core dumps, there are a few ways to create crash dumps. When the system does this, it is of course disruptive. Usually a crash dump is created as part of the system's *panic routine*. Normally, when the kernel encounters an error that could pose a threat to data, it has three objectives to pursue, in priority order:

- Protect the data
- Inform the user
- Keep the system running

When the cause of the problem is a process or something the kernel can "correct" (for example, by killing a process), it can meet all three criteria. When the problem appears to exist in the kernel itself, all bets are off. Protecting data comes first; informing the user comes second. The panic routine manages these tasks in part by calling a kernel-level sync routine to flush the program from memory into the dump device. The dump device on Solaris 11 is here:

```
# zfs list rpool/dump
NAME          USED   AVAIL   REFER   MOUNTPOINT
rpool/dump    416M   1.78G   403M    -
```

It has no mount point because it is only intended for the kernel's use. In earlier versions of Solaris, the swap device doubles as a dump device, unless the system is configured to host a dedicated one using a separate partition. Thanks in part to ZFS's integration as the root file system, there's no need for separate disk space. Solaris 11 is configured by default to host a dedicated space for crash dumps just by claiming space from the root pool.

Once the image has been flushed and stored, the panic routine writes a shutdown message to the system log to notify the administrator. It then reboots the system. Built in to the startup process is a service, svc:/system/dumpadm:default, that checks the dump device for a valid image. If it holds one, the service retrieves this image, assembles it into a file, and deposits it in the /var/crash directory. The bounds file is used to add the numeric extension to the dump file, after which the number in the bounds file is incremented by one.

You can also create a kernel program image using a program called savecore. Without any options, savecore emulates the behavior of the panic routine, writing out the kernel image to the dump device and writing a message to the log file. With the -L switch, it will not call reboot or write to the log. This option requires a dedicated dump device, and so in prior versions of Solaris additional configuration is necessary to enable it. With Solaris 11, it is available out of the box. Here is an example of that process:

```
# savecore -L
dumping to /dev/zvol/dsk/rpool/dump, offset 65536, content: kernel
 0:15 100% done
100% done: 103099 pages dumped, dump succeeded
savecore: System dump time: Sun Aug 26 09:36:38 2012

savecore: Saving compressed system crash dump in /var/crash/vmdump.1
savecore: Decompress the crash dump with
```

```
`savecore -vf /var/crash/vmdump.1'
# savecore -vf /var/crash/vmdump.1
savecore: System dump time: Sun Aug 26 09:36:38 2012

savecore: saving system crash dump in /var/crash/{unix,vmcore}.1
Constructing namelist /var/crash/unix.1
Constructing corefile /var/crash/vmcore.1
 0:32 100% done: 103099 of 103099 pages saved
4301 (4%) zero pages were not written
0:32 dump decompress is done
# ls /var/crash
bounds    unix.0    unix.1    vmcore.0  vmcore.1  vmdump.0  vmdump.1
# cat /var/crash/bounds
2
```

The process takes time based on the number of memory pages that must be pushed to disk. The empty line shown between the reported dump time and saving the dump to file is where a reboot would otherwise occur. To save bootup time and a bit of disk space, the process leaves behind a single vmdump file that can be extracted into a symbol table and memory map file at the administrator's discretion. The second crash dump has an incremented number, and the bounds file now holds the value 2. The dump file generated here was about 120MB in size. I extracted a symbol table of 3.3MB and a core file of 430MB from it. My dump device now shows 1.26GB full. These images quickly add up in storage cost.

CERTIFICATION OBJECTIVE 14.05

Managing Core and Crash Dumps

Keeping many user core files on hand can get messy as well as expensive to store. You can't store them all in one place, much less identify them quickly if they have the same name, and it might be difficult to determine on a multiuser system who (if anyone) wants to analyze them. One consideration an administrator has to make, therefore, is how to name and locate these files, and perhaps how much space to allow for storing them, too.

With crash dumps, naming may be less of an issue, but storage requirements are a bigger one. A crash dump can be significantly larger than what I've shown if it includes more than its kernel pages. If maintaining sufficient disk space is a problem, you may need a policy that prevents depositing a crash dump in the /var/crash directory if it will take up more space than you want to allow.

Solaris 11 provides separate tools for managing either type of core file. The coreadm utility lets you define how you want process core files handled. The dumpadm lets you configure the system to manage crash dumps.

Using the coreadm Command

The coreadm command provides two forms for arguments. The first form lets a privileged user set global policy for core names and locations, as well as other options. The second form lets all users change the preferences on a process they own or are allowed to control. Using the second form, you can query a process and determine what policies are currently in effect for it. The following output shows that my shell program, if it dumps, will produce a file named core with the default content for a failed process:

```
$ coreadm $$
1502:    core    default
```

Let's say I want a core file's name to include the process's PID and UID. The -p option lets me configure the resulting name with variables that resolve to process-specific values. Once the kernel signals a process to dump a core image, the coreadm utility abstracts these values from the process in question and appends them to the resulting file:

```
$ ksh
$ coreadm $$
1590:    core    default
$ coreadm -p core%p_%u $$
$ coreadm $$
1590:    core%p_%u    default
$ kill -s 11 $$
Segmentation Fault (core dumped)
$ ls
core1590_60004
```

The %p token stands for the PID; the %u token stands for the UID. The resulting file includes the correct values along with a literal underscore I included for readability. Note that the gcore utility applies its own options with an -o switch, but uses the same token conventions as the coreadm utility. Table 14-1 lists all these available tokens.

on the Job

These variables offer a great deal of flexibility in managing the resulting files. For a useful strategy to apply them, consider how you might like to filter or sort through such files if you had a large number of them.

The administrative settings are numerous, as you will see by running the coreadm command without arguments:

```
$ coreadm
       global core file pattern:
       global core file content: default
         init core file pattern: core
         init core file content: default
             global core dumps: disabled
        per-process core dumps: enabled
         global setid core dumps: disabled
    per-process setid core dumps: disabled
       global core dump logging: disabled
```

TABLE 14-1	Embedded Variable (coreadm/gcore)	Resulting Value
	%d	Executable file's directory name
Embedded Variables Used by the coreadm and gcore Utilities	%f	Executable file's name
	%g	Effective group ID
	%m	Machine name (same as uname -m)
	%n	Node name (same as uname -n)
	%p	Process ID
	%t	Time (decimal form)
	%u	Effective user ID
	%z	Zone the process ran in
	%%	Literal %

The first four lines manage the default pattern and content on a global basis and for the init process alone. The next two settings for core dumps are *not* mutually exclusive; if you want, you can allow up to three core dumps for one process: one according to the global policy, one according to the per-process settings, and one inside a non-global zone if it was running there. Disabling these settings will reduce the number of copies made.

The setid configurations have to do with processes that allow the user to obtain extra privileges only while the process is running. The passwd utility is one such program. In order to change your own password, you must be able to edit the /etc/ shadow file, which is only accessible to the rootuser. The passwd program assumes the root role for the express purpose of modifying passwords on the user's behalf. A crafty user could try to get this program, or one like it, to dump its core. If successful, he could then examine the contents for data a non-privileged user doesn't otherwise have access to. Sneaky, huh? So as a safety precaution, core dumps for these files are disabled by default. Use due caution before enabling setid core dumps.

You can also configure your system to write to the system log when a global core file attempt occurs. This notification can be a useful hedge against failed attempts, such as when insufficient space is left to hold the file, or you might use it just to add the report to a system log that is regularly monitored.

For each of the settings that can be enabled or disabled, you use the -d and -e options with the appropriate option, as shown in Table 14-2.

You can address several of these options at once in a single command, as shown here:

```
$ sudo coreadm -d process -e global -e log
$ coreadm
Ö
              global core dumps: enabled
         per-process core dumps: disabled
         global setid core dumps: disabled
   per-process setid core dumps: disabled
        global core dump logging: enabled
```

TABLE 14-2	Core File Option	Property
	global	(Dis)allow global file pattern
Options for Enabling/Disabling coreadm Facilities	global-setid	(Dis)allow dumps of setid programs globally
	process	(Dis)allow per-process file patterns
	proc-setid	(Dis)allow dumps of setid programs per process
	log	(Dis)allow writing to log when writing global cores

In this example, global dumps are allowed, per-process dumps are not, and the coreadm facility will write to the system log when a core dump occurs. You can change these back any time. The svc:/system/coreadm:default service tracks any changes and enforces the policies set immediately.

The switches that let you modify the naming pattern and content type for each policy type are shown in Table 14-3.

Setting the content type for a core file is an advanced topic. I've mentioned key segment types that are common to all processes: the text, data, stack, heap, and anon segments. These total roughly one-third of all segment types that can be configured.

---

e x a m

ⓦ a t c h   *Consult the coreadm(1) man page for the full list of supported types. You won't be tested on these types; doing so would assume you know the full*   *meaning and use of segment types that can appear in a core file. It's helpful knowledge, in my opinion, but not required for the exam.*

Using the dumpadm Command

The dumpadm command allows you to configure the environment for crash dump files. As mentioned previously, naming is handled by automatically incrementing the file extension of each successive dump. Other aspects, including the type of content

TABLE 14-3	coreadm Switch option	Description
	-g/-G	Global file and init process pattern/content
coreadm Switches	-i/-I	Default per-process pattern/content
for Managing	-p/-P	Per-process pattern/content for specified PIDs
Dump Naming		
and Content Type		

dumped, its location, the device that captures the pages flushed from memory, the availability of the savecore feature, and some other resource-oriented settings, can all be managed through the dumpadm utility. The default output for the command includes five key settings, as you see here:

```
$ sudo dumpadm
       Dump content: kernel pages
        Dump device: /dev/zvol/dsk/rpool/dump (dedicated)
Savecore directory: /var/crash
   Savecore enabled: yes
    Save compressed: on
```

These settings are kept in the file /etc/dumpadm.conf. The urge of many old-school admins to manage such files with a text editor aside, it's strongly recommended you use the dumpadm utility only to change this file. This practice ensures that typos and other format errors don't create unexpected results for subsequent crash dumps.

The content type for a crash dump has three valid settings: kernel, all, and curproc. The curproc setting allows the dump to capture kernel pages and the image of the process on the CPU as the crash dump started. It's assumed with this setting that the current process may provide some clues to why the crash dump occurred.

Historically in Solaris, the default location for the dump device has been the swap device. Because the swap device has no useful purpose during a system shutdown and reboot, using it as a kernel memory repository provided a clever savings on disk space. It also prevented administrators from using the savecore utility, which operates during run-time and therefore can't use the swap device to do its work. Administrators had to create a separate disk partition and point to it as a dedicated device, using dumpadm. Starting with Solaris 11, this extra step isn't required. The installation process automatically creates a dedicated dump device using space from the root pool. You can still specify an alternate dedicated device if you want, possibly from another pool you create, if you want to return storage space back to the root pool.

TABLE 14-4   List of dumpadm Options

dumpadm Command Option	Description
-c [kernel | all | curproc]	Content type (kernel, all, or curproc)
-d [dump-device | swap]	Dump device (dedicated dump-device or swap)
-m [#k | #m | #%]	Minfree value (in KB, MB, or as a percentage of remaining space)
-n | -y	Disable/enable savecore on reboot
-r *dir*	Alternate root directory
-s *dir*	Savecore directory
-u	Force update kernel to /etc/dumpadm.conf

The options for each setting that appears in the dumpadm utility's output are listed in Table 14-4.

The minfree value specifies how much headroom the system should maintain when handling a new crash dump. It can be specified in kilobytes, megabytes, or as a percentage of remaining capacity. If the new crash dump would impinge on the space reserved by the minfree value, the system will not add it to the savecore directory.

You can disable the work savecore does with dumpadm's -n option and enable it with -y. These switches acknowledge that an SMF service, svc:/system/dumpadm:default, provides a monitor and restart capability for the utility's file-based configuration.

CERTIFICATION SUMMARY

Handling process core and system crash files is primarily a configuration and storage management job for beginning administrators. Using the information they contain to determine causes may be beyond your current skills, but they are still just files that need a name, a location in which to reside, and some amount of disk space available. To prepare for the exam, study the utilities and configuration files that manage these files and the options you have to change default settings.

Understanding the makeup of these files is also important. You may not be called upon to analyze them, but knowing what kind of information they contain helps you understand why they're made and who in your organization might be interested in using them.

TWO-MINUTE DRILL

Understanding Core Files

❑ A core file is a snapshot of a running process, usually one that failed in an unexpected way. By default, its name is core. Its location is the last working directory of the process.

❑ You can use the file command and some mdb options to learn where a core file comes from and possibly what event created it.

Generating Core Files

❑ The kernel uses signals to abort a process that appears confused. This may result from conditions that indicate the program may soon corrupt its data.

❑ The gcore command allows a user to create a core image of a program without terminating it.

Understanding Crash Dumps

❑ Crash dumps caused by a system panic must be saved to disk before the system shuts down and cannot be recovered to a file until the boot process starts. If the dump is saved to a location other than one used for swap, you can recover additional copies using the savecore utility.

❑ In Solaris 11, a dedicated ZFS file system, named rpool/dump by default, is provided to capture crash images created either by the panic routine or by using the savecore utility.

Generating Crash Dumps

❑ The kernel has a panic routine that will flush kernel memory to the dump device, write a note to the system log, and then reboot the system.

❑ The savecore command emulates the work of the panic routine but can also be used to generate a crash dump without forcing a system reboot.

Managing Core and Crash Dumps

❑ Use the coreadm utility to name and locate process core files as they are generated. Without arguments, the command shows its current configuration.

❑ Use the dumpadm utility to name and locate crash dump files and set limits on how much space they consume. Without arguments, the command shows its current configuration.

SELF TEST

The following questions will help measure your understanding of the material presented in this chapter.

Understanding Core Files

1. Which two tools can you use to read the segment map of a process or core file?

   A. pstack

   B. mdb

   C. pmap

   D. gproc

2. Which of the following segment types is backed by a file?

   A. anon

   B. heap

   C. text

   D. stack

3. How does a program normally induce a segmentation fault?

   A. By executing an instruction the CPU doesn't support

   B. By accessing an unpopulated area of the program map

   C. By executing an instruction in the wrong part of the map

   D. By linking in the wrong segment with the dynamic linker

Generating Core Files

4. Which of the following is not an embedded variable supplied by the coreadm utility?

   A. %m, the machine name

   B. %p, the PID

   C. %d, the date

   D. %n, the node name

5. Which of the following commands can tell you the cause of a process core dump?
   A. file
   B. gcore
   C. mdb
   D. kill

6. Why is it unsafe to enable core dumps for setid processes?
   A. They have to be force-attached, which can disrupt the currently attached process.
   B. Someone could change their password and cause a core dump.
   C. It's possible to expose system data to a non-root user.
   D. Enabling the option increases the chances a setid program can crash.

Understanding Crash Dumps

7. Pick the true statement regarding dumpadm.
   A. You can switch from a dedicated dump device to using a swap device.
   B. You can use it to modify the number in the bounds file.
   C. The default minfree value is 2%.
   D. You can use it to write a notice to the system log every time a crash dump is saved.

8. Which files contain only the names that are aliases for memory addresses in a crash dump?
   A. vmcore
   B. bounds
   C. unix
   D. vmdump

Generating Crash Dumps

9. What happens if you disable the svc:/system/dumpadm:default service?
   A. The system will no longer flush kernel pages to the dump device.
   B. The system will reboot following a panic.
   C. The savecore command won't work.
   D. On a default Solaris 11 system, nothing.

10. What is the most core dumps the system can make from a single abnormal process termination?

   A. 1
   B. 2
   C. 3
   D. 4

SELF TEST ANSWERS

Understanding Core Files

1. ☑ **B** and **C.** The pmap command reports the segment mappings of an active process. Using the ::mapping command of the mdb utility, you can see the mappings in a core file.
    ☒ **A** and **D** are incorrect. **A** is incorrect because the pstack command reports the stack traces for each thread in an active process. **D** is incorrect because the gproc command will create a core file from an active process but doesn't have a facility for reporting its contents.

2. ☑ **C.** A text segment is composed of code, which by definition must come from a file.
    ☒ **A, B,** and **D** are incorrect. The stack, heap, and anon segment types represent run-time data specific to an active process. They cease to exist when the process terminates.

3. ☑ **C.** A segmentation violation occurs when the code tries to apply an instruction to the wrong kind of segment, such as trying to write data to a text segment.
    ☒ **A, B,** and **D** are incorrect. **A** is incorrect because this option describes an illegal instruction fault. **B** is incorrect because this condition could be a null pointer exception, but any time a program wants to access memory that hasn't been allocated yet, it's a clear sign of a big problem. **D** is incorrect because problems that occur with the dynamic linker could manifest a variety of ways. None of them are pretty for a junior administrator who just recently learned what the dynamic linker does.

Generating Core Files

4. ☑ **C.** The coreadm utility does support the date in decimal format via the embedded variable %t. It does not have an embedded variable to provide a human-readable date.
    ☒ **A, B,** and **D** are incorrect. Each of these options is a correct and available embedded variable.

5. ☑ **C.** The mdb utility's ::status command extracts the reason for a core dump from the file.
    ☒ **A, B,** and **D** are incorrect. **A** is incorrect because the file command can only read a file's magic number and report which program the core dump comes from. **B** is incorrect because the gcore utility only produces core dumps; it doesn't inspect them. **D** is incorrect because the kill command can initiate core dumps with the right signal, but it doesn't read them.

Understanding Crash Dumps

6. ☑ **C.** It is possible to dump a process's core by sending it the right signal. Enabling dumps for a program that runs as root, on the behalf of non-root user, could end by recording privileged data into a file that a non-privileged user can read.

   ☒ **A, B,** and **D** are incorrect. **A** is incorrect because enabling setid programs to dump core has nothing to do with attaching to the process. **B** is incorrect because normal operation of a stable command should never dump core merely because the system is configured to support it. **D** is incorrect for the same reason as B.

7. ☑ **A.** Although it's hard to come up with a good reason for doubling up the swap device as the dump device, the dumpadm command does allow that configuration.

   ☒ **B, C,** and **D** are incorrect. **B** is incorrect because you cannot modify the contents of the bounds file through the dumpadm command. **C** is incorrect because the default minfree value is zero. **D** is incorrect because writing to the system log upon generating a core file is an option in the coreadm utility only.

8. ☑ **C.** The unix file of a crash dump contains only the symbol names that map to addresses in the kernel image that was dumped.

   ☒ **A, B,** and **D** are incorrect. **A** is incorrect because the vmcore file contains the kernel image itself. **B** is incorrect because the bounds file keeps the number that will be assigned to the next crash dump. **D** is incorrect because the vmdump file contains both the unix and vmcore files.

Generating Crash Dumps

9. ☑ **D.** A default Solaris 11 installation installs a dedicated dump device. Disabling the dumpadm service should therefore have no effect.

   ☒ **A, B,** and **C** are incorrect. **A** is incorrect because the only time the system will not flush kernel pages to the dump device is if it's a savecore operation and the dump device uses the swap device. **B** is incorrect because whether the system boots after a panic has nothing to do with dumpadm configuration. **C** is incorrect because unless you've reconfigured the default Solaris 11 installation, savecore will operate normally whether the dumpadm service is enabled or disabled.

10. ☑ **C.** With all the right options enabled, a single process failure can be responsible for three core dumps: one global, one per-process, and one zone-based if the process was running inside one.

    ☒ **A, B,** and **D** are incorrect. They are mutually exclusive options to **C** and therefore are incorrect.

15
Managing Network Resources

N etwork administration was, at one time, considered an advanced topic for beginners. First you'd learn how to manage a single workstation, then how to get systems on a small network to talk to each other, and then how to get systems on different networks to talk to each other. As a training model, even for a company whose motto was once "The Network is the Computer," it made sense to widen the scope of services available on a Solaris system one step at a time.

The Internet has changed all that, of course, as the people who developed Solaris thought it would. Many people now manage their own complex networks at home. Most of us can just buy devices that reduce the configuration process to a few clicks and maybe a phone call. You can exercise as much or as little control over this domain as you like.

To support a business or some other community of users, however, an administrator has to become a more knowledgeable buffer between users and the network service provider. Far more people who want to know something about connecting to networks can learn it. An administrator should know why and how the system works as well as how to verify its operation and determine if a system's configuration is correct, and therefore not the cause of a connection problem. In this chapter, I'll guide you through the basics of the network model and operations to do just that.

CERTIFICATION OBJECTIVE 15.01

Understanding TCP/IP Networking

One difference between using a Solaris system and administering one is that you need an understanding that goes beyond what a command can do and what output you should expect from it. You need to know which commands do what, of course, but you also need to understand the system elements required for a command or application to work properly. In network operations, there are a lot of players, each with specific roles to manage one aspect of a multifaceted task:

- Receiving signals from a physical medium
- Decoding the signal into data your system can interpret

■ Determining if the data was intended for your system
■ Separating the delivery metadata from the payload data
■ Directing the information to its intended application

It's a long-established practice in operating systems to assign these tasks to individual software components in the kernel, known collectively as the *network model* or *network stack*. The de facto model for the Internet is called Transmission Control Protocol/Internet Protocol (TCP/IP). This model defines the functional responsibility assigned to each component and the facilities it provides to connect two processes that run on different systems (such as your browser and an HTTP server). It is also used as a visual model to help us understand in general terms how our systems convert signals taken from the wire (or from the air) into data our applications can use.

Analyzing the TCP/IP Model

The TCP/IP network model was first described formally in the Request for Comments (RFC) 1122 document. This document, and others like it, are maintained and communicated by the Internet Engineering Task Force (IETF). The IETF is a noncommercial body that promotes standards and practices so all participants on the Internet work together in a community-oriented fashion. RFC 1122 was written in 1989 and has been updated by other RFC documents along the way, but remains a useful reference for understand the roles and responsibilities of each defined network layer.

RFC 1122 defines a link layer, an Internet Protocol (IP) layer, and a transport layer. The link layer is the connection between some physical medium, such as an Ethernet or wireless network, and the operating system. When it receives data from the medium addressed to the physical link (through a Media Access Controller, or MAC, address), the data link processes and sends that data to the IP layer, which determines if the host is the intended destination for the message. (It is also at this layer that firewall software works, rejecting undesirable messages or requests intended for your system.) The IP layer removes the host addressing metadata from the packet and passes the result to the transport layer. The transport layer determines how the data has been communicated, as a standalone message (called a *datagram)* or one that is associated with an ongoing stream of them (called a *TCP packet)*.

From this point, what remains of the message metadata determines the destination process. The document RFC 1123 defines protocols to support the most common tasks, such as remote terminal connections (Telnet protocol), file transfer protocol (FTP), e-mail (Simple Message Transfer Protocol), and more. You might imagine that new applications invent new protocols at this layer, but most applications use the protocols that already exist and build on them. For example, a bare-bones HTTP conversation is just plain text running over a Telnet-like service. You can fool some HTTP servers using a Telnet session instead of a browser if you know the text:

```
$ telnet amazon.com 80
Trying 72.21.194.1...
Connected to amazon.com.
Escape character is '^]'.
GET / HTTP/1.1
<Press Enter twice>
HTTP/1.1 400 Bad Request
Date: Sun, 16 Dec 2012 17:24:38 GMT
Server: Server
Content-Length: 11
Cneonction: close
Content-Type: text/html; charset=iso-8859-1
```

In this example, I connected to an Amazon website using a Telnet client and asked for the home page content using the HTTP 1.1 protocol. The server rejected my request, probably because it couldn't identify my browser type, but returned proper HTTP syntax. All your browser does is parse the response as instructions to render a graphic view. At the networking level, the conversation is just structured text. You might also notice the word "Cneonction" in the response. The expected value is "Connection," but it turns out some network load balancers purposely change this word to avoid a technical issue that can slow a server's response to the client.

Figure 15-1 shows a full network stack with TCP/IP connecting the physical medium to the target process. The descriptions here are general, but are sufficient to understand the intent of the model. As you'll discover when you are ready to study network administration more deeply, there is a great deal more information in the details than anyone can comment on in a brief space. If you are interested in details right now, you can find a wealth of useful information on the Internet to guide you.

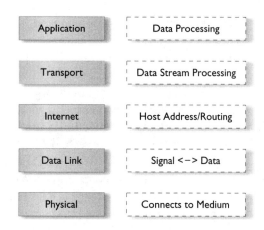

FIGURE 15-1

The TCP/IP
network model

For the rest of this chapter, I focus on the bottom three layers: the physical, data link, and IP components. These are all you need to see how a Solaris system connects to the network and supports processes that can communicate over a network. The tools you learn about in this chapter support configuring these layers and help you verify that network operations are in good working order.

Defining the Physical Layer

First, let's assume your machine is somehow connected to a network. You should always remember your system is a network client. It relies on some medium that will help you discover and connect to other systems. The way you confirm this connection is typically physical as well. If you connect with a cable, the physical port should have a link light (usually amber in color) that stays on or flashes to show you're seeing traffic. For wireless transceivers, your system may or may not have a physical link-status indicator.

The physical link is defined generally by a network interface controller (NIC) that attaches to your medium of choice. For cabled access, the common choice is Ethernet, which operates on a specific model called Carrier-Sense Multiple Access/ Collision Detect (CSMA/CD). This term identifies three primary attributes of the Ethernet protocol itself:

- **Carrier Sense**   The NIC identifies the medium and its signal automatically.
- **Multiple Access**   Multiple stations take turns using the wire.
- **Collision Detect**   NICs detect simultaneous use of the wire and compensate for it.

Because your system is only a network client—that is, all you have to do is to connect to use the service—a low-level protocol that receives, transmits, and corrects errors automatically takes a lot of responsibility out of your hands. It's an easy thing to take for granted, too—until it doesn't seem to work.

To operate at this level, your NIC uses a station identifier called a Media Access Control (MAC) address. This address is a 48-bit datum usually expressed in hexadecimal digits separated into pairs. The first 24 bits are an Organizationally Unique Identifier (OUI); the second 24 bits identify the NIC instance, or Device Identifier. Each MAC address is intended to identify devices on a global scale so that machine-to-machine communication can be unambiguous regardless of their relative locations. Although logical addressing occurs at the IP layer for host-to-host communication, this level of address is needed to identify a machine even before the operating system has prepared the system for higher-level communication.

The MAC is a value that comes from your NIC hardware, not the operating system. You can report the value in Solaris 11 in a couple of ways. The dladm show-phys command with the -m option reports the NIC's MAC address:

```
$ dladm show-phys -m
LINK              SLOT      ADDRESS              INUSE CLIENT
net0              primary   8:0:27:a3:33:93      yes   net0
```

The ADDRESS column shows the MAC address (with leading zeroes removed) for my net0 link. You can use the OUI portion to identify the vendor. Several different websites offer this service, such as http://macvendorlookup.com. The manufacturer for the address shown turns out to be Cadmus Computer Systems.

You can also report this value by asking for the ether property from the ifconfig utility, but root access is required to get this same information:

```
$ sudo ifconfig net0 ether
net0: flags=1004843<UP,BROADCAST,RUNNING,MULTICAST,DHCP,IPv4> mtu 1500 index 2
    ether 8:0:27:a3:33:93
```

Your system uses the MAC addresses of other local network devices to communicate with them, so it maintains a small cache to avoid looking them up repeatedly. Your system discovers these addresses using the Address Resolution Protocol (ARP). Most UNIX operating systems have a utility called arp that dumps the contents of this cache, including an entry for the local system:

```
$ arp -a
Net to Media Table: IPv4
Device   IP Address            Mask             Flags    Phys Addr
------   -------------------   --------------   -------- ----------------
net0     10.0.2.15             255.255.255.255  SPLA     08:00:27:a3:33:93
net0     10.0.2.2              255.255.255.255           52:54:00:12:35:02
net0     224.0.0.251           255.255.255.255  S        01:00:5e:00:00:fb
net0     igmp.mcast.net        255.255.255.255  S        01:00:5e:00:00:16
```

If you looked up the MAC addresses of the bottom three entries, you'd learn there is no vendor assigned to these numbers. The guidelines for MAC addressing reserves some numbers for use as virtual and pseudo network devices; this way, you can emulate such an address in software for your own convenience instead of hoping you don't hit a valid number. It's always good form to choose an OUI outside the valid range when you need a placeholder.

Defining the Data Link Layer

According to RFC 1122, the data link layer is responsible for communications between systems on the same local network. Whereas your NIC contains the MAC address, the data link layer provides the means to implement the ARP cache. This layer also converts the signal-oriented data received from the network medium into frames of local network data. These frames can be passed between machines that share a physical network, but are not suitable for internetwork communication.

The data link layer is also known as *Layer 2*, and it is where many network devices, such as hubs and simple switches, support connecting machines into local area networks (LANs). A hub will accept a data-link frame from one machine and propagate it to all other machines also connected to the hub. A switch will generally pass frames directly to the intended data link, reducing the amount of traffic on the wire that other machines have no interest in.

At this layer, you should think of your network connection as a logical link instead of a NIC. It may seem like mere word substitution at the moment, but it is useful for keeping the functions of the full network associated with the right layer. The value of this distinction will become more apparent in Chapter 16. In the meantime, notice that the dladm utility supports the show-link subcommand, appropriate to the data link layer, as well as the show-phys subcommand shown previously:

```
$ dladm show-link
LINK              CLASS    MTU     STATE    OVER
net0              phys     1500    up       -
```

The component net0 is the same one, although now you are seeing it displayed in the context of a logical link: with a supporting class type, a Maximum Transmission Unit (MTU) or frame size, and an activity state. I explain the meaning of the OVER column in Chapter 16.

Prior to Solaris 11, observing the data link layer as a distinct entity wasn't supported as clearly as it could have been. Historically, this area has been a network programmer's direct concern. The primary administrative tools, the ndd and ifconfig utilities, divided the tasks of managing low-level TCP/IP properties and NIC properties, respectively. The responsibility for managing data-link properties falls somewhere between these two tools. If you wanted to change a setting of a TCP/IP layer, you used the ndd utility to configure the kernel module. If you wanted to manage the MAC and/or IP address, you used the ifconfig utility to configure the adapter settings. If you wanted to manage the ARP cache, you used the arp utility, and so on.

Solaris 11 creates a clearer administrative distinction between these layers. Consequently, long-time Solaris administrators have about as much to learn to adapt to these new tools as new administrators have to learn to become familiar with them. But it's good news for all in the long run. With the dladm utility, you have a single tool for managing data links. There's a separate one, the ipadm utility, for managing the host addresses you assign to them.

Other benefits are attached to making the data-link layer a configurable interface that have to do with creating virtualized network resources. You'll learn about those in Chapter 16. But even for experienced Solaris administrators, this approach is new. Unless your administrator colleagues have already had some training on the Solaris 11 implementation, or time to learn it on their own, what you learn about the dladm utility may be news to them. The ndd and ifconfig utilities work the same, for the most part, but they will be deprecated before too long.

Defining the Internet Protocol Layer

Each network device, or NIC, has a unique MAC address. The data link (logical) layer supports devices on the same medium to communicate frames of data, using these addresses as source and destination values. To connect machines on different networks, you need the Internet Protocol layer, also known as Layer 3. The IP layer defines address schemes that allow each host to identify itself, the network it is connected to, and a mask value that divides a given IP address into its host and station elements.

A MAC address should be unique. It normally is, but it's possible to override a NIC's assigned value. A single NIC, however, can have only one identifier assigned. An IP address, on the other hand, is a value you configure on top of a data link. You can assign multiple IP addresses to a working data link, provided they aren't being used by another data link on the same network or any other network that is reachable. *Reachability* refers to one network's ability to route its traffic to or through another network.

It's commonly said that the IP layer is responsible for addressing and routing, but only some devices route the network data they receive. A station that allows other stations on the same network medium to pass data through it to another network is called a *gateway*. Dedicated Layer 3 devices, such as routers, come equipped with at least two NICs and can store routing tables that help them forward data intended for other networks along the best available path. Routing itself can be a complex topic to understand, as routing devices are just the beginning. There's also the matter of choosing the best algorithms for directing traffic across networks, and more.

In Solaris 11, the options for managing IP interfaces change considerably. Using the ipadm utility, you can observe both the data links available to the IP layer and the addresses assigned to them. At this layer, the data link can be used to create an IP interface. Each address you assign to an IP interface is also an object in its own right. Here is sample output for the ipadm show-if command:

```
$ ipadm show-if
IFNAME     CLASS       STATE     ACTIVE OVER
lo0        loopback    ok        yes    --
net0       ip          ok        yes    --
```

Here, you see two IP interfaces defined by their name, class, status, and activity state.

This information is more concise than ifconfig output because it is pertinent to the interface alone, not all the information you might want to understand an interface's full configuration. To see the IP addresses that are configured, use the ipadm show-addr command:

```
$ ipadm show-addr
ADDROBJ        TYPE      STATE      ADDR
lo0/v4         static    ok         127.0.0.1/8
net0/_b        dhcp      ok         10.0.2.15/24
lo0/v6         static    ok         ::1/128
net0/_a        addrconf  ok         fe80::a00:27ff:fea3:3393/10
```

Notice that each address has a name, or address object, in which the interface type appears as a path. This means different interfaces could use the same local name, whether it is "v4" or something more descriptive. The output also lists each address's configuration type and current state. The address itself is a property of the named object; its full meaning is outlined in the next section.

For one host to connect to another using IP addresses, they must agree on the addressing scheme (that is, how to interpret the address number). It is this relationship, coupled with each network's routing capability, that enables communication between any two systems on an internetwork. For the rest of this chapter, you'll learn the aspects of the IP layer that concern addressing. Some aspects of switching become relevant in Chapter 16. Routing is an advanced topic you won't need to learn until you are ready to administer connections to other networks.

IP Addressing

On a contemporary operating system that implements the TCP/IP model, the IP layer governs the assignment and interpretation of network addresses to outbound and inbound data. In order to interpret an IP address, your system needs to know how to parse it. Some part of the address data on an inbound packet identifies the destination network, which supports routing the data to the right area. Another part identifies the intended station on the target network. Because the address itself is a single number, you also need something to identify the separation between these network and station identifiers.

Two addressing schemes are in use today: version 4 (IPv4) and version 6 (IPv6). Each one has its own numerical range and scheme for dividing network and station identifiers. To prepare for the exam—and to become a useful administrator—you'll want to learn the basics of these schemes by memory. Although it's a common tactic among busy administrators to look up rarely used commands when necessary, handling the TCP/IP model this way is a poor tactic. There are simply aspects about it you cannot afford to reason out while you are establishing or restoring network service.

Understanding IP Version 4

For many networks, the IPv4 scheme is the default. An IPv4 address is 32 bits wide, which would allow for 2^{32} addresses, or just under 4.3 billion. To make these addresses easier to read, they are expressed as four 8-bit numbers, which range from 0 to 255, separated by periods. It's far easier for the average administrator to remember 10.0.1.150 or 192.168.15.25 than 00001010000000000000000110010110 or 11000000101010000000111100011001.

At the introduction of IPv4, several billion addresses was far more space than anyone could imagine needing, so IPv4 was also designed to support network classes, each with a different address range. The idea was to allot a very large range of addresses to a very large company, a large range to a large company, and an appreciable range to smaller companies.

To make the computation of an address class inexpensive, just reading the first four bits of an IPv4 number allowed a device to determine its address class. Table 15-1 lists the details for each class.

TABLE 15-1 IPv4 Address Classes

Leading Bits	Decimal Range	Class	Stations
0000	0–127	A (Very large)	16,777,216 (2^{24})
1000	128–191	B (Large)	65,536 (2^{16})
1100	192–223	C (Small)	256 (2^{8})
1110	224–239	D (Multicasting)	N/A

The signature of these four bits implied the class, and by extension the number of high-order bits reserved for the network identity; the remaining bits defined the range available for station addresses. Class A addresses reserve the highest 8 bits to identify the network, the 24 lowest for the station. Class B addresses reserve the highest 16 bits for the network and the lowest 16 for stations. Class C addresses reserve the highest 24 bits for the network and the lowest eight for the station. An administrator could also infer the address class by reading the first 8-bit value in decimal form: an address starting with 10 is class A; one that starts with 192 is class C, and so on.

As demand for Internet addresses intensified, so did the need for a flexible (or classless) range of addresses. This was supported by declaring an explicit range with a number called a *mask*. The mask can be expressed as the number of bits that define the network, such as 10.0.0.0/8 or 192.168.15.0/24. In binary form, it is simply all the bits that are set to 1 to identify the network, so /8 means the first 8 bits are all ones. You can also express the mask in a dotted format (255.0.0.0), also called a *subnet mask*.

With a configurable mask, a low-numbered network can address a small range of stations. The network address 10.0.1.0/24, for example, refers to the network 10.0.1.0, which supports up to 255 stations. The network address 192.168.0.0/16 identifies the network 192.168.0.0, with support for up to 65,536 stations.

The lowest address in either a class or classless network always identified the network itself and is not assigned to one station. The highest address in any range is reserved for broadcasting messages to all stations and also is not usable by a single station. Every station within a network that has an address actually listens to all network traffic that passes through its physical connection. At the IP layer, your station will discard packets addressed to other stations. It will accept packets that match either your address or the network broadcast address.

A likely address for your home network, if you use a standard router to your home stations to an Internet service provider, uses 192.168 for the high-order 16 bits. For the third octet, as the numbers are called, you might use zero or something else. If your subnet mask is /24 (or 255.255.255.0), you have support for 24 addresses. Let's say you are using 192.168.43.0/24 for your network. The first address in that range, 192.168.43.0, identifies the network. The last address, 192.168.43.255, is the broadcast address.

In contrast to the broadcast address, all others are called *unicast addresses* or *point-to-point addresses*. Part of the message a station receives includes the source address. Every message can be understood, in part, by whether it comes from a unicast or a broadcast source. These two address types make it possible to use send a message on a one-to-one or one-to-all basis without needing different message types for each.

A lesser known but equally important form of communication is *one-to-many* or *multicast addressing*. For this case, there is no specific address range, just an IP address between 224.0.0.0 and 239.255.255.255. Multicast addresses require a subscriber-based approach: Any station that wants to listen to multicast traffic must know at which address to listen. Network devices that communicate their state, such as routers, will use multicast traffic so other routers can listen to like devices and share information.

You can determine your current IP address a couple of ways in Solaris 11. On the command line, you can use the ifconfig utility; the -a option will report all the initialized (plumbed) network interfaces your system has:

```
$ ifconfig -a
lo0: flags=2001000849<UP,LOOPBACK,RUNNING,MULTICAST,IPv4,VIRTUAL>
 mtu 8232 index 1
        inet 127.0.0.1 netmask ff000000
net0: flags=1004843<UP,BROADCAST,RUNNING,MULTICAST,DHCP,IPv4>
 mtu 1500 index 2
        inet 10.0.2.15 netmask ffffff00 broadcast 10.0.2.255
lo0: flags=2002000849<UP,LOOPBACK,RUNNING,MULTICAST,IPv6,VIRTUAL>
 mtu 8252 index 1
        inet6 ::1/128
net0: flags=20002004841<UP,RUNNING,MULTICAST,DHCP,IPv6>
 mtu 1500 index 2
        inet6 fe80::a00:27ff:fea3:3393/10
```

The output shows two network interfaces, lo0 and net0, listed in order by IPv4 and IPv6 configuration. The inet values are 32-bit addresses; the inet6 values, discussed in the next section, are 128-bit addresses. The broadcast value shows you the address available to communicate with all stations at once. The netmask, which is reported in hexadecimal, is nonzero for all bits that identify the network address and zero for all bits that represent station addresses. Each digit in a hexadecimal number covers 4 bits of information, so you need eight hexadecimal digits for 32 bits of range.

on the
ⓙob

The conditions listed in parentheses are the cumulative, current state of the interface. You can read the documentation for the ifconfig command to learn more about them.

Solaris assigns the identity lo0 to what is called the *loopback interface*. This is a pseudo-network interface, useful for allowing two processes on your system to communicate using network semantics, even when you are not connected to a physical network. The well-known address for a loopback interface is 127.0.0.1 and has the default name *localhost*. In the absence of a physical connection, for example, the loopback interface supports using a browser to connect to an HTTP server on the same machine.

The net0 name is one that Solaris 11 assigns to your first network interface (NIC), regardless of its actual type. Prior versions of Solaris named the NIC by the device driver that supported it, meaning you had to know what one was called if it wasn't set up for you automatically. As the ifconfig command output tells you, you can have two IP types configured to an interface at once. In fact, you can also have addresses of either type assigned to the same NIC, emulating the appearance of multiple stations to the physical network. I'll discuss this more in the next chapter.

As I stated earlier, the ifconfig utility combines information from several layers into one view because Solaris 10 and prior versions did not have a clear administrator view of the data link layer. If you just want IP-specific information, use the ipadm utility to observe your current interfaces.

Understanding IP Version 6

You can tell by the inet6 values that an IPv6 address is quite a bit longer than an IPv4 address: 128 bits altogether. It was devised once it became apparent a 32-bit address range, even with modifications that permitted the subdividing of some address spaces and the reuse of others, was insufficient to support global demand for addresses. What's more, the community that supports the backbone of the Internet needs controls that make it easier to route traffic efficiently, and folding that purpose into the address scheme has several benefits.

An IPv6 address looks like this:

```
fe80::a00:27ff:fea3:3393/10
```

The first 48 bits, or first three delimited sections (fe80::a00), define a site prefix. Some of these prefixes have a predetermined meaning. Any address that begins with fe80:: and ends with a /10 suffix is called a *link-local address*; it has no meaning to a larger network. An address that begins with 2001:db8: and ends with a /32 suffix is an example address only and is not valid on an IPv6-managed network. Certain other prefixes at the highest range all have special meanings assigned.

The suffix indicates the number of bits reserved to identify the network, just like it does with IPv4. The remaining bits identify the station. The address ::1/128 thus is the IPv6 version of the loopback interface; because there is only one localhost for any station, the full bit range is used in the suffix to signify a network of one.

Note that 128 bits alone is enough to allow each person on the planet (in 2012) about 4.8×10^{28} IP addresses. I don't need more than a dozen myself, so I would have just under 4.8×10^{28} addresses I could spare if addresses get scarce again. But beyond providing a virtually unlimited supply of addresses, the IPv6 protocol also simplifies the way addresses are assigned. It is commonly expressed as 32 hexadecimal digits, which are divided into quadruplets with colons. Leading zeroes can be omitted, so my NIC's IPv6 address reduces to fe80::a00:27ff:fea3:3393. To avoid any ambiguity in the address, however, the double colon (all zeroes) can only be used once in an address, and it's typically applied to the first quadruplet that is all zeroes.

As with IPv4, the full addressing scheme may divide implicitly into parts. If the address is a unicast station identifier and has no suffix, the first 64 bits identify the network; the second 64 bits identify the station. The first 64 bits may also identify a subnet within the network, depending on how the network administrator applies it. Unlike IPv4, IPv6 does not support a broadcast mode. It has instead an anycast mode that applies to any number of interfaces assigned to a group. The closest member on a network may be selected as a target for packets addressed to the group.

Another benefit to IPv6's format is that IP addresses, such as link-local addresses, can be automatically assigned. The IPv6 address assigned to my net0 data link, for example, ends in a3:3393, the same as the last six digits of my NIC's MAC address, also known as the Device Instance portion of the address:

```
$ ipadm show-addr net0/_a
ADDROBJ          TYPE     STATE        ADDR
net0/_a          addrconf ok           fe80::a00:27ff:fea3:3393/10
$ dladm show-phys -m
LINK             SLOT     ADDRESS          INUSE CLIENT
net0             primary  8:0:27:a3:33:93  yes   net0
```

There are several other features and benefits to the IPv6 scheme, including a way to address a host that builds on its IPv4 address. That said, the measures taken to delay the depletion of IPv4 addresses have worked very well. Most of the world still uses IPv4 and has no immediate reason to convert. In 2012, it was estimated that IPv6 networks accounted for about 12 percent of all Internet traffic. It's safe for most users to think of it as alternative scheme they can select if its complexities are outweighed by its benefits. In either case, IPv6 has been available on Solaris for several years. You should become as familiar with it as the networks you can use will allow.

Working with Data Links

The traditional Solaris tools that identify and configure its network connectivity still work. In Solaris 11, however, you have utilities that clarify each layer's role. They also add many new objects to the system in virtualized form. Many of these objects are virtualized instances of physical network devices and allow the experienced Solaris administrator to create (or re-create) complex network topologies all within a single physical computer, assuming it has the CPU and memory capable to support them.

These virtual objects are new to Solaris 11. A small number of them appear in the most recent updates of Solaris 10. A few more were originally implemented in open-source versions, such as OpenSolaris, before Solaris 11 was released. Administrators who have focused on commercially supported releases, however, are seeing these resources for the first time; you may not see them widely adopted except by sites that have been working with open-source and trial versions of the code.

The dladm utility, like many tools in Solaris 11 that bear an -adm suffix, supports a variety of subcommands that have a verb-object format, making it easy to see which components it manages and what actions you can execute on them. Table 15-2 lists these objects, except those the dladm utility can list but cannot otherwise manage.

You may not be familiar with many of these objects, which is okay. You're not expected to learn most of them in preparation for the OCA exam. As with many features I present throughout this book, however, I think you should be aware of them. Even if they don't come into play for the OCP exam, you'll be a far better administrator if you are at least mindful of the features you haven't yet studied.

In this chapter, you don't need to concern yourself with any of these advanced objects. Your goal with this tool is to learn how to verify your network configuration

TABLE 15-2   Layer 2 Network Objects Managed by the dladm Utility

dladm Object Name	Type	Description
aggr	Link aggregation	Combines multiple links into one virtual link
bridge	Virtual bridge	Connects two networks into a virtual single medium
etherstub	Virtual switch	Connects two or more data links
iptun	IP tunnel	Connects two disjointed IP networks
part	Infiniband partition link	Subdivides an Infiniband physical link
secobj	Security object	Stores passkeys used for Wi-Fi
vlan	Virtual LAN	Divides a network into virtual domains
vnic	Virtual NIC	Creates a logical network stack
wifi	Wireless access	Accesses wireless media

and test it for correct operation. In Chapter 16, you'll begin to create virtual network objects using virtual NICs (vnics) and switches (etherstubs). You may wish to study the wifi object if you plan to run Solaris 11 on a machine with a supported wireless transceiver device.

In data link parlance, the phys object represents the physical view of a network interface. The link is a Layer 2 view of the same thing. The output of the show-phys and show-link subcommands gives you an idea, by the properties listed, of the attributes meaningful to each view. Let's take a closer look at output for a physical view:

```
$ dladm show-phys
LINK            MEDIA               STATE       SPEED   DUPLEX      DEVICE
net0            Ethernet            up          1000    full        e1000g0
```

Reading from right to left, the DEVICE column lists the driver instance that supports the network adapter. The e1000g0 interface describes a gigabit interface supported by a Generic LAN Driver (GLD) based driver, hence the name. The DUPLEX mode tells you whether the interface can handle inbound and outbound network traffic simultaneously. At half-duplex, the interface must switch between the two modes. In some circumstances, this setting reduces efficiency by far more than half. The SPEED column tells you the maximum bandwidth, in megabits of data per second, the interface can transfer.

The STATE column tells you whether or not the interface is currently active. This state depends on the card being plumbed, or available for use. Once an interface is plumbed, which is normally handled during system boot, it can be brought up or down as you wish. If down, the interface does not process traffic, but maintains statistical data of its use up to that point. If the interface is unplumbed, that usage information is dropped. The MEDIA column is self-explanatory and not modifiable.

You have seen the dladm show-link command output already, which seems terse by comparison. However, dozens of properties are associated with a data link. You can list them all with the dladm show-linkprop command:

```
$ dladm show-linkprop net0
LINK       PROPERTY         PERM VALUE      DEFAULT     POSSIBLE
net0       speed            r-   1000       1000        --
net0       autopush         rw   --         --          --
net0       zone             rw   --         --          --
net0       duplex           r-   full       full        half,full
net0       state            r-   up         up          up,down
net0       adv_autoneg_cap  rw   1          1           1,0
net0       mtu              rw   1500       1500        1500-16362
net0       flowctrl         rw   no         bi          no,tx,rx,bi,pfc,
                                                        auto
```

<continues>

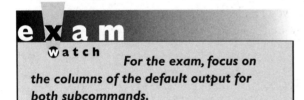

In this partial output, you see each property is listed with its permissions mode (showing whether it is readable and/or modifiable), its current and default value, and the possible values (if there is a discrete list or known range to them). There are 65 different properties altogether, many of which you may have no need to manipulate.

There is also an SMF service that oversees certain changes made at data link layer. The documentation for the daemon process dlmgmtd, which it manages, does not provide much detail on its purpose, but is started by default during the boot process:

```
$ svcs -p datalink-management
STATE          STIME    FMRI
online         Dec_14   svc:/network/datalink-management:default
               Dec_14        47 dlmgmtd
```

Working with IP Interfaces

The ipadm utility supports the IP layer and has relatively few primary objects to manage. They are listed in Table 15-3.

IP objects are supported by data links that have been initialized as IP interfaces. To find such data links, use the ipadm show-if command:

```
$ ipadm show-if
IFNAME      CLASS       STATE    ACTIVE OVER
lo0         loopback    ok       yes     -
net0        ip          ok       yes     -
```

The ipadm utility also lets you list the properties of an interface:

```
$ ipadm show-ifprop net0
IFNAME   PROPERTY          PROTO PERM CURRENT  PERSISTENT DEFAULT  POSSIBLE
net0     arp               ipv4  rw   on       --         on       on,off
net0     forwarding        ipv4  rw   off      --         off      on,off
net0     metric            ipv4  rw   0        --         0        -
net0     mtu               ipv4  rw   1500     --         1500     68-1500
net0     exchange_routes   ipv4  rw   on       --         on       on,off
net0     usesrc            ipv4  rw   none     --         none     -
net0     forwarding        ipv6  rw   off      --         off      on,off
net0     metric            ipv6  rw   0        --         0        -
net0     mtu               ipv6  rw   1500     --         1500     1280-1500
net0     nud               ipv6  rw   on       --         on       on,off
net0     exchange_routes   ipv6  rw   on       --         on       on,off
net0     usesrc            ipv6  rw   none     --         none     -
net0     group             ip    rw   --       --         --       -
net0     standby           ip    rw   off      --         off      on,off
```

TABLE 15-3   IP Objects Supported by the ipadm Utility

ipadm Object Name	Type	Description
addr	IP address	Defines static IPv4 or IPv6 address assignment
if	Data link interface	Describes a usable Layer 2 object
ip	IP interface	Provides an IPv4/IPv6 addressable object
ipmp	IP multipathing	Provides a failover group
vni	Virtual network interface	Emulates a legacy link interface

Five of these properties are maintained separately for IPv4 and IPv6 addresses that can be assigned to an interface: forwarding, metric, mtu, exchange_routes, and usesrc. The arp property is specific to IPv4 addresses. The group and standby properties are the same for either address type on the same interface. These properties are described in the ipadm man page.

To list the current address objects on your system, use the ipadm show-addr command:

```
$ ipadm show-addr
ADDROBJ          TYPE      STATE   ADDR
lo0/v4           static    ok      127.0.0.1/8
net0/_b          dhcp      ok      10.0.2.15/24
lo0/v6           static    ok      ::1/128
net0/_a          addrconf  ok      fe80::a00:27ff:fea3:3393/10
```

The IPv4 and IPv6 addresses are shown according to the formats described earlier in the chapter. Notice the type for each object shows how it was derived. A static type is defined by configuration. A Dynamic Host Configuration Protocol (dhcp) type is configured with the help of a DHCP server on the network during the boot process. The addrconf type associated with the net0/_a object is an automatic IPv6 configuration of a link-local address.

To see the properties associated with an address object, use the ipadm show-addrprop command. Remember to include the object name, which is seen as a path extension of the underlying interface:

```
$ ipadm show-addrprop net0/_b
ADDROBJ   PROPERTY    PERM CURRENT      PERSISTENT   DEFAULT         POSSIBLE
net0/_b   broadcast   r-   10.0.2.255   --           10.255.255.255  -
net0/_b   deprecated  rw   off          --           off             on,off
net0/_b   prefixlen   rw   24           --           8               1-30,32
net0/_b   private     rw   off          --           off             on,off
net0/_b   reqhost     r-   --           --           --              -
net0/_b   transmit    rw   on           --           on              on,off
net0/_b   zone        rw   global       --           global          --
```

The properties reported indicate the state of the address as it is currently configured and used. These are documented in the ipadm man page.

To create an IP interface, you need a data link that isn't yet initialized as one. It may be a little confusing at first, however. For starters, the interface you create will have the same name as the data link you use. What's more, although you'll use the ipadm create-ip command to initialize a data link, you'll use the ipadm show-if subcommand to observe its state as an addressable interface. Here's an example using a virtual machine I configured with more than one NIC:

```
$ sudo create-ip net1
$ ipadm show-if
IFNAME     CLASS      STATE      ACTIVE OVER
lo0        loopback   ok         yes    -
net0       ip         ok         yes    --
net1       ip         down       no     --
```

Once initialized, the net1 interface appears in a down state. To make it active, you can add an address object to it, including an IP address and a name for the address object:

```
$ sudo ipadm create-addr -T static -a 10.0.2.41/8 net1/oca0
$ ipadm show-if
...
net1       ip         ok         yes    -
```

I've declared the type of the address, the address and network mask, and named the address object oca0. Assuming the address object is reachable on the network it's connected to, it's now available to send and receive traffic. You can observe the address status using the ipadm show-addr command:

```
$ ipadm show-addr net1/oca0
ADDROBJ       TYPE       STATE      ADDR
net1/oca0     static     ok         10.0.2.41/8
```

Your options for practicing these commands are limited with a single network interface because you may not want to experiment with your one connection to the outside world if you're not completely sure of your ability to restore it. If you're using VirtualBox, you're in luck. You can configure the virtual machine with multiple network interfaces if you like and then boot up the VM and experiment on the secondary ones as you wish.

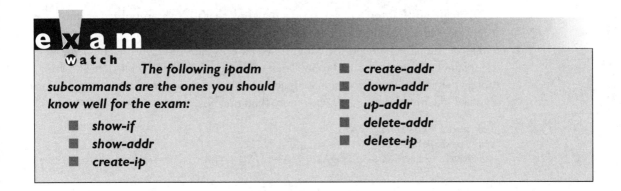

ⓦatch *The following ipadm subcommands are the ones you should know well for the exam:*

- *show-if*
- *show-addr*
- *create-ip*

- *create-addr*
- *down-addr*
- *up-addr*
- *delete-addr*
- *delete-ip*

Similar to the support for the data link later, there is also an SMF service that watches administrative events for the IP layer using a daemon process as a monitor:

```
$ svcs -p ip-interface-management
STATE          STIME     FMRI
online         Dec_14    svc:/network/ip-interface-management:default
               Dec_14         72 ipmgmtd
```

This daemon is documented in the same language as the dlmgmtd process and is not intended for direct use by systems administrators.

CERTIFICATION OBJECTIVE 15.04

Verifying Network Operations

Most people who have had to troubleshoot a network issue have learned to use the ping utility. Given a proper IP address for a target, the ping utility will tell you if the target heard you. This conversation, however, relies on quite a few assumptions that may not hold. Those assumptions include the following:

- Your system is connected to a network.
- Your system is configured correctly.

■ You are testing a reachable system.

■ The target system is responding to ping requests.

■ The target system is configured correctly.

Assuming you don't control the target system, you can only adjust for three of those assumptions if they are wrong. With that fact in mind, it makes sense to verify your own operating methodically, one layer at a time. If you know your configuration is correct and you still can't get a response, you can assume the problem may be the network itself, and not the way you're connected to it.

In Solaris 11, the things you check include using commands you have already seen: The physical link, the data link, and the IP interface and its address object(s) are all elements you need to understand if they have the right configuration. You also need to know if you are using an available IP address and applying the correct subnet mask to it. You also need to know the following:

■ Whether you are using static or dynamic IP assignment

■ Whether there are other link-level devices available on your network

■ Whether you can communicate with other networks

■ Whether you are sending and receiving network data correctly

■ Whether you can address each remote systems by name as well as IP address

In the following sections, I guide you through each of these steps and the tools you can use to verify their operations. You already know how to check the physical, data link, and IP interface setups, so these steps assume their proper configuration as well as a physical, usable connection to some medium (wireless or Ethernet).

Using Network SMF Services

You have two ways to assign an address to an IP interface. You can assign a static address, which is an address dedicated to your system. In contemporary networks, static addresses make sense for systems running services that other services rely on. For individual workstations or laptops, using the IP address for a network identity usually isn't important; you just want access to the network itself. For this purpose, many network service providers use a Dynamic Host Configuration Protocol

(DHCP) service, which can assign any unused IP addresses on demand to any system that attaches to the network and asks. Solaris 11 offers one as well; it's just not installed by default in a Live Media setup:

```
$ pkg info -r dhcp
        Name: service/network/dhcp
     Summary: BOOTP/DHCP Server Services
 Description: BOOTP/DHCP service and commands.  Uses the BOOT Protocol
              and/or Dynamic Host Configuration Protocol to provide network
              configuration parameters to BOOTP/DHCP clients.
    Category: System/Services
       State: Not installed
...
```

Your Solaris 11 system will detect this service when you attach to a network. If you watch your desktop after logging in, you may see pop-ups invoked by a graphic figure that looks like a physical network port. This figure represents the process nwam-manager, where nwam is short for Network Auto-Magic. If you double-click this app, you'll see a dialog box (like the one in Figure 15-2) with your current configuration, including IPv4 and IPv6 addresses and network speed.

Network
Preferences
dialog box

FIGURE 15-3

IP address
assigned from a
DHCP server

If you want to see the configuration in sequence, you can open a terminal
window and restart the SMF service svc:/network/physical:default. Watch the dialog
boxes as the network state progresses from no connection, to finding the network,
to acquiring an address. Figure 15-3 shows the dialog box that appears once net0
has been assigned its addresses. It doesn't matter if you also leave the Network
Preferences panel up while this transition takes place: It will also get updated at each
state transition.

If all goes well at this level, there's little work to do—that's one reason the service
is called "Magic." I have used this service in various forms, since it was first released
in OpenSolaris, for a couple years. The one time it failed me, at a hotel in the
Denver Tech Center, I dug into the provider's network configuration (in an utterly
safe and friendly manner) and noticed a router table entry that didn't make sense.
I passed this observation along to tech support, who said no one else had problems
with it. The next day, however, the router table had changed and I connected with
no problems.

Testing Another Device on the Network

Using either the dladm/ipadm commands or the SMF service, you can manage your
system's network configuration. Next, you want to see whether other devices on the
same network will respond. An efficient way to do this is by sending an echo request
to known devices on your local network and see who responds.

The ping utility is a popular tool for this task. It uses an echo message type
specified by the Internet Control Message Protocol (ICMP) and is a simple and
effective way to find listening devices. If you send an echo request to the broadcast
station of your local network, every device will hear it (including your own). It is
possible none of them will respond, but you can be sure they heard it. You will know,

in a general sense, if they pass an echo reply. This message will include their MAC address, which you'll find in your ARP cache:

```
$ ping 10.0.2.255
10.0.2.255 is alive
$ arp -a
Net to Media Table: IPv4
Device   IP Address             Mask            Flags    Phys Addr
------   -------------------    ---------------- -------- ----------------
net0     10.0.2.15             255.255.255.255 SPLA     08:00:27:a3:33:93
net0     10.0.2.2              255.255.255.255          52:54:00:12:35:02
net0     224.0.0.251           255.255.255.255 S        01:00:5e:00:00:fb
net0     igmp.mcast.net        255.255.255.255 S        01:00:5e:00:00:16
```

Another way administrators use ping is to time network responses. If you know your network configuration is right but the network seems sluggish, use the ping -s command to see the response time of multiple echo requests:

```
$ ping -s 10.0.2.2
PING 10.0.2.2: 56 data bytes
64 bytes from 10.0.2.2: icmp_seq=0. time=0.210 ms
64 bytes from 10.0.2.2: icmp_seq=1. time=0.674 ms
64 bytes from 10.0.2.2: icmp_seq=2. time=0.669 ms
64 bytes from 10.0.2.2: icmp_seq=3. time=0.389 ms
64 bytes from 10.0.2.2: icmp_seq=4. time=0.615 ms
64 bytes from 10.0.2.2: icmp_seq=5. time=0.438 ms
64 bytes from 10.0.2.2: icmp_seq=6. time=0.456 ms
^C
----10.0.2.2 PING Statistics----
7 packets transmitted, 7 packets received, 0% packet loss
round-trip (ms)  min/avg/max/stddev = 0.210/0.493/0.674/0.170
```

In this example, I used the IP address of the machine VirtualBox assigns to my host machine, so my instance of Solaris 11 can use it to reach the outside world. The responses show the number of bytes received, the sequence number assigned to each response, and the round-trip time taken to supply it. In a busy or convoluted network, each of these values might tell us something different. I could, with other options, change the size of the byte packet and see if that affects network performance. If I received the responses out of sequence, I'd know something was going on to hold up certain messages but not others. A big change in the round-trip times might indicate bursts of traffic affecting my test.

After interrupting the process, it reports the whole exchange, including packet loss and an breakdown of the best, average, worst, and standard deviations of response time. The times shown here are slow for an up-to-date network, but tolerable for an aging laptop allocating half its RAM and CPU cores to run a virtual machine.

You can also use ping to send an echo request to a machine on another network. Chances are you know the name assigned to the remote system, such as coderanch. com, but not the IP address. Fortunately, chances are your system is already configured to convert names to IP addresses, so you can try and see if it works:

```
$ ping coderanch.com
coderanch.com is alive
$ ping -s coderanch.com
PING coderanch.com: 56 data bytes
64 bytes from saloon.ejip.net (64.78.181.5): icmp_seq=0. time=59.124 ms
64 bytes from saloon.ejip.net (64.78.181.5): icmp_seq=1. time=57.947 ms
^C
----coderanch.com PING Statistics----
2 packets transmitted, 2 packets received, 0% packet loss
round-trip (ms)  min/avg/max/stddev = 57.947/58.535/59.124/0.832
```

The response from the ping -s command includes a different system name, indicating coderanch.com is an alias for saloon.ejip.net. We also get the IP address back with the ping statistics, so somewhere along the way, some agent found the real name of the target system and the IP address of that system and then rolled them back to us. How did that work?

Testing for DNS Response

Remembering systems by name rather than by IP address is a lot simpler for most people. We're generally better with words that evoke associations for us than we are with arbitrary numbers. To bridge the gap between what works for us and what is most efficient for the computer to process, Solaris 11 uses what it calls a *name resolver library*. It is not a system to convert names to IP numbers and back. Rather, it's a system that configures the mechanism you want to use for those conversions.

The de facto mechanism for the Internet itself is the Domain Name Service (DNS). DNS servers propagate name-to-IP information from one network to another. This process takes time, of course, and sometimes you get what's called a "nonauthoritative answer" when you ask a local DNS server for an address. When you get such an answer, it means the server passing it to you is just telling you what it has learned from other servers; most of the time, that's fine.

It's easy to check whether your Solaris system has a DNS client and is using it. It has an SMF service you can query, as you see here:

```
$ svcs dns/client
STATE           STIME    FMRI
online          8:39:33 svc:/network/dns/client:default
```

However, this service only tells you the prerequisites for using a DNS server are in place. To use one, you need a client application (such as the nslookup utility) to attach to a DNS server your system can query, as follows.

```
$ nslookup
> coderanch.com
Server:     192.168.11.1
Address:    192.168.11.1#53

Non-authoritative answer:
Name:       coderanch.com
Address: 64.78.181.5
> exit
$
```

In querying the server for the IP address associated with coderanch.com, the response includes the server IP address (192.168.11.1) and port (53). The nonauthoritative answer shows the server relies on information received from another DNS resource. Finally, you see the name and IP address. If you don't want an interactive session, pass the hostname as an argument on the command line.

You might also store name and IP addresses in the /etc/hosts file of your system. This approach is particularly useful for large private networks that don't use Internet-assigned addresses. Some sites also use a combination of hosts entries for identifying local systems and DNS for systems on other networks. Relying on the nslookup utility, then, means you assume you will find the addresses you need on a DNS server.

If you have a hybrid solution to this lookup service, the getent utility is a more flexible choice. It relies on whatever configured resources your system has in place. You can simply specify the kind of information you're looking for and the data. The getent utility will determine which mechanism provides the information:

```
$ getent hosts orca
127.0.0.1  orca localhost loghost
$ getent hosts coderanch.com
64.78.181.5coderanch.com
```

In this example, I asked for the IP address of my own system, which is stored in the /etc/hosts file, and the IP address of coderanch.com, which I know is only available from a DNS resource. The getent utility figures out the correct mechanism and returns the result for each query.

Testing Network Activity

It's a good idea from time to time to assess how well your system interacts with the network it's attached to. The netstat utility offers statistics that may help you understand why a network seems slow, or generally how much you're using it to send and receive data. Several options are available with it. With the context of this chapter in mind, I focus on the netstat -i command, which reports on the network interfaces as follows:

```
$ netstat -i
Name  Mtu   Net/Dest       Address       Ipkts  Ierrs Opkts  Oerrs Collis Queue
lo0   8232  loopback       orca          1828   0     1828   0     0      0
net0  1500  10.0.2.0       10.0.2.15     2204   0     50706  0     0      0
Name  Mtu   Net/Dest       Address       Ipkts  Ierrs Opkts  Oerrs Collis
lo0   8252  orca           orca          1828   0     1828   0     0
net0  1500  orca.local./10 orca.local.   2206   0     50708  0     0
```

The primary interest here is the report on inbound (Ipkts) and outbound (Opkts) packets. The number of errors and collisions are a concern, if there are any. Both are a consequence of doing business on a busy network, so they are usually measured as the percentage of occurrences against the total number of packets processed. If you see error rates that represent, say, 5 percent or more of all packets processed, chances are you're spending a lot of time sending or receiving them a second time.

CERTIFICATION SUMMARY

The basics of the TCP/IP protocol suite—the model architecture, the responsibilities assigned to each layer, and the communications protocols—are considered common knowledge for any Internet-savvy systems administrator. What you will learn over time about the roles of the data link, Internet Protocol, and transport layers will apply to all but a few systems that connect to networks that connect with other networks. RFC documents are your primary source for filling out the details of your understanding.

The tooling that Solaris 11 offers to configure these layers, however, has taken a big turn, not just from other traditional UNIX platforms but prior versions of Solaris too. Take some time to understand how tools such as dladm and ipadm differ from tools such as ifconfig. This difference marks a big shift in the way you'll administer Solaris systems. You only need to understand how your system connects to the network and how to verify operations for the OCA exam, but understanding the scope and application of these tools will take you a long way to forming good practices around them.

TWO-MINUTE DRILL

Understanding TCP/IP Networking

- ❑ The five layers that link data on a network to data an application can use are called the physical, data link, IP, transport, and application layers.
- ❑ Data-link communication allows systems on the same network to communicate with each other; each system uses a MAC address to identify itself on the physical medium.
- ❑ IP communication allows systems on different networks to communicate with each other; each system may use an IPv4 (32-bit) or IPv6 (128-bit) address to identify itself on an internetwork.

Working with Data Links

- ❑ The dladm utility refers to the physical link objects as phys components, and data-link objects as link components.
- ❑ The phys component properties include the object's media type, speed, and network device type. The link component properties include the Maximum Transmission Unit (MTU), or frame size, and the current communications state of the device.

Working with IP Interfaces

- ❑ The ipadm utility's term for an active data link is an IP interface, or if for short. Any valid interface object can be assigned multiple IPv4 and IPv6 address objects.
- ❑ An IPv4 address includes a network and station identifier. The bits that are reserved for each are defined by a network mask. A simple network mask declares how many high-order bits of the address identify the network.

Verifying Network Operations

- ❑ The SMF service svc:/network/physical:default supports the nwamd process, which can assign an address to the system automatically on a network that supports DHCP services.

❏ The ping utility uses an echo message, defined by the ICMP protocol, to test for an echo server. You can also use it to gauge the time it takes to send small packets of data across a network.

❏ The nslookup utility is a DNS client. You can use it to determine the IP address of any machine by its hostname, provided the name is registered with and shared by a DNS server. The getent utility does the same kind of work but can render the underlying support (DNS server or /etc/hosts file) transparent.

SELF TEST

Use the following questions to test your recall and understanding of the chapter's material.

Understanding TCP/IP Networking

1. Which TCP/IP model layer accepts or rejects messages addressed to a host?
   A. Physical
   B. Data link
   C. IP
   D. Transport

2. Which layer in the TCP/IP model uses frames of data to communicate?
   A. Physical
   B. Data link
   C. IP
   D. Transport

3. Which of the following expressions implies a valid class B network address?
   A. 255.255.0.0
   B. 192.168.15.0/24
   C. 161.24.0.0
   D. 0.0.255.255

4. How many network devices can be added to the 192.168.15.0 network?
   A. 254
   B. 255
   C. 256
   D. 257

5. Which two utilities can you use to read the MAC address of your network adapter?
   A. ifconfig
   B. dladm
   C. ipadm
   D. netstat
   E. nslookup

Working with Data Links

6. Which of the following options is not a data-link object as defined by the dladm utility?

 A. bridge

 B. vni

 C. ipmp

 D. aggr

7. Which option identifies a difference between the phys and link objects reported by the dladm utility?

 A. Only the phys object reports the MTU.

 B. Only the link option reports the media type.

 C. Only the phys object reports the network speed.

 D. Only the link object reports the duplex mode.

Working with IP Interfaces

8. Can you create an address with the ipadm utility without assigning it to an IP interface? Pick the correct answer and explanation.

 A. Yes, an IP address is a standalone object; it can be assigned after it is created.

 B. Yes, an IP address will be assigned to a default interface if one isn't specified.

 C. No, an IP address is a required attribute of an IP interface.

 D. No, an IP address needs an IP interface to provide a namespace.

9. Which SMF service monitors the nwamd process?

 A. svc:/network/physical:default

 B. svc:/network/physical:upgrade

 C. svc:/network/physical:nwam

 D. svc:/network/nwam:default

Verifying Network Operations

10. Which option is a valid reason why you'd get no echo response from a valid ping command?

 A. You pinged a station that is already listed in your ARP cache.

 B. You pinged an unassigned address.

 C. You pinged a non-Solaris station on another network.

 D. You pinged your own station.

SELF TEST ANSWERS

Understanding TCP/IP Networking

1. ☑ **C.** In order for a host to know whether network data is intended for it, it has to read the IP information that identifies the destination address.
   ☒ **A, B,** and **D** are incorrect. **A** is incorrect because the physical link just establishes a connection to the network medium. **B** is incorrect because, although the MAC address identifies the link device, on a local network level, it will pass packet data to the IP layer for review. **D** is incorrect because the transport layer only receives data that is accepted at the IP layer.

2. ☑ **B.** The unit of data at the data link layer is called a frame.
   ☒ **A, C,** and **D** are incorrect. **A** is incorrect because, although specific physical media may define a unit of data, there is not a general data unit that applies to all media. **C** is incorrect because the data unit specific to the IP layer is called a packet. **D** is incorrect because at the transport layer, each transport type defines its own data unit.

3. ☑ **C.** Class B addresses uses their upper 16 bits to identify the network and their lower 16 bits to identify a station. If the first part of the IP address falls in the numeric range 128–191 and has no explicit mask, it is an implied class B network.
   ☒ **A, B,** and **D** are incorrect. **A** is a network mask written in dotted notation. **B** is in the right range, but the mask /24 limits the number of station identifiers to 255. **D** is a value that has no meaning to the IPv4 scheme.

4. ☑ **A.** An 8-bit range allows for 256 addresses. The lowest and highest numbers are reserved for the network identifier and broadcast address, respectively, leaving room for 254 devices only.
   ☒ **B, C,** and **D** are incorrect. Each one does not allow for the network and/or broadcast identifiers or presumes more device space than an 8-bit range can accommodate.

5. ☑ **A and B.** The MAC address is associated with the data link layer. The dladm tool is concerned with link object attributes; the legacy tool ifconfig reports a blend of data link and IP layer properties.
   ☒ **C, D** and **E** are incorrect. **C** (ipadm) reports interface-level attributes and higher. **D** (netstat) is only concerned with physical interface statistics, not attributes. **E** (nslookup) is only concerned with IP layer information.

Working with Data Links

6. ☑ **C.** The ipmp object is a group object that associates one or more IP addresses with one or more IP interfaces. It does not know how to use a data link object unless it is available as an IP interface object.

☒ **A, B,** and **D** are incorrect. All are link-level (Layer 2) objects.

7. ☑ **C.** The speed at which a physical interface operates depends on the medium it attaches to. The link layer concerns itself with the frame size.

☒ **A, B,** and **D** are incorrect. Each one describes an attribute that belongs to the other object type of the two given.

Working with IP Interfaces

8. ☑ **D.** A shorter answer might be that the ipadm facility has no subcommand that will let you create an unassigned IP address. In practical terms, however, each address object has a name that requires the namespace provided by an interface. There is no global namespace for addresses.

☒ **A, B,** and **C** are incorrect. **A** and **B** are incorrect because you can't create a global address, so the explanations given are irrelevant. **C** is incorrect because you can have an interface with no addresses assigned; you cannot have the reverse.

9. ☑ **A.** Changes to the services that support network control in Solaris 11 put control of the nwamd process under the physical:default service.

☒ **B, C,** and **D** are incorrect. **B** and **C** are both valid service names (in Solaris 11 11/11). **C,** in particular, is an intuitively appealing choice, but it does not manage the nwamd daemon. **D** is a made-up service name.

Verifying Network Operations

10. ☑ **B.** You can ping any valid IP address you want. If no device is there to accept the echo request, however, nothing will happen.

☒ **A, C,** and **D** are incorrect. **A** is incorrect because an echo response updates your cache with the responder's MAC address; it doesn't keep you from pinging again. **C** is incorrect because the echo request/response protocol works across networks and across computing platforms. If the remote system doesn't respond, it's because it doesn't want to, not because it can't. **D** is incorrect because you can always ping your own system, even in the absence of a physical connection. That's one benefit of having a loopback interface available.

16
Managing Virtual Network Resources

I n Chapter 15, you reviewed a broad enough scope of material to cover the requirements for the OCA exam. You'll need to demonstrate a command of the tools you can use to review your network configuration, determine if you are connected to a network, and assess the usability of that network. This scope helps you demonstrate foundation knowledge and practical (if rudimentary) skills. A nonobvious technique or two are included, such as using the broadcast station address to ping all devices on a network at once and look up MAC device vendors. These tidbits can help you to learn more about your network than what is immediately apparent.

That said, a lot of networking goes on behind the scenes on your system, particularly when you create zones on it. Solaris 11 implements several labor-saving defaults in creating a zone that are welcome conveniences. They should not, however, be treated as auto-magic by a Solaris administrator (beginner or otherwise). Having this information in hand before you study zones, I think, will simplify that topic as well. It's the same motivation behind studying projects and resource management as independent topics.

In this chapter, you'll learn how to create virtual network objects that are building blocks for virtual network topologies—the foundation for a simple, small, but cloud-like infrastructure. Then, coupled with Chapter 17, you'll learn how Solaris Zones automates the use of these features to save you the trouble.

CERTIFICATION OBJECTIVE 16.01

Understanding Virtual Networks

You learned in Chapter 15 that Solaris 11 adds new features to the networking utility suite. These additions include tools for managing the data link layer (dladm) and IP interface layer (ipadm) as distinct objects. There are also new conveniences such as the nwamd process which will adapt your configuration to any network that supports a Dynamic Host Configuration Protocol (DHCP) server.

It is worth mentioning as well that some network service configuration data is no longer read directly from a file, but from the SMF repository. For example, Solaris has long used the /etc/nsswitch.conf file to show how the system resolves a hostname lookup: using a local file, a DNS service, or some other service. Now this file is obsolete but maintained for backward compatibility. The configuration is now stored as a property that belongs to the SMF service svc:/system/name-service/switch:

```
$ svcprop -p config/host system/name-service/switch
files\ dns\ mdns
```

You can use the svcprop utility to name a property and the service that contains it. The output is the value of that property. This output tells us that the system will try a local file to resolve a hostname to an IP address. If that fails, it will try a standard DNS server (if one is configured) and then a multicast DNS service. Editing the /etc/nsswitch.conf file will have no effect.

on the job

This change in configuration might catch some legacy Solaris administrators by surprise. Starting with Solaris 11, however, the SMF repository plays an increasing role in managing this data. Consult the man page for the nsswitch .conf file for more information.

In short, a lot of changes are afoot in Solaris 11 networking. Some add clarity to the roles in the TCP/IP model. Some shift the responsibility for maintaining configuration data. But the most profound change has to do with virtualizing the network stack. It is now possible to create a virtual network topology inside a single Solaris 11 instance using the new tools. Furthermore, it is possible for other features such as zones to leverage and automate these features, making it easier and faster to create self-contained, virtualized Solaris environments.

Managing the Physical Layer

In Chapter 15, you learned the physical layer is responsible for connecting the operating system's networking layers to a physical medium, such as Ethernet. This layer includes a Media Access Controller (MAC) with a globally unique address that identifies one network device as the source or destination for data frames passed along the medium. The cable that connects to the network adapter on one end usually connects to a switching device on the other end. Most people never see this part of the network they use. Figure 16-1 illustrates one likely small office scheme for connecting desktop systems to each other and the outside world.

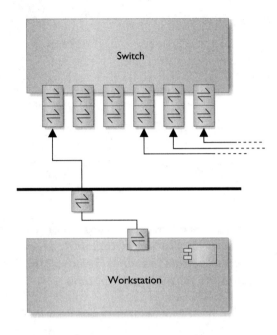

For client use, a single network connection and IP address is usually sufficient.
But if you're providing some kind of service to remote users—a relational database,
HTTPd server, web application server, or messaging server, for example—you
have to provide a location, in the form of a port address, that lets clients connect
that service, and not just the machine itself. Many of these port addresses are well
known and used by default, such as port 80 for an HTTPd server or port 1521 for an
Oracle database listener. What do you do, however, if you then want to run multiple
instances of these services, such as an Apache 1.2.x HTTPd server alongside a 2.2.x
server? What do you do if you have different users, each of whom needs free rein to
run a network stack of their own?

Solaris administrators could address this need by adding IP interfaces to a network
link using the ifconfig addif subcommand:

```
$ ifconfig net0
net0: flags=1004843<UP,BROADCAST,RUNNING,MULTICAST,DHCP,IPv4> mtu 1500 index 2
    inet 10.0.2.15 netmask ffffff00 broadcast 10.0.2.255
```

```
$ sudo ifconfig net0 addif 10.0.2.16
Created new logical interface net0:1
$ ifconfig net0:1
net0:1: flags=1000842<BROADCAST,RUNNING,MULTICAST,IPv4> mtu 1500 index 2
     inet 10.0.2.16 netmask ff000000 broadcast 10.255.255.255
```

In this example, I added the address 10.0.2.16 to the net0 instance. The netmask and broadcast address values are derived from the implied class A address. I could have added a /24 mask to set the address correctly for the network. I could also have chosen an address for a completely different network, assuming I could reach it through the physical medium provided. There are also options to enable the interface, get an address from a DHCP server, and so on. In pre–Solaris 11 terms, remember, the device interface was not understood as a pure data link, but as a hybrid of physical and data link properties.

When first introduced, this feature was called a *virtual interface* but is now called a *logical interface*. This feature made it possible for one NIC to host multiple IP addresses, each with its own network identity and range of network ports. You could also "move" these addresses from one network adapter to another, either on the same machine or to a different one, so long as the application and the data that relied on it could still be accessed. Figure 16-2 illustrates two NICs with an IP address and a third IP (192.168.0.101) that could be assigned to either one using a logical interface. The availability of this "roving" third IP is a safeguard against network adapter failure.

FIGURE 16-2

Two NICs with a virtual/logical interface in a failover model

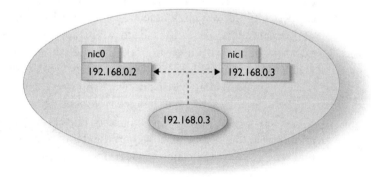

Using this approach, you can share the physical device and allow each of your key applications the appearance of their own network presence. However, all the properties that belong to the physical device, such as the MAC address, are also shared. Changes to the device state affect all the logical IPs assigned to it, as you'd expect. More importantly, if any process using one logical interface wants to communicate with a process on another logical IP, they must use the network adapter to do it, even though no external network communication is necessary.

Software that works within the network stack presents different limits. A kind of firewall known as an IP filter is one example. To block unwanted packets efficiently, an IP filter uses a rules table that is loaded into kernel memory. When a request from a blacklisted IP address comes in, the rules winnow out and block that request. For these rules to operate correctly, they have to be enforced below the IP layer itself, and thus before a target logical interface can be identified.

The filtering rules for each logical interface, therefore, have to be managed using one global table. If the requirements vary for each interface, those differences have to be managed and reconciled in that table, making it cumbersome to manage at best and impractical at worst to update the table on a rule-by-rule basis. Logical interfaces are still better than nothing, but they present constraints that can only be addressed with a solution that operates further down the network stack.

Virtualizing the Physical Layer

In Solaris 11, the data link layer can now virtualize the resources of the physical link. In short, the physical link behaves like a virtual network switch, able to connect multiple data link objects. Using the dladm utility, you can create virtual network interfaces, or VNICs. Each VNIC appears to the system as an independent network adapter with its own properties, including MAC address, activity state, speed, MTU, duplex mode, and many others. Even with a single network adapter, you can create as many virtual network interfaces as your system resources can support, varying each one to behave as you see fit.

On top of each VNIC, you can add IP objects and modify their properties using an interface that is more robust than the ifconfig utility and less obscure than the ndd utility. Now each major application you manage can have its own TCP/IP stack.

FIGURE 16-3

Comparison of
VNICs and logical
interfaces using
a NIC

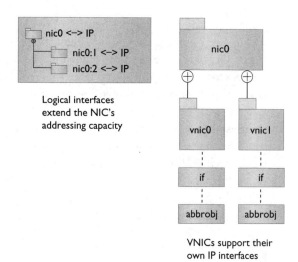

Logical interfaces
extend the NIC's
addressing capacity

VNICs support their
own IP interfaces

This arrangement allows for the VNICs tied to one NIC to see each other and other
network devices as peers. Figure 16-3 illustrates the difference in concept between
logical interfaces created with the ifconfig addif command and VNICs created with
the dladm create-vnic command.

The networking facility in Solaris 11, however, takes these capabilities even
further. Using the dladm utility, you can also create a virtual switch called an
etherstub. You can connect one or more VNICs to an etherstub, giving them a
virtual medium to share and creating what amounts to a virtual network with no
necessary relationship to a NIC. It is now possible, in Solaris 11, to create your
own network without the need for additional physical equipment, cabling, or NIC
adapters.

Let's say you have a machine with several CPU cores and a large bank of
RAM memory designed to host multiple resource-intensive applications, such as
a database, an application server, and an HTTPd server. You want your clients
to access pages through the HTTPd server, which in turn proxies work requests
to the application server, which in turn accesses the database. With network
virtualization, you can enforce these relationships on a single physical system by

assigning VNICs to each application. You could assign two VNICs to the HTTPd server, one connected to the NIC, and the other to an etherstub that it shares with the application server and the database. The only path possible to these back-end services from the outside world must then go through the HTTPd server. Figure 16-4 is a logical diagram that illustrates this concept.

As you can see by reviewing the subcommands available in the dladm and ipadm utilities, there is support for several other Layer 2 and Layer 3 network objects you can use to virtualize a network. What's more, you can use additional tools such as the flowadm utility to modify the properties and application of those devices. These capabilities, however, take us even further beyond the scope of the OCA exam into the realm of networking itself.

I've taken you this far past the exam requirement for another reason—to support what you'll learn about Solaris Zones in Chapter 17. Each of the last three chapters

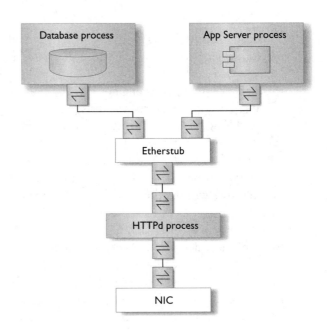

FIGURE 16-4

Multi-tiered applications using VNICs

is designed for that purpose. There will be plenty to learn about zones in the last chapter: what purpose they serve, how to create them, configure them, manage their state, and monitor their demands on the system. What you have learned about projects and resource management makes it easier to see how a Solaris Zone leverages these concepts into a more elaborate unit of service. The Solaris Zone didn't come out of nowhere. It is a logical next step that incorporates and improves upon service models available in Solaris for many years.

Network virtualization completes the Solaris Zone model. Using VNICs, you can assign each zone you create not just with an IP address, as you can in Solaris 10, but with its own TCP/IP stack. In Solaris 10, you can assign a zone a shared IP resource, which is supported by adding an interface to a NIC, using the ifconfig addif command, and supplying it to the zone. Using VNICs, it is possible instead to give an exclusive IP resource to the zone; that is, it is allowed to operate as if it had a physical NIC resource. This change gives the administrator of a zone more power and flexibility to manage and change network status at will.

It's easy to treat these network resources as just one configuration detail of a zone, but the changes in Solaris 11 alter the power of a zone a great deal. The OCA exam does not require you to understand the implications of network virtualization to this depth, but without it you might not appreciate how a Solaris Zone has become a more powerful tool. I'll say more about these capabilities in Chapter 17.

Virtualizing the Data Link Layer

In Chapter 15, I listed a variety of Layer 2 objects you can emulate using the dladm utility. Now that you have an idea what VNICs and etherstubs are for, it's worth a moment to describe these objects so you know how they might be applied. The object types I discuss are:

- Aggregations
- Bridges
- Virtual LANs (VLANs)
- IP tunnels

An *aggregation* collects one or more links into a single device entity. When you want to use the speed of multiple links in concert, an aggregation provides the logical control you need to spread network traffic across those links without managing it directly. To make this work, you need to connect the links to a switch that knows how to communicate with the system and coordinate the traffic appropriately. The administrator configures the aggregation so the links and the switch agree on protocol communications and tracking the state of the aggregation itself. Figure 16-5 illustrates the concept of an aggregation setup.

You'd normally use an aggregation to get greater bandwidth than a single link offers, often because getting an adapter and/or switch with faster link speeds is impractical or too expensive. This same rationale doesn't mean much when you're using VNICs and etherstubs. You could create a virtual aggregation with them, but you don't have the physical limit of a network link to work around. With physical links, however, Solaris 11 gives every administrator the ability to configure one. Prior versions of Solaris required additional software to implement trunking, which is synonymous with aggregating links.

FIGURE 16-5

Aggregation of physical links to a network switch

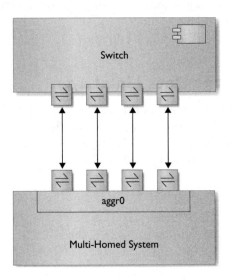

A *bridge* connects network segments together. Unlike a router, which connects independent networks by directing IP-layer packet traffic, a bridge lets you merge two physical networks at the data link level. A router manages traffic using rules and by discovering available paths from one network to another. A physical bridge operates by a firmware- or hardware-based algorithm that defines its strategy for efficiency. You might use a bridge, in fact, to connect two routers and extend the number of devices they serve. Figure 16-6 illustrates one possible use for a bridge in a network.

A *VLAN* usually divides a larger physical LAN into smaller segments, each with its own broadcast domain. Using a physical switch, you could configure some of its ports to create one address space, and the remaining ports to support another. Used another way, a VLAN can bring together a number of different hosts, which connect through a centralized console, into one network scheme. Many people who work remotely and connect to an office environment rely on a VLAN implementation to provide this service. VLANs also make sense for small workgroups that share a switching device with many ports. Figure 16-7 shows a single switch that is configured to support four separate group networks.

An *IP tunnel* allows two dissimilar networks that have no common routing protocol to pass messages to each other. A tunnel operates by encapsulating the packets issued from one network so they can be read by the receiving network's protocols. One well-known type of tunnel encapsulates IPv4 packets so they can be understood by an IPv6 router.

FIGURE 16-6 Bridging two networks together

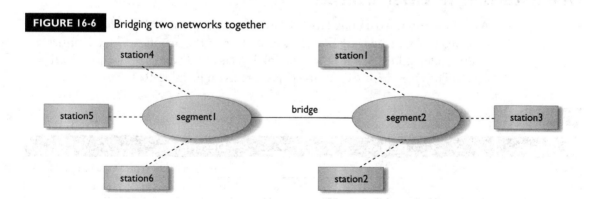

FIGURE 16-7 Using VLANs to share a switch's port resources

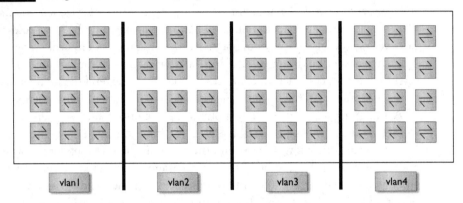

Each of these data link types makes it possible to customize or enable communication among network devices at the data link layer. A few remain that I haven't listed here. Although you may not have use for the types in this material, you can use them to emulate network topologies you would otherwise need additional equipment, cabling, and power outlets to implement. You can learn a great deal more about the roles real-world components play by exploring these types through the dladm utility.

Understanding IP Layer Objects

As it does with the data link layer, Solaris 11 cleans up the IP layer tools. The preferred tool for managing IP interfaces shifts from the ifconfig and ndd utilities to the ipadm utility. As with the data link layer, several types are supported by this utility. The types discussed in this chapter are listed in Table 16-1.

TABLE 16-1 IP Layer Types

IP Type	Name	Description
addr	Address	An object that represents an IP address
if	Plumbed interface	IP layer term for a data link
ip	IP interface	Plumbs the interface
ipmp	IP multipathing	Collection of interfaces
vni	Virtual interface	Contains an IP address only

It seems a general convention that Solaris utilities named with an -adm suffix have subcommands written with a verb-object structure. For each of the types listed in Table 16-1, actions are available that may take a moment to get accustomed to. They are easier to grasp, in my view, once you have the concept that informs each type.

In the legacy view, an administrator made a network device available by plumbing its device driver instance with the ifconfig plumb command. With no further instructions, this act promoted the card as an interface and gave it a default address of 0.0.0.0. The administrator could add an address to the interface, enable or disable the interface's accessibility, and modify other attributes associated with the NIC as needed.

The ipadm utility, on the other hand, treats a plumbed object and an addressable object as separate types. This arrangement means you have to configure each element in a separate step unless you allow the nwamd process to do it for you. The ipadm utility also maintains an IP-layer view of the interface that is separate from the data link view. As a result, an object name such as net0 will refer to both a data link and an IP interface, but you can't refer to the net0 object as a data link with the ipadm utility; the same is true for the IP interface named net0 and the dladm utility.

This arrangement also leads to a command interface in the ipadm utility that may seem odd at first. You'll notice, for example, that the subcommands create-ip and delete-ip exist, but there is no subcommand to list an IP object. All you do with these commands is create (plumb) and destroy (unplumb) available interfaces. Unplumbed interfaces simply disappear from view:

```
$ ipadm show-if net3
IFNAME     CLASS    STATE     ACTIVE OVER
net3       ip       ok        yes    --
$ sudo ipadm delete-ip net3
$ ipadm show-if net3
ipadm: cannot get information for interface(s): No such interface
$ dladm show-link net3
LINK                CLASS    MTU    STATE    OVER
net3                phys     1500   up       --
$ sudo ipadm create-ip net3
$ ipadm show-if net3
IFNAME     CLASS    STATE     ACTIVE OVER
net3       ip       down      no     --
```

In this example, I delete the net3 IP object, after which the ipadm utility does not recognize the interface name. The dladm utility shows the net3 data link is alive and well; it is merely unplumbed at the moment. I can plumb it again with the ipadm create-ip command, after which it is available as an interface. So, with the ipadm utility, you can make and delete IP objects, but manage them as interfaces. The word *interface* is already overloaded, so keeping your terms clear at this layer isn't always straightforward.

Address objects are assigned to an interface, but two more types are available. If you want to create an address without assigning it to a working IP interface, you can use a VNI object instead. The VNI type was introduced in Solaris 10. It doesn't attach to hardware—you can just name one—and it has no MAC address. A VNI object is like the loopback interface in this regard. It can route traffic from one point to another, but cannot send or receive packets itself.

If you instead wanted to create an address that could be assigned to one of several interfaces in a group, you can use an IPMP object. An IPMP object can treat its multiple interfaces like a pool, using any available interface to handle traffic destined for any IP address it is assigned. Figure 16-8 illustrates the differences among data link interfaces, virtual network interfaces, and IPMP interfaces.

Finally, there is the address object itself. Most people are used to thinking of an IP address as a flat value: 192.168.15.25 is what it is, although most people might use a hostname that resolves to that address. In Solaris 11, address objects are named; the

FIGURE 16-8

IP Interface types that accept address objects

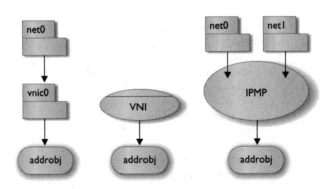

IP address is an important property but does not identify the object itself. To allow address objects a local name, the interface that contains it provides a namespace. The default names aren't memorable, as you can see from the following output:

```
$ ipadm show-addr | grep net0
net0/_b          dhcp      ok        10.0.2.15/24
net0/_a          addrconf  ok        fe80::a00:27ff:fea3:3393/10
```

This listing shows the address object name along with the type, state, and address configured for the object. I used the grep utility to show just the address objects assigned to the net0 interface, but the listing headers are stripped along with the six other listings currently on my system (IPv4 and IPv6 addresses for the loopback, net1, and net2 interfaces). Notice it is insufficient to supply an interface or address object name alone. With no argument to the ipadm show-addr command, you will list all configured addresses. You can supply instead one fully qualified address object name to see its listing, or use the grep utility as I did.

To review, once you plumb a data link (that is, an IP interface), it becomes an addressable interface. You can declare a VNI object or create an IPMP object to manage one or more data links (you cannot add a VNI object to an IPMP group because they serve opposing purposes). You can attach multiple address objects to one interface, similar to the way you can add multiple logical interfaces to a network driver with the ifconfig addif command. Remember that although address objects and logical interfaces serve the same purpose, they are not interchangeable elements.

Understanding Vanity Naming

The network object model for TCP/IP in Solaris was simpler before virtualization. In Solaris 10 and prior, a NIC is named using the device driver filename followed by an instance number. Sometimes these names follow the maker, sometimes they are acronyms of the project name: There was no single convention for naming new drivers. A Cassini Ethernet interface, for example, has the prefix ce. If you had multiple adapters of this type, they'd be named ce0, ce1, and so on.

You learned the name of each driver through documentation or other source because the name might derive from the manufacturer, the project, or even the chipset used on the adapter. Table 16-2 lists some current and legacy drivers.

TABLE 16-2	Driver Name	Description
	bge	BCM57xx (Broadcom) chipset Gigabit Ethernet
Solaris Current and Legacy Network Drivers	e1000g	Intel PRO 825xx chipset Gigabit Ethernet
	eri	RIO GEM chipset Gigabit Ethernet
	ce	Cassini (Sun Gigaswift) Ethernet
	hme	Sun Fast Ethernet (aka Happy Meal)
	qfe	Sun Quad Fast Ethernet

Vanity naming in Solaris 11 lets you alias these driver names. By default, network interfaces are assigned the general name "net" along with an instance number. You can observe the relationship between a physical NIC driver and its link alias with the dladm show-phys command:

```
$ dladm show-phys
LINK          MEDIA            STATE        SPEED   DUPLEX    DEVICE
net0          Ethernet         up           1000    full      e1000g0
```

I am running a Solaris 11 session on VirtualBox, which I configured to emulate the physical device reported here. The driver type is identified as an Intel PRO interface capable of operating at Fast (100 Mbps) or Gigabit (1000 Mbps) speed. The allowable speed is negotiated with the switch (or hub) that connects other network devices together. The link name, net0, is a default for adapters. Although you can change this name to suit you, you cannot do so while the device is active.

To illustrate the naming scheme, you can use the VirtualBox Manager interface to enable up to four network adapters as part of the virtual machine's resources. To follow the scheme of my first adapter, I configured the others as attached by way of Network Address Translation (NAT) to the host operating system. Figure 16-9 shows the configuration panel for Adapter 2, available under the Settings | Network selection for my LiveMedia installation. It includes a MAC address that VirtualBox has created to distinguish it from other virtual machines I might run, as well as from the host operating system's network adapter.

I have to shut down the session to enable these settings, but immediately after boot I can list the new links using the same command as before:

```
$ dladm show-phys
LINK          MEDIA            STATE        SPEED   DUPLEX    DEVICE
net0          Ethernet         up           1000    full      e1000g0
net1          Ethernet         up           1000    full      e1000g1
net2          Ethernet         up           1000    full      e1000g2
net3          Ethernet         up           1000    full      e1000g3
```

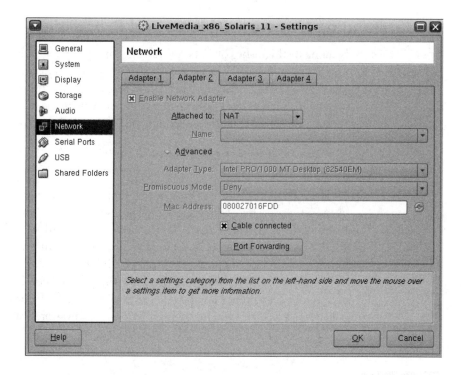

Network settings
for Adapter 2 in
VirtualBox

Each of the new links is operational because the Network Auto-Magic service
used the DHCP service available to initialize them. Notice the device names are
incremented, as are the vanity names. If for some reason I had a mix of device types,
however, the default link naming scheme would mask those differences using the
alias "net."

on the
job

*There is no default naming scheme for VNICs or etherstubs. It's a good idea to
choose one that suits your purpose and stick to it. Lots of online examples use
vnic0, vnic1, and stub0, stub1, and so on. It may help you to name things this
way on your first learning pass, but I hope you don't apply the idea outside
of a tutorial, for the same reasons I'd hope you don't name your pets cat0
and cat1, or dog0 and bird0, and so on. You can remember the type of a thing
without keeping an explicit type reference. A name that reminds you of the
key quality of, or purpose for, the object will be more helpful in the long run.*

Understanding Network Objects and Properties

Naming distinguishes objects of the same type, of course, which in turn creates an implied namespace. This namespace is used in Solaris networking to manage each object's configuration as a property list. Aside from the properties you see with commands such as dladm show-link, there may be many more properties you can list through the show-linkprop subcommand. A data link has over five dozen properties:

```
$ dladm show-linkprop net0 | wc -l
     65
```

The full list of properties may not be supported by the underlying hardware, but even so there's a lot of detail. Access to these properties has historically been the realm of the ndd utility. Since Solaris 11 does away with the idea of a single, global TCP/IP stack, however, it is assumed administrators will prefer the flexibility of viewing and managing properties on a per-link basis.

You can reduce the output of the show-linkprop subcommand by using the -p option to specify properties and the -o option to specify the property fields that interest you. Some properties you may wish to know right away are listed in Table 16-3.

TABLE 16-3   Selected Link Properties

Link Property	Settable?	Description
speed	No	Maximum rate of transfer (Mbps)
duplex	No	Can send and receive in parallel
mtu	Yes	Maximum frame size (1500–16362)
maxbw	Yes	Configurable limit on available speed
protection	Yes	Prevents spoofing (altering) an address
allowed-ips	Yes	Valid IP addresses for this link

To list just these properties along with their current and possible values, you can use the following command:

```
$ dladm show-linkprop -p speed,duplex,mtu,maxbw,protection,allowed-ips \
> -o property,value,possible net0
PROPERTY          VALUE          POSSIBLE
speed             1000           --
duplex            full           half,full
mtu               1500           1500-16362
maxbw             --             --
protection        --             mac-nospoof,
                                 restricted,
                                 ip-nospoof,
                                 dhcp-nospoof
allowed-ips       --             --
```

The output shows the default maximum bandwidth is the limit of the speed; you can set this property to a lower value if you wish. The protection property monitors attempts to change a MAC, IP, or DHCP-assigned address. You can apply more than one of these values at a time. The allowed-ips property, if set, determines which IP addresses are covered by the ip-nospoof value when it is also set. For a description of all the properties available and their meanings, consult the man page for the dladm utility.

The property list for an IP address object includes seven items:

- broadcast
- deprecated
- prefixlen
- private
- reqhost
- transmit
- zone

The prefixlen property holds the number of leftmost bits in the address that identify the network. The broadcast property holds the station address reserved for broadcast messages. The zone property identifies the zone to which the address object belongs; the default value is global. See the ipadm man page for details on the remaining properties.

The ipadm command supports the same reporting options as the dladm command, so you can choose which properties and fields you want to display. The following example shows just the properties you are familiar with for the IPv4 address object attached to the net0 interface:

```
$ ipadm show-addrprop -p broadcast,prefixlen,zone \
> -o addrobj,property,current,default net0/_b
ADDROBJ           PROPERTY    CURRENT        DEFAULT
net0/_b           broadcast   10.0.2.255     10.255.255.255
net0/_b           prefixlen   24             8
net0/_b           zone        global         global
```

CERTIFICATION OBJECTIVE 16.02

Managing Virtual Data Links

To create a VNIC, you need two things: a physical link or etherstub to provide a connection to a network and a name for the VNIC. You can also specify how the MAC address is defined and whether to associate the VNIC with a VLAN ID. You can also set specific properties for the VNIC at creation time. The syntax digest for the dladm create-vnic command follows:

```
$ dladm create-vnic
dladm: usage:     create-vnic       [-t] -l <link> [-m <value> | auto |
                  {factory [-n <slot-id>]} | {random [-r <prefix>]} |
                  {vrrp -V <vrid> -A {inet | inet6}} [-v <vid> [-f]]
                  [-p <prop>=<value>[,...]] <vnic-link>
```

The MAC addressing options start at the -m option and continue to the end of the third line. The default scheme for generating a VNIC is random, which is suitable for a start. As with many facets of Solaris, it's good to be aware of this additional information, but you're not expected to have mastered it to perform well on the OCA exam.

To get started, you use the net0 link to support a VNIC and show the results:

```
$ sudo dladm create-vnic -l net0 public0
$ dladm show-link public0
LINK             CLASS     MTU    STATE    OVER
public0          vnic      1500   up       net0
$ dladm show-vnic
LINK             OVER      SPEED  MACADDRESS      MACADDRTYPE    VID
public0          net0      1000   2:8:20:96:9b:77 random         0
```

In this example, I named the VNIC public0 to suggest its intended use. Notice the VNIC can be viewed as a link; the CLASS field makes it clear what kind of link it is, as does the OVER field. The MTU field value is derived from the net0 link. You can display a VNIC-specific view using the dladm show-vnic command. This output includes the MAC address assigned to the VNIC and the way it was generated. If the VNIC is also associated with a VLAN, the tag number for that VLAN appears in the VID column.

In most respects, you can simply treat a VNIC as a link. You can rename it, so long as it is not currently plumbed, and of course you can limit the display to just the fields you are interested in:

```
$ sudo dladm rename-link public0 pub0
$ dladm show-vnic -o link,macaddress
LINK             MACADDRESS
pub0             2:8:20:96:9b:77
```

Whereas a physical link has several dozen properties to display, a VNIC has 25. These properties are a subset of a physical link, and many values display virtual limits derived from those settings. If the MTU of the adapter is set to 1500, for example, it stands to reason the VNIC cannot set a higher value. The same applies for the maxbw property. The properties listed in Table 16-3 are the same ones you should be familiar with for VNICs.

Removing a VNIC is also a simple act:

```
$ sudo dladm delete-vnic pub0
$ dladm show-vnic
$
```

If you want to create a network of devices that can see each other but have no direct relationship to a physical adapter, you can use an etherstub. Etherstubs, like VNI objects at the IP layer, are simply declared. There is no hardware support for them; they are simply named, logical conduits that VNICs can use as switches.

Without at least two VNICs attached to an etherstub, there's not much point to using it.

An etherstub is still a type of data link, and it maintains the properties appropriate to one that behaves as a conduit between two or more network devices. In this example, I create an etherstub called intern0 and display it using the dladm show-etherstub and show-link commands. I also use the dladm show-linkprop command to display a selection of properties:

```
$ sudo dladm create-etherstub intern0
$ dladm show-etherstub
LINK
intern0
$ dladm show-link intern0
LINK                  CLASS     MTU    STATE     OVER
intern0               etherstub 9000   unknown   --
$ dladm show-linkprop -p state,stp,protection \
> -o property,perm,value intern0
PROPERTY          PERM VALUE
state             r-    unknown
stp               rw    1
protection        rw    --
```

Notice an etherstub has a default MTU value of 9000. It has no adapter-determined limit, so it defaults to this larger frame size; you can reduce it to 1500 if you prefer, but because you're not constrained by a physical medium, there's no need to do so. Along with the state and protection properties, I included the property stp (short for Spanning Tree Protocol), just for the sake of variety.

Next, I add some VNICs to the etherstub:

```
$ sudo dladm create-vnic -l intern0 mars0
$ sudo dladm create-vnic -l intern0 earth0
$ sudo dladm create-vnic -l intern0 venus0
$ dladm show-vnic -o link,over,speed,macaddress
LINK              OVER        SPEED   MACADDRESS
mars0             intern0     0       2:8:20:d2:b1:d5
earth0            intern0     0       2:8:20:9c:60:5f
venus0            intern0     0       2:8:20:4b:fa:7a
```

With just this much work done, I've created an internal network of data links. To make use of them, I can add an IP layer so I can use ping and other tools to test connectivity.

CERTIFICATION OBJECTIVE 16.03

Managing Virtual IP Interfaces

From an IP layer perspective, a VNIC is just an object that can be plumbed as an IP interface. The ipadm create-ip command makes no distinction among the Layer 2 virtual objects that behave as data links:

```
$ sudo ipadm create-ip mars0
$ sudo ipadm create-ip earth0
$ sudo ipadm create-ip venus0
$ ipadm show-if | grep -v net
IFNAME      CLASS      STATE    ACTIVE OVER
lo0         loopback   ok       yes    --
mars0       ip         down     no     --
earth0      ip         down     no     --
venus0      ip         down     no     --
```

In this example, I used the grep -v command to exclude the physical links already initialized. Although the ipadm command does not use the term "plumbed" in its syntax, the operation produces the same result as the ifconfig plumb command. In fact, you can view the properties of an interface made with the ipadm utility using the ifconfig utility:

```
$ ifconfig earth0
earth0: flags=1000842<BROADCAST,RUNNING,MULTICAST,IPv4> mtu 9000 index 8
    inet 0.0.0.0 netmask 0
```

The mtu value has been derived from the intern0 etherstub, as you would expect. Other flag values you see here are default property values for a newly plumbed interface. The inet and netmask values have not been set, so the value of the broadcast property is undefined.

You can now assign address objects to each of the interfaces. Because they belong to a common switch, the simplest arrangement would have them share a network identity and choose station addresses within it. I will use the 192.168.66.0/24 network and number the interfaces in the last octet according to planetary order.

Managing IP Address Objects

You have three ways to create an IP address. You can assign a fixed address and network mask, as you saw in Chapter 15, by declaring a static type. You can also supply a hostname, provided it matches an entry in the /etc/hosts file. To demonstrate this method, I created an entry for the host venus in my /etc/hosts, which I can look up using the getent utility. I then specify the name venus as the local address and assign an address object name:

```
$ getent hosts venus
192.168.22.2     venus
$ sudo ipadm create-addr -T static -a local=venus venus0/ex
$ ipadm show-addr venus0/ex
ADDROBJ          TYPE     STATE      ADDR
venus0/ex        static   ok         192.168.22.2/24
```

You can also request an address from a DHCP server (known as *leasing*), assuming you have one to connect to. The arguments for this option let you specify the duration you want for the lease and the host machine that provides the service. Here is the syntax digest for this option:

```
create-addr[-t] -T dhcp [-w <seconds> | forever] [-h <hostname>] <addrobj>
```

If you use this option on your local machine or another host where no DHCP service is available, this command will hang until your DHCP client process times out. If you want to install this service yourself, you'll need to install the package pkg://solaris/network/dhcp/dhcpmgr to get started.

You can also get an IPv6 address using the addrconf type:

```
$ sudo ipadm create-addr -T addrconf venus0/temp6
$ ipadm show-addr venus0/temp6
ADDROBJ          TYPE     STATE      ADDR
venus0/temp6     addrconf ok         fe80::8:20ff:fe4b:fa7a/10
```

To demonstrate that two interfaces connected to the same switch are connected, you can add an address object to another IP interface on the same etherstub, ping their broadcast address, and see if both MAC addresses appear in the arp cache:

```
$ sudo ipadm create-addr -T static -a local=192.168.22.3 earth0/ex
$ ipadm show-addr | grep ex
earth0/ex        static   ok         192.168.22.3/24
venus0/ex        static   ok         192.168.22.2/24
```

```
$ ping 192.168.22.255
192.168.22.255 is alive
$ arp -a | grep 02:08:20
venus0 venus                  255.255.255.255 SPLA      02:08:20:4b:fa:7a
earth0 192.168.22.3           255.255.255.255 SPLA      02:08:20:9c:60:5f
```

I created the address object earth0/ex just so I could search for the string "ex" in the output of the ipadm show-addr command and keep the results brief. After pinging the broadcast address, I filtered the output of the arp -a command using the portion of the MAC address that identifies the vendor, or in this case a random address generated when I made the VNIC objects. In this instance, there wasn't a good alternative; because I assigned an IP address to the venus0/ex address object using the /etc/hosts file, my system reports that hostname instead of the IP address, as it does for the earth0/ex object. Notice the arp utility is unaware of the address object itself; it only understands a hostname or IP number value for the second column.

The address object is just a named entity that holds an address, among other properties. It is not itself recognized as a formal TCP/IP entity. Also keep in mind that one interface can hold multiple address objects. If the concept of one interface to many addresses works for you, a naming scheme will become increasingly important. The object names you see in many examples just name the address type (such as lo0/ipv4) or are machine-generated stubs (such as net0/_a). Name these objects according to their purpose, or use a mnemonic scheme that makes them memorable.

It is the address object that has a full lifecycle state you can manage through ipadm subcommands. Aside from creating, deleting, and showing address objects, you can also do the following:

- Enable or disable them (enable-addr, disable-addr)
- Set them up or down (up-addr, down-addr)
- Refresh them (refresh-addr)

Enabling an address object causes the system to read its properties from the persistent store. The interface that supports the address object must be enabled first; there is no recursive option that will silently restore the interface. Disabling an address removes it from the active configuration and clears its performance counters. Disabling is stronger than marking an interface down, which keeps it in the active configuration but unavailable to send or receive data packets.

Marking an address object up makes it available to send and receive data packets. The interface it is attached to must be enabled first. The system will mark an interface down if you configure it with an IP address that is already in use. The system will return an error if you try this operation on an address of type addrconf.

How an address is refreshed depends on its type. For static addresses, refreshing makes sure the current address is not a duplicate of one currently in use. For dhcp types, refreshing attempts to extend the lease on the address. This command will return an error for addresses of type addrconf.

There is not much left to do but try these command options yourself and use the ipadm show-addr command to observe any changes. Although the OCA exam does not focus on questions that test your recall of command-line invocations or output, it's good preparation to know the names of defined state values and to recognize the effects each command can have on a static, dhcp, and addrconf type address.

CERTIFICATION SUMMARY

This chapter covered a broad foundation for understanding the virtual network objects Solaris 11 supports. You learned how data link objects relate to IP objects through the dladm and ipadm commands, and how to build a virtual network connection from VNIC up to the IP address object. As mentioned, the end result doesn't change; you can still observe objects made with these new utilities using the ifconfig command. The big difference is in the object model and their persistent storage, which makes it easier for administrators to inspect layer-specific properties and keep their configurations across reboots with no additional effort.

You also got an overview of some Layer 2 and Layer 3 objects Solaris 11 supports. You will need to master these for the OCP exam. In the meantime, awareness of these objects now will give you more time to think about how they come into play when you want to build or maintain your own virtual network scheme.

TWO-MINUTE DRILL

Understanding Virtual Networks

❑ The ipadm and dladm utilities separate responsibilities for administering TCP/IP objects into clear roles. The dladm utility manages Layer 2 objects and properties. The ipadm utility manages Layer 3 objects and properties.

❑ Some configuration files, such as /etc/nsswitch.conf, have been deprecated in favor of keeping data in the SMF configuration repository. The files are maintained for backward compatibility only.

❑ Vanity naming lets the administrator enforce a local naming scheme for network objects. Network interfaces are named "net" by default.

❑ The ipadm and dladm utilities both provide customized reports with options for specifying the properties and fields the administrator wants to see.

Managing Virtual Data Links

❑ The dladm command supports several virtualized Layer 2 objects, including aggregations, bridges, VLANs, and IP tunnels.

❑ A VNIC is a data link object that attaches to a NIC or etherstub. It can be used in most respects just like a NIC.

❑ Using etherstubs, you can create a network of devices with no direct connection to any NIC, and therefore can't be seen from the external network.

Managing Virtual IP Interfaces

❑ You can create an IP object by initializing a data link with the ipadm create-ip command. This command is synonymous with the ifconfig plumb command.

❑ Each interface behaves like a namespace for address objects, which have three types: static, dhcp, and addrconf.

❑ Address objects have a lifecycle scheme that includes create/delete, enable/disable, up/down, and show/refresh actions.

SELF TEST

Use the following questions to test your recall and understanding of the chapter's material.

Understanding Virtual Networks

1. What is a logical interface?
   A. An IP-addressable interface added to a network interface
   B. Any address object added to an IP interface after the first one
   C. A physical link that cannot support VNICs
   D. A pseudo IP interface that cannot send or receive data packets

2. Identify the correct statement regarding link properties.
   A. The speed property value must be greater than or equal to the maxbw property value.
   B. Only one protection mode can be in effect at one time per data link.
   C. Full duplex mode is only available when the speed property value is 1000 or greater.
   D. The maxbw property value must be greater than or equal to the speed property value.

3. What object type could you use to collect multiple remote devices into a single network?
   A. Aggregation
   B. IP tunnel
   C. VLAN
   D. Bridge

Managing Virtual Data Links

4. Which statement identifies a difference between a VNIC and a physical link?
   A. A VNIC can communicate with an external network device.
   B. A physical link has a fixed speed.
   C. A VNIC must have a random MAC address.
   D. A physical link cannot use the protection property.

5. What kind of Layer 2 object combines two network segments into one?
   A. Aggregation
   B. IP tunnel
   C. Bridge
   D. VLAN

6. Which statement identifies a difference between the ifconfig and dladm utilities?

    A. The ifconfig utility only lists active data links.

    B. The ifconfig utility doesn't save configuration changes.

    C. The dladm utility only lists unplumbed data links.

    D. The dladm utility doesn't save configuration changes.

7. Which of the following Layer 2 objects cannot be used to create an IP interface?

    A. Etherstub

    B. VNIC

    C. Physical link

    D. Aggregation

Managing Virtual IP Interfaces

8. Which of the following IP objects can route data packets but cannot send or receive them?

    A. Etherstub

    B. IPMP

    C. IP interface

    D. VNI

9. Which given behavior will occur if you use the ipadm refresh-addr command on an address object of type dhcp?

    A. A new address and lease will be assigned.

    B. The assigned address may be held longer.

    C. The current IP is checked for duplicates.

    D. The system searches for a new DHCP server.

10. Which option is a type of address object?

    A. mdns

    B. manual

    C. static

    D. dns

SELF TEST ANSWERS

Understanding Virtual Networks

1. ☑ **A.** You can create a logical interface using the ifconfig addif command. It has the form net0:1, where the value after the colon is the logical interface number. You can assign an IP address to a logical interface.
☒ **B, C,** and **D** are incorrect. **B** is incorrect because the ipadm utility does not track order among the address objects assigned to an IP interface. **C** is incorrect because all accessible physical links support VNICs. **D** describes a virtual network interface (VNI).

2. ☑ **A.** The value of maximum bandwidth is less than or equal to the speed of the physical link. When set to 0, the maxbw property is considered off.
☒ **B, C,** and **D** are incorrect. **B** is incorrect because you can set multiple protection modes for any one link. **C** is incorrect because the duplex mode is not determined by the speed of the adapter. **D** is incorrect because you cannot define bandwidth that is greater than the adapter's available speed.

3. ☑ **C.** A virtual LAN can be made from a subset of switch ports. You can also make a VLAN from an arbitrary arrangement of ports so connecting devices belong to a single network.
☒ **A, B,** and **D** are incorrect. **A** is incorrect because an aggregation combines data links into a single virtual link. **B** is incorrect because an IP tunnel encapsulates packets so a receiving network can understand them. **D** is incorrect because a bridge combines two network segments.

Managing Virtual Data Links

4. ☑ **A.** If a VNIC is created on a physical link that is connected to an external network, it can be made accessible to that network.
☒ **B, C,** and **D** are incorrect. **B** is incorrect because a physical link's speed is negotiated with the switch it is connected to. **C** is incorrect because a VNIC may have a randomly assigned MAC address, but there other options too. **D** is incorrect because the protection property is valid for physical links.

5. ☑ **C.** A bridge is the alternative to a router, which connects two independent networks.
☒ **A, B,** and **D** are incorrect. **A** is incorrect because an aggregation is a collection of data links used as a combined, single data link. **B** is incorrect because an IP tunnel encapsulates packets from one network so a network of a different type can interpret them. **D** is incorrect because a VLAN divides a switch into two or more independent networks.

6. ☑ **B.** Any interface configuration work you do with ifconfig is not stored for future sessions.
☒ **A, C,** and **D** are incorrect. **A** is incorrect because the ifconfig command only lists plumbed interfaces. **C** is incorrect because the dladm command lists all configured data links, regardless of their current use. **D** is incorrect because the dladm command does persist configuration changes across reboots.

7. ☑ **A.** You can use an etherstub like a physical link to support VNICs. You cannot use it like a physical link to support an IP interface.
☒ **B, C,** and **D** are incorrect. These are all object types that can be initialized (plumbed) to accept address objects.

Managing Virtual IP Interfaces

8. ☑ **D.** The virtual network interface can be used like a conduit, similar to the loopback device. Because it does not have hardware to support it, it cannot itself process data packets.
☒ **A, B,** and **C** are incorrect. **A** is associated with data link objects, not IP objects. **B** is an IP object that can contain multiple interfaces; it is the functional opposite of a virtual network interface. **C** is an object that can send and receive data packets.

9. ☑ **B.** Refreshing a dhcp address object issues a request to the DHCP server to extend the lease. It is not, however, guaranteed that the server will honor the request.
☒ **A, C,** and **D** are incorrect. **A** is incorrect because a refresh request does not include a call for a new IP address. **C** is incorrect because it is assumed the address assigned by the DHCP server will not be given to more than one client. **D** is incorrect because there is no facility in the ipadm command to discover other DHCP servers.

10. ☑ **C.** The three address object types are static, dhcp, and addrconf.
☒ **A** and **D** are lookup services you might use to resolve a hostname into an IP address. **B** has no meaning as a network type or property.

17
Administering
Solaris Zones

CERTIFICATION OBJECTIVES

ongratulations! You've made it to the final chapter of this book. You are about to learn how to create and configure a Solaris Zone, observe it in its various states of being, and manage it as it runs on your system. For those of you who need to get on with learning about other virtualization techniques available on Solaris and other operating systems, learning how zones work will give you a solid conceptual foundation for those subjects.

You've been learning about zones already—or at least the key parts that make up one. For example, you've learned to configure projects, an abstraction for treating a group of processes as a workload. You've learned how to set limits with process, task, and project resource controls, and you've learned about global resource controls such as memory caps, process scheduling, and CPU provisioning. You can create a new ZFS file system with its own property controls for any occasion you deem fit. And you know that you can now create virtual NICs whenever you need a new logical network resource.

Using properties or attributes as a meme, each of these subsystems provides a common quality, *isolation*, that contributes to zones. Projects and resource controls let you separate a workload from other processes in your system. ZFS file systems give you configuration management as well as a separate namespace for files. VNICs let you create a network presence that looks like another station on the network.

Congratulations if you're now asking, What else could I possibly need to create a zone? You've come to exactly the right place.

CERTIFICATION OBJECTIVE 17.01

Understanding Solaris Zones

Let's cut right to it: What is a Solaris Zone? If I'm talking loosely, I'd say it's a special kind of project that runs in its own boot environment (BE). That is, it runs its own operating system and its own file systems. It maintains its own process scheduler, its own service repository, and it can support its own network services. There are a few subtler elements as well that can make it virtually separate from the machine-level operating system that supports it. From now on, I'll refer to this machine-level environment as the *global zone*.

A zone takes the isolation concept a step further by partitioning its operations from all other processes running on the same machine, whether those processes run in the global zone or in another non-global zone. This additional level of separation means you can run multiple versions of some service, such as an HTTPd server, by using zones as separate process- and namespaces. It means you can run a slew of processes in one zone without fear that misconfiguration, process failures, or other anomalies can cause failures in other zones, including the global zone.

But let's back up for a minute. A lot of computing technology in the last decade, and all of this one so far, has focused heavily on virtualization. When Solaris Zones debuted in 2005, a lot people asked how they related to virtual machine technology such as VMWare. It became common to pitch zones using illustrations such as Figure 17-1.

This figure suggests the roles in a traditional multitiered environment could be fulfilled by zones running on one machine instead of running on separate physical systems. If each software package here supports its own HTTP and HTTPS services, it's no problem. Each zone can have its own network stack (and therefore its own range of ports), its own resource configuration, and so on. This picture is appealing for managers who want to consolidate their software processes, but still lots of people ask, What other operating systems can you run in a zone?

The short answer: not too many. In Solaris 11, zones running either late update versions of Solaris 10 or Solaris 11 are supported. A zone does not run on a *hypervisor* as many virtual machine implementations do. The analogous term sometimes applied to the global zone is *supervisor*, meant to suggest a facility that is much closer in form to a custom BE manager than a resource provider to different operating

FIGURE 17-1

Multiple non-global zones

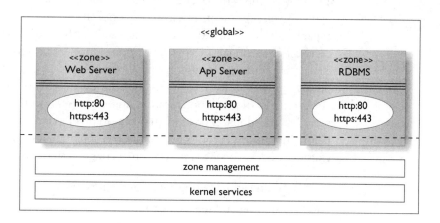

system instances. In Solaris 10, there was some support for Solaris Zones running an instance of Linux, but it didn't seem to attract an audience. Bottom line: Thinking of zones as a kind of virtualization misses the point, at least in my view.

What you can create instead are as many Solaris instances as your current hardware will support; that's not a small benefit. Each one can run a workload that is, from a resource perspective, unrelated to other workloads. More to the point, it can be configured specifically for the workload(s) that it hosts: a database, an HTTP server, a batch-processing application, or something else. Many resource settings that once had to be made in the global /etc/system file are now applied to a zone, thus removing the implied dependency of all processes on global settings. Consolidation, after all, is not much of a benefit if your database has to work with the same resource configuration as your HTTP server.

Zone isolation doesn't just protect the workload, either. All non-global zones rely on the global zone for kernel resources. Those resources are shared in the sense that every zone relies on them, but they are also moderated in the sense that only the global zone permits every other zone access to them. In addition, Solaris 11 extends the idea of a zone as a separate user space with what is called *delegated administration*. Each zone can be configured for access to a specific non-root user in the global zone. Each zone's resources derive from the global zone, but it's otherwise reserved for the user(s) as a separate process space they can use without fear of conflicting with other non-local zones.

Understanding the Global Zone

The global zone is the operating system instance that manages your physical operating environment (or virtualized one). It therefore has certain privileges and capabilities that other zones you create will not have. For one, only the global zone can host and manage another zone. You cannot create a zone inside a non-global zone. Also, although non-global zones share many aspects of a BE, you cannot boot off the hardware using one. Non-global zones can only run when the global zone runs.

A non-global zone configuration, in one sense, is just a list of resource requests passed to the global zone at startup time. The global zone validates each request before initiating the zone's boot. Some resource requests may even fail without causing the zone boot to fail too. The general actions you can perform include:

- Adding and deleting zone configurations
- Installing and removing zone files
- Booting, halting, restarting, and shutting down zones

You use the zonecfg utility to create, modify, and delete zones (we'll examine this tool in the next section). When you create a new zone, its configuration is stored in the /etc/zones directory in an XML file format called a *manifest*. The full contents of this directory on a freshly installed system are shown here:

```
$ ls /etc/zones
index                    SYSdefault-shared-ip.xml  SYSsolaris10.xml
SUNWdefault.xml          SYSdefault.xml
SYSblank.xml             SYSsolaris.xml
```

This directory includes an index file that records the name and current installation state of every zone. The global zone is listed in the index but is not represented with an XML manifest by default. If, however, you use the zonecfg utility to add resource controls to the global zone, it will write a global.xml file that reflects the changes. Other XML files that start with SUNW or SYS are templates for stock configurations, including legacy Solaris 10 types.

Zone manifests can be modified at any time. However, changes made to a manifest cannot be pushed into the running zone; doing so requires a zone reboot. Resource control changes are different. Any control you can modify using the rctladm and prtcl utilities will take effect on a running zone.

Understanding Zones and Resource Management

The benefit of applying resource controls and caps to suit a zone's workload is hard to overstate. The term Solaris Container, often understood as a synonym for Solaris Zone, is actually meant to describe a zone that has been configured with resource controls and caps to accommodate its workload. Given some of the architectural differences between projects and zones, zones are even better suited to using the Fair-Share scheduler and operating on memory caps, CPU shares, and CPU pools.

As mentioned earlier, each non-global zone is responsible for its own process scheduling. By default, a zone will just inherit the default scheduling class of the global zone, which you can change with the dispadmin -d command, as shown in Chapter 10. You can also assign a scheduling class specifically to a zone to override the global zone default. Or, you can run the dispadmin -d command inside a local zone and reboot. If you assign a CPU pool to a zone and the pool itself has a scheduling class configured, that will also take precedence over the global zone's default scheduling class. It's a mess to sort out all these options and the precedence among all of them. Fortunately, you're not responsible for preparing that on the OCA exam.

This complexity of control is due in part to the non-global zone scheduling design. Non-global zones manage their process demands through a process called zsched. This process only runs inside a non-global zone. All processes in all zones, however, remain visible in the global zone. Non-global zones can't hide what they're doing from the global zone, only from each other. Processes in non-global zones must work through their local zsched process to get CPU time, which is only supplied by the global zone. Figure 17-2 illustrates this relationship, along with the various ways a scheduling class can be assigned to a zone.

The Fair-Share scheduler, when applied to one or more zones, makes it easy for the global zone to guarantee some minimum chunk of time to each zone, which in turn can distribute the time among its processes, according to the local scheduler of choice. It's not required that global and non-global zones run the same scheduler, but it does make sense that the global zone distribute resources to zones using a system that does not take individual process priority into account but rather the relative importance of each zone as expressed in shares. The same logic holds for distributing time to various projects.

FIGURE 17-2

Non-global zones running zsched processes

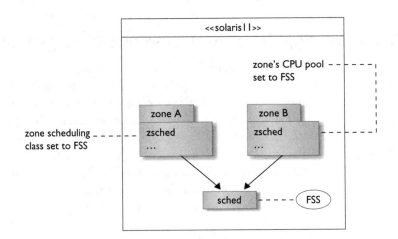

Understanding CPU Caps, Assigned CPUs, and Pools

Allocating CPUs, as opposed to CPU time, can take several forms in zone configuration. You can cap CPU resources with the resource control zone.cpu-cap. This control virtualizes the power of a CPU, treating 1 percent of the CPU (available to user processes only) as its unit of measure. There are 100 units of CPU power for every CPU on the system. Using this control, it's possible to assign a fraction of a CPU to a zone, irrespective of its scheduling class or other allocations.

A Solaris 11 zone has a configurable property called capped-cpu. It is an alias for the zone.cpu-cap resource control, but uses fractional values instead of integers to express a portion of a CPU. If you had planned to set the zone.cpu-cap control to 125, you could set the zone's capped-cpu property to 1.25 and achieve the same effect. The configuration property is recorded in the zone's manifest file, so it's a little easier to track than the resource control.

Solaris Zones also have a dedicated-cpu property that is different. It takes two values: an integer representing some number of available CPUs and an importance property, which is optional. With this property set, the global zone will allocate the number of CPUs declared by the non-global zone at startup, place them in a pool that it constructs on the fly, and then assign the pool to that zone. This approach to making a pool for a zone is not only fully automated, it is also constructed and torn down according to the zone's current state. The administrator only has to make sure the CPUs requested are available when the zone is started; if they aren't, the zone will not run. The importance value is applied by the poold process only if the number of CPUs required by a zone is defined by a range. Importance tells the poold process the degree to which a pool should receive all CPUs it will take or just some of them.

Chapter 10 briefly discussed that creating and using pools is mutually exclusive to creating psets by hand. It simply puts undue complexity on the system to moderate between managing psets by hand (using the psradm utility) and using pools to contain them. A similar tension exists between configuring pools by hand and letting the system configure them for zones that use the dedicated-cpu property. You can also define pools by configuration at the same time the system defines them on startup, just not for the same zone. That said, administration may be kept simple by preferring one approach to the exclusion of the other.

For any one zone, then, you may leverage the cpu-shares property, or assign a preconfigured pool to it, or use the dedicated-cpus property. You do not have to choose one way for all zones, but it may be difficult to keep all your CPU configurations straight if you mix and match configuration approaches as you go.

Understanding Zone Networking

The VNIC brings a completely new dimension to configuring network resources for a zone in Solaris 11. Early releases of Solaris 10 supported a shared-ip network configuration only. With a shared-ip attribute, the zone receives a logical interface that is created and added to a NIC controlled by the global zone. These interface names have a format such as bge0:1. The zone has no administrative control over the NIC and only some control over the IP interface supplied to it.

Later versions of Solaris 10 introduced the exclusive-ip interface. Using this property, the zone received complete control of the network interface, including the ability to plumb it, create logical interfaces, and assign IP addresses to it. As a control, the zone could also be configured with a restricted range of IP addresses and a default router address. This arrangement gave the zone administrator more control, but at the cost of removing the NIC, more or less, from the global zone view.

Solaris 11's fully virtualized network components have changed all that, and along with it the Solaris view of what the shared-ip and exclusive-ip properties represent. Now that you can create a VNIC on demand, there is no real need to use a shared-ip arrangement, just as there is no longer an either/or arrangement necessary for this NIC. You can, if you wish, simply assign any zone its own VNIC in exclusive-ip form. The global zone retains full visibility of the physical NIC, and the local zone gets full administrative flexibility. It's a win-win outcome.

In fact, Solaris 11 takes this new flexibility one step further with an automatic network resource, or anet, added to the default zone template. In short, when you create a zone, install it, and boot it, the system will create and configure a VNIC on the fly, get an IP address for it, bind it to the zone, and tear the whole thing down once the zone halts or shuts down. Similar to the effects of the dedicated-cpu property, Solaris Zones have a built-in convenience to make much of the process look like "Things Just Work."

You can continue to use the shared-ip setting or add net resources into a zone configuration, but in most cases there is probably no need. Where you have a custom configuration in mind, you can just remove anet resources from a zone or use a template that doesn't include them.

Understanding Zone Memory

In Chapter 10, you learned a bit about the difference between a process's virtual and resident memory sizes. Process virtual size (or SIZE in ps and prstat command output) is the total memory space the process requires the system to account for. Resident size is the amount charged against system RAM, and in many cases is a smaller number. By applying the rcap.max-rss resource control to a project (or zone), you can regulate the resident memory demand a workload makes against the system. You can also tune the vigor of the system's enforcement policy, which pages resident memory out to swap space (disk) until the workload demand falls below its cap again.

One unfortunate side effect of rcapd's enforcement behavior is that paging memory to disk can cause delays to other processes that get hung up on disk activity due to excessive paging. There are remedies, such as relaxing enforcement or raising the cap limits, but the threat of an unexpected system slowdown from abusive paging doesn't build confidence in the system. The problem is that swap space is a global resource governed only by the global zone. When local zones process pages heavily, the system reaction might impose delays on all other processes as a result. What's needed is a control to limit swap space as well as resident space. With both controls in play, a memory-hungry zone could run out of memory without getting a chance to exhaust the global supply. Figure 17-3 shows the difference between a zone that can access all of system swap and one that can't.

FIGURE 17-3 TZone with system swap vs. zone with limited swap

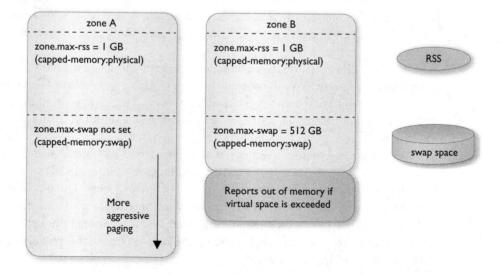

A zone with 1GB allotted for RSS and 512MB for swap has a total of 1.5GB available for all process maps. If the workload exceeds 1GB of RAM, the rcapd process kicks in and attempts to lower it. If the process demand still increases up to 1.5GB and tries to go further, all subsequent memory requests are denied; the zone cannot start more processes until some memory is released. The zone that places no limit on swap exhibits the same behavior, but to the limit of swap that has been made available for the entire system.

To that end, zones have a capped-memory property with three sub-properties: physical, swap, and locked memory. These sub-properties are aliases for the resource controls zone.max-rss, zone,max-swap, and zone.max-locked-memory, respectively. The zone.max-locked-memory control defines the total physical memory a zone's processes can pin down (that is, prevent from being paged out). If you enable capped-memory, you must define at least one of these three sub-properties to go with it.

Understanding Zone States

You use the zoneadm utility to install and remove zone files or to change the run state of an installed zone. I glibly said earlier that a zone is a lot like a project inside a customized BE, and in concept there are a lot of similarities. In technical terms, however, a zone that has been configured but not yet installed is in actuality an IPS *target*. That is, it's a location suitable for receiving and installing packages from an IPS repository. When a zone installs, it applies an image to the file system created for the zone. When the installation completes, you can then review it through the log messages that are recorded during the process, just as you would with a machine install. The process doesn't take as long as a machine install, or shouldn't, but it covers the same steps.

Figure 17-4 illustrates the stages from creating a zone to changing run states from the global zone's perspective. Note that this flow of changes is observed and enforced by the utilities in both directions. That is, the tools will not delete a running zone without halting it first, or let you delete a zone before you uninstall it, and so on. The current state is protected simply by recording it in the /etc/zones/index file.

Changing a zone's state is a nontrivial assignment, and it's not handled by the sched process in the global zone. The zoneadm process instead will spawn a zoneadmd process to handle the state transition of any one zone. The zoneadmd program, stored in the /usr/lib/zones directory, is not intended for administrative use. It shuts down once the task assigned to it is done, and it's managed through the SMF service svc:/system/zones:default. You are most likely to observe this process while a zone is booting or shutting down.

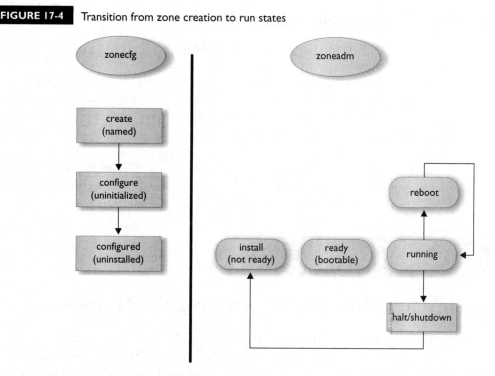

FIGURE 17-4   Transition from zone creation to run states

Understanding Branded Zones

Although Solaris Zones were not designed with virtual machine hosting in mind, some variations from the global operating system environment called *branded zones* are supported. In Solaris 11, *branded zones* support Solaris 10 instances. This support makes it possible to migrate existing Solaris 10 zones (or physical installations) to hardware that is running on Solaris 11. If you have applications with heavily customized, nonportable configurations, or a setup that is hard-coded to Solaris 10 features and services, a branded zone gives you a way to take advantage of more recent hardware—or at least to not be stuck running on a legacy system that Solaris 11 does not support.

The template for a Solaris 10 branded zone is SYSSolaris10.xml. All templates include the brand attribute, but the SYSSolaris10.xml file is the only one whose brand value isn't "solaris" but "solaris10." The Solaris 10 zone implementation used brand as an optional attribute. You don't have to do anything special to create a branded zone other than use the appropriate template. The mechanisms that support a Solaris 10 branded zone are baked into the kernel and are only otherwise evident by the features and behavior of the branded zone when it runs.

Understanding Access to Non-Global Zones

A local (or non-global) zone resides in the global zone. So how do you access it? It depends on who you are. Users in the global zone with sufficient privileges can treat the zlogin utility as console access, which requires superuser login and authentication by default. To get this type of access, use the -C switch. With the switch, the zlogin utility will access the zone using a baked-in sudo operation; there is no authentication challenge in that case. The utility takes the zone name as a parameter.

All other users can access a zone like any other remote system. A Solaris Zone will generate its own keys for SSH validation. If you set up services inside a zone, clients' systems can of course access them like another network station.

CERTIFICATION OBJECTIVE 17.02

Configuring and Reporting on Solaris Zones

Quite a few configuration options are available with a zone. A good zone configuration is one that complements well the workload you plan to run in it. It's then a matter of learning what each control does and how each can help you create a more complementary environment for your workload.

---

e x a m

w a t c h

Items in the OCA exam are specifically checked against what are called memory stunts, or questions that emphasize your ability to recall a diverse amount of technical detail. That means you won't (or shouldn't) receive questions that ask you to pick a bogus resource control out of a list or something similar.

Solaris 11 does *not* support the sparse root model that was popular in Solaris 10. A so-called sparse-root zone consumed very little disk space—less than 100MB. Although default zones in Solaris 11 are nothing like the Solaris 10 whole root zone model in size, they also aren't small: about 350MB. Then again, most people don't have the same concerns over storage space these days as ten years ago. Most people won't miss a 200MB here or there, not in a time when new laptops are shipping with 1TB drives in them.

The configuration process for a zone is straightforward: decide where you will support it (on disk) and what special resource requirements it may have. These requirements may include:

- Additional storage dedicated to the zone
- Multiple network interfaces
- Resource controls to support middleware or databases
- Direct access to physical devices in the global zone

These requirements fall into the realm of advanced configuration and fall outside the scope of introduction. For any requirements below this level of complexity, the following section will cover the proper technique for configuring a zone to accommodate them.

Remember that the zone configuration is just that: a manifest file that does not interact with an active zone. If you want to make changes to a zone, it's a good idea to incorporate those changes into the zone manifest, so they can be quickly read in when the zone is restarted. You cannot change the configuration of a running zone, other than its resource controls.

Reporting Zone Utilization

Once you have zones up and running. You can observe them in more or less detail for their resource consumption. The prstat -Z command will give you output similar to what the prstat -J command does for projects:

```
$ prstat -Z -c 1 1
Please wait...
   PID USERNAME  SIZE  RSS STATE  PRI NICE    TIME  CPU PROCESS/NLWP
  8342 mfernest   98M  41M run      1    0  0:00:35 2.6% plugin-containe/3
  1543 mfernest   77M  53M run     59    0  0:22:23 1.3% java/20
...
ZONEID    NPROC  SWAP  RSS MEMORY     TIME  CPU ZONE
     0      119 2841M 738M    47%  0:42:46 8.0% global
     1       31  155M  88M   5.6%  0:01:37 0.6% oca17
Total: 150 processes, 918 lwps, load averages: 0.18, 0.14, 0.27
```

Notice that a local zone without additional configuration runs a modest complement of processes (31) and consumes an equally modest amount of resident memory (88MB). For anyone who thinks comparing a zone to a virtual machine is reasonable, feel free to start here! It's very cheap on system resources to idle a zone.

For more detailed analysis, Solaris 11 offers the zonestat utility. It's a rich tool; you can report on CPU, memory, networking, and resource control utilization against one, many, or all of your zones. You can also define which columns you want in your output and manipulate the report intervals in some rather subtle ways. The reports are also quite busy on the screen. Here, for example, is a summary of zone demand over one five-second interval:

```
$ zonestat 5 1
Collecting data for first interval...
Interval: 1, Duration: 0:00:05
SUMMARY                    Cpus/Online: 1/1   PhysMem: 1571M  VirtMem: 2595M
                 ---CPU----  --PhysMem-- --VirtMem-- --PhysNet--
          ZONE  USED %PART  USED %USED  USED %USED PBYTE %PUSE
       [total]  0.22 22.6% 1300M 82.7% 1590M 61.2%     0 0.00%
      [system]  0.21 21.6% 1232M 78.4% 1532M 59.0%     -     -
         oca17  0.00 0.94% 67.9M 4.32% 57.9M 2.23%     0 0.00%
```

The summary line shows aggregate values for memory against which the consumption by zones is easier to interpret. The global zone, signified by [system], is eating the lion's share of system resources at the moment. The zonestat utility comes with many different options for producing more specialized reports and greater detail. For the sake of the exam, familiarize yourself with the kinds of information you can retrieve with the zonestat utility.

CERTIFICATION OBJECTIVE 17.03

Administering Solaris Zones

Understanding how zones bring workgroup isolation and resource management together with a BE-like operating state is the hard part. Getting a zone up and running, by contrast, is easy work. The first time through might seem like a lot of details you have to handle, but that fog lifts for most people very quickly. In this section, we'll walk through the steps illustrated in Figure 17-4:

- Configuration
- Installation
- Booting
- Logging in

- Exiting a zone
- Halting
- Removing and deleting

We'll stick to straightforward actions in each step. Bear in mind there are variations of all sorts. Now that you know generally what resources a zone may include, the goal is to get a simple one up and running that you can mangle and re-create as much as you like.

Configuring a Zone

To configure a zone with the fewest possible options, you will need:

- A name for your zone
- A location for the zone's file system

That's it for starting a zone in Solaris 11. Most values require no initial setting or have a default that suffices for simple configurations. You can use the zonecfg utility in interactive mode to declare the zone, configure it, validate it, and write the configuration to a file. The whole session looks like this:

```
$ sudo zonecfg -z oca17
oca17: No such zone configured
Use 'create' to begin configuring a new zone.
zonecfg:oca17> create
create: Using system default template 'SYSdefault'
zonecfg:oca17> set zonepath=/export/oca17
zonecfg:oca17> verify; commit; exit
$
```

The -z switch introduces the zone you want to add (or modify). In interactive mode, the zonecfg utility builds and maintains a zone configuration in memory during the session. You can write the contents of this session to file using the commit subcommand, so long as the in-memory configuration is complete and valid. You can use the verify subcommand to do this on demand, but if you intend to exit the session, the calls to verify and commit are implied. The tool will warn you if you attempt to exit with an incomplete configuration.

The create subcommand invokes a template to give a new zone a starting point. You can also choose another template available in the /etc/zones directory. After that, all you require is a zonepath, which the global zone will guard against use by other processes or newly declared zones.

TABLE 17-1	Select Zone Properties Reported by the zonecfg info Command	

Zone Property	Default	Description
zonename	*None*	*Assigned name*
zonepath	*None*	*Install location*
brand	solaris	Version supported (10 or 11)
autoboot	False	Boots with the system
pool	None	Assigned CPU pool
scheduling-class	global default	Process scheduler
ip-type	exclusive	Control type for network resource(s)
anet	linkname: net0	Multiple link properties

You can review your current configuration at any time with the info subcommand. The output is about 30 lines long and includes all the default or blank settings a zone can have. About half of this output is the properties from the anet resource, few of which concern us for the OCA exam. Some of the properties included in the output are listed in Table 17-1.

You can also call the zonecfg info command without an interactive session to see what's what. The command requires that you name the zone before passing the subcommand, like so:

```
$ zonecfg -z oca17 info
zonename: oca17
zonepath: /export/oca17
brand: solaris
autoboot: false
...
```

You can also observe the state of the zone with the zoneadm list command. You can specify whether you'd like to see (c)onfigured or (i)nstalled zones, along with ones that are running, but the switches themselves become redundant for zones in an advanced state. In other words, all zones that are installed are, by definition, configured. All running zones are of course already installed. You only need the -i switch to list zones that are not yet configured, and the -c switch to list zones not currently running. Also, be sure to use the -v option; otherwise, you'll just get a list of zone names, nothing more:

```
$ zoneadm list -cv
  ID NAME           STATUS       PATH              BRAND     IP
   0 global         running      /                 solaris   shared
   - oca17          configured   /export/oca17     solaris   excl
```

If you run this output for yourself, you'll notice that several of the properties discussed earlier, such as capped-memory, aren't listed by default. What you see in the default output are simple top-level properties. Property keys that may have more than one value (or sub-property) are added using the add subcommand. If you wanted to configure a capped-memory control in the oca17 zone, it would look like this:

```
$ sudo zonecfg -z oca17
zonecfg:oca17> add capped-memory
zonecfg:oca17:capped-memory> set physical=1g
zonecfg:oca17:capped-memory> set swap=512m
zonecfg:oca17:capped-memory> end
zonecfg:oca17> verify; commit; exit
$ zonecfg -z oca17 info capped-memory
capped-memory:
        physical: 1G
        [swap: 512M]
```

The zonecfg command has an add subcommand that requires a valid property. It opens a scope for setting the properties it contains and is closed with an end subcommand. The explicit verify and commit subcommands are unnecessary here, but I've gotten in the habit of spelling out what's happening. Also note you can limit the info subcommand output to the property you name.

Delegating Zone Administration

In Solaris 11, you can delegate some zone privileges to a non-root user in the global zone. The property name is admin. It hosts keys for a user and the auths you want to assign to the user. The auth values are login, manage, and copyfrom; this last authorization lets the authorized user clone the zone. The manage authorization gives the user root privileges inside the zone:

```
zonecfg:oca17> add admin
zonecfg:oca17:admin> set user=mfernest
zonecfg:oca17:admin> set auths=login,manage
zonecfg:oca17:admin> end
zonecfg:oca17> exit
Found user in files repository.
UX: /usr/sbin/usermod: mfernest is currently logged in, some changes may not
take effect until next login.
Found user in files repository.
```

You can add other users with an additional admin property, if you like. You can also use the delete subcommand to remove a property. If there's more than one property type, specify a key-value that matches your target.

```
zonecfg:oca17> add admin
zonecfg:oca17:admin> set user=joe
zonecfg:oca17:admin> set auths=login,manage
zonecfg:oca17:admin> end
zonecfg:oca17> remove admin user=mfernest
zonecfg:oca17> exit
Found user in files repository.
Found user in files repository.
```

Once the zone has been installed and started, the user joe may use zlogin from the global zone and enjoy root privileges inside the zone.

Installing a Zone

To install a zone, use the following command:

```
$ sudo zoneadm -z oca17 install
```

The process starts by creating a ZFS file system at the zonepath and opening a log to record the install progress. The initial output looks like this:

```
A ZFS file system has been created for this zone.
Progress being logged to /var/log/zones/zoneadm.20130129T051134Z.oca17.install
       Image: Preparing at /export/oca17/root.

 Install Log: /system/volatile/install.4249/install_log
 AI Manifest: /tmp/manifest.xml.m8a4ri
  SC Profile: /usr/share/auto_install/sc_profiles/enable_sci.xml
    Zonename: oca17
Installation: Starting ...
```

If you're short on storage space, the installation could fail. Otherwise, the process resembles an image install. The process will create a plan, "download" the files necessary, and install them to the zonepath. Once it is finished, your new zone will appear in an installed state and will be ready to boot.

The installation may also proceed slowly if the origin for your solaris publisher is still http://pkg.oracle.com/solaris/release. You're installing at Internet speed, if that's the case. If you're also running the process in a virtual machine with a modest memory complement, it might be worth your while to go for a short walk while the installation does its thing.

Booting and Accessing a Zone

Once you're past the installation, access to a zone is largely unsurprising and straightforward. To boot a zone, for example, simply name the zone and invoke the action:

```
$ sudo zoneadm -z oca17 boot
```

The first time you boot a new zone, it must initialize the services repository and perform some other housekeeping, just like a regular installation. Here, it's important to remember the distinction between the zlogin *zonename* and zlogin -C *zonename* commands. The first command behaves like an su command and lets you assume zone credentials, assuming you have the right credentials in the global zone. The second command gives you a console view of the system, which includes a view of the sysconfig process. *Note that you cannot see this setup process without the console view.* If you use the zlogin command to enter a zone and there doesn't seem to be anything going on, back out and try the zlogin -C command instead:

```
$ sudo zlogin -C oca17
[Connected to zone 'oca17' console]
112/112
```

The numbers show the count of installed SMF services to expected services. After a short pause, you should then see the first screen of the System Configuration Tool Wizard, as it appears in Figure 17-5.

System Configuration Tool Wizard screen

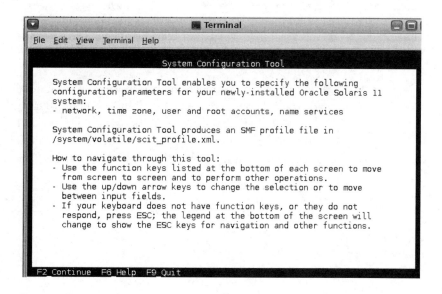

Refer to this screen progression in Chapter 2 if you need a refresher. The differences between system configuration and a global zone are minor and do not require additional scrutiny here.

In general, a fresh Solaris Zone doesn't hold too many surprises. It is just a replica of the global zone. A zone is supposed to behave transparently in most respects so that applications don't have to be "zone sensitive" by default. Local zones, however, are under no obligation to make their configuration invisible. You can use several commands to determine if you're operating in a non-global environment. Once you've configured your zone and let it reboot, log in and try the following commands:

```
mfernest@michaelz:~$ hostname
michaelz
mfernest@michaelz:~$ zonename
oca17
mfernest@ michaelz:~$ ifconfig net0
net0: flags=1004843<UP,BROADCAST,RUNNING,MULTICAST,DHCP,IPv4> mtu 1500 index 4
        inet 10.0.2.16 netmask ffffff00 broadcast 10.0.2.255
mfernest@michaelz:~$ zpool list
NAME    SIZE  ALLOC   FREE  CAP  DEDUP  HEALTH  ALTROOT
rpool  5.94G  1.09G  4.85G  18%  1.00x  ONLINE  -
mfernest@michaelz:~$ zfs list
NAME                         USED   AVAIL  REFER  MOUNTPOINT
rpool                        370M    398M  30.9K  /rpool
rpool/ROOT                   369M    398M  30.9K  legacy
rpool/ROOT/solaris           369M    398M   339M  /
rpool/ROOT/solaris/var      28.0M    398M  27.0M  /var
rpool/export                96.1K    398M  31.9K  /export
rpool/export/home           64.2K    398M  31.9K  /export/home
rpool/export/home/mfernest  32.4K    398M  32.4K  /export/home/mfernest
```

That's more than enough indication we're in a different operating space. Incidentally, I configured my net0 VNIC to get an IP from the DHCP server. The pool size derives from a separate 6GB logical volume that I attached to my virtual machine and am using to host the zones I create. From the local zone's perspective, it's the rpool. From the global zone, it looks like this:

```
$ zpool list bloom
NAME    SIZE  ALLOC   FREE  CAP  DEDUP  HEALTH  ALTROOT
bloom  5.94G  1.09G  4.85G  18%  1.00x  ONLINE  -
```

Notice, however, that the file system's perceived space is much smaller. I applied a quota at the zonepath of the local zone from the global zone, limiting the entire space to 768MB. From the zfs list output, you can see that 370MB or so is consumed by files installed in the rpool, leaving (in this case) just under 400MB to use. I included this part to show there's no zone configuration control that limits storage space. The local zone administrator could impose one, but it would be effectively voluntary.

Exiting a Zone

If you have used zlogin to access a zone, you can just type **exit**. You'll be dropped back into the global zone, just as if you had exited a shell or terminal session:

```
$ sudo zlogin oca17
[Connected to zone 'oca17' pts/3]
Oracle Corporation       SunOS 5.11    11.0   November 2011
root@michaelz:~# ls
root@michaelz:~# exit
logout

[Connection to zone 'oca17' pts/3 closed]
```

If you connected using zlogin -C, escaping the zone is a little trickier. A console session in a local zone behaves like a hard-wired, serial connection. If you type **exit**, the session will simply issue a new login prompt:

```
$ sudo zlogin -C oca17
[Connected to zone 'oca17' console]

michaelz console login: mfernest
Password:
Last login: Tue Jan 29 07:08:08 on console
Oracle Corporation       SunOS 5.11    11.0   November 2011
mfernest@michaelz:~$ ls
mfernest@michaelz:~$ exit
logout

michaelz console login:
```

To break out altogether, you have to signal the terminal controller (managed within the zone) and interrupt it. Pressing the tilde and dot keys, one after the other, will do the trick, but it can take more than one attempt. Sometimes the terminal controller is interrupted, does not catch your two-key sequence, and appears to ignore you. It's best to keep trying so you signal to the controller that the session is done:

```
michaelz console login: ~.
[Connection to zone 'oca17' console closed]
```

Halting and Deleting a Zone

The zoneadm and zonecfg utilities provide a built-in protection for the state transitions of a zone, as mentioned earlier. You might not think you'll catch yourself trying to delete a running zone. The protection isn't there for intentional acts, however, but for accidents committed in haste and the like. Try this out on your own installation: Use zonecfg to delete a running zone and see what happens. Nothing bad will happen, promise.

On the other hand, the steps for removing a running zone may seem tedious when you know you want to remove it and prefer not to waste time. It's a double-edged sword, of course: One that errs on the side of caution. Even if you follow the steps in the correct order, you'll be challenged each time you want to destroy zone data. In the following example, I uninstall the zone I created and then delete it. I use the zoneadm list command before and after to confirm the state of the zone I am dismantling:

```
$ zoneadm list -cv
  ID NAME            STATUS        PATH                          BRAND      IP
   0 global          running       /                             solaris    shared
   - oca17           installed     /bloom/oca17                  solaris    excl
$ sudo zoneadm -z oca17 uninstall
Are you sure you want to uninstall zone oca17 (y/[n])? Y
Progress being logged to /var/log/zones/zoneadm.20130129T085457Z.oca17.uninstall
$ sudo zonecfg -z oca17 delete
Are you sure you want to delete zone oca17 (y/[n])? Y
Found user in files repository.
$ zoneadm list -cv
  ID NAME            STATUS        PATH                          BRAND      IP
   0 global          running       /                             solaris    shared
```

You can also examine the log file, which records the progress in both directions, building up and tearing down.

CERTIFICATION SUMMARY

Solaris Zones use something from nearly every new technology we've covered in this book. I've repeated a few times that a zone is a project, more or less, running in its own boot environment with its own file system and network resource. Coupled with resource controls, caps, and pools, a zone uses almost everything Solaris has to offer. It's an excellent mode for reviewing all the concepts and skills you need for the OCA exam.

Speaking of the exam, keep in mind that you'll be tested on the basics of zones: how they operate; what a branded zone is; how to configure, install, boot, and shut down a zone; where configuration files are kept; and which commands provide zone-specific reports (such as zonestat). If the idea that zones are mostly a composite of other Solaris technologies seems right to you, I think you're in good shape to review a few questions and get yourself ready to pass the exam. Good luck!

✓ **TWO-MINUTE DRILL**

Understanding Solaris Zones

❑ Solaris Zones add partitioning and run-state management to the project/resource controls paradigm, adding stronger isolation to the workload concept.

❑ The global zone acts like a supervisor, managing the requests non-global zones make for resources and monitoring their behavior and state.

❑ The gateway to the global zone from a local zone is the zsched process.

❑ The zoneadmd process manages local zone transitions from the global zone's process space.

Configuring and Reporting on Solaris Zones

❑ All zone models in Solaris 11 are a form of whole root.

❑ A local zone is an IPS image, or installation target.

❑ The prstat -Z and zonestat utilities provide high-level and detailed views of zone resource consumption, respectively.

Administering Solaris Zones

❑ The only required elements to configure a new zone are a name and zonepath; everything else can be configured later.

❑ Some zone properties are top level, are always visible with the zonecfg info subcommand, and can be modified with the set command. Other properties must be added because they involve setting multiple sub-properties or more than one value.

❑ The zlogin and zlogin -C commands are different ways of connecting to a local zone. Without the -C argument, the user invokes operation, similar to what the su utility does, that overrides the authentication process. The -C option forces a console-like access routine that must be broken with the tilde-dot (~.) key combination.

SELF TEST

Use the following questions to test your recall and understanding of the chapter's material.

Understanding Solaris Zones

1. Which three items are kept in the /etc/zones directory?

   A   A global zone configuration file

   B   A blank template file

   C   A Solaris 10 branded zone

   D   An index file

2. Which two options cannot be made into a zone and hosted on a Solaris 11 machine?

   A   A Solaris 10 zone

   B   A Linux virtual machine

   C   A Solaris 10 physical instance

   D   A Solaris 11 boot environment

3. Under what circumstances can a local zone host another zone?

   A   None

   B   If the global zone detaches it

   C   If it is configured but not yet installed

   D   If it is defined but not configured

Administering Solaris Zones

4. Which of the following zone properties is an alias for one or more resource control?

   A   admin

   B   capped-cpu

   C   scheduling-class

   D   importance

5. Which of the following methods will set a zone's scheduling class to FSS?

   A   Deleting the /etc/dispadmin.conf file

   B   Putting the zsched process in FSS

   C   Putting zoneadmd in FSS

   D   Changing the global zone's default scheduler to FSS

6. Which two are properties of the capped-memory control?

    A   crypto

    B   swapped

    C   physical

    D   locked

Configuring and Reporting on Solaris Zones

7. Which option is not a valid authorization of the admin property?

    A   copyto

    B   login

    C   copyfrom

    D   manage

8. Which two zone properties must be unique to one zone?

    A   zonename

    B   vnic

    C   pool

    D   ncpus

9. Which command-subcommand pair is not valid?

    A   zoneadm halt

    B   zoneadm info

    C   zonecfg boot

    D   zonecfg add

10. How many zones can participate in a shared-ip arrangement?

    A   OneTwo

    B   All the zones on the system

    C   None in Solaris 11

SELF TEST ANSWERS

Understanding Solaris Zones

1. ☑ **A, B,** and **D.** The /etc/zones directory maintains an index that tracks all zones on the system, templates for stock zone configurations, and XML files for any local zones. It will also host an XML file for the global zone if resource controls are applied to it.
☒ **C** is incorrect. No zones are stored in the /etc/zones directory.

2. ☑ **B** and **D.** Solaris 11 does not support branded zones for Linux as Solaris 10 did. There is no method for converting a BE into a zone.
☒ **A** and **C** are incorrect. Either one is the target candidate for a branded zone.

3. ☑ **A.** Only the global zone can host and manage other zones.
☒ **B, C,** and **D** are incorrect. There are no conditions under which any zone other than the global zone may manage another zone.

Administering Solaris Zones

4. ☑ **B.** The capped-cpu property is an alias of the zone.cpu-cap resource control that uses a different unit of measure.
☒ **A, C** and **D** are incorrect. **A** and **C** are incorrect because they have no counterparts in the resource controls. **D** is incorrect because it is part of the ncpus property.

5. ☑ **D.** If the global zone boots up with the FSS scheduler as its default, local zones will follow suit and use the same scheduler.
☒ **A, B,** and **C** are incorrect. **A** is incorrect because deleting /etc/dispadmin.conf will revert the global zone to the TS scheduler after a reboot. **B** and **C** are incorrect because changing the scheduling class of the zsched and zoneadmd processes will not force other processes to follow suit.

6. ☑ **C** and **D.** The three memory controls for the capped-memory property are physical, swap, and locked.
☒ **A** and **B** are incorrect. **A** is incorrect because there is no zone property that addresses crypto memory. **B** is incorrect because the control defines swap space, not swapped memory.

Configuring and Reporting on Solaris Zones

7. ☑ **A.** The three available auths of the admin property are login, manage, and copyfrom.

☒ **B, C,** and **D** are incorrect. These are all correct auths for the admin property.

8. ☑ **A** and **B.** The zone namespace is flat, so every zone's name must be unique. Each VNIC can be assigned to one zone.

☒ **C** and **D** are incorrect. **C** is incorrect because any number of zones may be assigned to the same pool. **D** is incorrect because zones are not constrained from declaring the same number of CPUs for themselves as another zone.

9. ☑ **C.** The zonecfg utility cannot boot a zone. The zoneadm utility is solely responsible for managing the lifecycle of local zones.

☒ **A, B,** and **D** are incorrect. These are all valid command/subcommand combinations.

10. ☑ **C.** All local zones can "share" the NIC controlled by the global zone. Each one will receive a different logical interface on which to support an IP address.

☒ **A, B,** and **D** are incorrect. **A** and **B** are incorrect because there is no exclusive or limited relationship between the local zones and a global zone and a NIC. **D** is incorrect because Solaris 11 does support the shared-ip configuration. There's just not many compelling use cases for it.

Appendix

About the CD-ROM

The CD-ROM included with this book comes complete with MasterExam and an electronic copy of the book in PDF format (the electronic book). The software is easy to install on any Windows XP/Vista/7 computer and must be installed to access the MasterExam feature. To register for the bonus MasterExam, simply click the Bonus MasterExam link on the main launch page and follow the directions to the free online registration.

System Requirements

Software requires Windows XP or higher and Internet Explorer 8.0 or above as well as 200MB of hard disk space for full installation. The electronic book requires Adobe Acrobat Reader.

Installing and Running MasterExam

If your computer CD-ROM drive is configured to auto-run, the CD-ROM will start up after you insert the disc. From the opening screen you may install MasterExam by clicking the MasterExam link. This will begin the installation process and create a program group named LearnKey. To run MasterExam, use Start | All Programs | LearnKey | MasterExam. If the auto-run feature did not launch your CD, browse to the CD and click the LaunchTraining.exe icon.

MasterExam

MasterExam provides you with a simulation of the actual exam. The number of questions, the type of questions, and the time allowed are intended to be an accurate representation of the exam environment. You have the option to take an open-book exam (including hints, references, and answers), a closed-book exam, or the timed MasterExam simulation.

When you launch MasterExam, a digital clock display will appear in the bottom-right corner of your screen. The clock will continue to count down to zero unless you choose to end the exam before the time expires.

Help

A help file is provided through the help button on the main page in the lower-left corner. An individual help feature is also available through MasterExam.

Removing Installation(s)

MasterExam is installed to your hard drive. For best results removing programs, use the Start | All Programs | LearnKey | Uninstall option to remove MasterExam.

Electronic Book

The entire contents of the book are provided in PDF format on the CD. This file is viewable on your computer and many portable devices. Adobe's Acrobat Reader is required to view the file on your PC and has been included on the CD. You may also use Adobe Digital Editions to access your electronic book.

For more information on Adobe Reader and to check for the most recent version of the software, visit Adobe's website at www.adobe.com and search for the free Adobe Reader or look for Adobe Reader on the product page. Adobe Digital Editions can also be downloaded from the Adobe website.

To view the electronic book on a portable device, copy the PDF file to your computer from the CD and then copy the file to your portable device using a USB or other connection. Adobe does offer a mobile version of Adobe Reader, the Adobe Reader mobile app, which currently supports iOS and Android. For customers using Adobe Digital Editions and the iPad, you may have to download and install a separate reader program on your device. The Adobe website has a list of recommended applications, and McGraw-Hill Education recommends the Bluefire Reader.

Technical Support

Technical Support information is provided here, by feature.

LearnKey Technical Support

For technical problems with the software (installation, operation, removing installations), please visit www.learnkey.com, e-mail techsupport@learnkey.com, or call toll free at 1-800-482-8244.

McGraw-Hill Technical Support and Customer Service

For questions regarding the electronic book, e-mail techsolutions@mhedu.com or visit http://mhp.softwareassist.com.

For questions regarding book content, please e-mail customer.service@ mcgraw-hill.com. For customers outside the United States, e-mail international_cs@mcgraw-hill.com.

INDEX

D

n